# Speaking the Unspeakable

SUNY Series, The Margins of Literature
Mihai I. Spariosu, editor

# Speaking the Unspeakable

*A Poetics of Obscenity*

Peter Michelson

STATE UNIVERSITY OF NEW YORK PRESS

ACKNOWLEDGMENTS

*Another Chicago Magazine, Continuum, The New Republic*, and *TriQuarterly* magazines, where portions of this book have appeared in somewhat different form.
Grove Weidenfeld, for permission to quote from William S. Burroughs, *Naked Lunch*, 1966; Henry Miller, *Nexus*, 1965 and *Sexus*, 1965; The Marquis de Sade, *Justine, Philosophy in the Bedroom & Other Writings*, 1965 and *The 120 Days of Sodom & Other Writings*, 1966; Jean Genet, *Our Lady of the Flowers*, 1964.
Olympia Press, for permission to quote from Frank Newman, *Barbara*, 1968.
Random House, for permission to quote from Pauline Réage, *Story of O*, 1965.
Sterling Lord Litristic, for permission to quote LeRoi Jones/Amiri Baraka, "Poem for Speculative Hipsters," *The Dead Lecturer*, 1964.

Published by
State University of New York Press, Albany



Printed in the United States of America



For information, address State University of New York Press,
State University Plaza, Albany, N.Y., 12246

Production by Marilyn P. Semerad
Marketing by Theresa A. Swierzowski

**Library of Congress Cataloging-in-Publication Data**

Michelson, Peter.
Speaking the unspeakable : a poetics of obscenity / Peter Michelson.
p. cm. — (SUNY series, the margins of literature)
Rev. ed. of: The aesthetics of pornography. 1971.
ISBN 0-7914-1223-7. — ISBN 0-7914-1224-5 (pbk.)
1. Erotic literature—History and criticism. 2. Erotic films--History and criticism. 3. Pornography—Aesthetics. I. Michelson, Peter. The poetics of obscenity. II. Title. III. Series.
PN56.E7M5 1993
809'.933538—dc20 91-46954
CIP

10 9 8 7 6 5 4 3 2 1

# Contents

# Preface

The first incarnation of this book was published in 1971 as *The Aesthetics of Pornography*. Since then there has been a significantly expanding corpus of literary and cinematic works that identify themselves as products of a poetics of obscenity. Likewise, social discourse on the subject has taken on new perspectives. In 1986 the Attorney General's Commission on Pornography issued its report, which was at considerable variance with that of the 1970 President's Commission on Obscenity and Pornography. To a large degree this was due to the influence of the Women Against Pornography movement and its vigorous national campaign for an anti-pornography ordinance in the early and middle 1980s. But in 1984 an opposing feminist perspective was synthesized in the Feminists Against Censorship Taskforce *amicus curiae* brief to federal court arguing against the anti-pornography ordinance. The contemporary perception of the pornography "problem" has been profoundly informed by this feminist debate.

Meanwhile, at least since the mid 1970s, women had been producing a body of sociological and fictive literature that was exploring female sexuality, its fantasies and its artistic expression. Prominent among early works were Shere Hite's sociological study *The Hite Report*, Nancy Friday's survey of women's sexual fantasies, *My Secret Garden*, and Erica Jong's novel, *Fear of Flying*. The subsequent years have witnessed the growth of a female poetics of obscenity from small presses, little magazines, commercial journals and mainstream publishers. Additionally, in the last twenty or so years feature films have addressed pornography in an unprecedented way. For example, Bertolucci's *Last Tango in Paris*, Oshima's *In the Realm of the Senses*, and Wertmuller's *Swept Away* in various ways have all been controversial but broadly distributed. This situation derived from an antecedent cinema of sexuality in avant-garde films and the parodies of Russ Meyer, not to mention such arrant pornographic features as *Deep Throat*.

These developments have provided occasion to reconceive the original study. This new perspective explores a historical rationale for the evolution of obscene poetics, a progress including pornography's increasing aesthetic and sociological functions. For example, the Marquis de Sade's writings reflect a view of nature so modified by the materialist science and philosophy of the eighteenth century as to induce his peculiar theories of the obscene. Later in the nineteenth century Sade's influence is manifest, sometimes parodically, in such marginal works as the Comte de Lautreamont's *Les Chants des Maldoror*, Guillaume Apollinaire's *The Debauched Hospodar* and the British journal of "Voluptuous Reading," *The Pearl*. Apollinaire brought Sade to Andre Breton's attention, who designated Sade a surrealist antecedent and touchstone in 1919. Georges Bataille's erotic fiction and theory drew at once on Sade, surrealism and existentialism. Similarly with Antonin Artaud. In the 1960s works by Pauline Réage, Jean Genet and William Burroughs reflected Sadean dispositions. In the 1970s Angela Carter extended Simone de Beauvoir's earlier apologia and undertook a sort of female reclamation of Sade in *The Sadeian Woman*. And by the early 1980s Sade was providing basic premises for the feminist lesbian S/M literature of the Samois group in the United States. These are instances of how, between the eighteenth and late twentieth centuries, one line of obscene poetics took recognizable shape. My purpose in this book is to contextualize such poetics in relation to the history they share with mainstream poetics.

This attention to obscene poetics—as distinct from though inclusive of pornography—should relieve a certain semantic strain. Some reviewers of the earlier work, for example, were either unwilling or unable to recognize my distinction between hard core pornography and obscene poetics in the work of a Sade or a D. H. Lawrence or a William Burroughs. Similarly, my designation of work by Lawrence, James Joyce or Anais Nin as pornographic is not so antithetical to their own poetic theories as it might seem. While these writers abhorred what they understood to be pornography, their conceptions of it were not in the perspective of the historical matrix for obscene poetics that I am positing. I think that the more elaborate contextualization in this version makes my conception clearer in itself and my vocabulary more negotiable with that of such writers.

Also, given the proliferation of "theory" in literary studies since 1971, it seems prudent to situate my approach in that matrix. Historically, my premise is that obscene poetics are the coherent (as distinct from aberrant or ephemeral) product of the continuing dialogue between aesthetic idealism and materialism and that their emergence as a genre of legitimized literature and art is a reflection of the modern and especially contemporary assertiveness of the latter. In structuralist terms it might be described as a study of how traditional signifiers of the obscene are reconstituted to assume the function of traditional signifiers of the beautiful. As the aesthetic signifying system persists, perhaps perversely, in admitting new or different signs a more complex hermeneutic burden is assumed by the system. In post-structuralist terms that burden forces an elasticity or expansion which effects a decentering of the system. In the process of realignment obscenity's legitimization—the extent to which it is assimilated by legitimized literature—serves to deconstruct the aesthetic imperatives of the system. Where my address tends to differ from that of scholarly theory is in treating poetics as a creational rather than interpretive phenomenon. The first concern of the writer/artist is articulation, i.e. poetics. He or she may adopt, adapt, reject or reinvent the known modes of articulation. He or she will be informed by many other things—politics, gender, economics, psychology, etc.—but the first principle of making is making, *sine qua non*. Accordingly, I have given priority attention to the works made and to the writers' suppositions about their making. Correlatively, I have sought to identify the historical logic whereby diverse works and artists might warrant the category of an obscene poetics.

Readers familiar with *The Aesthetics of Pornography* might want to know where this book differs from it. Four chapters, by volume more than half of the book, are completely new and replace their original counterparts. Chapter 1 is a historical overview of how the development of cultural liberalism and materialist conceptions of aesthetics and sexuality cultivated the emergence of obscene poetics. Chapter 8 addresses the feminist dialectic that precipitated a female "pornorotica," largely since the mid 1970s. Chapter 9 hypothesizes a cinematic poetics of obscenity evolving from the avant-garde film makers of the 1950s and 1960s into both hard-core and mainstream feature films. Chapter 10 puts liberalism's principle of free speech into the historical contexts of its litigation, especially in the U.S. Supreme Court since Justice Woolsey's *Ulysses* decision, of recent research on the pornography-violence nexus, of the feminist pornography debates of the early 1980s, and of the modern tension between liberal and conservative political perspectives. Chapters 2, 3 and 6 are substantively revised versions of their originals. Chapters 4, 5 and 7 have minor revisions, mainly deletions. It is also pertinent to call attention to the note on usage which follows this preface and presents working definitions of obscenity, pornography and their poetics.

It is also appropriate to repeat that inasmuch as this book proposes neither a representative survey nor a critical bibliography of obscene literature, the body of works discussed is not supposed to be comprehensive. My criterion of address has been what I thought of particular or illustrative interest in connection with the development of the poetics of obscenity as I understand it. As my approach to the subject is essayistic rather than scholarly, I have avoided footnotes. I have identified my sources, materials and intellectual debts in the text and bibliography.

For their generosity and good counsel I am grateful to several friends and colleagues, and am pleased to be able to acknowledge my thanks here: to novelist Alix Kates Shulman, for extensive and insightful conversation on the feminist debate and female pornography; to Michele Barale, feminist scholar and critic, for highly informative suggestions about developments in female pornography; to literary historian John Graham, for fruitful suggestions about the work of Edith Wharton; to Kathi George, former editor of the feminist journal *Frontiers*, for incisive criticism of chapter 8 on female obscene poetics; to writer and film scholar Bruce Kawin, also for incisive criticism on chapter 9, on cinema; to film maker Stan Brakhage, for access to his avant-garde film archive and for penetrating commentary on film history and aesthetics; to poet and fictionist Marilyn Krysl, for adroit criticism of much of the new material in this book and her sustaining encouragement of the project. Lest they be associated with such malapertnesses or blunders as may linger, I should add that all of these people have taken exception to one articulation or another in this book.

# A Note on Usage

Obscenity and pornography are quarrelsome concepts in general and no more tractable in the context of poetics. I would not hazard something so imperious as definition if it were not for the fact that lately they have been designated especially significant social problems, and discussion surrounding them reflects a confusing and contentious variety of semantic orientations. I do not presume to still the waters but want rather to identify the approach that informs this study. I use obscenity in the Greek sense of bringing onstage what is customarily kept offstage in western culture, for example, the Oedipal bedroom or Jocasta's suicide or Oedipus' blinding. Custom and obscenity both are relative to time, so nowadays violence is problematic as obscenity except where it is specifically connected to sexuality. Violence is graphically pervasive in our culture in a way that sex is not. The Three Stooges whacking one another over the head is standard slapstick. Clyde's bullet-riddled death, rendered balletic by slow motion in *Bonnie and Clyde,* is a movie convention. John Kennedy's assassination, like that of Lee Harvey Oswald and many others, is a television staple. Violence is professionalized as entertainment in boxing and football. While a close-up visual of a shotgun blasting someone's face away *might* be considered obscene, in general violence is primarily made obscene by its association with sex. Thus obscenity is essentially pertinent to sex and its vocabulary. It also applies, of course, to the privy parts, their excretory functions and epithets about them.

An aesthetics of obscenity implies a perceptual alteration whereby the obscene, a species of the ugly, is reconstituted to a function akin to that of the beautiful. In that sense it is a *contemplation* of the unspeakable and counterpoints traditional aesthetic assumptions. Traditionally the beautiful is associated with an idealist synthesis or transcendental revelation. The obscene counters by redirecting attentions from the ideal to the material nature of human being and doing. That is, it tempers or displaces idealist assumptions. A D. H. Lawrence tempers them; a Jean Genet displaces them. A poetics of obscenity, then, describes *speaking* the unspeakable and is defined by the artistic strategies used to change assumptions and perceptions. These will vary according to artist, but what they will have in common is the disposition to make the obscene function aesthetically. This will frequently, if not necessarily, bring them to the magnetic field of pornography. Pornography is the representation of sexuality so as to make its obscenity conspicuous, to the point of evoking its transgression of conventional taboos. It is a principal strategy of obscene poetics, and both develop out of the western evolution of aesthetics and their dialectic—philosophical materialism's progressive encroachment on the territory of philosophical idealism.

Being a particularly troublesome concept, pornography requires some comment. The now traditional designations of "hard-core" and "soft-core" continue to be plausible, with the qualifications I discuss in the main body of text. Hard-core pornography represents explicit sex, usually depicting genitalia in action and usually to the end of eroticizing its readership or audience, though it may also employ other subordinate motifs. Soft-core pornography may represent explicit sex but will usually depict sex within what is perceived to be an acceptable standard of taste and will usually subordinate sex to other motifs, particularly sentimental or parodic ones. While hard-core's principal function is to evoke sexual obscenity, soft-core tends rather to allude to it and is consequently more restrained or decorous.

In addition to these standard, though not necessarily standardized, concepts I propose a third, which can be called artistic pornography. It may and frequently does represent explicit genital sex but integrates sexuality as a theme or rhetoric into an aesthetic context for an aesthetic purpose. This mode, with which I am primarily concerned, tends to use obscenity as a dialectical term counterpointing a phenomenology of human sexuality with cultural configurations that tend to sublimate, disguise, suppress or divert cognition of it. These definitions obviously have their ambiguities. The determination of what is obscene or eroticizing or an acceptable standard of taste or aesthetic is unavoidably subject to interpretation, which is in turn subject to inclination or predisposition. Moreover, the works that these definitions try to corral are frequently disobliging and disconcertingly jump the fences. Such are the habitual risks of definition in the arts.

The link between pornography and obscenity and their dialectical function means that I distinguish between pornography and erotica on a functional rather than a valuative or legal basis. Pornography functions in terms of the obscene, while erotica functions in terms of sexual love. As a rule of thumb, the difference can be measured by the context and character of a work's focus on explicit sex. Radclyffe Hall's novel, *The Well of Loneliness,* is about sexual love but subordinates sex to love so as to be unequivocally erotic. Pauline Réage's *Story of O* is also about sexual love, but casts love in terms of an obscene sexual imperative that is unequivocally pornographic. Of course there are many more equivocal cases, particularly in works where sexuality has an occasional or minor presence. In William Faulkner's *Pylon*, for example, I take its famous cockpit/parachute scene to be a pornographic apostrophe to an otherwise erotic relationship. Again, such distinctions depend on context and interpretation. There is also another usage of erotic as a verb, to eroticize, in reference to sexual arousal, which I use in its conventional sense. While the general distinction between pornography and erotica may or may not be important in itself, it assumes significance in reference to those polemics that define pornography as that which is damaging to society, particularly to women, and erotica as that which is not. I take up these issues in due course but for now merely want to note the particular terms from which my analysis proceeds. I trust that the framework of discussion will clarify in practice what will very likely continue to be problematic in theory.

# 1

# The History of Sexuality and Poetics

## LIBERALISM AND THE PROBLEM OF PROBLEMS

Eroticism, Georges Bataille says in the most philosophically incisive study of the subject to date, is "the problem of problems. In that he is an erotic animal, man is a problem for himself. Eroticism is the problematic part of ourselves. . . . Of all problems eroticism is the most mysterious, the most general and the least straightforward." Pornography, for better or worse the aesthetic configuration of eroticism, is one measure of the problem's social dimension. And if we take the commercial printing press as a demarcation of modernity, pornography is coextensive with modern life and its vexations. In 1524, some fifty years after the introduction of the press to Italy, Pietro Aretino punctuated Giulio Romano's erotic drawings, called *Posizioni*, with pornographic sonnets. The publication was promptly suppressed by the Church; its engraver-printer in Rome was jailed, and Aretino avoided the same fate by skipping town. When he returned, a Vatican hit man wounded him in an assassination attempt. Aretino left Rome and settled in Venice, which in the spirit of variable community standards had something of a free-press tradition already. Thus Aretino, the first modern pornographer, presented Renaissance society with problems that nag us still.

Aretino was also among the first professional writers, one who wrote for pay as distinct from patronage. He produced verse, plays, satire, political and religious tracts, and libels. In fact, so thriving was the latter business that for a price he would *refrain* from writing libels, thereby inventing the "kill fee" and possibly the model for what later became the English common law concept of obscene libel. From the start, pornography was integral to both the professional writers' arsenal and popular literature. Especially the *Positions*, as his sonnets quickly became known in England, were read throughout Europe. He spawned a school of imitators, the self-styled "Aretines." Others attacked him even as they exploited his example. That his imitators had a certain success of their own confirms that the master, whose *Positions* and *Dialogues* are notorious even now, pioneered a genre that from the beginning had a broad appeal.

Moreover, as David O. Frantz argues *(Festum Voluptatis)*, Aretino was distinctly a part of the great humanistic enterprise of his epoch. Renaissance humanism had two strains, the mainline scholarly one recovering pre-Christian classicism and the popular one exploring and exploiting human nature. Modern pornography is prefigured in the former and explicitly realized in the latter. The one produced a tradition of learned erotica developing out of Italy's academies. After hours the eggheads got together over *vino* and regaled one another with dirty jokes and tales. For example, Poggio's famous *Facetiae* is a compendium of these. But pornography per se got its start in the less rarefied atmosphere of politics and commerce, where Aretino hung out.

Frantz demonstrates that pornography was rather more central to Renaissance concerns than scholars have let on, not only in the writing of Aretino and the Aretines but also in the graphic arts, where among others such artists as Perino del Vaga and Agostino Carracci rivaled Romano's explicitness.

Humanism included rather than transcended the varieties of sexual imagination, and this means pornography, not just the erotica or bawdry with which it is usually lumped and trivialized as a whimsical distraction from the period's prime humanistic business. Aretino's *sonetti lussuriosi*, the *Positions*, are unequivocal: "Put a finger in my asshole, dear old man, and push the cock in little by little, lift up this leg, and make a good game. . . ." While the recreational spirit of these sonnets does not advance the verse form, it is a part of the form's history.

Frantz further makes the intriguing claim that the sonnets served another aesthetic function. They subverted two centuries of Petrarchan tradition and helped establish an anti-Petrarchan one. Aretino's women are not neo-Platonic ideas on a pedestal, they are down and dirty and enjoying it. That attitude informs an epistemological function today in certain lines of feminist pornography. Aretino was no feminist ("What wrong is there," he writes in a letter, "in beholding a man possess a woman?"), but he was on to something. Similarly with his *Dialogues*, which by volume are about one part pornography to seven parts satire on the Church and the situation of women vis-à-vis wiving and whoring, and which even include some rudimentary class analysis. Aretino's reputation and works survive primarily because he brought sexuality within the purview of the humanism of his age. What's more, his satirical posture foreshadows the deconstructivist spirit characteristic of such successors in the pornographic tradition as the Marquis de Sade, Bataille, and Jean Genet.

That modern pornography developed along with the commercial press, a professional as distinct from a patronized literati, increasing general literacy, and popular forms of prose fiction indicates its general human appeal. That suppression accompanied its development indicates how problematic its appeal is. Indeed, Bataille contends that taboo is imperative to its existence. To those who would remove restrictions, he scoffs that one might as well eliminate the hygienic axiom that you don't shit where you eat: Pornography is as atavistic as sexuality itself, and both require mediation. Negotiating eroticism's magnetic field of appeal, taboo, and their mediation is precisely what makes the problem of problems problematic.

Western civilization has had a long problematic history with eroticism, pornography, and obscenity. Today the discourse is as polarized as ever, although the conservative view has been complicated by a feminist perspective. Two such contrasting approaches to the problem as Wayland Young's *Eros Denied* and Susan Griffin's *Pornography and Silence* are illustrative. Young, reflecting a rationalist liberalism, argues that the hypocritical suppression of candid sexual expression in Western culture has produced false and unhealthy sexual attitudes and practices in both men and women. Griffin, reflecting a feminist conservatism, challenges liberalism's laissez-faire expressionism by charging that the whole history of the West reveals the "pornographic ideology" of patriarchy, the consequence of which is suppression of women. As we shall see, these positions are not necessarily gender specific. The irony of their collision is that Griffin's feminism is as much a product of Western liberalism as is Young's latitudinarianism. I will return in a later chapter to the matter of gender, but I want here to explore the conundrum of liberalism and how it has brought us to this point by helping cultivate a poetics of obscenity to mediate between the traditional taboos and the aggressive emergence of eroticism's appeal.

Obviously Aretino did not invent that appeal, but he did give it momentum, with the assistance of printing. His own appeal lasted into the seventeenth century and received a peculiar boost from the post-Reformation division of taste between puritan censoriousness and high church wit. John Donne, for example, satirizes the Aretino vogue in *Ignatius His Conclave* (1611). Aretino was erotically uninventive, Donne chides playfully, because he was ignorant of the licentious "treasure of Antiquitie." What's worse, Aretino deflects the curiosity of youth, who think this ignoramus is an authority on the subject.

But, notwithstanding occasional works by such writers as Thomas Nashe, the Earl of Rochester, or even John Cleland, eroticism was essentially a bauble until the late eighteenth century. By then the novel had become a popular form, and materialism had sufficiently influenced science and philosophy, including aesthetics, to question idealism and provide a preliminary basis for a poetics of obscenity. All of this was concomitant with developing liberalism, the modern milestone of which in England might be dated from 1695 with the expiration of the Licensing Act.

Obscene poetics, a functional rather than gratuitous linking of art and obscenity, were catalyzed in an atmosphere profoundly informed by increasingly assertive materialism, the Enlightenment, and the French and American revolutions, and the prologue to capitalist liberalism. If Sade was the first to synthesize the components of obscene poetics, there were nonetheless others probing them more circumspectly. But it will be useful to get at those developments from the perspective of "the end of history," announced two centuries later in 1989 by Francis Fukuyama, a policy planner for the United States State Department. He thereby launched a debate about whether *glasnost*, *perestroika*, and the collapse of Communism signified this dénouement. Representatives of both the political left and right for rather different reasons insisted that Communism and history still lived. But Fukuyama adroitly evoked Hegelian semantics in declaring that Marx's long end run around Hegel had gone for no gain and the Marxist totalitarians had had to punt. The capitalist liberals now had the ball, and the lead, and would run out the clock. In short, the ideological game was all but over, liberalism could claim the egalitarian trophy instituted by the American and French revolutions and was therefore the culmination of Hegelian history. Daniel Bell, author of *The End of Ideology*, in the *New York Times* dismissed the whole affair as a "farce." Possibly so, but then Marx, the Dadaists, and Charlie Chaplin have not been alone in suggesting that farce is the most salient form of modern times.

It was certainly a peculiar extension of that end point in history when Czechoslovakian playwright Vaclav Havel addressed a joint session of the United States Congress in February 1990. Of the scribbling tribe, only a white-haired Carl Sandburg had been accorded this forum, and that predictably to croon Lincoln glory. Havel spoke as the new democratic president of his country, and he had no elegiac intentions. Whether or not he had been aware of the "end of history" debate, he brought the weight of his status down on the side of Fukuyama. Capital was so obviously his objective that he didn't have to mention it. He was, though, apprehensive that Americans might not recognize their moment of historic destiny, and of course the corollary function of liberal capital. He lectured them from the sober perspective of one who had survived Communism and appealed to them on the high ground of ontological homily. So grim was the "nightmare" of Communism that it had given Havel, the age of uncertainty notwithstanding, "one great certainty: Consciousness precedes Being, and not the other way around, as the Marxists claim."

Oddly, his analysis of the world situation seemed to demonstrate the reverse. Capitalists and Communists alike, he said, persist in rendering the natural, political and cultural environments dysfunctional. "From time to time," he scolded both East and West, "we say that the anonymous megamachinery we have created for ourselves no longer serves us, but rather has enslaved us, yet we still fail to do anything about it." Neither, he emphasized, has moral conscience prompted responsibility in the face of macrodisaster. In short, he described being as holding consciousness in thrall. And although he appealed to a quasi-religious higher "order of Being, where all our actions are indelibly recorded and where, and only where, they will be properly judged," this did not seem to change the material circumstances, as the Marxists might say.

The very intensity of Havel's cheerleading for consciousness to assert itself qualified his "one great certainty." Indeed, even Havel's own plays, where the state, society, the work place, dominate consciousness are a measure of his posture's desperation. Economically, politically, and aesthetically, Havel would seem to illuminate the same situation, where being determines consciousness. Why, then, would he express such certainty that it is otherwise? Could it be his own material circumstances, a writer turned politician who had just emerged battered from under the hammy fist of Communism but apprehensive about putting himself and his country under the prosperously gloved but distinctly meaty paw of capitalism? And what of his invocation of the Big Recorder in the sky—was that just residual theism or a shrewd pitch to the schizophrenic conscience of a high-rolling nation whose currency proclaims its trust in God? Given the end of one sort of materialist ideology, did he hope to induce consciousness of Judgment Day in a capitalism whose ideology is notorious for its own version of materialism? Did he wonder, after all, about liberal capitalism's blithe equation of the free market with the free spirit?

Whether or not political economy has reached the end of history and therefore the beginning of ideological consensus, President-playwright Havel's uneasy posture is a paradigm at once historical and contemporary.

His phenomenological project of urging allegiance to both the world's body and its idea is emblematic of the long dialogue between the philosophies of idealism and materialism. And if liberal capitalism has now made the world safe for Havel's idealist *cri de couer*, so has it made the world safe for obscenity and pornography. Pornography has always flourished under the entrepreneurship of capital, for liberalism is not merely secular, it is downright profane.

In the progress of liberalism it is no coincidence that modern pornography developed out of the Renaissance, when the Roman Church began to lose its theocratic grip, when humanism, science and technology began their offensive, when navigation got more able, the world got round, and commerce went global, when commercial printing induced a more demotic literature, when the vernacular validated itself and induced increasingly more popular literacy, when, in short, the Western world view began to be more material, various, and liberal.

Modern pornography, among other things, was the beneficiary of incipient liberalism's tolerance for the materialist encroachment on prevailing idealism. By the end of the eighteenth century, the dialectic between idealism and materialism had sharpened sufficiently to pose metaphysical and epistemological problems for poetics. Skepticism had challenged idealist ontology, and empiricism gathered credibility. This also helped deconstruct conceptions of nature, which could no longer be the univocal icon of fixed and permanent forms. Neither could art, claiming an epistemological function, be the mere mirror of nature but must assume the interior role of illumination. Correspondingly, this compounded the much-worried neoclassical and Romantic concern with distinguishing the universal natural truths from aberrations, the essential from the accidental. In short, the skeptical materialization of ideas precipitated a crisis of the idea that undermined the theoretical foundations of the beautiful itself, to say nothing of taste.

A convenient index of the evolution of this aesthetic problem is in Sir Joshua Reynolds' annual *Discourses* to the Royal Academy of Arts between 1769 and 1790. In the early discourses, Reynolds is unequivocal in his insistence that only the universal is the source of beauty, but by the last discourses he feels obliged to acknowledge that the aberrant, too, may be a source. That is, in the course of about twenty years the "official" premises of beauty had shifted implicitly from univocal idealism to materialist relativity. This was crucial to the development of obscene poetics. The aberrant, or unnatural, was associated with the obscene. So its aesthetic validation implied new artistic possibilities. Except for William Blake and Sade, these implications were slow to be realized. Meanwhile, they perturbed the univocal idea of nature, suggesting the erasure of distinction between the natural and the unnatural.

## THE COVERT HISTORY OF POETICS

Writers and artists confronted the "crisis of the idea" in various ways. Some neoclassicists, like Dr. Johnson, temporized in the face of it, emphasizing reason and common sense as if they were immune to the virus of materialist implications. Others, like Reynolds, accommodated without really engaging the problem. Both sorts simply lived with the contradictions, for example those inherent in the coincidence of the beautiful—implying God, order and coherence—and the sublime—implying the thrill of wildness, terror, and pain. But such evasions wouldn't do for long. When Friedrich Schiller divided the poetic house between classical naivete and modern sentimentalism, it was a demarcation too exclusive for coexistence. And when he characterized the latter as a sick man seeking the health of the former, he put his finger on the dialectical key—the nostalgic appeal of vestigial idealism in the face of decentering materialism.

Schiller's own response to the crisis, though, was at least as heroic as it was nostalgic. Given the modern difficulties of a univocally idealist nature, he posited a dialectically binary nature. Physical nature constituted a kind of bondage against which intelligent nature had to assert itself. The resistance to suffering bondage was the function of reason and was a manifestation of the beautiful. The existential resolution of nature's dialectic was the transformation of suffering via rational action, which asserts freedom and thus the sublime. This theoretical process is worked out programmatically in *William Tell*, for example. The Swiss Tell first suffers the oppression of the Austrian interloper; his resistance is in one sense reasonable but in a larger sense petulant, individualistic and ineffective; his suffering is transformed only when he finally takes the more rational action of joining collectively with his fellow Swiss to overthrow the oppressor. Schiller's dialectic solves several problems. By shifting the imperative from universality to freedom he avoids idealist sticking points. If freedom is an idea, it is one materially validated by the American and French revolutions. At the same time he is able to restore idealist reason in the context of an acknowledged materialist situation. In his scheme beauty and the sublime complement rather than contradict one another. But after all it would seem that Schiller had co-opted materialism into latent idealism, where the material world was heroically transcended by an ideal action. In that sense Schiller was his own sick man yearning for pre-lapserian health.

Schiller's project of accounting materialist implications yet keeping them subordinate to the synthesizing utility of idealism was similar to that of the mainstream of English Romantics. For them, too, the epistemological was the most absorbing problem posed by the crisis of the idea. Given a dialectical rather than univocal nature, the character and reliability of poetic knowledge was necessarily in question. Schiller's paradigm connected poetic knowledge to the sublime, achieved in the final phase of transforming the pathetic bondage of material nature into intellectual freedom from it. In making epistemological authority rational, this was consistent with revisionist Platonism, which was also the English model. But if the English poets were preoccupied with the imagination as the locus of authority, they too recognized the need to take materialism into account in order to sustain idealism.

Coleridge had perhaps the most profound agon with the problem and lent his considerable intelligence to making Platonic method not only user-friendly to science but in fact the very basis of scientific method. His key to knowledge was the Platonic principle of unity, i.e., of synthesizing ideas. The problem of knowledge was that of discovering law, the master or universal idea. Ideas necessarily preceded observation and experimentation, and therefore the latter were validated only by their methodological reliability in confirming the idea. Whatever problems there are in this subordination of the empirical to the ideal (e.g., whether our idea of electricity does in fact precede our observation of it) are resolved idealistically. They are negotiated by imagination—that highest exemplastic power of mind—the arbiter for transforming empirical observation and experiment into law, i.e., idealist knowledge. Indeed, imagination itself is idealistically constituted. Association is its material basis but is too mechanistic; association is not a direct product of consciousness interacting with the world, it is rather an immaterial "disposition" to associate. That is, association is the idea of associating. If there are slippages in this theory derived from the Platonic "principle of unity," we need only recall the yearning in modern science for a unified field theory to see how elusive yet appealing that idea is.

The Romantic struggle to contain creeping materialism is also evident in Coleridge's debate with Wordsworth about the law of rusticity. The irony of this dispute is that Wordsworth seems to have supposed he was on safe Platonic ground when he proposed that, because nature was the source of the "beautiful and permanent forms," the rustic or natural man was the "most philosophical," i.e., the essence of human nature. But Coleridge perceived that Wordsworth had inadvertently fused a materialistically tainted nature with the forms. So hybrid a conception implied very dubious quality control; Wordsworth's idiosyncratic designation of the "rustic" was an example. So far from being "philosophical" the "rustic" was ignorant, inarticulate, and unimaginative. He may be quaint, but that appeal was purely accidental and not a law of human nature. Such exceptions as there were, Coleridge argued, were either educated as with Swiss mountaineers, or were edited of their quaintness and grossness. Nature, particularly the hybrid Wordsworth version, did not in itself produce the master idea of human being. If for Wordsworth "The Idiot Boy" was a natural phenomenon, for Coleridge he was not only an aberration but a violation of epistemological law. Coleridge was trying to hold a line that even Reynolds had abandoned, and not without reason. If idiots were a product of natural law, what was to preclude sadistic "monsters" of the sort Sade was even then inventing? And if, then, art were to imitate nature . . . ? No, monsters could not be natural, and art's business was to illuminate distinctions, not merely reflect deceiving appearances. If Coleridge was perhaps deficient in negative capability, he was also more attentive to philosophical history than his colleagues. And he was acutely aware of the cadence in the dialogue of idealism and materialism. He noted that metaphysics were in recession by the late Renaissance and that Thomas Hobbes and David Hartley signified the materialist boom of the post-Renaissance, especially of the eighteenth century. And he was anxious lest materialism negate the coherence provided by idealism.

In general the English Romantics responded to the crisis of the idea by co-opting materialism as the valet of idealist epistemology. The acme was Shelley's *Defence*. While Coleridge may have been the most laborious with philosophical implications, they were all more or less attuned to the same discourse. This was an approach altogether too pedestrian for William Blake, however. Contemptuous of philosophy, whether idealist or materialist, Blake had no patience with reasoning one's way to truth. Contradictions? Of course. His visionary epistemology married them and presented co-equal partners. "Without contraries is no progression." Innocence needs experience; beauty, the ugly; love, hate; good, evil; reason, energy; soul, the body. The cosmos is in motion and contraries are its impetus. In terms of poetics Blake simply erased trivial distinctions en route to a dialectic of dynamics between energy and reason, the ugly and the beautiful. His sense of nature was coextensive with Creation's sublime energy, featuring a Creator who made both the tiger and the lamb, and pronounced it fitting. For Blake the problem of aberration was no problem; it was subsumed in the contrariety of Creation. Moreover, in the tussle of energy and reason, sexuality was not only unleashed, it had a precociously naturalistic importance. Blake did not write pornography, but it was not outside at least his theoretical ken:

> Abstinence sows sand all over
> The ruddy limbs & flaming hair,
> But Desire Gratified
> Plants fruits of life & beauty there.

---

In a wife I would desire
What in whores is always found,
The lineaments of Gratified desire.

---

What is it men in women do require?
The lineaments of Gratified Desire.
What is it women in men require?
The lineaments of Gratified Desire.

Then, too, there is "A Divine Image":

Cruelty has a Human Heart
And Jealousy a Human Face,
Terror the Human Form Divine
And Secrecy the Human Dress.

---

The Human Dress is forged Iron,
The Human Form a fiery Forge,
The Human Face a Furnace sealed,
The Human Heart its hungry Gorge.

This is the verse incarnation of Edmund Burke's "sublime," and it is thoroughly compatible, as is Burke (and others who are of the "Devil's Party" without knowing it), with the Marquis de Sade's diabolical conception of nature.

If Blake had written pornography it is conceivable that it would have had affinities with that of Sade. Blake's obsessions were rather different than Sade's, but both were convinced of a sublime nature that was essentially energy, more tainted with materialism and embracing more aberrations than Reynolds or Coleridge or Wordsworth or even Shelley ever dreamed on. Their respective poetics were consequently in some senses idiosyncratic, but in another sense they are logical, if impatient, products of the idealist/materialist dialectic. As Sade's psychology would have it, he pursued the obscenity/pornography axis and produced the pertinent models. I will return to Sade later, but here it suffices to note that the correspondence between two such different writers suggests that an obscene poetics evolved quite organically out of the philosophical preoccupations of the eighteenth century.

Madame de Staël, whose attention to the relation of social institutions and literature at the turn of the nineteenth century helped establish preliminary terms for a materialist criticism, contended that the courtly and stylish traditions of French society produced a "genius" for comic literature (e.g., Moliere), while the democratic yeoman traditions of England produced a genius for the "sublime" (e.g., Richardson, Shakespeare). Among other things this meant that English literature was the more likely to transcend the limitations of mere "taste." Ironically, even as she was writing these assessments, her countryman Sade was making a calculated assault on taste and its implications at every conceivable level, surely the single most relentless such assault in the history of Western literature. Sade, too, admired the English sublime, most especially its manifestations in Richardson. Making a somewhat perverse use of his model, Sade confronted French taste with nature's combustible sublimity and did it with a quite literal vengeance.

If Madame de Staël was accurate about pre-revolutionary French literature, the post-revolutionary situation was about to change dramatically. Since Sade, it has been the French rather more than the English who have led the attack on taste, quite likely in reaction to the condition Madame de Staël described. A lineage runs from Sade through Baudelaire, Lautréamont, Zola, Jarry, Apollinaire, Breton, and the Surrealists to Bataille, Pauline Réage, and Genet. All of them have targeted conventional taste as an idol of the mind. All, possibly excepting Zola and Réage, have shared variations on or extensions of Sade's contrapuntal sense of nature's sublimity. All have made significant use of pornography and/or obscenity. It is along this line that obscene poetics have most self-consciously developed. And that development is an index of materialism's corollary swelling of the idealist mainstream.

To be sure, materialism was in continuous dialogue with idealism, but increasingly it gained an equal footing, and its perceptions were catalytic for poetics. Sade's categorically materialist determinism was of course extravagant, but that made his volcanic sense of nature all the more portable. Increasingly, too, the problem of poetics was not to co-opt materialism in the service of idealism but to harmonize the two as equal contraries. Baudelaire, in his simultaneous attraction to heaven and hell, body and soul, was "spiritualist and materialist all in one," as Marcel Raymond observes. The poetic problem was to negotiate the space or whatever it was between the two realms, to discover and articulate *les correspondances*, "the raptures of the spirit and the senses." The goal of poetry was "superior beauty," the signs and symbols of which were the sensuous images of nature but the comprehension of which could only be spiritual. Baudelaire is a slightly more neurotic and slightly less idiosyncratic version of Blake, both of them admirers of Swedenborgian syncretism.

Similarly, for Breton later on the dream was equally a material phenomenon in the Freudian sense and a noumenous revelation of spiritual being. He simultaneously embraced the magical and irrational power of mind to make (sur)reality and Marxian historical materialism. Surrealist poetics could neither quite realize nor survive the programmatic attempt to harmonize contraries, as the instances of Louis Aragon and Salvador Dali suggest. Aragon forfeited the dream to cast his lot with Marxism. Marxism was never much of a temptation for Dali, who redefined the surrealist dream as a "paranoiac" idealism and exploited it so adroitly that Breton came to call him Avida Dollar.

But even before that the materialist/idealist dialogue had flipped the crisis of the idea into the crisis of reality, signified by the more or less complementary emergences of Einsteinian relativity, Heisenbergian indeterminacy, and the Surrealist "crisis of the object." For the symbolists, materialism had been associated with utility, and, following Baudelaire, they cast the dialectic in terms of pedestrian utility and mystical beauty. Mallarmé's famous "struggle with the ideal," for example, was an attempt to make a "divine transposition of the fact into the ideal." Utility warped the beauty of primordial being, and his impatience with utility, even more than Baudelaire's, matched Blake's. But Mallarmé's preoccupation with the primordial was looking backward, and the modern quest for reality, in the face of the machine age and quantum physics, could not indulge atavistic nostalgia. Later, with Bataille, atavism would shed nostalgia and take on the hard edge of ontological materialism. Meanwhile, at the skeptical turn of the twentieth century, humor and caprice seemed the best antidote for either spiritualism or positivism. For Alfred Jarry and Guillaume Apollinaire, positive reality hovered somewhere between menace and nuisance. Jarry's "pataphysics," the "neo-scientific" investigation of "the laws that govern exceptions and . . . explain the universe that supplements this one," parody both scientism and metaphysics. Similarly with his Ubu plays, where social reality and its power premises are reduced to absurdity, to say nothing of obscenity. The *ubu* image, in fact, seems literally to evoke the medieval *saccus stercorum* homily, the world as a sack of shit.

Apollinaire's interrogation of reality was directed more toward problems of poetics, both graphic and literary: "The art of the modern painters takes the infinite universe for its ideal, and it is to the fourth dimension alone that we owe this new measure of perfection which enables the artist to endow objects with proportions in conformity with the degree of plasticity he wishes to give them." Having predicated this fourth-dimensional function, Apollinaire appropriately coined the term *surrealiste*. His literary caprice manifested itself both in "concretist" typography and more profoundly in imagistic conception, where he infused symbolist technique with his peculiarly chancy juxtapositions:

A stammerer with two jets of flame on his forehead
Went by, leading a sickly people for the pride
Of eating quail and manna every day
And of having seen the sea open like an eye.

Here reality is given the plasticity of Apollinaire's fourth dimension, the challenge to conventional perception achieved by the chop-logic conjunction of disparate imagistic components. Breton, in formulating a surrealist poetics, specifically adopted humor and caprice as principal weapons for his revolution of reality. To him realism was the villain for its monadist commitment to the illusion of the object. He could embrace materialism because of its dialectic between the object and the mystery of its implications, most conspicuously in the situation of the dream. Surrealism constituted a kind of Summa Poetica for the crisis of the idea. Materialism had been assimilated, and idealism's focus shifted from determining fixed reality to exploring the cosmic mystery. In surrealist hands the idealist function had become, via a combination of Freudian dream research and Baudelaire's *correspondances,* a scientific interrogation of reality. It was not only the age of relativity and indeterminacy, but also of the Oedipus complex and archetypes.

If such works as Lautréamont's *Les Chants des Maldoror* and Zola's *Nana* had confirmed aberrance and obscenity on the docket of French poetics, pornography per se had been marking time since Sade. Apollinaire left off speculations on the fourth dimension long enough to reclaim the genre. His complex legacy includes two pornographic novels and considerable bibliographic attention to pornography. His novel, *The Debauched Hospodar,* is especially pertinent here because it revived Sade, along with touches of Sacher-Masoch.

Predictably, in the context of Apollinaire's humor and caprice, the novel is a parody of Sade. Where Sade pursues a pleasure-pain-power nexus relentlessly as a demonstration of nature's sublime indifference and inexplicability, Apollinaire approaches the motif as cavalierly as he did what he called "the game of verse," to say nothing of his life itself. Although the novel's protagonist indulges pretty much the complete catalogue of Sadistic manias, it is as if the reader were watching Sadean narrative sped up to 64 frames per second. The caricature is further heightened by Apollinaire's deletion of anything like Sade's extended philosophic and pseudo-philosophic apologetics. Perhaps anticipating Bataille's later impatience with Sade's apologists, Apollinaire was determined simply to evoke Sadistic images in the face of contemporary community standards. The execution of his protagonist (one of Sade's tongue-in-cheek self-defenses was that vice was always punished in his works, a claim notably contradicted by *Justine,* which he did not acknowledge publicly) is an instance of how Apollinaire baits several dispositions, including his own, with Sadism:

> At the 2,000th blow, Mony gave up the ghost. The sun was radiant. The songs of the Manchurian birds made the spring morning even more gay. The sentence was executed and the last soldiers struck their blows on a mere formless tatter, a sort of pork mincemeat in which one could no longer distinguish anything except for the face which had been carefully respected and whose wide open glassy eyes seemed to contemplate the divine majesty of the world beyond.

Here he parodies, in order, the benign idealization of nature, the body itself, and by implication materialist positivism, the symbolist romance of death, and simultaneously his own post-symbolist project of the fourth dimension. In the process of satirizing competing ideologies, Apollinaire put Sade back on the poetic agenda. It certainly was a reminder to Breton, for whom Sade was to be a surrealist touchstone.

If Louis Aragon was indeed the author of *Irène,* a pornographic novel with touches of both Lautréamont and Sade, it would confirm the Surrealist link in the pornographic chain. But Bataille, whose novel *Story of the Eye* was published in the same year, 1928, will more than suffice to indicate the connection. I will discuss his work in detail in a later chapter, but I want here to note its historical context in the progress of a poetics of obscenity. Bataille was connected to both surrealist and existentialist sensibilities, and brought Breton's "convulsive beauty" together with existentialist ontology. Convulsive beauty was an analogue of orgasm and served the emancipation of sexual desire. Bataille extended its Sadean implications and provided it an erotic metaphysics. In that form he passed the pornographic baton on to Genet and Réage. Bataille's is arguably the single most profound synthesis of sexual theory, in *Eroticism,* and pornographic practice in his fiction. He takes Sade well beyond reductivist obsessions to a highly sophisticated philosophy and poetics. In fact, his seems to be the only comprehensive formulation of a poetics of pornography or, in his vocabulary, eroticism. Still, it is distinguished by its erotic exclusiveness and features a whole ontology built upon a theory of sexuality. Perhaps it is this extravagance that led Bataille's colleague Roland Barthes to observe that Bataille achieves a "subtle subversion" of conventional discourse whereby he "eludes the idealist term by an *unexpected* materialism in which we find vice, devotion, play, impossible eroticism, etc.; thus Bataille does not counter modesty with sexual freedom but . . . with *laughter*." If Bataille's mode is laughter, it is a rather different laughter than that of his predecessor Apollinaire or of his contemporary Henry Miller or of such successors as William Burroughs or the recent writers of *Ladies' Home Erotica.* Bataille's extremity raises a distinction important to the development of obscene poetics.

In general, serious, as distinct from genre, writers incorporate pornography into a diffuse poetics where pornography has the complementary function of configuring the obscene. D. H. Lawrence and Anaïs Nin would be conservative examples, that is, writers who had to resist the idea of pornography in order to subdue it to their other purposes. Henry Miller would be a liberal example, that is one who rather casually and organically fused pornography into his practice. Bataille, of course, is a radical example, that is one for whom pornography is prior even to obscenity and is a philosophical imperative. The French pornographic tradition (e.g., Genet, Réage) inclines to the radical, whereas the British tradition (e.g., Beardsley, Joyce) inclines to the conservative, and the American (e.g., William Faulkner, Philip Roth) to the liberal. The measure is the degree to which pornography per se has philosophical necessity and the degree to which it is organically compatible with a writer's other aesthetic assumptions. Philosophy is somewhat elastic in this context. The American Alix Kates Shulman, in *On the Stroll* for example, is concerned not with philosophy as such but with a feminist sociology. Similarly with several lesbian S/M writers, whose work may have an implicit ontology but who more directly are polemical. Or Pauline Réage's *Story of O*, which explores a female psychology of love. So in this context philosophy is meant to be broad enough to include something as general as the intellectual perspective that informs the work. Obscenity is the key to the distinction. In Bataille's *Story of the Eye* sexuality insists on its obscenity, indicating a radically obscene poetic. Lawrence, in *Lady Chatterley's Lover*, wants to recuperate sexuality from obscenity, indicating a conservative obscene poetic. These polar positions tend to have theoretical dispositions toward sexuality and/or obscenity. The centrist liberal posture has little or no theoretical inclination. In Henry Miller's work sexuality has a pragmatic quotidian function, in itself neither obscene nor otherwise. It is integrated with other human activities, and its ethical implications are better or worse according to situation. In a liberal spirit, I make no theoretical claim for these distinctions, which of course have exceptions and overlappings, but they are useful in understanding the range and aesthetic dynamics of obscene poetics.

Just as English history has no equivalent of the French Revolution, so the English pornographic line has no equivalent of Sade. Until the twentieth century obscene poetics as such had no particular appeal for British writing. It was characterized by the robust sexual comedy, masculine in the most conventional sense, of Thomas Nashe, the Earl of Rochester, and John Cleland. And this was essentially the sort of bawdy amusement later produced by "the other Victorians." Cleland had made an overture to a female persona, but Fanny Hill is more a convenient caricature than a character. It was Samuel Richardson's more imaginative, howevermuch stereotyped, address to female sensibility that inspired Sade and ironically set the pornographic agenda. In Richardson there is an anxiety about the menace of eroticism that simultaneously evokes and suppresses its potency. And, as *Clarissa* is the homiletic tragedy of unbridled eroticism, *Pamela* is the comedy of eroticism brought to heel, facilitating domestic order by harmonizing aristocratic class structure with upward mobility. Henry Fielding—whose common-sense natural treatment of sexual hypocrisy, e.g. in *Tom Jones*, also influenced Sade—was contemptuous of Richardson's commercialization of virtue, but he was an old-fashioned man, a rational classicist. Richardson, a sentimentalist, anticipated the psychic potency of commerce and put his finger on the extended social dynamics of erotic power that so fascinated Sade.

The future was to be an age of ascendancy for both Britain and capital, and the domestication of erotic power served the purposes of banking, industrialism, and imperialism, the great pillars of British hegemony and stability throughout the nineteenth century. Queen Victoria, the long-lived symbol of potency discreetly skirted, presided over that econo-erotic code for most of the century. Occasionally the erotic component would rear its literary head. It threatened disruption in the passion of Heathcliffe and Catherine in Emily Brontë's *Wuthering Heights*, for example. But then that novel is a requiem for libido, not a paean. Thackeray's Becky Sharp was more enterprising. She is a shrewd and calculating variation on Richardson's Pamela, who uses sex to co-opt and corrupt both her class superiors and the commercial ethos itself. Thackeray clearly targeted the code but kept Becky's erotic carryings-on off the page.

The French, in the wake of Sade and their revolution, with its contrapuntal reverberations through the nineteenth century, were more disposed to an aggressive obscenity. Where the British, in their social stability, seemed to want either to criticize or aestheticize the world, the French, in the throes of a disruptive environment, seemed more focused on aesthetic revolution, the de- and reconstruction of perception itself. Obscenity had a distinct function, as Baudelaire, Lautréamont, and Zola demonstrated directly, Gautier, Huysmans, and Rimbaud more obliquely. In this regard the French obscene agenda was on the table, while the British was underneath and camouflaged by skirted legs. But even in that demimonde, as Steven Marcus adroitly examined it, when the British got obscene, they merely got smutty. They did not mix their covert amusements with their poetic business, although the implications occasionally emerged in such works as Aubrey Beardsley's *Under the Hill*. Beardsley demonstrated pornography's aesthetic nexus, as we shall see, but then literature was not really Beardsley's art, and the more complex issues of obscene poetics were left dangling until James Joyce and D. H. Lawrence addressed them. That they both denied the aesthetic validity of pornography as they defined it, even as their practice counterpointed their theory, is less a semantic problem than an index of the modernist engagement with the crisis of reality.

The British modernists were rather more disconcerted by materialism than were the French. Like Pound's Mauberly, trying to peer through a cinematic flicker back to the chiseled sculpture of rhyme, their reaction to the corporate industrial manifestations of materialism was profoundly conservative. Joyce, for example, deliberately invoked an archaic Thomistic aesthetic rooted in classical idealism. While this effectively informed his sense of artistic mission, it did not sit so lightly atop his fictive inclinations. That is, it is one thing to profess Thomistic *claritas* as aesthetic model, rather another to produce Molly Bloom's "smellrump lickshit" as an instance of it. Joyce's poetic formula of pressing forth beauty from the gross earth implies a material cause quite different from the understandings of either Aristotle or Aquinas. His grafting of medieval vocabulary onto materialist implications—e.g., his positivist interest in psychoanalysis and dream phenomena and interpretation, notwithstanding his distrust of Freudianism—was a willful attempt to invest a material perspective with a dignity and truth otherwise debased by modern, especially Irish, culture. Joyce's aesthetic seems to have been at least as much a product of his antagonism to atrophied religiosity and cultural nationalism as it was of a working poetics. His project was similar to that of the Romantics, co-opting materialism in the service of idealism.

Lawrence's approach to the critical problem was less cohesive than Joyce's, largely because it was more modern. His idealist connection was his Jungian sense of the psyche, which he saw in a dialectical relationship with mechanistic industrialism. The human problem was achieving a holistic synthesis of *anima* and *animus* in the face of the culture's insentient machinations. The poetic problem was to represent the dialectical dynamics and their for the most part destructive effects. In *Lady Chatterley's Lover*, especially, the opposition is between an idealist nature and the machine's implacable progress. Given Lawrence's relentless attentions to the situation of eros and psyche, it was logical that he would address sexuality per se in this context. The poetic problem here was evoking sexuality without succumbing to its mechanistic physicality. Philosophically he solved the problem by equating sex with the sentient potency of an idealist, even Wordsworthian, nature, on the one hand, while making problematic its prospects for survival vis-à-vis cultural determinism, on the other. Imagistically, he solved the problem by garnishing sex and its organs with ceremonial flora and personification so that a sexual spectacle evoked Dionysian cult rather than materialist libido.

Lawrence tended to hedge the philosophical bet with his use of archetypes, but his critical perspective was based on a cultural materialism, an analysis of cultural dynamics and their mechanization of human spirit. His idealist disposition induced the mythy costume with which he dressed the anatomy of sex. Joyce's representation of sex, conversely, was naturalistic. Molly Bloom is a highly sentient being, but she is also a lusty one who has little patience for metaphysics and is more at home in her knowledge and meditation of eroticism's nitty-gritty. Similarly with Leopold, whose cerebral character is punctuated by a moment of unmediated masturbation. Joyce's aesthetic is more self-consciously idealist than Lawrence's, but both are characteristically modernist in their adaptation to the pressures and appeals of materialism. They are also another index of how obscene poetics were, and are, not some perverse quantum jump, but rather evolved from the general matrix of culture and aesthetics. The dialogue of idealism and materialism continues, of course. It is in Genet's peculiar iconography of crime, to say nothing of Sartre's encomium, *Saint Genet*. It is in the feminist debates about pornography, both those about pornography's feminist validity in general and those about lesbian S/M in particular. Even William Burroughs, whose ontology seems to be at least as ruthlessly materialist as Sade's, postulates the function of control addicts like Dr. Benway to be the eradication of "other-level experience," a concept implying that consciousness left to its own devices might well be prior to the situation of being.

But of course consciousness is never left to its own devices, which brings us back to Vaclav Havel and the poet in the world, a world in dialectical tension. His Pyrrhic declaration of mind's pre-eminence is plaintive because the failure of Communism is after all the failure of its idea in the face of material demands. And he rightly fears that the ideas of democracy and its current corollary, capitalism, are merely playing roles in a masque where the plot is driven by the material circumstances of productivity and distribution. His one great certainty whistles in the dusk of the skeptical trope of our time, indeterminacy. Like Havel, we all continue to live in the crisis of reality. We test our hypotheses and then test the tests. At present, wherever that may be in world-historical terms, we apparently now have the one hypothesis of liberal capitalism. If history is a measure—and if capitalism stays liberal—that should continue to expand the prospects for obscene poetics.

Since at least the time of Aretino pornography has been an international commodity, as has prostitution, at least for a certain stratum. Already the new Soviet liberalism has induced a significantly higher incidence of prostitution than previously. Many of its practitioners acknowledge that their objective is to snag a presumably rich foreigner and become a matrimonial ex-patriot. As the United States Immigration and Naturalization Service testifies, this is not an unusual arrangement in other parts of the world as well. Since the Vietnam War, especially, the practice has been democratized a bit. Asian brides are advertised to American men at affordable rates. American brides on lease to Asian men are somewhat more pricey, but that market is probably skewed by the vexatious situation of Hong Kong. Whatever the progress of liberalism over the past two hundred years, it has not managed to leave all that far behind the conditions that inspired Richardson or Sade or Zola. And if I have discussed obscene poetics as a product of ontological and aesthetic discourse, I have not meant to obscure their obvious derivation from life as well.

## THE PROLIFERATION OF PERVERSITIES

Still, in *The History of Sexuality*, Michel Foucault argues that sexuality is not so much a biological, sensual or even emotional fact of life as it is a formulation of discourse. Although it tends to operate behind a facade of data, it is essentially a rhetorical articulation of sexual assumptions serving the purposes of the cultural power matrix that produces it. He contends that sex is so wrapped in the discourse of sexuality that in itself it has no being as such. Rather, "the imaginary element that is 'sex'" has been created as a "deployment" enforcing historical power dynamics. Foucault accordingly deconstructs the liberal perception of power; as with sex, power is not what it seems. It is not simply a matter of hierarchical oppression. It is a complex insinuation of cultural interests, i.e., not one power but several, and those generally competing. With regard to abortion or pornography in the United States, for example, there are competing powers within and between the executive and judicial branches of government, within and among political parties, religions, genders, even feminists. Similarly, he deconstructs the liberal humanist assumption that sexuality has been repressed and that sexual freedom is a liberation from power's oppression. Power being what it is, it is not so simply relieved. And so far from being repressed, sexuality has in fact been created by the supposed oppressor, namely the Church. What is true, however, is "that Western man has been drawn for three centuries to the task of telling everything concerning his sex; that since the classical age there has been a constant optimization and an increasing valorization of the discourse on sex; and that this carefully analytical discourse was meant to yield multiple effects of displacement, intensification, reorientation and modification of desire itself." So sexuality is a kind of behavior modification. In the process, Foucault says, it has functioned as an *ars erotica*, and an *ars erotica* is not all that far from an *ars poetica*.

Foucault's historical analysis suggests intriguing parallels between the progress of sexuality and that of obscene poetics. It is not surprising, for example, that the development of sexuality parallels an ascendant materialism. Sexuality emerged from religious preoccupations with the flesh, and by the seventeenth century had found a form in pastoral instructions for dealing with the subject in the confessional. These established the form of discourse that is still with us: they directed pastoral attentions meticulously to interrogation about not only the act itself, e.g. postures, but also about the stimulus of desire; they were also concerned, of course, with the flesh as the root of sin, which influenced conceptions of the natural and unnatural. By the late eighteenth century sexuality was becoming secularized, and developed a technology along the lines of pedagogy (e.g., child sexuality), medicine (e.g., the physiology of women and "nervous disorders"), and economics (e.g., demography and birth control). In the nineteenth century the medical model was dominant and induced an elaborate pathology of sex, culminating in the psychoanalytic approach. Normalizing sexuality, its *ars erotica* function, was an abiding interest but found especially fertile ground in medicine, where perversions and aberrations were particularly compelling. Normalization has continued into the twentieth century but has been modified to accommodate the more elaborated diversity of the cultural power matrix—e.g. sciences and scientists, feminists, gays and lesbians, racial groups, etc. Thus sexuality in this century has been characterized by a proliferation of "polymorphous perversities," where the moral connotations of perversity and aberrance have all but disappeared.

Throughout this history the sex-pleasure nexus has been troublesome, primarily but not exclusively in regard to women. Pleasure is an index of the corresponding development of sexuality and materialism. The history of sexuality suggests the gradual materialization of pleasure, which is to say that pleasure gradually gained an existential independence from traditional morality. In the theocratic phase pleasures of the flesh were equated with sin and were essentially a theological violation. They were proscribed by the procreative function. In the scientific phase the moral imperative remained but was masked by a shift of attention from first principles to empirical validation, from the model of God to the model of nature. Nature was still a unified idea (as much for Einstein as it had been for Coleridge) and procreation its sexual standard. But deviation became not so much a sin as a disease, implying diagnostics. The diagnostic framework made the sex-pleasure nexus the subject of proliferating material analyses—pathology, physiology, sociology, political economy. In fact the positivist standard for scientific method and the pathological preoccupations of medicine posed particular problems for an epistemology of pleasure.

Richard von Krafft-Ebing, whose *Psychopathia Sexualis* in 1882 was a pioneering study, is an instance. He gathered an impressive volume of case history data on sexual behaviors but put it exclusively in the category of pathological aberration, derived from the then prevalent theory of "degeneration" and the assumption that sexual abnormalities were caused by vague brain dysfunctions of some sort. In this context pleasure was either criminal or insane. He steadfastly refused to recognize the implications of "perversions" for "normal" sexuality, which created obstacles for the younger generation, especially Sigmund Freud and Havelock Ellis. Krafft-Ebing was disdainful of Freud's hypotheses connecting sexual development with neurosis, calling them "a scientific fairy tale." At the same time that his scrupulous empiricism led him to be perhaps the first to clinically note that the clitoris was the primary source of erotic pleasure for virgins, Krafft-Ebing's aberrational agenda led him to say that, "Since woman has less sexual need than men, a predominating sexual desire in her arouses the suspicion of its pathological significance," especially when, "passing beyond the limits set by good breeding and manners, [this] becomes quite noticeable." There is little or no room for pleasure in this analysis, where sexuality is merely a need for men and a pathology for women. And it is a familiar amalgam of empirical discipline and ideological acculturation by which nature is protected from aberrations.

Obviously pleasure does not readily lend itself to positivist investigation. Freud's own approach to female sexual pleasure, in clitoral versus vaginal orgasm for instance, was a combination of physiological rigor and ideology. The anatomical frame of discussion in *Three Contributions to the Theory of Sex* is a distinctly materialist address to pleasure. However, Freud's interpretation of the transference from childhood to adult sexuality—that the shift from clitoral to vaginal orgasm marked the mature woman—had the ring of moral imperative. This was enforced by his notion that anesthesia in the mature woman, where "the clitoric zone refuses to give up its excitability," is "brought on by profuse sexual activities in infantile life." Here it seems that material analysis is at the service of a moral stigma assigned to masturbation. Still, however compromised by the study of pathology and by a moral subtext, Freud's approach permitted him to place the sex-pleasure nexus in an essentially materialist context.

But it was the scientific humanism of Havelock Ellis' *Studies in the Psychology of Sex* that sought to remove sexology from its preoccupation with pathology, morbidity, and normative morality. He published the first volume, *Sexual Inversion*, in the wake of the Oscar Wilde trial, and its conclusion is characteristic:

> What, then, is the reasonable attitude of society toward the congenital sexual invert? . . . On the one hand, it cannot be expected to tolerate the invert who flouts his perversion in its face, and assumes that because he would rather take his pleasure with a soldier or a policeman than with their sisters, he is of

> finer clay than the vulgar herd. On the other, it might well refrain from crushing with undiscerning ignorance beneath a burden of shame the subject of an abnormality which, as we have seen, has not been found incapable of fine uses. Inversion is an aberration from the usual course of nature. But the clash of contending elements which must often mark the history of such a deviation results now and again—by no means infrequently—in nobler activities than those yielded by the vast majority. . . .

He is not always so overt an apologist, but in his preface he does disclaim scientific objectivity, acknowledging a "moral fervor" because, anticipating Bataille and Foucault, he regards "sex as the central problem of life." In his introduction to *The Sexual Revolution* Aron Krich notes that, "before Ellis' first cases on homosexuality were published in 1894 'not a single British case unconnected with the asylum or prisons had ever been recorded'." Ellis' work was essentially a mission to document and thus persuade society that sexual abnormalities were generally within a standard deviation of nature and thus could and should be accommodated, a mission consciously counterpointing the pathological shadow cast on abnormal sexual pleasures, particularly by Krafft-Ebing. Ellis was not, however, simply a liberal polemicist. His studies of homosexuality and female sexuality, especially, are still cited respectfully by such influential positivist sexological researchers as William Masters and Virginia Johnson. He expanded the spectrum of what might be considered socially, as distinct from naturally, normal sexual pleasures. In this regard, as Krich also notes, his "therapy of acceptance," helping people live with rather than repressing their abnormalities, established a foundation for existential psychoanalysis. If this laissez-faire approach did not quite morally neutralize sexual pleasure, it did shift the moral ground from normative reconstruction to tolerance.

Liberal tolerance is, of course, the agency for the proliferation of polymorphous perversities that Foucault finds characteristic of twentieth-century sexuality. So thorough has this process been that by the last decade of the century one is tempted to say that perversity has been cancelled as an operative term. But the corresponding proliferation of power centers has ironically complicated the dialectic. The AIDS epidemic is an instance. On the one hand, it has confirmed popular negative assumptions about homosexuality and is perceived as a kind of natural retribution for unnatural acts. This perspective has been marginalized in the discourse of sexuality but is not without even scientific advocates. On the other hand AIDS has catalyzed homosexual activists to a vigorous rebuttal, inducing a body of polemical and aesthetic works validating homoeroticism as normal love.

The irony is that even as this point of view prevails in the liberal discourse of sexuality, it revitalizes its nearly moribund antagonist, perversity. Rape, a crime implying perversity, complicates the discourse even more. One line of feminism, for example, defines rape as a violent rather than sexual act, which has certain advantages for litigation. But the matter is muddied by those cases of date or acquaintance rape where an inebriated "victim" whose will is unclear or inarticulate is either "raped" or "seduced" according to interpretation. Those who take a hard line on violence, as with the more traditional condemnation of the brutal beating of the Central Park jogger, say cases against "date rape" trivialize the issue; those who want to cast a wider legal net say otherwise. And the date rape defendants—a developing power locus corresponding to new definitions of rape—contend, possibly in good faith, that they had consensual sex with the plaintiffs. What if we factor in the problematics of marital rape? Or those of feminist lesbian practitioners of sado-masochism? Or Bataille's theory of eroticism, with its imperative of violence and violation . . . ? The rights of homosexuals and women and lesbians and the accused and of thinkers are all covered by the legacy of liberal tolerance, a legacy that has multiplied, as Foucault says, diversities of both power and "perversion."

In general the proliferation of perversities has had the effect of dissociating sexual pleasure from normative morality. In 1989 an AIDS-infected bisexual ex-convict was interviewed on national media and provided a chilling signal of how far dissociation might go. He said that it was his pleasure to have sex with as many people as possible, that he felt no obligation to inform them of his affliction, and that if he had to die he had no compunction about taking others with him. If this is an extreme hedonist perversity, it is not without a certain modern logic. Among other things, it is a perversion of the liberal doctrine of sexual liberation, the kind of warp that Foucault saw was built into it.

Ellis and Freud had launched a sexual revolution, but they were both rather moderate. Ellis' humanistic fervor was always tempered by scientific and moral responsibility; similarly with Freud, whose theoretical speculations were after all rooted in case histories and data. Wilhelm Reich, a Freudian analyst, brought a more charismatic style to sexuality, and the movement that formed around him between the two world wars became apocalyptic. Sexual repression was a kind of cosmic disease, and the cure for everything from the body to the body politic was free expression of sexual impulses. Orgasm released "sexual stasis" and "sexual fluids" and thus purged personal neuroses like necrophilia and political ones like naziism. Orgasmic therapy apparently has a certain validity for appropriate maladies. But cranked to the level of theory it implies an ethic of orgasm, and that is only a short-circuited synapse or two from the liberal perversity of our ex-con. If we can equate orgasm with pleasure, however, Reich did validate pleasure in an amoral if still pathological context. And the Reichian function of pleasure was distinctly materialist. His "discovery" of orgone energy—then and now regarded as Reich's white whale—in 1939 precipitated his unhappy end as well as increased skepticism about the potential quackery of the general theory of orgasm.

Reichian assumptions about sexual liberation probably had more lasting impact on popular discourse than on the scientific. They certainly informed the liberal side of the censorship battles of the 1950s and 1960s in the United States, where works by John Cleland, D. H. Lawrence, Henry Miller, William Burroughs, Allen Ginsberg, Edward Dahlberg, and others, as well as several literary magazines, were embroiled in obscenity litigation. The courts were a propitious forum, since the doctrine of free speech coincided conveniently with that of free sexual expression. These cases had considerable publicity and, along with the Kinsey reports, catalyzed both artistic and popular dialogue on sex.

By the mid-1960s, liberal discourse was taking an aggressive stance. An instance is Lars Ullerstam's *The Erotic Minorities*, translated from Swedish and published here in 1966 (1964 in Sweden, 1965 in France) by Grove Press, an especially activist publisher in this area. The book was a polemic for the liberation of sexual deviations primarily, but also of pornography as an aid to sexual pleasure (Ullerstam was a physician). "'Perversion' is a word that should be discarded," says the author, "It has been made to order for obscurantists and demagogues. It is saturated with superstition, and it is an insult, to boot." Ullerstam's prevailing assumption was that pleasure is the logical conclusion of Western history:

> We in the West now live in an age which is about to make Bentham's old dream of the hedonist society come true. The profane needs of men, their pleasure and displeasure, hold the foreground in the preoccupations of our politicians—or at least in their official statements. Our social institutions are no longer designed to please preachers and gods, but to create tolerable conditions for the individual in society. . . . There is really only one principle that is still in serious competition with the pleasure principle, and that is the principle of justice.

"Minorities," the politically operative word in the book's title, brought the principles of pleasure and justice together. Pleasure, an extension of the pursuit of happiness, is a democratic right for everyone, including religious, racial, and sexual minorities. Ullerstam is reminiscent of Havelock Ellis' inversionist apologetics, although he raises the ante considerably: "In order to abolish the myth that the 'perverted' pleasures are of a low and tawdry nature, I intend to give a few samples of the inner experiences that these 'perverted' acts can create. Their spiritual level is often very high: practices now termed sexual offenses can satisfy the same elementary human cravings as religious rites." The religious claim here is another instance of the sort of systemic circularity for which Foucault criticized the doctrine of sexual liberation; that is, the reclamation of religious validation hardly seems an advance, let alone revolutionary. But we might also see this as a materialist's appeasement of the loss of religious idealism. Ullerstam has taken Ellis' liberal tolerance to its logical conclusion, installing profane pleasure as the culmination of historical process, making it independent of any testament morality except that of secular liberalism and, the religious gesture notwithstanding, validating pleasure's function on existential ground.

In the 1950s the scientific discourse of sexuality showed a surge of behavioral, experimental, and clinical approaches. The behavioral Kinsey reports had been an unanticipated bombshell. Life during World War II in the United States had been faster and looser than ever before; those who weren't in uniform were working in war industries that operated around the clock, especially women in unprecedented numbers, and entertainment spots kept pretty much the same hours to accommodate swing and graveyard shifts. The country kept itself going on a kind of crazed energy. By the 1950s things were supposed to have returned to normal, symbolized by Ike's old-fashioned paternalism. But Kinsey reported a dramatic change in the norm, or at least what it had been thought to be. Promiscuity, it turned out, was not limited to men or even to adults. Pre- and extra-marital sex was common, if not quite so common for females as for males. Increasingly, homosexuals did not regard their disposition as pathological, and reported that their primary problem was not sexuality but social reaction to it. Moreover, Kinsey reported, moral standards were relative to social class. People were taking their pleasures and their morals as they liked, not necessarily as prescribed. Was sexual behavior taking its cue from morality, or vice versa?

Scientific sexologists were mostly interested in behavior. In fact, if they were to objectively understand sexual behavior, they were obliged to dissociate it from morality. The acme of this approach were the human sexual response studies by Masters and Johnson. They were the first to subject human sexual activity to laboratory conditions. People copulated in every possible position, masturbated and manipulated, performed fellatio and cunnilingus, were sodomized by machines, fantasized, pored over pornography, all under clinical observation, measurement, and recording. Never was sex submitted to such coldly calculated voyeurism. Obviously these proceedings violated social conventions, and every state then had sodomy laws, so they also violated the law. And, since sodomy laws derive from moral codes, morality too was violated. But so scrupulously positivistic were these studies that it is almost impertinent even to raise the issue of morality. Human subjects, albeit volunteers, were studied as lab monkeys or rats would be. An ecology of sex—i.e. its full panorama of postures, excitations, and activities—was assumed and investigated quite apart from moral considerations. The sex-pleasure nexus was recorded, calibrated, described, quantified, and thus validated in categorically existential terms. Pleasure, in short, had been rendered materialistic.

## SPEAKING THE UNSPEAKABLE

At about the same time that sex was set on its own two feet, literary battles over obscenity in the courts reached a new peak, as noted earlier. Notwithstanding the *Ulysses* decision in the 1930s by Judge Woolsey (to be discussed in more detail later), older works by such writers as Lawrence and Miller as well as new works by such writers as Ginsberg and Burroughs were being prosecuted. Post-war culture in America was alerted to sexuality and obscenity. Just as its young avant-garde writers were working a poetics of obscenity, so were its young avant-garde film makers. Aesthetics, too, were alerted. The historical correspondence along materialist lines between developments in the discourse on sexuality and those in the poetics of obscenity suggests more than complementarity. In combination they make a comprehensive discourse of sexuality. And Foucault's critique of liberation sexuality, the modern culmination of its discourse, is useful for a perspective on some political functions of obscene poetics.

Foucault charges liberation sexuality with being under three illusions: first, that power is a simple hierarchical structure of imposition; second, that sexuality is a psychosexual phenomenon suppressed by power; third, that sexual liberation is analogous to, or a significant step toward, revolution of power relationships. But power, says Foucault, is a complex matrix of powers within a larger liberal bourgeois system. The system cultivates an increasingly inclusive evolution of sexual discourse (hence, the proliferation of perversities); it manipulates discourse by tying sex to desire, which it modifies to sustain itself and its ends. The proliferation of perversities gives the illusion of liberation from a universal idea of sexuality and its oppressions, but in fact the discourse is a historical formation preoccupied with its own terms. Thus the discourse functions within itself and never disturbs the system. This is not to say that sexual discourse does not refer to the world but rather that the aspect of the world to which it refers is contained in desire and its systemic modifications. *Cosmopolitan* magazine, for example, sustains a running discourse of liberation sexuality for women. How to be sexy, how to combine sexiness with the conventional demands of careers, etc. Don't be fat, don't be wrinkled, don't be drab, or, conversely, be fat and feminine, wrinkled and racy, though you probably cannot ever get away with being drab: Drabness denies desire, and the point is to keep raising the ante on female desire. The proliferation of perversities—let's say, for example, female sexual aggressiveness or obese beauty—have the appearance of liberation but are in fact contained within the scheme of desire for sexiness or success or aesthetic acceptance sustaining the bourgeois system.

Foucault's perspective, though, is somewhat Olympian and tends to discount tactical analyses in the absence of revolutionary strategy. For folks in the trenches tactical advances may have their own validity. One sort of feminist writer, as reflected in the work of Alix Kates Shulman, for instance, regards any female definition of female being and sexuality as an imperative objective. Shulman's early work deconstructs male definitions of femaleness by parody. Her later work is more analytical of the political economy of female sexuality. When the protagonist of *On the Stroll* escapes her pimp-lover, there may be no strategic implications in her story, but there certainly is a significant liberation. And her story does put psychosexual and sociological contradictions in high relief. Since raising the consciousness of contradictions is a revolutionary tactic, Shulman's poetics here may reasonably be said to be revolutionary. For this feminist project, then, putting women at parity with men in sexual power relations is a crucial advance in political economy. And, as Shulman has said, in the context of the feminist pornography debate, the availability of pornography and obscenity to women is a necessary aesthetic and political tool. Similarly with feminist lesbian writers of sado-masochism. In their work sado-masochism is constituted as a theater where shifting power ratios can be explored through the roles of dominance and submission. On that stage consciousness of contradictions is endemic to the material. Moreover, their approach to the subject establishes a dialectic with the hegemony of traditional feminist assumptions about power and sexuality.

Any persons or groups who perceive themselves to be at best on the margins of power are likely to find Foucault's conception of power a bit promiscuous. If the proliferation of perversities has proliferated power, it is also true that power is relative. A given tactical sense will be conditioned by its relative numbers and positioning in the social matrix. Pedophiles, for example, will probably not suppose that any revolution would substantially increase their power. Not that its proliferation has totally passed them by. The furor of reaction to the Robert Mapplethorpe photographs in the late 1980s galvanized a counterpointing support rhetoric of some volume. It tended to focus on free speech and aesthetic validity rather than apologetics for pedophilia itself. But then those were also the early foci of Havelock Ellis' appeal to tolerance for homosexuality. Whatever the aesthetic virtues of child nudes, and however little correlation there may be between such works and pedophile practices, they necessarily serve a function of existentially validating those particular tastes, whether aesthetic or sexual. This ontological tactic is another aspect of obscene poetics, especially in lyric form. Allen Ginsberg's poem, "Please

Master," for example, is simultaneously an elegiac love poem and a celebration of masochistic submission. In that sense it confers a double legitimacy on perverse pleasure. At the same time, too, the poem's self-conscious extravagance implies a wink at the straight world, complicating perverse legitimacy with a dialectical edge interrogating normal pleasures. In "A Supermarket in California," Ginsberg brings Walt Whitman out of the closet, validating a perversity-poetics nexus in the most normal of contexts. His conclusion to "America"—"America, I'm putting my queer shoulder to the wheel"—is another quickie deconstruction by parody of normative assumptions about perversity and the good order of political economy. One hallmark of Ginsberg's career has been his use of more obscenity or less toward the ontological validation of homosexuality. And one measure of how such poetics can act on the world is the degree to which, in Ginsberg's lifetime, homosexuality has gained public acceptance and corresponding power. In his two major poems, "Howl" and "Kaddish," Ginsberg uses obscenity tactically to expand the scope of his cultural critique. But in those works the obscene trope is madness rather more than sexuality. An implicit motif in those works, however, is cultural desexualization. In "Kaddish" Naomi's madness is generated by the conflict of moral idealism and *realpolitik*; madness subsumes her vitality, the sexual aspect of which is suggested by her youthful sensuous spontaneity, her alienation from her husband and the poet's brief moment of Oedipal temptation when Naomi's gown slips up revealing her vagina. In "Howl" madness and self-destruction victimize a generation, precipitated by the cultural materialism symbolized in Moloch. Moloch's sapping of vitality is countered by Neal Cassady, the poem's "secret hero" who has so "sweetened the snatches of a million girls trembling in the sunset" that the poem pays tribute "to the memory of his innumerable lays of girls." Still, notwithstanding Cassady's vitalistic ministrations and the poet's final exorcisms, Moloch and madness prevail. So Ginsberg suggests the tactical function of obscene poetics in both sexual politics and the larger cultural critique.

Obscenity and sexuality have also served an important tactical function in the development of black poetics, especially in its self-conscious formulation in the 1960s. The radical black analysis was that the first step toward racial liberation required blacks to define themselves and identify with their blackness. Hence, the change in nomination from "Negro," a white euphemism, to "nigger" or "black." For writers this entailed the use and validation of black language. The most identifiably black language was street argot with its frequent obscenity. The epithet "motherfucker" was especially suitable, not only because it combined linguistic obscenity with taboo but also because it carried a whole lexicon of signifying expressions, such as "yo momma don't wear no underpants" or "that ain't what yo momma said last night in bed." The obscenity, like the idiolective grammar, spelling, and syntax, had the political purposes of dismissing white standards and validating black ones. Given black stereotypes, sexuality was somewhat more complicated. Amiri Baraka (then LeRoi Jones) took on the problem in his plays. In *The Baptism*, for example, he addressed sexuality itself, without particular reference to race. It satirizes a Christian sociology where religious fervor is a hypocritical sublimation of sexuality and its motives. That fervor also masks a confusion of love and hate. Christ, who in his second coming is a compulsive masturbator, is first revered and then attacked by the minister and the female acolytes Christ has seduced. In retaliation Christ kills them. But the real protagonist is a character called Homosexual, who further deconstructs the idealism of Christian love by reducing it to a materialist pleasure principle. In the process, of course, he challenges the hegemony of heterosexuality. The challenge is elaborated and given racial context in *The Toilet*. There the association of black virility, violence, and heterosexuality is interrogated when the black gang leader reveals his homosexual love, a love he has betrayed. This play, modifying the black ethos of virility and violence, restores a now humanistic love to sexuality.

In these two early plays Baraka establishes a sexual ground for black identification and morality. He has, first, to deconstruct majority assumptions, both black and white, and then install new terms—humanism for religiosity, love for virility. Violence, understandably, remained a constant. As his work became more overtly political, sexuality as such was subordinated. In *The Slave*, black revolutionary violence is pervasive but cross-examined by personal relationships and liberal humanism. Sexuality, specifically interracial sexuality, is in the background as a liberal legacy. The play is a requiem for both liberalism and its sexuality. They must, however painfully, give way to the revolution.

By the late 1960s the humanistic love Baraka had earlier evoked was a political imperative, as black poetry tried to close the gender gap. Black women poets were profuse in their praise of "Beautiful Black Men," and black male poets reciprocated in kind. But sexuality itself was politically problematic. Nikki Giovanni gave it a comic turn in "Seduction." Her man is preoccupied with black revolutionary analysis as she undresses them both, so the poem concludes, "then you'll notice / your state of undress / and knowing you you'll just say / 'Nikki, / isn't this counterrevolutionary . . . ?'" Don L. Lee turned the table in "The Revolutionary Screw," suggesting that black male revolutionary consciousness had not yet transcended sexual exploitation. Addressing the brothers, Lee ironically agrees that "when u ask for a piece / of leg / it's not for yr/self / but for yr/people . . . / & she wd be doin / a revolutionary thing." But one sister keeps her eye on the ball, "i mean / she really had it together / when she said: /

go fuck yr/self nigger. / now / that was / revolutionary."

Some of Baraka's poems synthesized the sexual-political dialectic his plays had explored, as in "A Poem for Speculative Hipsters":

> He had got, finally,
> to the forest
> of motives. There were no
> owls, or hunters. No Connie Chatterleys
> resting beautifully
> on their backs, having casually
> brought socialism
> to England.
>                 Only ideas,
> and their opposites.
>                               Like,
>                 he was *really*
>                 nowhere.

And in "Babylon Revisited" Baraka characterizes white women as diseased Whores of Babylon who suck the life from black men or, worse, reduce them to analogues of King Kong. By the mid-1970s Baraka could see the revolution being co-opted by money and sexuality. Black sexuality, so long an albatross, was suddenly paying off in white culture. In "Jim Brown on the Screen" he casts the football star turned movie star and sex symbol as a kind of sexy Jim Crow: "the eyes of our women and beast-women glued to yo thang, Jim / you can be more than that anyway, more than a new amos in space." Sexuality evolved from affirmation to negation in Baraka's poetics as racial politics intensified and redefined sexuality's role. But as feminism increasingly incorporated black women, and the end of the Cultural Revolution in China revealed a self-destructiveness in the Marxist-Maoist model, one significant focus of black poetics shifted from interracial to intraracial politics. Alice Walker's *The Color Purple* reconstituted the sexual dialectic, suggesting that the mutual admiration of black beauty between the sexes had been perhaps only skin deep. Black heterosexuality took as severe a beating as Walker contended black men had been giving black women for generations. Moreover, the stock of lesbianism, along with that of black female entrepreneurship, blew the roof off the Sex Exchange. Sexuality in black poetics was once again bullish.

Clearly, obscene poetics at once reflect and participate in contrapuntal political dynamics. But even when they divide the house, as with Walker's *The Color Purple*, they tend to carry the common stamp of the disaffected outsider. As we have seen, obscene poetics are in no sense exclusive to minority perspectives. But the organic aggressiveness of obscene poetics does seem to have a consistent appeal for culturally marginalized sensibilities. Still, while the liberal system cultivates the competition of their interests, obscenity constitutes a communal rite articulating their collective alienation. In "America," for example, Ginsberg—a white, Jewish intellectual—declaims: "America, when will we end the human war? / Go fuck yourself with your atom bomb." Twenty years later Baraka—at the height of his antagonism to whites, Jews, and bourgeois intellectuals—reclaims the lines in "Reprise of one of A. G.'s Best Poems": "America / Allen Ginsberg sd / 'Go fuck yrself w/ yr / Atom Bomb'—and yr doing / it!!" It is as if there is at the center of liberalism a Hydra myth with a head for every dissident to hack.

In *Mythologies,* Roland Barthes complained that bourgeois culture masquerades as a universal imperative of nature, whereas in fact it is a formulation of a particular historical moment. The process whereby the distinction is confused, or mystified, is mythification. Myth is a type of speech, defined by its form and not, as is often supposed, by truth or universality. That is, myth is not a self-constituted idea or archetype, it is a semiological formulation from the world's infinite suggestiveness according with the social uses history chooses myth to serve. Anything can be made into myth, and mythification transforms historical conditions into nature, hence myth's appearance of universality. For example, the designers of the Great Seal of the United States adapted Virgil's epithet, "God favors our enterprise," to invest the vision and works of the new republic with divine sanction. Virgil, as a classical poet with a pre-Christian theology, was a useful source for deists and a country proclaiming religious freedom. Thus the myth of the Republic made it the culmination of classical humanism under a pantheistic ordination. But myth, being historical, is subject to changing historical circumstances. As classical humanism evolved into bourgeois liberalism, and Christianity reemerged as the *de facto* religion of the West, history was subsumed into the myth that bourgeois liberalism was the political economy of nature (based on the competitive, acquisitive, and self-interested nature of human psychology) ordained by the Christian (sometimes Judeo-Christian) God.

Barthes' materialist analysis of myth is essentially the same as Foucault's analysis of sexuality. Myth and sexuality are analogous in that they are both functions of discourse. Indeed, Foucault's critique of liberation sexuality is that it developed along mythic lines, in Barthes' terms giving sex an "inflection" that made it seem to have a natural rather than historical-discursive relation to psychic and political liberation. In this sense, then, sexual discourse can be understood either to be or to operate as myth, and similarly with obscene poetics as a form of sexual discourse. Thus, Baraka's later formulation of white female sexuality mythifies it as naturally bestial or whorish. That is, white women are not merely metaphorical whores and beasts; Baraka represents those conditions as their nature. Moreover, as is characteristic of myth, the natural "fact" validates and disguises his political use of it. It is not that he simply chooses to so characterize white women for political purposes, but rather that, because they are what he says they are his politics are justified. Baraka's radical racial myth deconstructs the liberal American myth. The Christian ordination of the Republic is bound up with the sexual-religious confusion expounded in *The Baptism*, and that confusion informs and degrades bourgeois culture so thoroughly as to refute its claim to nature. When Alice Walker turns Baraka's myth back on itself by mythifying the bestiality of black men, it is an index of how fluidly myth, obscene poetics, and sexual discourse proliferate and interact in the power matrix of liberalism.

That there have been no black, feminist, lesbian, or homosexual revolutions may confirm Foucault's critique, that the discourse of sexuality even at its liberationist extreme has no effect on power relationships in the bourgeois system. The white male consciousness movement that developed around Robert Bly in the late 1980s, however, has an added irony. One aspect of that movement was to co-opt the claims of victimization by racial, feminist, and sexual minority groups. White men could now claim their own victimization at the hands of assumptions about their gender and sexuality. If this could be made to stick, it would eliminate the last human agency of oppression, white men. At that point, perhaps, attention would be directed to what Foucault says is the real source of oppression, which is the system itself. Then again, if liberalism has indeed triumphed over its opposite and ended Hegelian history, it may be that Foucault's point is moot. By the Ides of January 1991, however, it appeared that the infamously Eurocentric myopia of western liberalism had struck again.

The face-off between the United States and Iraq suggested that after all Hegelian history had not ended but had instead been recycled back to the Crusades, when the Mohammedan "Abstract One" challenged the "real culmination of Individuality" in Christianity by "outrageously" occupying the Holy Land. True, the Sepulchre now enshrined unholy oil, and the Jews as well as the Muslims had a new "objectivity," but the West was still as Hegel said it was then, in danger of its secular and spiritual alliances dissolving. Here once again in the face of outrage, the West could once again demonstrate that "secular pursuits are spiritual occupations." So, for that matter, could the Muslims, even though in Hegelian history their time in the sun had been eclipsed by the eleventh century.

Whatever the historical situation of this confrontation, it did demonstrate the dynamics of myth and of obscenity. In our side's mythification of

Saddam Hussein, the focus of "obscenity" was genocide and demagoguery. On their side, even for the Saudi Arabian friendlies, it was clear that female sexuality in the West was its own invitation to infidel demonology. Female American soldiers in Saudi Arabia were not permitted to drive vehicles, let alone bare their shoulders in the desert heat. Bob Hope's troupe could not include female entertainers. The Muslim myth of female sexuality prevailed. It was analogous in several respects to Baraka's myth. Accordingly, both black and white women soldiers countered with what was essentially the myth of liberation sexuality and in the media deconstructed the logic of liberalism's contradictory alliances. Back home their position was vigorously supported by the National Organization of Women. Sexuality and its myths became a very vocal item on the agenda of opposition to a Persian Gulf war. Here again, then, is an instance of the fluid interaction of myth, sexual discourse, and political economy. Meanwhile, Garry Trudeau's *Doonesbury*, frequently on the editorial rather than comic strip pages of the newspapers, ran episodes of a Gulf Rest & Recreation shipboard romance featuring Western infidels engaged in sexual infidelity, in Trudeau's running parody of contradictions in the Gulf situation. Befitting a family newspaper format, the pornographic motif was very soft-core. But this was nonetheless another index of how, whatever sort of history may have currency, obscene poetics will find inspiration and form in its flux.

"Ancient or not," Barthes argues, "mythology can only have a historical foundation, for myth is a type of speech chosen by history: it cannot possibly evolve from the 'nature' of things." While idealism and materialism continue their philosophical dialogue about the nature of things, the materialist "inflection" has been enormously influential on all forms of discourse. Thus even the ancient myths are subject to history. The Oedipal myth of Sophocles is not the Oedipal myth of Freud. The Freudian inflection not only makes the tragic potential normative—i.e. something we cannot avoid merely by moral example—but also invites our attention to its sexuality in a distinctively modern way. For sexuality's discourse, as Foucault says and history confirms, has been a hallmark of modern life. As with Freud, we find its attraction as imperative as its repulsion. Small wonder that Freud could neither face up to nor face down a sexuality of incest. Who can? Sexuality is, as Bataille says, the problem of problems. It will not go away. And we are in the dialectical situation of speaking the unspeakable.

It is an uneasy posture, and to maintain it we devise elaborate stratagems. Perhaps the most elaborate are the aesthetic. Literature and art reflect the panorama of collective and idiosyncratic mythologies more extravagantly and less cohesively than other discourses. In the last half of the twentieth century they have become the primary agencies of confirmation for a new ethos summed up in the fashionable phrase "cultural diversity." This is a logical extension of their modern function. Aesthetics derive from perception. Liberalism and materialism have cultivated increasingly various, interrogative, and skeptical perceptions of reality. T. S. Eliot, radically conservative modernist that he was, was quite right about the progressive dissociation of sensibility. It is manifest, as noted earlier, in the tension between James Joyce's aesthetic theory and his artistic practice. Marianne Moore was appropriately an admirer of Dwight Eisenhower; she and her modernist colleagues shared Ike's inclination for a forward-looking return to the past. But they were, after all, artists in history and willy-nilly ratified the dissociative myth of the modern. And modern reality is dialectical. At the very moment that capitalism is triumphant, for example, its exemplary capitalists—men like Charles Keating—are revealed to be public enemies. Or, just as liberation sexuality reaches its pinnacle, along comes AIDS to refute its myth. Contradiction and uncertainty are organic to our liberal ecology, a situation where univocal assumptions and values are necessarily challenged. Hence, the cultivation of challenges that Foucault characterizes as the proliferation of perversities.

Indeed, liberal aesthetics has cultivated a myth of perversity whereby, for example, it condescends to a Norman Rockwell for his lack of perversity and valorizes a Robert Mapplethorpe or Andres Serrano on its account. Perversity and the grotesque have had a long association with the arts, as in the works of Bosch, Goya, Swift, and Sade. But perversity's mythic status is largely a product of twentieth-century aesthetics, which launched a concerted challenge to univocal idealist assumptions about the natural, the beautiful, and their connection. Marcel Duchamp's self-conscious deconstruction of the concept of aesthetic taste was one of the first in this campaign. His Dadaist mustache on a copy of the *Mona Lisa* evoked both biological and aesthetic perversity. His "ready-made" *Fountain*, an inverted urinal, provided a slightly different twist to biological and aesthetic function. He waged a guerrilla war on the traditional myth of beauty, and in the process launched a counterpointing mythology of the perverse. Salvador Dali added to the myth with his lascivious mutilation of a dead donkey in *The Andalusian Dog*, as did Georges Bataille with *Story of the Eye*, Jean Genet with *Our Lady of the Flowers*, and William Burroughs with *Naked Lunch*. Pop art picked it up by representing mechanical urbanized landscape in traditionally natural terms. In Allan D'Archangelo's painting, *Evening Star*, for example, a Texaco star emerges from the darkening horizon to usurp nature's glory. By the late 1980s the myth of perversity was so well established that Serrano's photographs of Christian icons submerged in vats of piss, of flying sperm, and of used kotex pads had elicited no very extraordinary aesthetic attention. His modest reputation was not based on his subjects or materials, so to speak, but on his highly formal and aestheticized treatment of them. While Serrano's notoriety came from middle-brow outrage, his formalist style was in fact quite high-brow. In that sense he manifests a late or decadent phase of perversity; that is, one where perversity is a common aesthetic, as distinct from social, assumption, and validity depends on stylization.

Since obscene poetics represent obscenity as natural, they are obviously fellow travellers with the myth of perversity. The fluidity of myth poses some problems of focus and discrimination. Obscenity signifies a variety of things, and its designation changes in the flux of history. In some liberal analysis, for example, violence is an obscenity, but in the culture at large the representation of violence is far too commonplace for it to be obscene. While some kinds of violence are still obscene, e.g. child abuse, after public documentation of Nazi genocide camps, war atrocities and Hiroshima Maidens, there is not much representation of violence that goes beyond public tolerance. In fact, the discourse around violence has proliferated to at least the same degree that has characterized the discourse of sexuality. Accordingly, sex and violence have become the infamous Bobbsey Twins in the myth of perversity. Characteristically, that myth in itself neither confirms nor denies the linkage. Various inflections of it mark different, sometimes opposing, idioms. In Bataille's version, as we shall see, the linkage is at once imperative and dangerous via his radical ontology. In the version common to lesbian S/M pornographers, on the other hand, the linkage mediates and even neutralizes the violent term. Still, linkage and overlap notwithstanding, the poetics, discourses, and mythologies of sex and violence are distinct.

Sex and violence converge in the myth of animality, where the respective natures of humans and beasts—their instincts, urges and pleasures—are analogized. The crucial distinction is in the myth of sentimentality. The traditional distinction between the human and the bestial was reason. In the eighteenth century reason was augmented with sentiment. In literary contexts reason actually came to be subordinate: In Richardson's *Pamela* and *Clarissa* the villains are highly rationalistic in their conniving and are redeemed from villainy only when their higher and civilizing sentiments are evoked. Then in Laurence Sterne's *Tristram Shandy*, rationalism is rendered actually absurd in the face of fellow-feeling. Finally, sentiment transcends itself in Blake, for whom it becomes intuitive passion and cancels reason: The myth of sentimentality gives primacy to the feelings as the highest faculty of human nature. In the nineteenth century the influence of German thought gave sentiment ontological and psychological significance that culminated in the psychoanalytic focus on consciousness. Indeed, the myth of sentiment hovered above scientific and philosophical discourse, and, with permutations, it still survives. Sade had combined the myth of animality with that of sentiment by integrating sentiment with his brutal pleasure principle, as we shall see: The myth of animality counterpoints both reason and sentiment with its insistence on the brute sensuousness of human nature. This conception got a considerable boost, of course, from Darwin and Social Darwinism. In an age of high technology and micro-measurement the myths of sentiment and animality may now seem crude. Nonetheless, they continue to function, perhaps because of their very crudeness.

These two myths inform both the scientific and imaginative discourse of sexuality. I turn next to a discussion of how they provide context for the poetics of obscenity, particularly in the form of pornography. In general, hard-core pornography derives from the myth of animality, and soft-core from the myth of sentimentality. I propose a third term, artistic pornography, that derives at once from the myths of love and consciousness. The mythology of consciousness is what Vaclav Havel wanted to reify before the United States Congress and the world. And it is the mythology that essentially informs the aesthetic sensibility of the last two centuries. The rest of this book is an exploration of its artistic workings in our inexorable urge to speak the unspeakable.

# 2

# Pornographic Ways and Means

## *DE VULGARI* AND BEYOND

By insisting that storytelling be socially prescriptive Plato reduced poetry to rhetoric. As such it was not regarded as a mode of knowledge, only an instrument of persuasion or demonstration. He sought, of course, to neutralize the power of poetry. Aristotle articulated the counter-argument that not only was poetry a mode of knowledge but that it was one of the highest modes, the nature of which was evolving and precluded any sweeping interdictions against it. The history of aesthetics and poetics has been essentially a commentary on the debate between these two positions.

Because Plato's idealistic synthesis of all things has the appeal of cosmic unity and is consequently more socially portable, his view has dominated Western aesthetics. Aristotle, partly because his total philosophy was not until relatively recently understood, and partly because his method of differentiation is not so neat, and partly because the *Poetics* does not adequately develop the idea of poetic evolution, has been wrongly regarded and sometimes despised as a poetic formalist. Ironically Dante, neo-Platonic as he was philosophically, provided the pragmatic wedge in western poetics for an Aristotelian notion of evolution.

Once Dante had not only argued for the poetic propriety of native languages but demonstrated their possibilities in his poetry, it was only a matter of time before sociology caught up with poetics to provide Aristotle's view the substance it needed. Once poetry was released from the static citadels of church and academy, once it was put back into the languages people used, as Aretino used the sonnet, it was only a matter of time until someone like Dryden came along to argue the superiority of the "moderns" over the "ancients" on the basis of vitality. After that, it was a relatively short and easy critical jump to Schiller, Wordsworth, and then Arnold. Whatever anxieties Arnold may have had about popular literature and culture, which he shored up with such doctrines as "high seriousness," he knew the essential truth—that poetry was a mode of knowledge, that it had its own evolutionary rhythms of criticism and creativity, and that it would prevail perhaps even over religion as a cultural force.

If, then, literature is a mode of knowledge disobliged to the univocal presuppositions of an idealist dialectic, deriving its authority rather from the existential imagination, it is not only qualified to express mythic sensibility but it may help that sensibility to change, to assimilate the seemingly undammable stream of new truths being revealed to it. In this theory of "disinterested" poetics—a legacy of materialism—literature is disobliged not only to the dialectic, but as well to beauty, as we shall see in the following chapter. So it may as properly explore the ugly or obscene as the beautiful. Whereupon, pornography enters as a genre.

As a genre, pornography has a political implication that perhaps more than any other factor has locked it into a subcultural role and thereby obscured its artistic character. In his history of English censorship *(A Long Time Burning)* Donald Thomas astutely observes that, "There is an anarchic quality in obscene writing (as there is in satire), an urge to undermine what is intellectually or morally the accepted standard of the age." If Arnold was right about cultural rhythms of criticism and creativity, as I think he was, then we may see something more positive in the anarchic impulse of obscenity. More and more, as our cultural values are perverted (by militarism, capital punishment, poverty, chauvinism, racism), our arts use the obscene and the pornographic to let us see, in William Burroughs' metaphor, the "naked lunch" on the end of "that long newspaper spoon."

Western aesthetics have a long tradition of the grotesque. Aristophanes and Petronius early probed the connection between sex and social order. Contemporary art has been particularly preoccupied with a generic sense of the obscene—Burroughs' *Naked Lunch,* Jack Smith's "Flaming Creatures," Norman Mailer's *Why We Are in Vietnam,* Erica Jong's *Fear of Flying,* Amiri Baraka's plays and poems, Allen Ginsberg and Adrienne Rich's evocation of homosexuality and lesbianism, to cite only a few instances, all announce a reformation of mythic sensibility that requires a poetics of obscenity. The pornographic genre, precisely because of its moral anarchy, has provided a touchstone for a modern imagination disgusted with the blind and mechanical (or electronic) optimism of rich and powerful societies. If, as Kurt Vonnegut suggests, we must infect ourselves with humanity, and if, as Burroughs says, we have to get past shame (fig leaf as archetypal censor) to know our humanity, then our best artistic virus may be nakedness, and nakedness, perforce, means obscenity.

The erotic imagination is itself a species of the obscene—the unspeakable. The very act of speaking it, then, is aggressive and at least implicitly political. But its starting point is much darker and more private, dark and private enough that, although pornography has existed as long as literature, it could not be defined, or perhaps even recognized, as a genre until Freud, Jung, and subsequent depth psychology articulated the murky connections between sexual neurosis and human behavior and imagination. Beyond that, it perhaps needed also the more "objective" support of such studies as the Kinsey, Hite, and Friday reports and the Masters and Johnson investigations to document "normality" in sex activity and erotic fantasy. To discuss pornography as a genre, then, is simply to acknowledge that there is a substantial body of literature and other arts that are either wholly or in part pornographic, and that by inquiring into it we may discover something about both poetic evolution and erotic imagination.

Although obscenity, as an aesthetic concept, is not limited to sexuality—the explicit subject of pornography—pornography has become a popular analogue of the obscene. Thus, in the popular and frequently in the legal mind, while all obscenity may not be pornographic, all pornography is obscene. "Soft-core" pornography, such as that in *Playboy* or the novels of Harold Robbins or Jacqueline Susann, may attempt to dissociate itself from the obscene, but to a large segment of social taste even this is obscene. Consequently it seems more useful to provide a comprehensive basis for interpreting obscenity than to deny a deeply imbedded cultural association. The object of this study, therefore, is to demonstrate that obscenity is not simply a cultural aberration but a complex expression of human imagination, humanistically vital enough to have its own poetics. If one is to have any commerce whatsoever with this interpretation of obscenity, then one must necessarily be attuned to the materialist perspective of the modern mind. For it is this that has permitted a separation of the good, the true, and the beautiful, and made it possible to see that there is no necessary or constant equation between them. Rejecting that trinity of association also makes it possible to see that there may be positive connections between, for example, the good and the obscene.

There is a sense, however, in which we need to distinguish between the popular notion of pornography and the notion of it presented here. The quality by which pornography is usually identified is its inducement of autoeroticism. Autoeroticism is an important part of pornography, especially at its simplest levels, but it is not itself a defining characteristic. For one thing, eroticism is highly variable according to both gender and personality. A shoe fetishist and a homosexual will not likely respond to the same stimuli. And it is quite possible for a "straight" heterosexual to respond to both fetishist and homosexual or lesbian stimuli. More significantly, pornography as a mythic genre is too complex to be capsuled into a masturbation syndrome. The point is that pornography, in the sense that it is being discussed here, is a literary genre (pornographic film is discussed in a separate chapter), and like any such genre concerns itself with a full range of psychic and social dynamics, including the explicit sexuality by which we may recognize if not define it. My prefatory note on usage has defined pornography as a depiction of sexuality that consciously evokes obscenity. In its simplest hard-core form its obscene focus is usually exclusive and usually to the specific end of eroticising its audience, although other complicating motifs may be employed. In its soft-core form, obscenity is marginal to the work's general focus, usually although not necessarily more restrained in its sexual depictions, and sex is made compatible with the prevailing sentiments of the culture. In its complex artistic form sexuality is put in an aesthetic context to serve an aesthetic end, and in it obscenity will usually pose a dialectical contradiction between its functions and the cultural agencies deflecting or sublimating cognition of its functions. Obviously these distinctions depend on interpretation of what constitutes obscenity and of what a work's focus is, to name only the two most salient problems. While hard- and soft-core pornography stay more or less recognizably within their frameworks, essentially for marketing reasons, artistic pornography might well draw from both of those conventions and at the same time invent new ones. I will be primarily concerned with this latter complex mode, but as all three are associated, I will at this point attempt to clarify their relationship by describing their workings and their ends, and their most characteristic cultural and mythic implications.

That knowledge of human consciousness is never exhausted is the principal epistemological argument for literature. And in arguing that pornography is a mode of this exploration, I claim that, in greater or lesser degree, it is either spiritual or has the potential of telling us something of the human spirit. Such a notion of spirituality requires accepting the depraved, the perverted, the neurotic, the psychotic—in short, the obscene—as agencies of spiritual knowledge. There are precedents for this notion in Christian tradition—Augustine, John of the Cross, Abelard—but they have not been a part of its mainstream. They do, however, suggest that this view of the human spirit has a distinct if suppressed role in the history even of Christian humanism.

At its simplest level (whether "hard-core" or "soft-core"), pornography is not itself spiritual. However, even simple hard-core pornography does articulate the sexual aspect of what might be called "the myth of animality." The characteristic concerns of hard-core pornography, from its celebration of "normal" sexuality to its confusions of pleasure and pain in sado-masochism, document human intrigue with sexual animality. The persistence of simple pornography as a coherent genre and the expansion of its audience argue that there is a cultural myth of animality. Soft-core, the right wing of simple pornography, titillates its audience with animality, but seeks to socialize that myth by sublimating its physically egocentric energies into a materialistic culture's analogue of spirit, the myth of sentimentality. One must remember at this point that, while hard-core pornography has had a long—if underground—history, soft-core pornography is relatively recent, and its myth consequently is tied more closely to the materialism of modern culture than is that of hard-core. While hard-core looks back to the cave man for its model, soft-core looks ahead to technocratic and executive man. As discussed later, soft-core is probably best examined in the context of transformational psychology, because it provides a locus for the transformation of explicitly sexual energy from genital activity to "productive" energy in the more socially acceptable form of commodity. And commodity has come to be associated with a peculiarly moral sentiment in modern technological culture. Soft-core pornography has emerged from underground through its ability to make sexual energy contribute to the Gross National Product. In the myth of sentimentality, a man who keeps the economy churning is a man of implicit good will, that is to say, a modern equivalent of the man of feeling.

Finally, in the mythic structure of the pornographic genre, there is that artistic or complex pornography that has been around since at least King Solomon and is of course the richest pornographic source of spiritual knowledge: It presents the myth of love in the context of obscenity. It differs from soft-core in that it is culturally disinterested, not concerned to serve cultural sentimentalities. It differs from hard-core in that it is complex, committed to exploring the full consciousness of being rather than restricting itself to animality, however much it may use the imagery of explicit genitalia and genital activity characteristic of hard-core pornography. Although it is complex, and may include many other concerns than sexuality, this mode of the genre is pornographic by virtue of making sexuality at once obscene and a major metaphor in the construction of its myth of love. D. H. Lawrence's *Lady Chatterley's Lover* is an example (very likely over Lawrence's own semantic objections). Although the action of Lawrence's novel is not predominantly genital, it does image considerable genital activity to the end of exploring the antitheses of potency/impotency and man/nature to develop Lawrence's dialectic of love.

Whereas simple pornography tends to stereotype, flattening sexuality into conventions that will not disturb its audience, the myth of complex pornography varies, sometimes diametrically opposed to the conventional, according to the imagination of the writer. The erotic sensibilities of Jean Genet and D. H. Lawrence, for example, could not be more antagonistic, yet both of them can use the same themes, for example homosexuality and moral inversion, and the same explicit genital imagery, and both explore the possibilities and failures of modern love. The imaginative approaches to the theme of love are manifold, and this artistic mode, therefore, follows the dictates of imagination. As with any poetry of integrity, complex pornography is not obliged to confirm cultural norms of what love is. If, for example, Allen Ginsberg finds love to be homosexual, then his obligation as a poet is to pursue that idea and make as honest a story of it as possible. Not to do so because it threatens or contradicts the cultural norm is to fail not only himself but to fail his cultural role as poet.

## THE BEAST WITH TWO BACKS

To see how these mythic levels of the genre work, we may begin with the simplest and "dirtiest." In *Pornography and the Law*, Eberhard and Phyllis Kronhausen have so thoroughly analyzed the structure of hard-core pornography that their "formula" has become a model for commercial exploiters of the form. They have, in effect, articulated pornography's conventions. They define its fictive principle thus: "A book which is designed to act upon the reader as an erotic psychological stimulant ('aphrodisiac') must constantly keep before the reader's mind a succession of erotic scenes. . . . The characteristic feature in the structure of 'obscene' books is the *buildup of erotic excitement* in the course of the text." Verbal and imagistic conventions of hard-core pornography exist to implement this movement of action. The imagistic conventions that the Kronhausens identify are seduction, defloration, incest, the permissive-seductive parent figure, profaning the sacred, supersexed males, nymphomaniacal females, Negroes and Asians as sex symbols, homosexuality and flagellation.

Conventional hard-core narrative describes stereotypical actions performed by stereotypical actors. It is the predictability of pornographic action that permits the buildup of erotic excitement—one knows where the action is going, and it remains only to "see" it. In this perhaps Humean sense, "seeing" is believing (that is, an aphrodisiac) because sexual activity is imaged with an exclusiveness and purity that real-life experience of it does not have. Hard-core pornography focuses almost exclusively on the physicality of sex, animal desire, and animal pleasure. Consciousness is seldom or never evoked. Normal anxieties, for example, that a couple might expect to have in their first sexual experience are, if included at all, token overtures to verisimilitude. They do not interfere with spectacular sexual performances. There is little or no "mind" represented in hard-core pornography, and certainly none of its consequence—such as impotence or frigidity. Whatever diminishes sexual performance is excluded from the hard-core pornographic world view. The imagistic conventions of hard-core are not really imagistic at all. They are superimpositions of a pornographic thesis on images of nature, to the end of fictively reconstructing nature according to the myth of animality. There libido rules the universe. All the conventions of the genre testify to that, but especially the permissive-seductive parent figure, where libido is not only given opportunity but becomes an implicit moral imperative—one *should* indulge the libido, through the ethic of sexual frolic. In such a convention parental authority, at once the most intimate and cosmic kind, enforces the sexual ethic and thus provides a place for animality under the canopy of heaven.

One must remember that in this myth all manifestations of animality from affection to violence are approved. One must also remember that the morality is fictive—thus figurative, thus incomplete. All myths, for poetic and rhetorical purposes, represent their view of things as absolute. That selectivity makes art possible and, as any teacher knows, makes knowledge possible as well. The audience has the responsibility to place the special pleading of myth in the context of its total experience. This is at once the freedom and restriction of poetic imagination. Not being under obligation to the literal, it is free; knowing that its creations are bubbles, the audience is free; only the poet is bound to his art. Unlike the philosopher or scientist, the poet trades in proximate and suggestive truths, the value of which does not depend on exactness. Gravity is an exact truth, intimidating one's behavior accordingly. Animality is an inexact, even contradictory, truth, the knowledge of which may influence behavior but cannot intimidate it. Because society, for example, accommodates human animality, the policing of prostitution is correspondingly inexact. Neither prostitutes nor their customers are intimidated by the law or its enforcement, but they are influenced enough to be discreet about their behavior. The long history of pornography testifies to the archetypal truth of its animal myth. The irregular passing of laws against it and related activities, and the still more irregular policing of them, testify that although humans may want the myth out of sight, they don't want it destroyed. Pornography, in its hard-core form, invigorates humans' animal character, reminds us of it, suggests behavioral possibilities for it, approves of it. Morally, pornography not only certifies that humans have this nature, it serves to remind us of the curiously intriguing game of fast and loose that is played with the mythic sensibility.

The characteristic narrative of hard-core pornography consists in a series of sex scenes more or less inventively described. "Classics" of the form (*The Autobiography of a Flea, The Lascivious Hypocrite,* and so on) are for that reason usually rather short. The action, in E. M. Forster's terms, is all story and no plot. Plot requires a sense of causality, both immediate and cosmic. But in this form all causality is the same—animality. Everything sharing the same cause, there is no need to represent anything other than its effects, carnal pleasure in various modes. Thus, hard-core pornography's fictive representation rests in the inventiveness of its descriptions rather than the energy of its imagination. Its imaginative energy is in the myth of which it represents a particular variation. This is one reason why publishers of hard-core pornography tend to revive classics as often as they commission new works. One such publisher, Maurice Girodias of Olympia Press, complained that one of the problems of contemporary pornographers is that they get too "literary," consequently diminishing pornographic focus as they introduce psychic or moral complexities into the narrative. The principle of hard-core form is to tap into the myth of animality and derive its energy and appeal therefrom. Its audience directs its own imaginative energies, and the function of this mode is to provide the vehicle for surfacing the animal dimension of its audience's sensibility. Thus not only is animality acknowledged but in large part its subliminal power over the psyche is exorcised: Recognizing animality subjects us less to it.

Thus hard-core pornographic action is locked into its symbolic function. When we read it we know, roughly, what we want from it. We want its erotic stimulus to remind us of the animal nature we spend our civilized energies suppressing. And we want approval for it, with the pleasure implicit in approval. Thus, at best, hard-core pornography provides a psychic joy that transcends the bounds of its imagistic physicality, the joy of acknowledging our own lust, and of being figuratively assured that it is not necessarily destructive of our humanity. This is why John Cleland's *Memoirs of a Woman of Pleasure (Fanny Hill)* is and will remain one of Western literature's great books. It is a great work of art because it is a brilliant example of its genre, and it surpasses most other examples of its genre in its civilized celebration of sexual pleasure. It reminds us, apart from its trappings of eighteenth-century ecology, that sex, as sex, is a source of joy, and frequently enough, amazement. A professional lady of pleasure, the pornographic heroine Fanny Hill, manifests human animality and yet retains a compassion, generosity, and humanity that fictively argue the compatibility of man's animal and spiritual natures. But, because *Fanny Hill* has a literacy and grace that make it artistic or complex pornography, I want to use another example to illustrate hard-core pornography: "Frank Newman's" *Barbara* (Traveller's Companion Series, 1968) is an unequivocal instance of hard-core pornography. Where *Fanny Hill* reflects the stylistic gentility of its aristocratic eighteenth-century origins, *Barbara* reflects the contemporary flaunting of the pornographic imagination before social conventions. Like most examples of its kind, it does not have a plot, though it frequently parodies moral associations, and its story line is simply a convenience on which to hang a series of sexual descriptions. Each chapter is a variation on some form of hard-core convention, although by virtue of its up-to-date context (the action takes place in Provincetown, and it incorporates all the "hip" characters possible), it assumes a particularly aggressive posture toward social standards. Here is a scene from the first chapter:

> Max lying on the warm sand. The June wind cold on his back and he pressed his body against the smooth and yielding texture of the sun-warmed dune. Down in the hollow below, two college kids were fucking dog-fashion. . . . Max watched impassively as they fucked furiously throwing the sand around, the boy on his knees behind the crouched girl, bending his body like a bow while he fucked to bite her neck and her back, reaching around her body and grabbing at her tits; squealing, both of them squealing, she twisting her arse in jerky, rapid rhythm, he pounding faster and faster until he screamed, threw back his arms and fell on his back—lay there like dead. The girl quite still in the same position, on knees and elbows, eyes tightly shut, slowly let her legs and arms slide straight till she lay flat on her belly, face in the sand. Max watched . . . slowly got up and carefully, slowly walked down the dune, took off the faded cut-down blue jeans—all he was wearing—and dropped them on the pile of the kids' bathing suits and sun-tan lotion. He walked over till he stood behind the prone girl, her arse slightly elevated from the wind-blown sand. He watched her, eyes closed, slow shallow breathing. Stood astride her, his feet level with her knees, then carefully and quietly lowered himself to his knees so that his cock slid into her cunt from behind. She stayed quite still, her eyes still shut. Max began to fuck her with long slow strokes, rocking back and forth on his knees, until she began twisting her arse in time to his slow, regular strokes. . . .

Barbara illustrates the hard-core form so well because, unlike many others, it is maximally inventive within the framework of its conventions. It does not transcend those conventions as *Fanny Hill* does, unless one regards its peculiarly satirical ending as getting somehow beyond those limits. But its sexual descriptions are clearly good within the limits of the form. The ingenuity of this passage, "Max, still with only the tip of his cock in her, was decreasing his motions, making each outstroke slightly longer than each instroke, imperceptibly leaving her to the excitement of sucking," borders on inspiration, from perhaps a diabolical rather than divine muse. But of course it isn't quite, even diabolically, inspired. Its inventions simply bring readers into the framework of a libidinous world, where their interests and excitements may be pursued. Max organizes a pornographic cell of sexual novitiates, and their fun-and-games work systematically through the whole host of pornographic conventions—from Max's defloration of a more than willing twelve-year-old through homosexuality, lesbianism, incest, and group sex to conclude with a prodigious outrage to one of the greatest of all cultural taboos—incest between father and son, mother and daughter. After which we are given a bucolic family portrait—"They stood quite content on the peak of the last dune before the tidal beach. Arm in arm, Barbara and Franz between their mother and father." This is the mood with which the book closes, and its parodic absurdity reminds us of the distance between archetypal awareness and ethical instruction. Having belabored nearly every possible sexual act, position, and relationship, *Barbara* ends with the suggestion that when confronting our sexual fantasies we do well to keep our own ridiculousness in mind. And not the least of the joke is that the demands of our animality are such that we read to the end, to find ourselves and our fantasies, both the pornographic and sentimental ones, ridiculed.

But, unlike a pornographic novel such as *Candy*, satire is not the real business of *Barbara*. The apostrophe of *Barbara's* ending is merely the author reminding us that, after all, pornography is just another game, like metaphysics. But such fun is not the usual animal tone of either this novel or the form generally. *Barbara* evidences another dimension of the animality myth—violence. Violence, as Gershon Legman's *Love and Death* argues so persuasively, is a cultural sublimation of sexual impulses, and is a vital part of the pornographer's arsenal. In *Barbara* it has a particularly modern nuance; the fusion of violence and pleasure provides an appropriately modern sense of subtlety. It is a kind of hard-core analogue of Burroughs' far more complex treatment of Dr. Benway, who parodies the subtle fascistic sado-masochistic genius of technocracy.

In *Barbara*, violence gives what might otherwise have been rather flat pornographic conventions a suspense and tension appropriate to the nature of the "civilized" myth of animality, where this peek-a-boo game of intrigue constitutes a basic rhythm. As with sex, we at once want it and fear it. So sex and violence complement one another; in addition to which they are both very much a part of the act of sex, especially insofar as the violence is implicit or controlled. In the scene cited above Max violates Leslie, who mistakes him for her lover and enjoys it. Max then violates Tom, the lover, with similar results. His use of force universalizes sexuality by depersonalizing and ungendering it, and thereby asserts the transcendance of erotic power in animal being.

If violence may be defined to include the violation of another's will, then Max rides the thin ridge of it, molding Tom's and Leslie's wills by literally manipulating their pleasure, thus fictively acknowledging that archetypal relationship between pleasure and pain, will and submission, so crucial to the pornographic genre. One submits to one's animality under the aegis of pleasure, even if it must be forced upon him. The omnipotence of pleasure is precisely the excuse: Faust says of the Helen whom Satan has conjured to keep Faust from backsliding to salvation, "Her lips sucks forth my soul." This sado-masochistic pleasure is central to the pornographic ethos because it is so deep in our archetypal sense of self, however disturbing and therefore repressed.

Further, pleasure is given a kind of "purity"; that is, like beauty, in pornography it is its own excuse for being. In his "rape" of Leslie, Max demonstrates a depersonalized sexual pleasure both as a lesson to Leslie and analogously to the reader. Leslie experiences it unequivocally in mistaking Max, a stranger, for Tom, her lover. Aside from the parodic theme of the mysterious stranger, the point is that Leslie's pleasure is not tainted in this scene by affection for her sexual partner. Max does much the same with Tom, expanding the lesson in "pure" pleasure by making him enjoy buggery and homosexuality. In both lessons there is enough force used to make the reader wonder where things are going, but the anticipation of violence (in hard-core, unlike complex pornography, one does not fear violence—it is an aphrodisiac) is elevated into the novel's pornographic version of the flower-power admonitions to "love" one another. The final sublimation of violence comes in Max's creation of the *ménage à trois*, where Tom and Leslie learn that sex is not only pure pleasure (their first pornographic lesson), but is also art and knowledge (their second): "each more intensely aware of his individuality than ever before, while lost in a work of art." Only after these lessons have been learned by the neophytes does the master introduce himself, transforming bodies as instruments of pure pleasure into personalities. And then the chapter drifts with post-orgasmic bliss into a modern pornographic theme—don't get uptight, there's enough to go around. So much for the tragedy and violence of the eternal triangle. Here, then, is a "good" example of pornography—that is, one that uses the mythic conventions, gives them the dynamics of a tantalizing manipulation of violence, which is finally sublimated to the pornographically omnipresent and necessary theme that sex is good for you.

The verbal conventions of simple or hard-core pornography—what the Kronhausens call "'dirty' words in 'dirty' books"—are in fact the most complex and evasive aspect of that mode of the genre. Their brief but basic statement suggests the many implications in the use of dirty words:

> The use of taboo words in "obscene" books is closely related to the frequent mixture of the sacred and the profane. . . . Its chief attraction lies in the open defiance of the "superego," or conscience, the flagrant violation of the social conventions of polite discourse, the flaunting of one's independence, the

> throwing off of social responsibility, and the assertion of the instinctual primitive side of life against all the restraining and inhibiting forces of the environment.

Verbal pornographic conventions are used to remind the audience of what it is getting away with, and in that way heighten its pleasure. Dirty words are at once an aphrodisiac and a repudiation of social restrictions. Their thrill, therefore, is both psychic and political. The dynamics of this relationship are difficult to get at and would require an examination of language as a mode in the "transformation" of psychic energy. This is not the place for that, but we can suggest how that psychological context helps us see that pornography is not merely a subcultural sign of depravity but is in fact a relatively common way for individual personalities to relate to their environment and exorcise some of its power over them.

The history of the epithet "motherfucker" illustrates the complexity of dirty words in practice. Obviously it toys with the most pervasive of taboos and Freudian impulses. Originally in black argot it was used in opprobrium and may have developed out of the insult slinging of "signifying" contests (which have analogues in many linguistic and verse traditions). But in subsequent usage it is sometimes an insult and sometimes merely generic slang for "man," suggesting partly that with time the term has lost some of its cutting edge and partly that the incest taboo is less piquant than it once was, at least verbally. The latter usage frequently carries a tone of existential resignation, as in "We're all poor motherfuckers together," suggesting a racial fraternalism defiantly defined by the worst thing whites might say of blacks, though it occasionally also has the ironic implication of common racial humanity and/or comic exorcism of the insult. When it became a rad-lib fashion in the 1950s and 1960s to appropriate black styles, the term was adopted into white argot, where it additionally signified either political solidarity with oppressed blacks or was a more radical means of class distinction, whites dissociating themselves from the oppressive class of their birth. In short, the term indicates the intricacy of symbolic action characteristic of dirty words.

Similarly with the epithets "fuck you," "prick," and "cunt." In nonsexual contexts they are aggressive indictments. All three obviously carry the freight of age-old gender hostilities. "Getting fucked," which can be effected by either a "prick" or "cunt," certainly has the onus of deceit traditionally associated with seduction. It may also, as Andrea Dworkin insists especially for "cunt," signify masculine aggressiveness and assertion of power over women. But these terms clearly punctuate the holistic anxiety surrounding sex—whether it is giving or taking, loss or gain, entrapment or exaltation. In sexual contexts, however, these words can be transformed from hostile epithets to eroticizing endearments, as both men and women report. So the symbolic function of dirty words can range from politics to aphrodisiacs and from the cosmic to the intimate. At the very least their usage is an index of the entanglement of sexual mythologies with those of social order.

Another function of language is its use as a social index of knowledge of and ease with social propriety. Comedy and satire are by and large peopled with mismatched vulgarity and gentility, and the usual giveaway is language: Witness Eliza Doolittle in both the musical and dramatic versions of Shaw's *Pygmalion*. Dirty words, and the jokes and stories made from them, are a kind of transformation that permit people to "get even with" a social or cultural repression that they do not wish or dare to oppose directly. The preference in "lower-class" speech for dirty words probably derives from the preference of the Angles and Saxons (and the indigenous "lower classes" subsequently in their tradition) for their own words (e.g., "fuck") over Roman imports (e.g., "copulate"). But inkhorn pretensions and Christian sublimation prevailed, and now no socially ambitious man whose native tongue is English will "shit" if he can "defecate," and he will do neither if he can "go to the bathroom." If he is not much polished he will use the "men's room"; if a middle or working class wit and bon vivant he will use the "little boy's room"; and if he is socially hopeless he will "go to the toilet." If one feels either oppressed or boxed in by these linguistic niceties, he might very naturally—as a walk on the street or even a visit to a country-club locker room will show—advise such an intimidating system to "eat shit" or "get fucked." When he does, if he has not been too deceived by his education, he will be ripe for subscription to an obscene poetics. Actually, the culture is a good deal more prepared for a smutty poetics than it knows, considering that most of us are better equipped by it to enjoy a dirty joke than a Keats ode.

Another use of smutty language is its assistance in maintaining a psychic balance. Oppression and imbalance are of course closely related. If people can exorcise a sense of social oppression through language—their own or what they read or hear—that will surely help them maintain some kind of psychic balance. That is, it will help them channel psychic energy into socially acceptable modes of conduct, for instance swearing rather than bloodying somebody's nose. There is wide approbation for letting dissidents—from children to political radicals—"blow off steam," at least to a point. This device, administrators of colleges and governments have discovered much to their advantage, helps maintain order.

Dirty words too, then, are an aspect of the myth of animality. Animality implies naked power; in the case of dirty words it means the power to dare defy social conventions. There is also the more psychically complex role of language as aphrodisiac. If we may think of language as including phonemic noises, that is, voice sounds such as moans that do not signify anything outside a specific behavioral context, then there is no question but that language does act as a sexual stimulant. Sexual partners are certainly guided, one way or another, by vocal responses. Positive vocal responses such as moaning or heavy breathing induce heightened sexual excitement and activity. Language is both a guide and an encouragement in sexual conduct. Two soft-core examples show how pornographers imitate this fact of sexual life. In one, from Grace Metalious's *Peyton Place,* a girl at a peak of sexual excitement says to her partner, "Hurt me. . . . Hurt me a little," thus guiding and encouraging his activities. The other, from Harold Robbins' *The Adventurers,* is more specific. Here the passionate lady says to her partner, who has just called her a "dirty cunt," "That's right honey . . . eat me, hurt me, talk dirty to me, and fuck me. That's all I want," giving advice and consent for cunnilingus, sadism, vulgarity, and other delights of the animal nature.

Sex is a single-minded activity—the seeking of (frequently but not always at one with the giving of) pleasure. It is its own form of communication, and consequently does not usually involve discourse, which is a different form of communication. It is also at once intensely physical and also psychological. Thus language, in its service, is intense to the point of primitiveness, a primitiveness that taps the myth of animality. Dirty words in sexual intercourse, like any aphrodisiac, are a form of liberation—liberating the libido verbally as manipulation of the body liberates it physically. Erotic language approves the actions of the body, approval is encouragement, and sexual encouragement is the point of all aphrodisiacs. It may be that a greater intensity of such language marks a given person's greater need of an aphrodisiac, in which case it is perhaps slightly neurotic. Those who are completely satisfied sexually by language alone, like those who are satisfied by voyeurism or flagellation, are certainly abnormal, possibly psychotic, that is, in some psychic way dissociated from their total being. But it may also be, and this is no contradiction, that an intense use of dirty words is a lyrical celebration, primitiveness being at the very heart of lyricism, of the release of animality. There is very likely something of both behind the use of erotic language or dirty words.

## SOFT-CORE SOPHISTRY

The myth of animality being what it is, is threatening at once to personality and to society. Soft-core pornography evades both threat and fear by sublimating the primitive energies that are its source into socially approved activities. In modern culture the most socially approved activities turn on economic productivity and its corollary, a willingness to defend the capitalist faith with rhetoric and/or arms. This corollary is in some ways most potent because it provides the emotional wherewithal to sentimentalize economic materialism.

Patriotism, as a proper repository of virtuous emotionalism, has a long and distinguished history. Under its aegis, justice and power become synonymous, and thus power is sentimentalized, that is, it takes on the emotional value of justice. Any war that the social order undertakes becomes a just or even "holy" war defending the faith, the capitalist ethic. From the time of the "Church Militant" violence has been sentimentalized. In the sublimation of the means of economic production to moral virtue, the violence used in its "defense" becomes the sign of moral sensibility.

Unlike either complex or hard-core pornography, soft-core fortifies such social sentimentalities. It is not anarchical. It celebrates social order. In fact its pornographic character is only approved insofar as it associates itself with elevated cultural sentiments. The two staples of social elevation are, again, wealth and power. And soft-core pornography, from Samuel Richardson to Jacqueline Susann and Harold Robbins, focuses extravagantly on both. But naked wealth and power border on the obscene, so they need to be made presentable to "civilized" society. They need, in other words, to be dissociated from the myth of animality (scary) and connected to the myth of sentimentality (gratifying). Consequently, soft-core pornography uses "realistic" settings and actions, including explicit, if carefully controlled, sexuality. The control usually comes in providing a sentimental context for such titillating nakedness as it does show.

Most characteristically the context for sexual excitement created in soft-core pornography is some analogue of wealth and power. The heroes, then, of soft-core are the rich and the powerful, and the narrative structure of these novels, much more complex than that of hard-core pornography, builds on the timeless romanticizing of these qualities. To achieve one or the other, ideally both, justifies everything, including animality, that may be necessary to get there. Fictively, this means that society will readily approve a little obscenity if it is dressed elegantly and ultimately uses its animality for the good, true, and beautiful. Thus, soft-core pornography flirts with animality, but does not descend into its naturalistic depths. Rather, it connects animality with "proper" sentiments, and thereby sublimates it into the more socially acceptable myth of sentimentality. In it, animal energies are occasionally revealed (usually in short pornographic scenes paced more or less regularly through the story), but these are transformed into such productive contexts as making a fortune, becoming a successful politician, fighting for freedom (freedom somehow never has a rational basis, being always connected with the glorious gore of sentimentalized violence; that this violence derives from animality is not so much forgotten as hurriedly covered up by giving it a "civilizing" objective), and so on. The myth of sentimentality is based on the assumption that men are "civilized" creatures with "civilized" feelings.

The danger of that mythic ideal is that it easily becomes confused with the logic that, because men are civilized creatures, whatever they feel and do are consequently also civilized. That confusion permits, for example, genocide in such civilized countries as Germany and the United States. And fictive treatments of the myth of sentimentality tend, because their trappings are "realistic" and more broadly based socially than fictive treatments of animality, to assume a guise of ethical possibility. No normal person expects to live in a hard-core world of total sexuality; but he knows very well that he lives in one where wealth and power are premiums and do define a possible ethic. This ethical modeling is what makes the generalized sentimentality of the soft-core pornographic view so appealing. One popular fiction writer, Ayn Rand, who was occasionally a "soft-core" pornographer, has in fact argued in *The Romantic Manifesto* that Mike Hammer and James Bond are the proper heroic models for modern culture.

Soft-core pornography, then, happens most effectively in the context of popular romantic literature. Fictionally, its conventions are analogous to those journalistic conventions of *Playboy* and *Cosmopolitan*. It is necessary to place sexuality in context with a generally romantic rendering of life. The "realism" of violence and sexuality provide a "tough" realistic basis so that the reader (usually, bookstores report, middle-class women between 35 and 45) is titillated by this proximity to "life as it really is," which is to say, life as she in her boredom would like to imagine it. Wealth, or such analogues as detectives, politicians, movie stars, and other images of glamorous public life, provides an exotic assistance to the reader's fantasy elevation of animality to an admirable rather than fearful plane. In this sense, popular fiction follows the *Playboy* rule of thumb in its use of sex—giving it its place in a "well-rounded" bourgeois fantasy life.

Because it adroitly encompasses so many cultural sentimentalities and is also unequivocally pornographic, Harold Robbins' *The Adventurers* serves as a good example of the soft-core form of pornography. Its title suggests its theme, adventure; and the political, economic, jet-set, and sexual adventures of the novel are a brilliant springboard into the effect of "realistic" romantic fantasy that such a novel requires. Robbins' use of adventure makes it a vehicle of sublimation. Its story fuses many sentimental myths. He skillfully handles the Horatio Alger myth in the fortune of his hero, Diogenes Alejandro Xenos, Dax for short ("Diogenes after the fabled seeker of truth; Alejandro after the conqueror of the world . . ."). Dax, from Corteguay—yet another decadent Latin American republic in turmoil, rises from humble beginnings to become the heir-apparent to *el Presidente's* military dictatorship. His grooming for this position sends him to Harvard and then on to become part of the international jet set, where he conquers women, money, influence, and all the rest of it.

But Robbins knows the mythology well enough not simply to make a poor boy rich, sexy, and powerful. A hero needs the right sentiments. And, as Dax wearies of the venal life, he gets them. Having experienced all that wealth and power can provide, he is converted to the social gospel, and decides to return to Corteguay and topple the dictator, setting up a true republic in its place. But this, of course, involves the betrayal of *el Presidente*, who has been like a father to him, however evil otherwise. (To justify Dax and let us know just how evil and decadent *el Presidente* is, we are treated to a Turkish delight; when Dax breaks in to tell his surrogate "father" he is through, he finds *el Presidente* in *delicto flagrante* with Amparo, who as it happens is not only *el Presidente's* daughter but also Dax's wife: "They were naked on the bed, Amparo's legs wide, *el Presidente* on his knees between them, a huge black dildo strapped around his waist. In his hand a riding crop." Not, as they say, a pretty scene.) This kind of thing, that is, the father-son business, Robbins knows, is the stuff of pathos; and he gets the most from it. *The Adventurers* is not, therefore, a simple success story. It won't do to get away with treachery, even in the interests of justice. So, though Dax successfully engineers a coup and refuses the offer (thrice) of the presidency in order to institute a government by, for, and of the people, he is killed at the very moment of his selfless triumph by a bandit who wrongly thinks Dax is still an agent of *el Presidente*. Tragic irony, more or less.

If that sentimentality doesn't get you, the postscript chapter will. Dax may be dead, but not his son, also named Dax. He is in the care of his mother (not the infamous Amparo) and a foster father less adventurous than Dax Sr. But Robbins knows his Faulkner, and Dax Jr. will be a chip off the old block: This scene ends the book, as Dax Jr.'s mother says to the foster father, dropping Dax's Harvard ring down the incinerator, "'Now he is gone . . . and there is nothing left of him but a dream we all had when we were young. . . . She was wrong. And he knew that she knew it. There was always the boy upstairs."

But if Robbins is a genius at compounding sentimental formulas, he is no less skillful at lacing them with pornographic conventions. He may not use them all, but then he has a lot of fish to fry, and the ones he does use he uses inventively. The following scenes illustrate:

A little blood and rape:

> With an angry curse he let her go, then his hand came up with a knife. It slashed quickly down the front of the dress. The coarse shift fell away like the husk from an ear of corn. A thin pencil-like streak, starting at her throat and running down between her breasts and across her brown Indian

> belly into the heavy matting of pubic hair, suddenly began to well crimson. She screamed and tried to get away, scrambling on her hands and knees, but he laughed aloud and pulled her back by her hair.
>
> She tried to get away again. Quickly he reversed the knife in his hand and hooked the butt end viciously upward between her legs, and this time she screamed in pure agony.
>
> She crumpled to the floor at his feet, writhing in pain. The sharp blade end of the knife reflected the crazy yellow lights from the candle as it stuck upright from between her legs. He put his heavily booted foot on her belly to hold her still and started to pull at the rope belt that held up his *pantalones*.

A little candor about cunnilingus:

> Her voice was soft and slurry. "Honey, nobody, but nobody, eats me the way you do."
>
> Dax rolled over on his side and looked up at Sue Ann. Her eyes were almost closed and her mouth partly open. Her long blond hair spilled out over the pillow and her full breasts, with their oddly tiny pink nipples, rose gently with her deep breathing. . . .
>
> Her head fell back against his shoulder and her face twisted around to look up at him. Her eyes were almost closed again and her voice was very low. "No wonder they don't want you to fuck niggers!"
>
> He had been long enough in the States to know what she meant. It was all he could do not to hit her. "You dirty cunt!"
>
> Her eyes closed tight and she pressed herself against him. "That's right, honey," she whispered, "eat me, hurt me, talk dirty to me, and fuck me. That's all I want!"

A little theory of sports cars and sporting ladies:

> He grinned. It worked every time. No matter how sophisticated they were, no matter how snide about things American. All you had to do was get them beside you on that front seat. Whatever it was—the speed, the sense of power, the masculine smell of new leather—it never missed. . . .
>
> She fell on him almost before he had time to cut the motor, her fingers frantically tearing at the nonexistent buttons. He pulled down his zipper, and she gasped as his youth and life sprang free. Then her hot moist mouth covered him.

Thus *The Adventurers* gives us an enticing view of life as it might be, neatly balancing sex, money, and violence to provide a socially redeeming world view.

A later chapter will suggest that soft-core pornography of female authorship shifts the perspective slightly on the myth of sentiment. Wealth and power are staple motifs, but women tend to be more preoccupied with the process of their acquisition. Since cultural sentiment prescribes a different situation for women, women writers of soft-core pornography are more disposed to address the problematics of the nexus of career success and love. Still, while there are gender inflections, soft-core pornography by both sexes tends to confirm the mythology of sentimentality.

## CONSCIOUSNESS AND LOVE'S BODY

Complex or artistic pornography differs from hard-core or simple pornography in not being exclusively committed to the myth of animality and its explicit sexual imagery. And, while soft-core pornography offers ethical encouragement to the sentiments of the status quo, complex pornography, like most artistic modes, explores the moral recognition that necessarily precedes and informs true ethical perception. In the sense, then, that art is moral rather than ethical, artistic pornography is moral. It may use both soft- and hard-core conventions, but is distinguished from both by the degree to which it meets the criteria of all serious art—how honestly and thoroughly it pursues its imaginative vision. Formally, when complex pornography appears in more sophisticated modes, as in Molly Bloom's pornographic soliloquy at the end of James Joyce's *Ulysses*, it exhibits a corresponding formal sophistication. The conventions of complex pornography are, then, indistinguishable from those of whatever form it may take. And it has the same freedom available to it that any artistic mode has. It is generically distinguishable, however, by its matrix of consciousness, obscenity and the myth of love. Complex pornography is unique in synthesizing the myths of animality with those of love—while animality is a naturalistic premise, it is expanded to fuse with the more complex psychic consciousness of love. Such books, therefore, as D. H. Lawrence's *The Rainbow*, in which the theme of sexuality is used to help explore love but not through explicit genitalia imagery, are more erotic than pornographic. *The Rainbow* focuses on the consciousness of love rather than the act of love (which, though present, is treated on an archetypal level of consciousness rather than in the pornographically descriptive manner of *Lady Chatterley's Lover*), and therefore represents a modified pornographic mode of the myth.

Complex pornography may be said to preoccupy itself, appropriately for the Age of Anxiety, with a neurotic interpretation of love, although we must remember Freud's sound premise that neurosis is a normal phenomenon. As we have become increasingly aware of the range and influence of neurosis on behavior, we have come more and more to see love and love relationships as neurotically structured. Whether or not psychologists will agree to this generalization, there has developed a substantial body of literary and artistic works that turn on this theme. That some of them, such as Vladimir Nabokov's *Lolita,* have not only been best-sellers but transformed into popular movies argues that both the artistic and popular imaginations are highly conscious of the dynamic and dangerous association between neurosis and love. In fact, the narrative structure of Nabokov's novel hands the problem directly to society. When Humbert Humbert addresses his defense to the "ladies and gentlemen of the jury," he addresses the whole of modern culture. Humbert does not deny his guilt; he is guilty of crimes against both man and nature—the murder of his rival in "love" and the systematic violation of his juvenile "beloved," of both her body and, finally, her soul. Humbert's defense consists in defining the terms of his guilt, in explaining how the confusions of modern culture, an almost hopelessly mix-mastered paste of "decadent" Old World and "progressive" New World demonologies, made his crimes inevitable. He wants, he says, to save not his head but his soul. His murder of Quilty, his rival and fellow despoiler of Lolita, is a symbolic purge of the New World. Humbert's own execution, as inevitable as his crimes, is the symbolic purge of the Old World. And yet, as things of the soul are wont to be, it is only a symbolic purge. We, the ladies and gentlemen of the jury, are left with the neurotic modern culture that produced the neurotic characters that people the neurotic plot of Nabokov's brilliant telling of his neurotic version of the myth of failed modern love.

What makes the myth of love so fascinating for the modern mind is that, having lost confidence in its divine or idealistic nature, we do not know what to make of it. We do know, as the history of tragedy testifies, that it is often destructive. But we also know, from both mythic and personal history, that it makes the world go round. Our fascination comes from its dichotomous and ineluctable nature, like a cobra weaving and hypnotizing, luring us to some glorious demise. Since the invention of consciousness and its relativistic mythology, love has become a universalized idea in dialectical relation to its material perception. Thus, if it is a sometime transcendental affect, it is equally a four-letter word. Hence our perturbed consciousness of the antics of the narrow fellow in the grass.

Steven Marcus in *The Other Victorians* remarks the extravagant sense of phallic power so characteristic of pornography, where, as he puts it, "the penis becomes the man: it does the thrusting and not the man; it is its own agent." And in the world of pornography, where sexuality is the prime mover, the penis takes on a kind of omnipotence. When viewed in an archetypal context, this characteristic becomes an elaborate and central device of pornographic rhetoric. Theodore Reik, in *Love and Lust*, provides an interpretive context:

> Every analyst who has treated many women will have observed that most of them are often . . . assaulted by the conscious and often preconscious fear

> that their lover or husband will desert them, will not stay with them, but forsake them at a certain time. A fear . . . that is very rare with men. . . .
>
> I daresay that there is a pattern for this contrast of the two sexes in the psychology of the sexual act. The male who has shown such an immediacy, urgency, and intensity of sexual desire has very soon after the emission the wish to leave the body of the woman. The woman who has hesitatingly and much more slowly yielded to his and her own desires feels the wish that the man's genitals should stay within her. She now experiences a heightened affection for him and something akin to gratitude. . . .
>
> There is no doubt in our mind that in her wish to feel his body inside her long after ejaculation she identifies his genitals with . . . his person, as if it were not only part of him, but he, himself. Does she identify his genitals only with him or is there a yet undiscovered dynamic factor operating?

There is here the psychic basis for the symbology of phallic power and pleasure so significant in sexuality from ancient worship to modern pornographic rhetoric. Is it, in addition to a celebration of power and pleasure, a figure also for the social and cultural role of the penis, that is, the reproduction of the race and state? Is it an ironic figure subconsciously trying to exorcise a masculine fear of impotence? Does, in other words, the popular and literary persistence of this figure document in some as yet untranslatable way Reik's sense of the "undiscovered dynamic factor" in the psychology of sex? In any event, it must be clear that this pornographic convention testifies to the psychic and archetypal human impulses which are themselves the origin of pornography. Marcus tends to regard this extravagant phallic metaphor as another sign of pornography's juvenility. But its psychological dimensions signify something well beyond the rhetorical crudeness of its masculine vanity. It symbolizes real human intercourse—fear and desire, fire and ice.

In her book *Psychic Energy* M. Esther Harding, a colleague and student of Jung, analyzes what might be called the sexual ages of man. She defines a progressive correspondence between emotional complexity and sexuality. The more advanced stages have a more complex emotional involvement in sexual relations. The earliest stages are phallic, in which man is synecdochically conceived as penis. There are also intermediate stages where sexuality is stylized and idealized. The graphic representations of the early stages are of course the graffiti of the ages—phallic imagery and symbology. The intermediate stages are represented in the expansion of man's image from penis alone to the whole body—e.g. in stylized nude statuary. The advanced emotional stages are where consciousness informs physicality. These are the stages of eroticism in its most comprehensive sense, and they evoke complex artistic pornography. Consciousness implies perception, and perception implies aesthetic perspective. Artistic pornography, then, derives from that psychic state where consciousness mediates sexual energy.

A comparison of the contemporary *Story of O* with the eighteenth-century *Fanny Hill* suggests the aesthetic potential of pornography. *Fanny Hill's* mode is one-dimensional, amiable and aesthetically minimal in ambition. It describes a prostitute's life, to the end of exploiting the obvious sexual doings. Fantasy is of course central to this end, and to induce it a kind of realism is affected through description of an occupation where rampant sexuality is believable. Thus the action adopts the epistolary narrative device, the trappings of a specific sociological setting (eighteenth-century London), and is resolved with a gratuitous moral apostrophe on virtue and honor. In these respects it parodies the techniques of the eighteenth-century novel.

The novel turns a standard eighteenth-century plot into a paradise of erotic fantasy. Fanny, a poor provincial innocent, goes to London where she is deflowered and debauched by urban decadence and aristocratic profligacy. The bulk of the action is description of the standard variety of sexual experiences. In tribute to those happy endings that caused Richardson grief in regard to *Clarissa,* the story is resolved when Fanny is reunited with her first despoiler and true love; they marry and live ever after in virtue, honor, and penitence. Although the standard situations of the early English novel are employed—Fanny's world is shot through with the vicissitudes of poverty and innocence in the clutches of City and Aristocracy—the story is altogether focused on fantastic sexuality. There is a suggestion of moral causality, but it is so slight and so overshadowed by sex that it signifies little. There is no attempt to explore any of the implicit moral or psychic problems.

The essence of *Fanny Hill* is simplicity, simplicity of theme and simplicity of description. *Story of O,* on the other hand, adopts the complexity of abstraction and metaphor so characteristic of the modern novel. *Fanny Hill* is the description of a prostitute's life; *Story of O* is a metaphor of love as libido. If that figure contains all the paraphernalia of pornography—whips, chains, tortures, sadism, masochism, masculine power, feminine submission, sexual anonymity (at one point O is blindfolded and brought into a room where "*A* hand seized one of her breasts, *a* mouth fastened on the tip of the other") and so on—it also contains the complex apparatus of the psyche. O submits herself to a brotherhood of sexuality which exploits and punishes her body, exorcises her will, dominates her total being, and finally is the cause of her self-destruction. Having been given away by her lover, she gives herself again to her surrogate lover, proving and taking refuge in her capacity to love; he abandons her also and she kills herself, but only after securing her master's permission.

The story provides, thus, two erotic points of view. From the masculine perspective it describes a complete liberation of the sexual libido.

Men possess and enjoy O anonymously, without consequence or emotional responsibility. Her need for love brings her to them, which is a male power fantasy. And once they are through with her she is simply discarded; they have in fact the power of life and death, another male power fantasy. But from the female viewpoint the story arouses intense anxiety, a sure antidote to pornographic fantasy. O's captivity may be ended whenever she wishes, but to wish it is to forfeit the love she so desperately needs. Thus she is confronted constantly by the fear of loss, that archetypal anxiety observed by Theodore Reik. And of course she does lose that love, twice. And the consequence is suicide. Here is another classic female anxiety, that love for a man will subsume self-identity, and the loss of the love will leave her without reason to be. The novel, then, employs a multidimensional and complex descriptive and metaphorical methodology, exploring simultaneously the antitheses of sexual fantasy and anxiety.

What is important here is that O becomes the ur-woman in quest of love. She is thus exposed to its complete domination and consequent agony. Is she, then, an allegorical figure, perhaps a post-Freudian Everywoman? Certainly everything about her is feminine stereotype—her love, her submissiveness, her sexuality, her annihilation of self, her anxieties. At one point in *Peyton Place* (also written by a woman), a young girl says to her paramour, "Come on Honey. Love me a little. . . . Come on Honey. . . . Hard. . . . Do it hard, Honey. Bite me a little. Hurt me a little." This is O's position; except she says, "Hurt me a *lot*." She is the archetypal woman in an archetypal situation. She has been described by every psychoanalyst who has written on the subject. On the one hand, she is the answer to the stereotypical secret dream of males. On the other hand, she is an object awful in her implications. It is the former quality that makes her story pornographic. And it is the latter quality that takes her story beyond simplistic exploitation of sexual fantasy and lets it metaphorically explore a fundamental human condition.

The dramatically different techniques of these two works parallel, of course, the narrative forms characteristic of their respective times. But more than that, they document the evolving psychic and artistic complexity of pornographic literature. Admittedly, these examples have higher artistic claims than most pornography. But I am interested here in its nature and artistic potential, and must consider therefore its highest stages of development. On the one hand, hard-core or commercial pornography is static. Its ends are served by the simplest of descriptive techniques and rhetorical gambits. But on the other hand, there is another and higher form of pornography. Rather than being only an exploitation of orgasm stimuli, it is rather an exploration of human sexuality. It may exploit its subject, but it does more than exploit. We are, as Freud observed, all of us more or less neurotic. One aspect of human neurosis is the rhythm of expectation and frustration which marks our sexual lives. Pornography on its lowest level exploits this rhythm by providing easy fantasy gratifications. But on its highest level it explores this rhythm, its moral and psychic implications, and to the degree that it does this, it is poetic in the highest sense. This kind, of course, is the pornography being absorbed into what we call literature, and it is represented by such works as *O*.

*Story of O* uses all the devices of hard-core pornography, but manages to transcend those conventions with its profoundly depressing explorations of the neurosis of modern love. In opening up the anxieties of love, in prodding its archetypal fears and desires, *Story of O* is not only a true statement of human experience, it is anarchical at a deep and distressing personal level. For it is, in effect, a cultural suicide note, articulating the failure of love in an allegory depicting an obsessive masculine need for the security of possession and an obsessive feminine need for the security of love. Ironically, masculinity can only prove itself by destroying what it most desires (and is most contemptuous of), woman—and thus its very need carries the seed of its own loss. And woman, needing as much to give herself over to that neurotic masculine irony, is at once gratified and destroyed by it. O's story records the disintegration of human personality as it clumsily thrashes and writhes in a death struggle with the incomprehensible antagonism of body and soul seeking a harmonious synthesis in love. But the idea of love that promised such a harmony was a dialectical chimera, and in the rough and tumble of psychic reality it often as not fails to deliver. As Plato knew, the only hope for the ideal of love lies in suppression and control of animality, harnessing it to the service of sweet reason. However, he also knew that this was pretty unlikely without the complete restructuring of society that he recommends in *The Republic*. But since no utopian social structure has proved amenable to human idiosyncrasy we are, twenty-five hundred years later, still left with the wars of body and soul, and the carnage it makes of tranquility. This, after all, is what the allegory of O is about.

O being the protagonist, her story is a largely feminine projection of the myth of love, but it has masculine implications. For, although the story represents the characteristic pornographic sense of gender—masculine domination and feminine submissiveness—these stereotypes take on bisexual ambiguities. O is completely feminine in relation to men, but she also plays a dominant lesbian role in relation to women. In fact, until she falls in love with René, her lover and master, she prefers lesbian sexuality, partly because of the simple pleasure she derives from caressing women and partly because of the more complex pleasure she gets from dominating them, and finally because of the highly ambiguous reassurance she gets from finding in her attraction toward women an analogy of men's attraction toward her. It is interesting that, again from this peculiarly feminine myth of love, while O's story includes a fair amount of lesbian activity, it has no homosexuality whatsoever. The yin/yang principle, Westernized to signify sexual ambivalence and perhaps neurosis rather than the personal harmony it suggests to the Eastern mind, operates only in women. But it is always overshadowed by their willing subservience to men. In E. M. Forster's critical terms, men in O's story are always "flat" (that is, predictable) characters, while women are "round"—capable of psychic changes and complexity within the framework of narrative action. The novel, then, brings a myth of female consciousness together with the myth of love. Men are used to represent one mythic quality, power. But it is a strangely complex power, symbolized by sexual domination, yet signified more ominously by its manipulation of feminine will, the ability to make that will consent to its own obliteration. O, having been imprisoned in a kind of obedience school for mistresses of a secret sexual society (not dissimilar in its murky international omnipotence to those political conspiracies Ian Fleming conjures), reflects thus on her bondage:

> And yet nothing had been such a comfort to her as the silence, unless it was the chains. The chains and the silence, which should have bound her deep within herself, which should have smothered her, strangled her, on the contrary freed her from herself. What would have become of her if she had been granted the right to speak and the freedom of her hands, if she had been free to make a choice, when her lover prostituted her before his own eyes? True, she did speak as she was being tortured, but can moans and cries be classed as words? Besides, they often stilled her by gagging. Beneath the gazes, beneath the hands, beneath the sexes that defiled her, the whips that rent her, she lost herself in a delirious absence from herself which restored her to love and, perhaps, brought her to the edge of death. She was anyone, anyone at all, any one of the other girls, opened and forced like her, girls whom she saw being opened and forced, for she did see it, even when she was not obliged to have a hand in it.

The invocation of love and death, in conjunction, is crucial. For love, in this anxious exploration of it, demands a corresponding death. O, the archetypal woman, must destroy her sense of self to secure love. She must consent to whatever men desire of her, even if it means forfeiting the consciousness by which any human being certifies existence. Thus the mythic statement is that there is only one consciousness possible in love, that of masculine authority. All power to masculine will—which means the anarchical destruction of a feminine reality. There is, in this vision, psychically only one sex, one reality, one essence. The feminine differential is an accident, suitable, like slaves in the Athenian democracy, only for service. Even O's lesbianism, in which she assumes a masculine role, argues for the myth of a masculine metaphysics.

Woman's need for love forces her into a masculine cosmos, where morality is defined by masculine power and desire. O is ordered by her lover to seduce Jacqueline—a haughtily confident and thoroughly feminine woman ("Since Jacqueline was sure of herself, she had nothing to redeem; she had no need to be reassured, all she needed was a mirror") who consents to O's lesbian ministrations because they give a "safe" animal pleasure—into the secret sexual society that metaphors the universe of love. O recognizes that to do so is to betray both Jacqueline's essentially feminine nature and the trust that Jacqueline has in her. To betray her is to don absolutely the masculine ethic, and O has still enough resistance to have this awareness. But her need for love, which means the approval of her lover, and her own "masculine" desire for the possession of Jacqueline (the proof of which in *Story of O*, it will be recalled, is a kind of primitive version of conspicuous consumption—that is, the ability to give to someone else certifies one's complete "ownership") force her to be

> obsessed with the burning desire to have Jacqueline at any price, even if attaining her goal meant handing her over to Sir Stephen. After all, she rationalized to herself, Jacqueline's beauty is quite sufficient protection for her, and besides, why should I get involved in it anyway? And what if she were to be reduced to what I have been reduced to, is that really so terrible?—scarcely admitting, and yet overwhelmed to imagine, how sweet it would be to see Jacqueline naked and defenseless beside her, and like her.

With this betrayal O moves unequivocally into the masculine world view. Her act parallels her own lover's betrayal of her into the secret society, into the demonic hypothesis that love demands complete surrender of being. So with this act O becomes the moral equal of her lovers, men. And she further enforces that morality by betraying Jacqueline, who with her mockery and self-containment threatens the masculine solipsism that has become for O love's salvation:

> O was happy that René had had her whipped and had prostituted her, because her impassioned submission would furnish her lover with the proof that she belonged to him, but also because the pain and shame of the lash, and the outrage inflicted upon her by those who compelled her to pleasure when they took her, and at the same time delighted in their own without paying the slightest heed to hers, seemed to her the very redemption of her sins.
>
> And what if, in spite of that, Sir Stephen was right? What if she actually enjoyed her debasement? In that case, the baser she was, the more merciful was René to consent to make O the instrument of his pleasure.

It is, then, imperative to the mythic view represented by O that she betray Jacqueline, that she does signifies the deep need in her. But she is in fact unsuccessful, for Jacqueline's animality is far greater than her need for love, and so is impervious to the satanic guiles and temptations of the secret society. Not being in love, she has no need for O's diabolical selflessness. In the dialectic of love's myth Jacqueline presents the only other option to the slavery of love, not being in love. But, although Jacqueline does not love, she is loved by someone outside the secret society. So her dialectical option is real, so far as the reader is concerned. It tells us that O's condition is not the result of a simplistic cosmic determinism, it is rather the result of her particular (perhaps neurotic) need for love. O's condition is a result of choice, however little, given her psychic needs, she is in control of that choice. O's decision, and the novel repeatedly emphasizes that she is free not to love, to choose love and its bondage may be the most terrifying dimension of the mythic sensibility she represents.

One of the great human aches is the desire to be free from oneself, to have the gratifications one associates with the self without the obligation of making the choices by which moral character and personality are defined. This is the sense in which *Story of O* is a suicide note, the ultimate anarchy, proclaiming the human will to self-destruction as a way to that constant state of felicity that has been promised in all our mythology, a state, if it exists at all, no more constant than Juliet's moon. Keats, "half in love with easeful death," knew that temptation, the temptation that somehow nature will make it possible "to cease upon the midnight with no pain." But he also knew he was talking in his sleep. For Aristotle hit the mark long ago when he told us that the object of human actions is happiness, and our choice of actions is what brings us happiness or the reverse, and no single choice (Christianity to the contrary) lands us in heaven. Life, Joyce said in a profound addendum to the *Ethics,* is every day, day after day. But O's mythic being testifies to the archetypal human fear of that great labor, the steady seeking after happiness. Like most of us, O does not want always to be in transit. She wants to be *there.* And our mythology also tells us that love is where it's at. O's story articulates at least one version of the price for a one-way ticket:

> In the space of a week she learned fear, but certainty; anguish, but happiness. René threw himself at her like a pirate at his prisoner, and she reveled in her captivity, feeling on her wrists, her ankles, feeling on all her members and in the secret depths of her heart and body, bonds less visible than the finest strands of hair, more powerful than the cables the Lilliputians used to tie up Gulliver, bonds her lover loosened or tightened with a glance. She was no longer free? Yes! thank God, she was no longer free. But she was light, a nymph on clouds, a fish in water, lost in happiness. Lost because these fine strands of hair, these cables which René held, without exceptions, in his hand, were the only network through which the current of life any longer flowed into her.

However fictively exaggerated, O's story spreads before us the dark terrors and the nearly nihilistic rewards waiting in the labyrinth of love. Hers is the story of the love-pilgrim's progress to a celestial city, the existence of which we are no longer sure. And thus the progress is understandably fearful, its severe demand promising so ambivalent a reward. Being fictive, her story sets out options before us with a clarity and force, however disturbing, that no other mode of knowledge can attain.

One might, then, discuss this novel in many terms other than its sexual theme, that is, without needing to be preoccupied with the explicit sexual scenes, because it deals with life as any poetic work does, on a level of significance beyond its literal imagery. Its sexuality at all levels is a natural part of the novel's narrative rhythm, and, once accustomed to its subject, one is not particularly conscious of pornographic spectacle. One is in fact a good deal more aware of its psychic ominousness, of its particular rendition of the myth of love. If one brings oneself to accept the possibility of a pornographic art, one may critically consider this novel as one would any other. And there are, of course, as many possible interpretations of the myth of love as there are artists to interpret it. Nor are they necessarily a product of philosophical naturalism. No artistic dimension of complex pornography is obliged to anything other than its art.

What I am arguing is that pornography, like any literature or art, is a way of knowing. Obviously this conception is rather different from those in the feminist critiques by Andrea Dworkin and Susan Griffin. Dworkin's approach seeks to isolate pornography from legitimate literature and art so that it might be perceived and prosecuted as a criminal act rather than protected as aesthetic or scientific expression. Her polemic is complemented by Griffin's historical analysis, which essentially sees Western culture dominated by the "pornographic" masculine mind: thus, the "pornographic mind" has developed a "pornographic ideology" and produced a "pornographic culture." For both, pornography is categorically vicious in effect and pejorative as a term. But where Dworkin's use of the term is arbitrarily prescriptive, depending entirely on her interpretation of the data, Griffin's is rather too inclusive. For her purposes, Sophocles, Juvenal, Sade, Byron, and Hitler all represent the same thing: pornography. Whatever the validity of Dworkin's and Griffin's perspectives, their approaches are exclusively preoccupied with the perniciousness of pornography and clearly preclude any prospect of its providing knowledge. But a more liberal feminist position, as already observed, takes up the notion that pornography has epistemological potential, and is, moreover, notably less condescending to that possibility than such prominent male writers on the subject as Steven Marcus, Morse Peckham, and George Steiner.

In a *Rolling Stock* interview novelist Alix Kates Shulman addressed the issue as follows:

> I myself see sex as one of the central ways in which women have been oppressed and continue to be used by men. And so sexual rebellion seems to me central to feminist rebellion. I think, for example, a lot of the moral majority, anti-abortion feeling has less to do with murder, as they would put it, than it does with keeping women's sexuality under control. And before that, the whole birth control movement was less about population considerations or moralistic prohibitions about the formation of new humans, than it was about keeping women's sexuality under male control. So in my writing I always explore sexuality. I seem often to be writing about sex as power; I often conceive the battle between the sexes as being essentially a sexual battle. . . .
>
> Traditionally, sex has been one of the few kinds of power women have been able to exert at the same time that men have exploited women sexually. I always want to be free to explore this subject in every way. . . . I think one of the things that fiction explores is unconscious impulse—a deeper level of secret data—and if anything, we need to encourage more exploration of it, not less. I think the few anthologies that are coming out now of women's own attempts at pornography, sometimes called erotica, are to be applauded, no matter how crude or restrained.

I earlier noted the themes of sexual power and submission as masculine and feminine archetypes in *Story of O*. Shulman's topics are similar, expressed in terms of sexual politics, feminist rebellion, and the unconscious. Feminist critics point out that the scientific and imaginative domination of sexual investigation by men has contributed monumental misinformation. Freud's preconceptions about female orgasm is a classic instance. Hemingway's famous earth-moving orgasmic romanticism is perhaps another. In any event, men will continue to explore the subject, and women will now add to it their own perspectives on the interaction between moral imagination and sexual being.

For both men and women, then, pornography has become artistically useful for exploring contradictions in perceived reality. As modern aesthetics has subordinated moral idealism, the truth with which beauty has been associated assumes a discourse with the false, the ugly, and the obscene. Thus the true and the false, the beautiful and the ugly, the bizarre and the quotidian, the innocent and the obscene, all co-exist simultaneously in a dialectic of relativity. In this respect aesthetics reflects the situation of physics and the material world. So a modern "perverse" aesthetic has evolved in complementarity to the proliferation of contradictions and interrogations so characteristic of liberalist modernity. Beauty has always kept occasional company with the obscene, as in Aristophanes or Petronius or Bosch. But as the development of scientific materialism provided theoretical foundation for obscenity and aberrance, they were incorporated into aesthetics. Zola analogized from medical diagnostics to fictive method, and by the early twentieth century Pound defined beauty according to its diagnostic and curative functions. The art of diagnosis was precisely to address the ugly, aberrant, and obscene.

Modern literature, art, and cinema continue to develop those aesthetic possibilities. By the early 1980s women had begun to produce not only pornography but sado-masochistic pornography, heretofore perceived to be the bane of women, with the declared intent of exploring power relationships as well as other personal and social dynamics. Moreover, they insist that the S/M experience is beautiful. This may be a peculiar taste, but then, as they said in the eighteenth century, there's no disputing taste. Certainly Sade would not have been surprised, nor would Krafft-Ebing. Einstein might have been, but very likely Niels Bohr would remind him, chuckling, "I told you so." Whether or not nature has the grand design Einstein surmised, its magnitude is such that we cannot perceive the big picture. Our perspective being relative to our limitations, the aberrance/normality ratio in nature also becomes relative. A sado-masochistic art asserting its beauty challenges at once traditional concepts of nature and beauty. That in turn is the challenge to the art. If it is persuasive, we will have learned something about both beauty and nature. That of course is the challenge of any art, but pornography carries a larger burden of credibility than most.

Perhaps sex is a ritual that is, as Freud suggested, always testing the culture's elastic limit. In 1985 the Supreme Court agreed to consider whether laws prohibiting consensual fellatio, cunnilingus, and like acts are constitutional. If sexuality itself is a sometime cultural outlaw, certainly pornography shares the onus. But their power on the imagination is punctuated by the fact that, at the very moment in history when women are vigorously asserting sisterhood and parity, a prominent schism has developed precisely around the issue of pornography. Moreover, there are schisms within the schism—between heterosexuals and lesbians, between orthodox lesbians and S/M lesbians. If there was what was called "the sexual revolution" in the 1960s and 1970s, by the 1980s it verged on anarchy, underscored by the AIDS epidemic and the abortion wars. Small wonder that our conservative instincts feel threatened by pornography; equally so that our liberal ones claim its utility. For sex is always with us even more than the poor. We should be no more surprised that pornography accompanies sexuality than that landscape painting accompanies the countryside. As with better and worse landscapes, so with pornography. The worst sort at the very least documents an indomitable sexual will; the best sort integrates that will with the inexorable cadences and contradictions of life.

Walter Benjamin describes the ancient story teller as a sort of mysterious stranger bringing news from the dark beyond the edge of the village firelight. If story tellers were to survive at this trade, they had to develop a pretty good nose for their audience's limits. But if they were any good at all, they stretched and added to its frame of reference. If the Greeks or Hebrews are any index, the story teller, we're told, risked speaking the unspeakable—rape, incest, sodomy, adultery, patricide. Pornography is something like that. It is the risky side of the story teller's art. If it is any good at all it will stretch our frame of reference. Lately it has been getting bolder, more aesthetically ambitious, and increasingly it insists on speaking the unspeakable.

# 3

# Decadence and the Poetics of Obscenity

## WHAT YOU SEE IS WHAT SHE GOT

Nat King Cole used to sing a calypso song about a homesick Trinidadian comparing the decadent, civilized States with healthy, natural Trinidad. Gringo women, he lamented, were submerged beneath their arty use of padding, cosmetics, and clothes. But with the Trinidad girl, "what you see is what she got." This topical calypso format presents the archetypal problem for all lyrical impulse—the antithesis of art and nature. From Plato to pop, this tension permeates the history of art and art theory. The vogue in the 1970s for Aubrey Beardsley articulated a version of this dilemma that is pertinent to the development of a poetics of obscenity.

His artistic elegance—both graphically and literarily—satisfies our inclination for the beautiful, while his pornography adds another raspberry to the popular assault on moral transcendentalism. The "decadent" art with which Beardsley was much involved made a direct hit against the monolith of aesthetic idealism. Beardsley, in keeping with the central principle of decadence, demonstrated that artistic beauty was not obliged to traditional morality in any way for its being. His two most extreme statements of this are of course the *Lysistrata* illustrations and his unfinished pornographic novel, *The Story of Venus and Tannhauser* (or, *Under the Hill*). Beardsley was one of the first to present pornographic satire in a lyrical guise and make both satire and lyricism convincing. His story of Venus and Tannhauser is at once a rebuttal of the transcendental melodrama of Wagner's libretto, on the one hand, and a parody of pornographic "romance," on the other. Simultaneously it is also a lyrical *tour de force* celebrating its own purely artistic beauty. Whereas Wagner's libretto is patterned on the morality play—Tannhauser's despair, for example, is at last resolved in Christian faith and spiritual beauty—Beardsley's treatment denies the artistic potency of moral conflict by simply dismissing it, and he thereby exorcises morality and celebrates style. Wagner's Tannhauser, for instance, is introduced in profound angst—"No more, no more. . . ./How long this nightmare?"; when Venus cloys, his conscience boggles. Not so with Beardsley's dandy, who is introduced thus:

> The Chevalier Tannhauser, having lighted off his horse, stood doubtfully for a moment beneath the ombre gateway of the Venusberg, troubled with an exquisite fear least a day's travel should have too cruelly undone the laboured niceness of his dress. His hand, slim and gracious as La Marquise du Deffand's in the drawing by Carmontelle, played nervously about the gold hair that fell upon his shoulders like a finely curled peruke, and from point to point of a precise toilet, the fingers wandered, quelling the little mutinies of cravat and ruffle.

The decadent Tannhauser, unlike Wagner's moralistic counterpart, relishes losing himself in the Hill of Venus, and is neatly poised in the face of his ambiguous perdition: "Goodbye, Madonna," he says casually, and then sighs to heaven for "the assurance of a looking glass before I make my debut!" In similar manner, Beardsley satirizes pornography and romance (antithetical variations on the same theme): "It is, I know, the custom of all romancers to paint heroes who can give a lady proof of their valiance at least twenty times a night. Now Tannhauser had no such Gargantuan facility, and was rather relieved when, an hour later, Priapusa and Doricourt and some others burst drunkenly into the room and claimed Venus for themselves." Beardsley proves the decadent thesis by creating a pornographic narrative at once denying the necessary connection between either pornography and vulgarity, or immorality and ugliness. Characteristically he casts pornographic images into elegance and wit; for instance,

> Venus allowed most of the dishes to pass untasted, she was so engaged with the beauty of Tannhauser. She laid her head many times on his robe, kissing him passionately; and his skin, at once firm and yielding, seemed, to those exquisite little teeth of hers, the most incomparable pas-

> ture. . . . Tannhauser, on his side, was no less devoted. He adored her all over . . . and crushed her in his arms, and slaked his parched lips at her mouth. He caressed her eyelids softly with his finger tips, and pushed aside the curls from her forehead, and did a thousand gracious things, tuning her body as a violinist tunes his instrument before he plays upon it.
>
> Priapusa snorted like an old war horse at the sniff of powder, and tickled Tannhauser and Venus by turns, and slipped her tongue down their throats, and refused to be quiet at all until she had had a mouthful of the Chevalier. Claude, seizing his chance, dived under the table and came up the other side just under the queen's couch, and before she could say "One!" he was taking his coffee "aux deux colonnes," Clair was furious at his friend's success, and sulked for the rest of the evening.

The appeal of Beardsley's starchy rhetoric to the literati in an age of fading aristocracy was ironically similar to his latter-day appeal. To his time, Beardsley represented the triumph of an aristocratic, classically oriented aesthetic taste over a modern moralizing utilitarianism. To a sensibility of the 1990s he recalls a traditional aesthetic—line, symmetry, highly stylized representation—without its vestigial moralism. He is another analogue of Ike's forward-looking return to the past. *The Story of Venus and Tannhauser* is a *tour de force* carrying formal poetic tradition to an extreme and at the same time ridiculing the moral idealism so long concomitant with that poetic tradition.

Of the four major treatments of the Venus and Tannhauser legend in the nineteenth century, Beardsley's has particular artistic potential for us today because his was the only treatment that was in touch with poetic evolution in a really vital way. He used pornography to make a statement about the nature of art. The others resorted to more acceptable traditions. William Morris's "Hill of Venus" (from *The Earthly Paradise*), for instance, uses allegory; it is an allegory of psychic despair in which Tannhauser leaves the Hill of Venus, and gropes his way to Rome where he is refused absolution by the Pope unless his holy staff should bloom. In despair, Tannhauser returns to his venal life. Meanwhile, back at the Vatican, the Pope's staff blooms. Unknown to Tannhauser, his salvation exists through the miracle of God's grace. Thus the poem argues allegorically the need for faith. But both its vision and its structure throw us back on tradition, not forward to either a new vision or a new poetic. Wagner's opera libretto is similarly unrewarding. It uses morality as resolution; where Morris resolves despair theologically, Wagner resolves it through Tannhauser's moral repentance. The ending is directly from the morality play, with Venus (Knowledge, evil) and Elizabeth (good, Innocence) contending for his will. Naturally, Elizabeth's Christian virtues win. Not even Swinburne could expand the tradition. His "Laus Veneris" articulates a sort of inverted Pascal's Wager in the lyric stoicism with which Tannhauser recognizes that he is doomed, but not doomed until the last judgment (and there is always the hope that there is not any judgment to come, in which case he is home free). Swinburne cannot seem to figure out whether there is a God or not; so he resolves the whole thing by going back to a lyric version of Dryden's "All for Love," on the hunch that the millennium is a long way off.

*The Story of Venus and Tannhuser* did for English pornography what *Tristram Shandy* had done for the English novel, gave it dimensions of artistic possibility hitherto unexplored. And it perhaps lay dormant so many years for much the same reason that *Tristram Shandy* did—because no one quite knew what to make of it. Unlike Sterne, however, he gave up everything for classical beauty. Even in his time it was a desperate investment. On the truth exchange, the politics and religion markets had already collapsed; science was ominously rising, and artists tried to head off a bull market by pulling everything out of politics and religion and investing in beauty. It was, despite its brief and glorious success (Beardsley, Beerbohm, Rossetti, Swinburne, Wilde, Symons, Pater, and Yeats in England; Rimbaud, Verlaine, Mallarmé, Gautier, Baudelaire, in France), a strategic failure. The rendezvous between the art of monolithic beauty and the art of analytic exploration was already begun with Claude Bernard and Emile Zola.

Beardsley's pornographic novel is important because it shows how completely the decadents were persuaded that, as Oscar Wilde put it in "The Decay of Lying," "Things are because we see them, and what we see, and how we see it, depend on the Arts that have influenced us." The decadents could produce Beardsley's effete *tour de force* because it affirmed for them what Zola denied, that art brings reality to man rather than bringing man to reality. But in fact it was a losing ploy because it showed that the logical conclusion of their poetics was nihilistic. In saying that nothing mattered but artistic beauty, they had sooner or later to confront the implication that beauty did not matter either.

One sees Arthur Symons wrestling with this when he says in "A Note on Zola's Method" that "He sees the beast in all its transformations, but he sees only the beast. He has never looked at life impartially, he has never seen it as it is. His realism is a distorted idealism. . . ." Symons really means that Zola' scientific-poetic formula challenges Symons' own symbolic-decadent formula. One must remember that Symons' idea of realism, of "telling it like it is," is Mallarmé's mystical "confidence in the eternal correspondences between the visible and the invisible universe." Symons did not understand that Mallarmé's mysticism, like any mysticism, is simply an idiosyncratic idealism, and that the very idiosyncrasy he so admired was an ominous fissure in his revered edifice of Beauty. For not only did Mallarmé write prose-poems, thereby refuting the necessity of artistic convention, but he also located beauty in the perceptions of his mind (in "the horror of the forest, or the silent thunder afloat in the leaves; not the intrinsic, dense wood of the trees"). Such beauty is not in a unified Nature; neither is it in artistic presentation of vision; it is in the vision itself. And the logical conclusion of Mallarmé's theory is that he not write about his visions at all, but that he simply have them. As Symons laments, this is pretty nearly what Mallarmé did. If beauty does not have its own form to control art, and if artistic convention is no authoritative vehicle for conveying the beautiful, then every person is his or her own artist and every vision has its own beauty. Symons' preference for Mallarmé over Zola is simply a matter of taste, not aesthetic necessity. Beardsley's pornography carried the grand decadence as far as it could go in creating a cosmos where morality was non-existent, sentiment was merely an ironic rhetorical device, and classical artifice was the nature of being.

## BUT WHAT DO YOU SEE?

When Schiller noted that the difference between classicism and modernity was in the latter's loss of confidence in a coherent sense of nature, he identified also that component in romanticism which revolutionized Western poetics. Once such philosophers as Kant and Hume had relocated reality from external space and time to perceived space and time, this opened poetic possibilities that recreated the imagination. In the poetic tradition that evolved from Plato's moral idealism and Aristotle's theory of artistic imitation, art was supposed to imitate nature. Nature was supposed to have an order more or less coherent and comprehensible. Correspondingly, art too was supposed to be ordered, and its truth lay in the rightness with which it represented the correspondence. Thus Dr. Johnson, one of the great products of this tradition, judged that *Tristram Shandy* could not last because "nothing odd will do long." Sterne's psychically idiosyncratic novel anticipated the Romantic modernity that Dr. Johnson could not be expected to appreciate.

Decadence, as I am using it, is a development from romanticism. There was never, of course, a comprehensive romanticism; if Schiller, for example, doubted a coherent natural order, that was certainly not true of Wordsworth. But if one can talk about a generalized and synthetic impression, then one can observe that, for all its revolutionary aesthetic potential, romanticism kept to a conventionally unified poetics as an expression of the coherent moral sense which still prevailed. And if we except a tendency to narrative and descriptive impressionism in such decadents as Gautier, Huysmans, Baudelaire, Swinburne, and Wilde, the structural poetics of decadence too was conventional enough. Early decadence manifested itself in subject and imagery rather than form. By introducing the ugly, the grotesque, and the "immoral" as agencies of beauty and "harmony," the early decadents refuted moral idealism, but maintained the poetic unity so long associated with it. Thus decadence attempted to "liberate" art from morality, and even life. A later decadence—beginning perhaps about 1915 (vorticism, Imagism, Dadaism, and others), subsiding in the new critical 1930s and 1940s, and strong again in the 1950s and 1960s—took the next logical step; having long since accepted the refutation of moral idealism, this "movement" proceeded to repudiate artistic unity and wholeness as necessary poetic principles. In this larger sense, then, decadence refers to the contemporaneous rejection of complementary moral and artistic unity, the heritage of Western poetics. It is analogous to existentialist absurdity, where epistemological uncertainty obliges us to conduct our affairs with "negative capability." We cannot indulge a passionate reaching after moral fact where such facts themselves are demonstrably dialectical and problematic.

A premise of moral unity derives from a univocal metaphysics (for example, Platonic idealism), or such Romantic analogues as Wordsworth's or Coleridge's moral transcendentalism. Decadence denies Romantic morality (that is, the upward Good for which Nature is figure) while extending the implications of Romantic poetics. Romantic theory (as in Shelley's *Defense*) holds that art leads to truth. Oscar Wilde, in "The Decay of Lying," implicitly reverses that with marvelous chop logic: Art is lying; art is truth; therefore lying is truth. Thus decadence confronts Romantic poetics with a radical contradiction. The result is the absurd paradox fundamental to decadence, the paradox that cuts romanticism off from its vestigial idealism.

Romantic poets, the popular front for Romantic theory, had been unwilling to make that break. They had instead wallowed in elaborate but unconvincing attempts to integrate deep psychology with Olympian morality. In so doing, as Byron says, they "proved unintelligible." It is true that Keats, for example, recognized an incipient decadence: "Negative capability" was Keat's unsystematic awareness that dialectical preoccupations like those of Wordsworth, Coleridge, and Shelley were an "irritable reaching after" facts that were clouded by the very presuppositions through which they were to be reached. But Keats, unfortunately, although true to the decadent tendency, died young, leaving doctrinaire decadence for a later generation in England. When Wilde, echoing Gautier, said that art expresses only itself, he was articulating the decadent wish to find a world of beauty that neither the natural nor moral worlds provided. Thus the decadents wanted essentially a Romantic beauty, but they denied its source in nature. Man, they said, defines nature and not the converse. So art, not nature, is the source of beauty. The later decadence simply makes the next logical assumption—that if there is no beauty in nature, neither is there any in art.

Thus, by our time, the basic generalities of poetic tradition—that art reveals the good and the beautiful—are largely disbelieved. Like the early decadents, we say that art expresses itself, but its "self" no longer necessarily implies beauty. Beauty, as an artistic concept, has largely become rhetorical. It was meaningful only when it applied to creation or formal analogues of creation. Since the author of nature has ceased to exist, it is no longer necessary to honor him by praising his works. And with his passing so too passed the analogy between his works and ours. Although the early decadents tried to grasp beauty a while longer without its metaphysical basis, they had to do so by appealing to an aristocratic sensibility, which was also doomed. When democracy caught on, it swept away the last refuge of monolithic beauty.

The decadent connection between art and metaphysics is that perception is controlled by the arts (for contemporary decadence, "art" is expanded to mean something like Marshall McLuhan's "media," hence, for example, pop art) which convey experience to us; we can therefore be informed only by what these arts intend or are capable of conveying to us. Thus we know only what we perceive; our perceptions are controlled by the arts that represent "reality" to our senses; reality therefore depends on the character of the art or medium that represents it; and consequently rather than art imitating Nature (the constant), nature (the relative) imitates or takes on the qualities of art, which has now become the arbiter of reality. Thus Wilde:

> Consider the matter from a scientific or a metaphysical point of view. . . . For what is Nature? Nature is no great mother who has borne us. She is our creation. It is in our brain that she quickens to life. Things are because we see them, and what we see, and how we see it, depends on the Arts that have influenced us. To look at a thing is very different from seeing a thing. One does not see anything until one sees its beauty. Then, and then only, does it come into existence.

If we substitute "irony" or "absurdity" for Wilde's "beauty" and expand Wilde's use of "Arts" to include popular culture and its "media," we have here a late-twentieth-century statement of decadent poetics. Nor is what McLuhan describes in *The Medium is the Massage* substantially different from what Wilde observed:

> We have all seen in our own day in England how a certain curious and fascinating type to beauty, invented and emphasized by two imaginative painters, has so influenced Life that whenever one goes to a private view, or to an artistic salon, one sees here the mystic eyes of Rossetti's dream, the

> ivory throat, the strange square-cut jaw, the loosened shadowy hair that he so ardently loved, there the sweet maidenhood of *the Golden Stair*, the blossom-like mouth and weary loveliness of the *Laus Amoris*, the passion-pale face of Andromeda, the thin hands and lithe beauty of the Vivian in Merlin's Dream. And it has always been so. A great artist invents a type, and Life tries to copy it, to reproduce it in a popular form, like an enterprising publisher.

In short, to say that life imitates art is to say that artistic media influence our perception and knowledge of complex reality and to that extent our lives.

These premises about the warp between reality, perception, and articulation have become commonplaces of modern theory. Thus, as noted in Chapter 1, Foucault characterizes sexuality not as a natural phenomenon but rather a product of the discourse of social power interests. Reality is but a function of the motives and manners of its describers. Everyone is an artist willy-nilly. This may make for a lot of bad art, as it did in the media coverage of the 1991 Gulf War where the antics of "smart weapons" were cast as a kind of video game and the ground assault as a turkey shoot. So it obliges us to interpretive ingenuities, Susan Sontag and Jonathan Culler to the contrary notwithstanding.

A classic instance is recorded in C. D. Bryan's *Friendly Fire*: when a soldier's mother received the official description of her son's death in Vietnam, it was coded in a language she could not comprehend, the key phrase being that he had been killed in the line of duty by "friendly fire." The military language was of course conceived to obscure the event that it was supposedly describing. Only by an agonizing perseverance was she eventually able to get the military to release the facts—that her son was killed in his sleep when a drunken American artillery unit inadvertently fired on his position in the middle of the night. Thus the reality was rather different than the art of the military correspondent had represented. When we add the artist who controls the art to the art which controls our perception, then we must get a very decadent idea of the reality of the house that Jack built.

Our continuing intrigue with documentary works, whether reportage or fictive, is an index of our fascination, not to say need, for the story of reality. Despite such antecedents as André Breton's *Nadja*, for example, Truman Capote claimed a new narrative form for his *In Cold Blood*. Moreover, both authors received the same criticism: Why didn't Breton attempt to help Nadja's neurosis, why didn't Capote attempt to stop the executions of his two hapless protagonists? In other words, why didn't these authors of reality give it a more salutary plot? Samuel Richardson got a similar complaint for *Clarissa*, Earnest Hemingway for *A Farewell to Arms*. Reality, of whatever sort, is always perplexingly problematic. We try to fix it with the story of Yahweh or Allah or Jesus. Even the uncertainty principle is an attempt to stabilize the plot of the deconstructing story. It is not enough to kiss your lover with your eyes open. You'll see something odd and amusing, a distortion. But when you see a Picasso figure with its eyes centered and stacked slightly askew you recognize another reality, the story of distortion and perspective. Plato lamented the epistemological distortion of appearances, how a straight stick appears curved in the stream. Well, yes, but then in the stream the stick *is* curved. The stick's story has two parts. Similarly with the story of the eyes. Over morning coffee your lover's eyes flank his or her nose as we're accustomed to seeing them. But last night, kissing with your eyes open, they were as Picasso depicts them. It's another part of their story.

The theory that art, as medial purveyor and reflector, controls reality means also—and more significantly—that it controls moral reality. Moral categories, the traditional method of moral knowledge, are consequently absurd. That is, they exist because of faith rather than necessity. Categories have a way of becoming disengaged from experience by way of their own "artistic" (that is, dialectical) structure and taking on their own intimidating existence. Contemporary decadents attempt to fight this intimidation by articulating the gap between real moral authority and chimerical moral faith. They assume the stance of an existential Socrates demonstrating that the Philistines, like the sophists, are epistemologically dangerous because they believe shadowy categories to be reality. Thus the dominant decadent motif is, in William S. Burroughs' words, "Let them see what is on the end of that long newspaper spoon."

## WITH THE HELP OF THAT LONG NEWSPAPER SPOON

Beardsley's early decadence conceived art as celebration. But, having lost moral faith, he was able to celebrate only elegance. The later decadence is analytic rather than celebratory, dubious that there is anything under the sun so true or beautiful as to inspire celebration. This subverts Art and Beauty because they, like transcendental morality, have proved incapable of the latitude necessary for dealing with a highly fragmented and incoherent reality. Here art's function is deconstructive, erasing both moral and aesthetic assumptions. Nor, with the rejection of beauty as artistic center, is it surprising that decadent art's primary imagery draws from the ugly and obscene. For instance, it is a culturally programmed generality that drug addiction is evil. Burroughs' *Naked Lunch* demonstrates by satiric disposition of images that it is human nature to be addicted, and that drug addiction is in fact simply the most easily recognized addiction. The novel's structure is a dialectical tension of obscene images designed to persuade us that the potential for addiction in all its manifestations is chillingly normal, and that ignorance of this makes one morally absurd.

We are morally absurd when our actions or ideals are dissociated or abstracted from the moral values authorizing them. As Burroughs presents it, for example, our programmed association of addiction with abnormality depends on our subsuming human nature under preconceived and simplified moral categories. He assaults this idol of the mind by counterasserting that the central issue of addiction is not moral vice at all, but rather the freedom of human will. Then he reconstructs our popular images of freedom through knowledge and order (for example, the scientist, the jurist, the police agencies, the political parties, the business corporations) and reveals them to be agencies of control addiction. They are all aspects of the Nova Mob. Thus not only are our cultural ideals recast in a criminal context, but we are also shown that complex reality (that is, the true nature of addiction) is falsified by popular image makers, whose art demands and whose purposes are served by programmatic simplifications of reality. Thus the deconstruction. And thus the title *Naked Lunch*: With reference to charges of pornography against his orgasm-death gimmick, Burroughs says,

> These sections are intended to reveal capital punishment as the obscene, barbaric, and disgusting anachronism that it is. As always the lunch is naked. If civilized countries want to return to Druid Hanging Rites in the Sacred Grove or to drink blood with the Aztecs and feed their Gods with blood of human sacrifice, let them see what they actually eat and drink. Let them see what is on the end of that long newspaper spoon.

In short, he conceived both the obscenity and the dialectic as devices to make people perceive the reality of cause and effect in such basic cultural addiction syndromes as capital punishment.

Burroughs defines the novel's central metaphor thus:

> Junk is the mold of monopoly and possession. The addict stands by while his junk legs carry him straight in on the junk beam to relapse. Junk is quantitative and accurately measurable. The more junk you use the less you have and the more you have the more you use. All the hallucinogen drugs are considered sacred by those who use them—there are Peyote Cults and Bannisteria Cults, Hashish Cults and Mushroom Cults—"the Sacred Mushrooms of Mexico enable a man to see God"—but no one ever suggested that junk is sacred. There are no opium cults. Opium is profane and quantitative like money. I have heard that there was once a beneficent non-habit-forming junk in India. It was called *soma* and is pictured as a beautiful blue tide. If *soma* ever existed the Pusher was there to bottle it and monopolize it and sell it and it turned into plain old-time JUNK. Junk is the ideal product . . . the ultimate merchandise. No sales talk necessary. The client will crawl through a sewer and beg to buy. . . . The junk merchant does not sell his product to

> the consumer, he sells the consumer to his product. He does not improve and simplify his merchandise. He degrades and simplifies the client. He pays his staff in junk. Junk yields a basic formula of "evil" virus: *The Algebra of Need*. The face of "evil" is always the face of total need. A dope fiend is a man in total need of dope. Beyond a certain frequency need knows absolutely no limit or control. In the words of total need: "Wouldn't you?" Yes you would. You would lie, cheat, inform on your friends, steal, do anything to satisfy total need. Because you would be in a state of total sickness, total possession, and not in a position to act in any other way. Dope fiends are sick people who cannot act other than they do. A rabid dog cannot choose but bite. Assuming a self-righteous position is nothing to the purpose unless your purpose be to keep the junk virus in operation. And junk is a big industry. I recall talking to an American who worked for the Aftosa Commission in Mexico. Six hundred a month plus expense account:
>
> "How long will the epidemic last?" I enquired.
>
> "As long as we can keep it going. . . . And yes . . . maybe the Aftosa will break out in South America," he said dreamily.

In a world whose chief business is JUNK, the object of humans is to profiteer. And in a world where JUNK is the principal industry, its end is to make of the human an addiction machine. The decadent absurdity of such a world is portrayed in the image of Bradley the Buyer, the narcotics undercover agent who destroys the institutions he was created to protect because their knowledge of reality has been so categorically deformed that they cannot comprehend or control the monster they have made. Bradley goes berserk, schlupping up the District Supervisor, other agents, junkies, and finally the Narcotics Commissioner himself. Finally Bradley is destroyed by Flame Thrower, "the court of inquiry ruling that such means were justified in that the Buyer had lost his human citizenship and was, in consequence, a creature without species and a menace to the narcotics industry on all levels."

The Algebra of Need, so central to this deformation, is a decadent phenomenon too. On its literal level, in reference to drugs, it means being controlled by physiological need. On the larger metaphorical level need is more subtle, more artistic, and so more decadent. Dr. Benway, himself a control addict, is perhaps the consummate artist at turning humans into the soft machine. Benway is a bureaucratic Frankenstein, the bourgeois scientist whose arts of power over human nature and reality describe a massive cultural obscenity. Here is Benway at work:

> "I deplore brutality," he said. "It's not efficient. On the other hand, prolonged mistreatment, short of physical violence, gives rise, when skillfully applied, to anxiety and a feeling of special guilt. A few rules or rather guiding principles are to be borne in mind. The subject must not realize that the mistreatment is a deliberate attack of an anti-human enemy on his per-

sonal identity. He must be made to feel that he deserves *any* treatment he receives because there is something (never specified) horribly wrong with him. The naked need of the control addicts must be decently covered by an arbitrary and intricate bureaucracy so that the subject cannot contact his enemy direct. . . .

"Many subjects are vulnerable to sexual humiliation. Nakedness, stimulation with aphrodisiacs, constant supervision to embarrass subject and prevent relief of masturbation (erections during sleep automatically turn on an enormous vibrating electric buzzer that throws the subject out of bed into cold water, thus reducing the incidence of wet dreams to a minimum). Kicks to hypnotize a priest and tell him he is about to consummate a hypostatic union with the Lamb—then steer a randy old sheep up his ass. After that the Interrogator can gain complete hypnotic control—the subject will come at his whistle, shit on the floor if he but say Open Sesame. Needless to say, the sex humiliation angle is contraindicated for overt homosexuals. (I mean, let's keep our eye on the ball here and remember the old party line . . . never know who's listening in.) I recall this one kid I condition to shit at sight of me. Then I wash his ass and screw him. It was real tasty. And he was lovely fellah too. And sometimes a subject will burst into boyish tears because he can't keep from ejaculate when you screw him. Well, as you can plainly see, the possibilities are endless, like meandering paths in a great big beautiful garden. I was just scratching that lovely surface when I am purged by Party Poops. . . . Well, 'son cosas de la vida.'"

Finally, of course, the system produces its logical consequence, a man who becomes the perfectly efficient soft machine—and is then banished as an unnecessary adjunct of the anal aperture: Here is part of the story of the "Man who taught his asshole to talk":

After a while the ass started talking on its own. He would go in without anything prepared and his ass would ad-lib and toss the gags back at him every time.

Then it developed sort of teeth-like little raspy incurving hooks and started eating. He thought this was cute at first and built an act around it, but the asshole would eat its way through his pants and start talking on the street, shouting out it wanted equal rights. It would get drunk, too, and have crying jags nobody loved it and it wanted to be kissed same as any other mouth. Finally it talked all the time day and night, you could hear him for blocks screaming at it to shut up, and beating it with his first, and sticking candles up it, but nothing did any good and the asshole said to him: "It's you who will shut up in the end. Not me. Because we don't need you around here any more. I can talk and eat *and* shit."

Human reality has now been subsumed so completely by function that the functioning parts themselves commandeer Being and exile humanity.

Thus the arts of addiction, the Algebra of Need, define and control complex human reality. We are all the junkie naked in sunlight; we are all the pusher; exploiter and exploited. This is the tension that defines nature. As Wilde saw, nature is not our voluptuous mother. Nature is the obscene, the naked reality of our personal being in conflict with impersonal being. Impersonal being, imaged as the Nova Mob, makes it a crime to manifest personality. Benway's arts, the arts of our culture, are designed to redefine identity in corporate terms. Thus the crime of separate life:

> The black wind sock of death undulates over the land, feeling, smelling for the crime of separate life, movers of the fear-frozen flesh shivering under a vast probability curve. . . .
>
> Population blocks disappear in a checker game of genocide. . . . Any number can play. . . .
>
> The Liberal Press and The Press Not So Liberal and The Press Reactionary scream approval: "Above all, the myth of other-level experience must be eradicated. . . ." And speak darkly of certain harsh realities . . . Cows with the Aftosa . . . prophylaxis. . . .
>
> Power groups of the world frantically cut lines of connection. . . .
>
> The Planet drifts to random insect doom. . . .
>
> Thermodynamics have won at a crawl. . . . Orgone balked at the post. . . . Christ bled. . . . Time ran out.

Here the "red shift" is paradigmatic for both physical and spiritual cosmos. The comprehensive dialectic of Burroughs' whole canon of work articulates the cause of disintegration. In *Naked Lunch* the culture industry merchandises addiction: Benway programs our interior isolation, dehumanizes us, defines our mechanistic reality for us. *The Soft Machine* explores the destructive human consequences of this reality—"Are these experiments really necessary?" *Nova Express* provides an antidote to nova control:

> I have said the basic techniques of nova are very simple consist in creating and aggravating conflicts—"No riots like injustice directed between enemies"—At any given time recorders fix nature of absolute need and dictate the use of total weapons—Like this: Collect and record violent Anti-Semitic statements—Now play back to Jews who are after Belsen—Record what they say and play it back to the Anti-semites—Clip clap—You got it?—Want more? Record white supremacy statements—Play to Negroes—Play back answer—Now The Women and The Men—No riots like injustice directed between "enemies"—At any given time position of recorders fixes nature of absolute need—And dictates the use of total weapons—So leave the recorders running and get your heavy metal ass in a space ship—Did it—Nothing here now but the recordings—Shut the whole thing right off—Silence—When you answer the machine you provide it with more recordings to be played back to your "enemies" keep the whole

> nova machine running—The Chinese character for "enemy" means to be similar to or to answer—Don't answer the machine—Shut it off—

And the Nova Mob, by articulating the criminal source and character of nova control, shows nature—the cosmos—in a state of total moral emergency.

We have come a long way, here, from Wilde's or Beardsley's aloof, aristocratic superiority to nature. And we have come still farther from the naive romantic idealizing of nature. But, though art and nature have lost coherence in their respective expansions, they still have design. Design is not univocal; it means simply that events happen according to cause and effect, or probability and necessity. The artist's business, that which makes him poet rather than mere artificer, is to locate causality in the events of nature. That is the center of poetic imitation. For Burroughs, and much contemporary sensibility, cause cannot be referred to such categories as the good or the beautiful. Knowledge of causal reality requires penetrating to those points in time where cause is revealed. Even plot, the long-time poetic agency of showing cause, is a falsification—because it means the artist must superimpose a linear and chronological order on the chaos of his perceptions. The maker of plots is, at least to some degree, the maker of causes rather than their discoverer. Dr. Benway represents the dangerous potential of giving life a plot. Our arts work on the premise that knowing requires ordering; Burroughs, realizing that the mind has greater perceptual capacity than we have thought, counters this by showing that superimposed order makes life take the shape we give it, and in so doing it prevents our perception of cause in natural events. Knowledge so derived is a chimerical self-indulgence.

Nakedness is all. Nakedness means images structured as little as possible—enough structure to show the artist's perception of causal connection, not so much as to provide an order that may gratify the mind's ease but which must falsify our knowledge of nature. Thus, direct experience and perception is the aesthetic base of Burroughs' poetic:

> I awoke from The Sickness at the age of forty-five, calm and sane and in reasonably good health except for a weakened liver and the look of borrowed flesh common to all who survive The Sickness. . . . Most survivors do not remember the delirium in detail. I apparently took detailed notes on sickness and delirium. I have no precise memory of writing the notes which have now been published under the title *Naked Lunch*.
>
> There is only one thing a writer can write about: *what is in front of his senses at the moment of writing*. . . . I am a recording instrument. . . . I do not presume to impose "story" "plot" "continuity." . . . Insofar as I succeed in *Direct* recording of certain areas of psychic process I may have limited function . . . I am not an entertainer. *(Naked Lunch)*

When he says that he is no entertainer Burroughs denies that component of poetic tradition which the earlier decadents grasped so desperately. When he declines to claim continuity, he rejects the traditional means by which art was supposed to instruct. How, then, to instruct?

Instruction occurs through an irregular rhythm of intersecting images that articulate causes and are, in their obscene nakedness, themselves the effects. By forcing us to concentrate on the imagistic connections—connections traditionally made for us by plot—we are kept, as he says, from taking our own pulse. The artist projects his montage, provides editorial control through the ironic inversion of beauty and obscenity, which serves as catalyst to the reader's imagination rather than the determinant of it. The rhythmic recurrence of coordinated intersecting images acts as objective correlative. Here is Burroughs' own description:

> You can cut into *Naked Lunch* at any intersection point. . . . I have written many prefaces. They atrophy and amputate spontaneous like the little toe amputates in a West African disease confined to the Negro race and the passing blonde shows her brass ankle as a manicured toe bounces across the club terrace, retrieved and laid at her feet by her Afghan Hound. . . .
>
> *Naked Lunch* is a blueprint, a How-To Book. . . . Black insect lusts open into vast, other planet landscapes. . . . Abstract concepts, bare as algebra, narrow down to a black turd or a pair of aging cajones. . . .
>
> How-To extend levels of experience by opening the door at the end of a long hall. . . . Doors that only open in *Silence*. . . . *Naked Lunch* demands Silence from The Reader. Otherwise he is taking his own pulse. . . .
>
> The Word is divided into units which be all in one piece and should be so taken, but the pieces can be had in any order being tied up back and forth, in and out fore and aft like an interesting sex arrangement. This book spill off the page in all directions, kaleidoscope of vistas, medley of tunes and street noises, farts and riot yipes and the slamming steel shutters of commerce, screams of pain and pathos and screams plain pathic. . . .
>
> This is Revelation and Prophecy of what I can pick up without FM on my 1920 crystal set with antennae of jissom. . . . Gentle reader, we see God through our assholes in the flash bulb of orgasm. . . . Through these orifices transmute your body. . . . The way OUT is the way IN. . . .

Given JUNK as existential metaphor, the images are necessarily obscene in character. For we are all junkie analogues, we all share—we all *must* share—his shamelessness and obscenity:

> Take a shot in front of D. L. Probing for a vein in my dirty bare foot. . . . Junkies have no shame. . . . They are impervious to the repugnance of others. It is doubtful if shame can exist in the absence of sexual libido. . . . The junky's shame disappears with his nonsexual sociability which is also dependent on libido. . . . The addict regards his body impersonally as an instru-

> ment to absorb the medium in which he lives, evaluates his tissue with the cold hands of a horse trader. "No use trying to hit here." Dead fish eyes flick over a ravaged vein.

Without that obscene vision of nakedness we know nothing.

But contemporary decadence is complicated by the peculiar nature of its spiritual vision. Burroughs' doctrine of separate life, that is, personality liberated from nova control, is a spiritual doctrine. But it presents spirit in psychic terms, spirit without theological apparatus, radically humanistic spirit. And the form of his fiction is much influenced, though indirectly through Swift, by a homiletic tradition. Swift's own sermons, of course, were far more humanistic than religious. And the tradition that both Swift and Burroughs share is the medieval *saccus stercorum* homily. Fundamental to this thinking is the image of the world as compost heap, decadent and obscene in the eyes of God. Burroughs even has his own test; his book of knowledge is his own profound experience of addiction and its obscenity. His novel, like the homily, takes its authority from this book. Specifically, it takes the form of his article on drugs in the *British Journal of Addiction*. Though naturalistic and inverted, it is still a "revealed book," and ultimately speaks to the human spirit. It tells us of new demonic gods, the technocrats, and their new arts. It explains their ways to man.

## THERE IS NO DISPUTING TASTE

This latter-day decadence, then, and the humanistic relativism behind it, are the root of an obscene aesthetics. In the modern recording of Truth, obscenity has become the flip side of Beauty. Thus deconstruction has provided the philosophic audacity necessary to deny the aesthetic synthesis of the good, the true, and the beautiful on which Western poetics have been based. So far as the "true" goes, Burroughs puts the function of poetry succinctly—"Let them see. . . ." Conrad said it before, but for him moral truth was still a gorgeous operatic melodrama, however forceful, profound, and experiential. Still, though he was afraid of its rhetoric, he had at times—as in *Lord Jim* or *Heart of Darkness*—a fundamental grasp of the artistic possibilities of obscenity. Many are now persuaded, as Swift was, that obscene rhetoric is a necessary probe in the search for true understanding. If this view of truth is exaggerated, it is the exaggeration of selection and focus that we expect in art.

Pornography has become, in effect, the principal genre of obscene aesthetics. Obscenity counters beauty in its dialectics, bringing "onstage" what heretofore was kept "off"; and sexuality is the imagistic, figural, and verbal basis of its rhetoric. The critical problem has been that, fearing the aesthetic implications of acknowledging that pornography was anything other than an artistic aberration, we have not been critically prepared to recognize its artistic integrity. Now we no longer have that choice. There are simply too many unequivocally good writers and artists using obscenity and pornography as vehicles of poetic statement.

Henry James rightly insisted that the art of fiction required a *"donné"* from its audience—that is, the audience must grant the fiction its subject, for questions of art are questions of execution, not subject. And if the audience will insist on "taking its own pulse," in Burrough's phrase, there can be no artistic engagement with the artist. This is perhaps most profoundly true of pornography, because it so often puts people off. But the artist has no obligation to confirm our own expectations. Rather, we want him or her to tell us something special. And the special thing that pornographic art tells us about is sexuality. If we are to have commerce with an artistic pornography, then, we must grant it its subject. While pornography has been around as long as any mode of art, it is only lately—perhaps since Judge Woolsey's *Ulysses* decision, where law joined new criticism to blend art and life—that we have had an aesthetic, social, and poetic climate that would permit us to recognize pornography's more than pathological role in human imagination—and in art, the deepest statement of imagination. Until then, while criticism had always recognized the "erotic" (Solomon, John of the Cross), the "bawdy" or "vulgar" (Chaucer, Rochester), the "gallant" (Casanova, Cleland), and the "depraved" (Sade), it had always marginalized them. They were attributable to human but not, for that very reason, aesthetic phenomena.

There is, sighed the Augustans, simply no disputing tastes. Even that grudging acknowledgement signified a remittance by the hegemony of good taste to the idiosyncrasy of variable or even low tastes. Dr. Johnson was suspicious of the upstart novel's influence on this account. And well he might be. For across the channel the form was about to be adapted to the Marquis de Sade's furious assaults on manners, taste and conventional morality. And Sade's model was precisely the sublime, the same sublime that Johnson's friend Edmund Burke had so intriguingly associated with terror and pain.

By the early nineteenth century the whole apparatus behind good taste—the great chain of being, the cohesive balance of ordained nature, social and class stability, religious orthodoxy—was already problematic, both in itself and in its aesthetic implications. This was obviously more recognizably so in France than England, although in the course of the century the French would backslide, yearning for the old order. Sade foresaw the inclination and sounded an alarm so obscene it could hardly escape notice even in the chaos of the revolution. The sublime indifference of nature was revealed, he warned, in the power-pleasure-pain cathexis endemic to sexuality, the dynamo that turned the world. The old order, both secular and ecclesiastic, exploited this and sustained itself on the naivete of conventional morality. Sade saw the revolution and the Enlightenment for the deconstructions that they were. Of course he was a bit crazed and had one foot in the old order himself. But not all that crazed. He had adapted his fiction from the most conventional of English authors, Samuel Richardson, who had domesticated the sex-power beast in *Pamela* and redeemed its abuses in *Clarissa*. Still, Dr. Johnson's suspicions lingered, and later Thackery classed Richardson with those who would make "Mrs. Grundy's hair stand on end." Sade was not so far out of the mainstream as has been supposed in developing the dark implications of Richardson's attentions.

In England, where Richardson and Blake were put on ice, Victoria's skirts covered piano legs, and her frown inspired "the other Victorians" to toss off their voluptuous discourses in *The Pearl* and other underground journals as *facetiae*. Not so in France, where Sade, especially, had put obscene sexuality on the agenda of serious poetics. Gautier, Baudelaire, Lautréamont, and Zola explored the motif in rather various ways. If Lautréamont's *Les Chants des Maldoror* is most indebted to Sade for its obscenely contemptuous attack on conventionality, Zola confirmed Sade's foresight in *Nana*, where he depicted the Second Empire as a gilded brothel presided over by a power-brokering prostitute. Apollinaire kept the spark of Sade's polemical obscenity aglow with his pornographic novel, *The Debauched Hospodar*, described earlier, and passed it on to the rest of the twentieth century along with the inspiration for surrealism. Similarly with Jarry's Ubu plays and, of course, pataphysics. Breton officially awarded Sade the laurel of Surrealist poetics, and Artaud revived his premises in the theater of cruelty. But Sade's most direct heirs, in the sense of a deconstructionist poetics of obscenity, were to be Bataille, Genet, Pauline Réage and the American Burroughs (first published in France).

Ironically, English Victorianism induced the facetious aestheticism of Beardsley's *Under the Hill*. Its very absence of content, nonetheless, subverts the complementarity of art and conventional morality. The late Victorian decadents at least gained that much for their substitution of effete elegance for Mme. de Staël's yeomanish vigor. There was a correspondingly languid aesthetic in France too, as in Marcel Proust, for example. But the Sadean line was eventually picked up and Americanized by Burroughs, who evoked the depressing but undeniably vigorous ethos of the street. As for subversion, his "cut up" collage structure rebukes assumptions of narrative form, and his coldly calculated ex-junky's scansion of the perverse forms of modernity's addictions simultaneously deconstructs morality, technology, and assumptions of social order. Beardsley and Burroughs, then, represent the antipodes of a poetics of obscenity as they developed out of nineteenth-century preoccupations in England and France.

Beardsley and Burroughs share an interest in moral subversion, but, where Beardsley aestheticizes obscenity, Burroughs renders it into congealed animal fat. This convergence and divergence pattern is characteristic of obscene poetics. Although D. H. Lawrence and Jean Genet both lyricize sex and its organs, for example, they are on most other points distinctly antipathetic.

Obscene poetics make strange bedfellows, but they do have a history in both mainstream and underground literatures. They are not always pornographic, but sexuality and violence both are at least implicit, when not explicit, in their broad spectrum of concerns. Their first principle, of course, is getting the trope of obscenity in your face. Several premises follow from this stance. First, the agency of obscenity is peculiarly well suited to the subversion or deconstruction of received wisdom, whether moral, aesthetic, economic, political, or social. The corollary is that obscenity by its very nature is anarchical. Both ideas imply that serious practitioners of the obscene are socially disaffected in some way, as Beardsley was from Victorian moralism and Burroughs from the sanitizing logic of technocracy.

Burroughs' first publisher was the Olympia Press, not now extant but seminal to literature after World War II for both its literary books (e.g. by Henry Miller, J. P. Donleavy, Lawrence Durrell, Samuel Beckett, Jean Genet) and its "d.b." or dirty books (e.g., by Bataille, Beardsley, Sade, Frank Harris). In his introduction to *The Olympia Reader* (1965), Maurice Girodias, the publisher and editor, describes the disposition of the expatriate writers for the press in the Paris of the 1950s:

> Writing d.b.'s was generally considered a useful professional exercise, as well as a necessary participation in the common fight against the Square World—an act of duty. What the Square World exactly was, nobody could have explained with any precision, but the notion was very strong, indeed; and it was not the usual routine of a new generation picking a quarrel with the old, it was a much stronger and deeper protest; not a protest against war or hunger, or against the bomb, but, beyond that, a protest against the mental weakness, the poverty of spirit, and the general lack of genius and generosity of a rich and sclerotic society. The colorful banner of pornography was as good as any other to rally the rebels: the more ludicrous the form of the revolt, the better it was, as the revolt was primarily against ordinary logic, and ordinary good taste, and restraint and current morals.

Naturally, there are also more particularized disaffections. In the 1980s, as noted earlier, a group of American lesbians developed a sadomasochistic pornography as a means of distinguishing themselves from not only heterosexual culture, including straight feminism, but as well from more conventional lesbian culture. In fact each of these groups—feminists, lesbians, and lesbian sado-masochists—include writers whose poetics reflect identification group interests. Insofar as obscenity is common, they share a poetics; insofar as their interests differ, so do their poetics. Polemics, whether individual or collective, are not imperative, but they do tend to accompany a poetics characterized by subversion, anarchy and disaffection.

Obscene poetics, then, are as uniform and various as any other. Certain attitudes toward nature, language, and figuration informed Romantic poetics, but there was considerable discrepancy between, for example, Wordsworth and Coleridge. If we add Schiller, Blake, and Poe to the equation it gets looser still. Similarly with naturalism, symbolism, or especially, modernism. The latter embraces imagism, Freudianism, surrealism, Marxism, and objectivism. On several points these poetics are antithetical. Ezra Pound's associational theory of the image is radically different from André Breton's dissociational theory. Likewise, Gertrude Stein's objective verbalism from Virginia Woolf's fluid interiority in narrative. As with modernism, obscene poetics overlap structural and moral dispositions. D. H. Lawrence's *Lady Chatterley's Lover* and Georges Bataille's *Story of the Eye*, for instance, were published at about the same time, and both use strategies of the obscene. But two novels could not be more different in their conceptions of nature or language or the obscene itself. Both might be said to have sought to naturalize sexuality, yet their ontologies were so opposed as to make their ideas of sexuality mutually exclusive if not unintelligible. It is a commonplace that one person's obscenity is another's truth, or one's pornography another's art. The poetics of obscenity, notwithstanding lexical quibbles, erase the contradiction between art and pornography, obscenity and truth. Indeed, that is precisely their purpose.

The conceptions of obscenity and pornography are often idiosyncratic, and consequently they have an elusive elasticity as terms. I am proposing an aesthetic construct where the obscene self-consciously calls our attention to what custom characteristically obscures or suppresses as malediction via sex, violence, or profanation. Pornography, in the three forms earlier described, is a mode of obscenity. A poetics of obscenity is pertinent primarily to artistic pornography. Artistic pornography calls our attention to sexuality in such a way as to evoke its actual (as in Bataille) or its perceived (as in Lawrence) obscenity and to configure the complexities of its being and doing. The rest of this study will attempt to give these concepts more particularity by outlining the poetics of obscenity in reference to writers and works that have made obscenity artistically integral to a greater or lesser extent.

I begin that outline with an inquiry into the moral and figural functions of obscenity, i.e., the use of obscenity and pornography as a deconstructive moral rhetoric, for example in Molly Bloom's soliloquy concluding James Joyce's *Ulysses*. Moral deconstruction implies both anarchy and regeneration; in that context I examine obscenity as a psychic component of the social dialectic of order and disorder, for instance in the works of Bataille and Genet. Then I consider the function of obscenity in tragedy and comedy. Obscenity informs tragedy, at least since the eighteenth century, by way of philosophical materialism and naturalism, for which the works of Sade have become a paradigm. Comedy provides catharsis, release from the oppressive "dirty little secret" of sex, as Lawrence called it, as can be seen in the work of Henry Miller, among others.

These broad topics in themselves are gender neutral, but a common presumption, especially in regard to pornography, is that they are products of male preoccupations. Historically this has been largely true, but particularly since the mid-1970s women writers have come out of the pornographic closet. I will discuss the ways in which female pornography has become a factor in feminist dialectics, particularly for the objective of a female definition of female sexuality, including consideration of works by such authors as Edith Wharton, Anaïs Nin, Diane di Prima, Erica Jong, and Alix Kates Shulman. One of the most pervasive cultural forms of modern times, the movies, has also been influenced by the poetics of obscenity. In films, spectacle poses a special poetic problem, which I discuss in the context of an evolution of cinematic sexuality from avant-garde film makers—e.g. Stan Brakhage—to the pornographic parody features of Russ Meyer, such hard-core features as *Deep Throat* and such general distribution feature films as *In the Realm of the Senses*.

The previous chapter noted that hard- and soft-core pornographies rely upon recognizable conventions, while artistic pornography is no more conventionally predictable than any serious aesthetic form, and a good deal less so than most. I conclude here by suggesting another differentiation marking a poetics of obscenity, the distinction between figuration and representation that Roland Barthes remarks in *The Pleasure of the Text*. As prologue to this distinction, he observes, "the text of bliss is never the text that recounts the kind of bliss afforded literally by an ejaculation. The pleasure of representation is not attached to its object: pornography is not *sure*." Pornography, by which here he means hard-core, is not sure because it is representation, and moreover represents "not so much the erotic scene as the expectation of it . . . and when the scene occurs, naturally there is disappointment, deflation." Pornography, being self-contained language, cannot be or even mimic its object, which is orgasmic sexuality.

Figuration, on the other hand, has "bliss" for its object, a bliss for Barthes analogous but not identical with ejaculation. It is the bliss of figuration, an orgasmic shudder of recognition, recognition of something far more deeply interfused than its actual source can intimate. But it can be made to intimate by the art of figuration. Thus Sade and Bataille, for Barthes, so construct their pornographies as to transfigure literal sexuality with reverberations beyond itself. Theirs are texts of figuration rather than representation. Similarly, for me, Beardsley figures sexuality as style, and Burroughs figures it, in the orgasm death gimmick for example, as just another term in the algebra of need, a quantum for control addicts. Transfiguration is not necessarily transcendental. It can, however, situate sexuality and other obscenities in the world. It is characteristic of obscene poetics and is what distinguishes artistic pornography from other kinds.

# 4

# Unspeakable Moral Rhetorics

## INTERROGATING CONSENSUS

Dedalus's famous aesthetic, in *A Portrait of the Artist as a Young Man*, argues for a pure aesthetic emotion in which the mind is arrested by its artistic perception and lifted momentarily beyond the "loathing" or "desire" caused by "improper arts," the pornographic and didactic. Beauty, he says, is the proper end of art, and the end of beauty is to induce an "ideal pity or an ideal terror" at last resolved by the "rhythm of beauty." He defines art: "to express, to press out again, from the gross earth or what it brings forth, from sound and shape and colour which are the prison gates of our soul, an image of the beauty we have come to understand—that is art." There is here the antithesis that has buggered artistic theory at least since the formulation of romanticism in the late eighteenth century. It postulates a naturalistic art ("from the gross earth") as the agency of an ideal beauty. Joyce has attempted to fuse the two poles of moral awareness—the transcendental and the naturalistic—and in so doing articulates the classic dilemma between flesh and spirit. His solution is a naturalistic idealism—faith that the gross earth must finally give us an image of beauty.

This is, too, the pastoral faith that the earth abides forever. In this respect Joyce articulates a paradigm of the Western aesthetic tradition. It is based on the Platonic analogy between the good, the true, and the beautiful. On the one hand, his premise is idealistic and so he must deny the beauty, truth, or good of desire and loathing. On the other hand, however, his artistic theory is sensual, rooted in the sound, shape, and color of the earth and what it brings forth. Surely desire and loathing are indigenous to that. The aesthetic dilemma, then, is whether our art presents to us a world preordinately beautiful—and therefore good and true—or whether it presents to us a world that predicates only its perceived existence, and is not necessarily either good or beautiful. But of course it does both, and we are left with the realization that there is no single satisfactory theory of art. For those who feel the truth of Plato's analogy, art does one thing. For those who do not feel that truth, it does quite another.

As artistic postures, obscenity and pornography proceed from a sense of moral dissonance rather than moral harmony. Because human nature is presented in exclusively sexual terms—sexuality in it is the metaphor of being—Pauline Réage's *Story of O* is an extreme statement of this perspective. If its figure for humanity is limited, it is the limitation of selection and focus that we expect in art. It is the limitation necessary to all literature conceived figurally. It is a limitation in kind with Camus' *The Stranger.* Although both Joyce and Lawrence opposed "pornography," they opposed it in its limited semantic context. But in our expansion of the concept, pornography creates an image of human sexuality that may or may not inspire erotic gratification but distinctly configures the archetypal and moral dimensions of sexuality.

In Lawrence's case, the pornographic image serves as the source of symbolic vitality central to his moral dialectic. His opposition to what he understood as pornography was based in his belief that such a pornography denied humane vitality. But we shall see that it need not. For Joyce, pornography was crucial to his extended epiphanal image of the existential comedy, as for example in Molly Bloom's soliloquy. In such instances pornography provides the means for positive moral statement. On the other hand, the pornographies of Sade, Genet, or Réage do not much feel vitality as a persuasive presence in life. Their sexual imagery is oppressive and destructive. They see vulgarity, hostility, and anxiety. This vision of life is ugly, but it is exploratory and authentic: authentic because it is experiential, and exploratory because it attempts to construct images from the subliminal erotic imagination.

We have here a philosophy of the ugly that is clearly operative, a philosophy that has been a long while with us—in, for example, the Gothic—but has only recently become predominant. If we continue to identify the beautiful with the true, the truth now explores the human meaning of the grotesque and the ugly. Whether it articulates an affirmative or negative morality, then, pornography is an important figural vehicle of moral statement.

At the transcendental pole of moral awareness, knowledge is dialectical, and subsumed therefore into axiomatic first principles. In Platonic dialectic the *idea* is the axiomatic first principle; in the Judaic-Christian dialectic it is *God*. In such systems knowledge is conceived as evidence for the truth of dialectically established first principles. Knowledge which does not so verify is ignored, considered chimerical, or dialectically reinterpreted. In the sense that it is within a dialectical parenthesis, then, knowledge is static in this system, and if any knowledge threatens the system, it is considered vicious. Thus Jesus and John of the Cross had to be dispatched because they brought a new threatening knowledge to the old dispensations.

Conversely, to a naturalistic moral awareness knowledge is scientific and is obliged to no ultimate truth. Its restraints are methodological rather than axiomatic. In this way of thinking sensory experience is the measure of things, and thus the virtuous scientist is one who has the widest range of experiential knowledge. Insofar, then, as naturalistic knowledge is without arbitrary limits, it is dynamic, and it is virtuous in proportion to the degree it realizes its undefined potential. In the one system of morality, the good, true, and beautiful prescribe what knowledge is; in the other, knowledge prescribes the good, true, and beautiful. Morality, then, is a way of interpreting the happenings of the universe. And one's sense of cosmic order or its absence will profoundly influence, perhaps even determine, a sense of what is good and how and to what extent knowledge is a part of or means to the good.

The artist, like everyone else, has his or her own more or less sophisticated moral sense. Moral vision will determine both the forms and themes of the art produced. When we speak of the artist's "vision or imagination" we speak essentially of this moral perception of things. And when we speak of an artist's "growth," we mean not only technical mastery but also the increasing consciousness and artistic use of moral awareness. Poets like Dante or Milton, for example, wrote in the context of specific moral dialectics, one highly Catholic, the other highly Protestant. The poetics of both the *Comedy* and *Paradise Lost* were conceived as testimonials to the truth and efficacy of their systematic moralities.

There is of course also a naturalistic artistic tradition. It began—for example, in Zola—as an artistic analogue to scientific method and it was an important step away from the aesthetic imagination's intimidation by assumed first principles. Naturalism has had its own evolution and has formed its own metaphysics and morality. The most coherent latter-day statement of this is probably an eclectic non-dogmatic existentialism. God is final cause in a Christian metaphysics, but in an existential metaphysics no final cause is predicated. Such writers as Camus, Beckett, and Genet deal only in temporal causality and distinct images of human ignorance of ultimate cause. *Waiting for Godot* and *Malone Dies* are two radical examples of a literature built on existential morality. Where Dante schematized a morality to the end of gaining for man the beatific vision of God, Beckett's Malone is without the options necessary for moral choice, and his end is quite simply his end. The plot of *Malone Dies* is that Malone dies. Of powers beyond his own impotence he knows only that a pair of hands deposit a daily tray of vittles. Camus' summation of such a natural order is that the universe maintains a "benign indifference."

That Dante and Beckett have antithetical moralities is merely a doctrinal difference. Both have a moral sense of good and evil, however disparately understood, as operative forces in the universe. Dante's good is an ideal; Beckett's is existential. Dante's good may be more hopeful and inspiriting, and we therefore may prefer his morality, but that is quite another matter. No person, and certainly no artist, is obliged to have a moral vision that pleases us. Their vision may not even please themselves. But when we penetrate the implications of dissident moralities, we often find a reality that gives us profound moral knowledge whether or not we subscribe to its particular metaphysics. It may be that, from a Christian point of view, a morality that refuses to transcend humanistic knowledge is highly limited. But, on the other hand, there will never be an Inquisition to enforce an existential truth.

## VISIONS AND REVISIONS

The lack of moral consensus that characterizes contemporary life and art indicates the viability of moral exploration, to say nothing of its need. In this process, art is a means of seeing what we are, what we think we are, and what we want to be. For, to use Joseph Conrad's definition, art is an

> attempt to render the highest kind of justice to the visible universe, by bringing to light the truth, manifold and one, underlying its every aspect. It is an attempt to find in its forms, in its colours, in light, in its shadows, in the aspects of matter and in the facts of life what of each is fundamental, what is enduring and essential—their one illuminating and convincing quality—the very truth of their existence. The artist, then, like the thinker or the scientist, seeks the truth and makes his appeal.

Conrad's analogy between the artist, the thinker, and the scientist is important because it designates art as a mode of knowledge. Since Western culture has been Christian, Western art has concentrated largely on rhetorical appeal; the artists' responsibility to delight and instruct largely meant that there was a truth available for them to instruct and their business was to make it appealing through invention. But we are now in the process of redefining ourselves, discovering what we are. Science has told us so much more than we previously suspected that the old definitions will not do. Now the business of art is actually, rather than rhetorically, to seek the truth. Schiller understood this in his famous essay on sentimental poetry when he distinguished between the ancients and the moderns by virtue of their relation to nature. Ancient culture, he says, has a simple existential relation to nature in which the poet *is* nature. The modern, or sentimental, culture has a moral relation to nature wherein the poet *seeks* nature. The ancients identified with nature and were confident of it and of themselves and of their proper relation. We are not confident in our knowledge of either nature or ourselves, and we are compelled therefore to seek where we have not previously been accustomed to finding. The artistic consequence, as Schiller stated it, is that "the power of the ancients consists in compressing objects into the finite, and the moderns excel in the art of the infinite." As we grope in the shadows of the infinite for its truth, one of the first principles of art will and must be that it is exploratory rather than persuasive.

Pornographic literature is one manner of artistic exploration—which is saying that pornography, as we have defined it, is a mode of knowledge in the way that any literature may be said to be. It deals in a dark knowledge, whose implications have been denied or ignored for a long time by philosophy and have therefore been largely unavailable to our literature. But science has provided us with information and procedures to verify our suspicions, and demonstrable natural truths—many of them sexual—have authenticated new directions for the imagination. So what we have thought of as simply perversion or titillation has been shown to have psychic, archetypal, moral, and therefore artistic significance.

The moral basis of pornographic literature, then, is that it is an imaginative avenue to greater knowledge of human being. Its point of view is of course naturalistic. But its methodology, like any literature, is the word. The difference between its use of the word and a transcendental use of the word lies in the different reality that each attitude envisions. The basis in each, however, for verbalizing its reality is the same.

There is a verbal strategy common to both religious and pornographic literature, what Erich Auerbach in *Mimesis* has defined as the figural interpretation of reality and it is similar to Barthes' concept cited in the previous chapter. Without going into the complex history of the concept, we may say that figural interpretation is similar to allegory and symbolism in that it is a device for interpreting scripture that has become as well a moral paradigm for literary structure. It is similar, too, in that it is a way to penetrate "deeper meanings" of both scripture and nature. It differs from allegory in having historicity, where allegory has abstraction, so prophecy is central to it. It differs from the symbol in that the symbol is more directly related to nature, having some kind of magical power, whereas *figura* is not a talisman and relates rather to interpretation of history (for example, the Old Testament) than to nature directly. These are Auerbach's distinctions. But, as he acknowledges, in rhetorical and exegetical practice the three methods of interpretation—allegory, symbolism, and the figural—tended to be synthesized. The important point here is that the figural method is a way of articulating an abstract reality (God, for example) by means of imagistic reference to an experiential reality (God as father, shepherd, or lover). It is in this respect the immediate ancestor of what we call figures of speech. But, unlike figurative language, it is not simply a rhetorical way of speaking; it is a means of getting at reality. Metaphor is comparison; *figura* is not similitude but an imaging of reality. My thesis here is that pornographic imagery is best understood in terms of its figural structure, that it has that structure in common with religious literature, and that both use it as a device of moral statement.

In mystical religious literature, for example, where the object is to communicate an ecstatic religious truth, it is common to employ sexual figures. John of the Cross is an excellent example of the use of figural sexual imagery through which to state the power of the soul's union with God. In John of the Cross' three major works—*The Ascent of Mount Carmel, The Dark Night,* and *The Spiritual Canticle*—he uses what we might call the vocabulary of figural sexuality in order to convey the ecstatic sense of divine love in terms of its figural analogue in human life—sexual orgasm. Mount Carmel is his symbol for the "union of a soul with God." To make its ascent one must first pass through three stages of the Dark Night, which are the mortification of the senses, the purgation of the spirit, and the "passive purgation" of the soul, effected by God. Although the end of this dark night is in fact the beatific vision, John does not use, as Dante does, the basic image of light and revelation. He wants something more emotionally persuasive than that, so he uses the "Song of Songs" as his scriptural base, rather than "Genesis." Thus his basic image turns on union with God rather than the revelation of God. This impels him, as a user of the word, to use a sympathetic instead of apocalyptic imagery. The only natural source with sufficient sympathetic force for his purpose is the imagery of courtship and sex.

Here is the figural theory as John himself describes it in *The Ascent of Mount Carmel*:

> The soul, naturally speaking, possesses no means other than the senses (the windows of its prison) of perceiving what is communicated to it, . . . because

> the faculties of the soul cannot of themselves reflect and operate except upon form, figure, and image, which would be the rind and accident of the substance and spirit, . . . For the aim of this activity is the reception of substantial understanding and love through those forms. . . . In these apprehensions coming from above (imaginative or any other kind . . . ) a person should only advert to the love of God they interiorly cause. He should pay no attention to the letter and rind (what they signify, represent, or make known). Thus he should pay heed not to the feeling of delight or sweetness, not the images, but to the feelings of love that are caused. Only for the sake of moving the spirit of love should the soul at times recall the images and apprehensions which produced love.

That such apprehensions may have a diabolical origin is the chance that a mere human being must take to perceive anything at all. Therefore, the figural method is the only effective way of understanding the highest moral good—union with God. With this figural methodology in mind, John wrote his "Stanzas" for the soul, which begin "One dark night,/Fired with love's urgent longings . . . " and conclude with this clear, though decorous, sexual imagery:

> Upon my flowering breast
> Which I kept wholly for Him alone,
> There He lay sleeping,
> And I caressing Him
> There in a breeze from the fanning cedars.
>
> When the breeze blew from the turret
> Parting His hair,
> He wounded my neck
> With His gentle hand,
> Suspending all my senses.
>
> I abandoned and forgot myself,
> Laying my face on my Beloved;
> All things ceased; I went out from myself,
> Leaving my cares
> Forgotten among the lilies.

And such images as this from *The Spiritual Canticle*:

> The bride has entered
> The sweet garden of her desire,

And she rests in delight,
Laying her neck
On the gentle arms of her Beloved.

Even the religious mystic finds the imagery of sexuality necessary to transmit understanding of the reciprocal love of man and God, when that prodigious union is attained. He is dealing with a reality for which there is no other suitable analogue. He has gone beyond dialectic and theology to explore the realm from which no traveler returns—the felt power of God's presence, mystical knowledge.

John of the Cross does not, of course, write pornography. But he does use for his own purposes the kind of imagery and subject characteristic of writers who do. John, however, unlike the pornographer, disengages the ecstatic effects of orgasm from its material cause and conceives it only in terms of its final cause. The moral purpose of figuring God's love as sexual love is to transcend the merely human to a love still better and more ecstatic. And to keep focus on God rather than on the analogical "delight or sweetness" of the love image, he refrains from an indecorous description of "love's urgent longings." In his commentary on this phrase he observes that it is neither "appropriate" nor "possible" for him to make a "description . . . of these longings of love." Morally, however, we are, he says, instructed about spiritual love by analogy from physical love:

> A love of pleasure, and attachment to it, usually fires the will toward the enjoyment of things that give pleasure. A more intense enkindling of another, better love (love of one's heavenly Bridegroom) is necessary for the vanquishing of the appetites and the denial of this pleasure. . . . For the sensory appetites are moved and attracted toward sensory objects with such cravings that if the spiritual part of the soul is not fired with other more urgent longings for spiritual things, the soul will neither be able to overcome the yoke of nature nor enter the night of sense.

This is not only a warning about the naturalistic world, it is also an analogical lesson in the great power of love and pleasure. The highest love and pleasure are therefore the proper concern of the religious man. But the access to their comprehension is necessarily physical love, because, as John says in another of his verses, "the act of love is on the arm, since by the arm the beloved is held and caressed."

Thus John of the Cross uses the imagery of sexuality in his spiritual dialectic as a means of knowing the divine love of which it is the figure or prophecy. Love is the key in distinguishing between his figural use of sex and the naturalistic figuration of sex in pornography. Religious figures prophesy that all the goods of earth—for example, love ecstacy—are such faint shadows of heaven that they are evil by comparison. And love, of course, is the central fact of Christian dialectic. Pornography is not necessarily concerned with love, although it may be (for example, the *Story of O*). Nor is it committed to a dialectical truth for which it acts as prophecy, although here again it may be *(Lady Chatterley's Lover)*. And, being naturalistic, pornography is inclined to use description and specificity in its treatment of sexuality, so its analytical concern is more immediately with the material cause of sexuality and its human effects. Its moral perspective will be determined, consequently, by the demands of its fictional function rather than by an external system.

To see pornography as a literary device for moral statement, let us look at William Faulkner's morally pornographic use of three characters—Laverne Shumann *(Pylon)*, Mink Snopes' wife *(The Hamlet)*, and Lena Grove *(Light in August)*. Faulkner's own moral vision is nicely synthesized in his famous Noble Prize acceptance speech. In that speech he consciously articulates the moral perspective from which he wrote and from which he thought all poetry must come.

> I believe that man will not merely endure: He will prevail. He is immortal, not because he alone among creatures has an inexhaustible voice, but because he has a soul, a spirit capable of compassion and sacrifice and endurance. The poet's, the writer's, duty is to write about these things. It is his privilege to help man endure by lifting his heart, by reminding him of the courage and honor and hope and pride and compassion and pity and sacrifice which have been the glory of his past. The poet's voice need not merely be the record of man, it can be one of the props, the pillars to help him endure and prevail.

Laverne Shumann, in *Pylon*, is one of Faulkner's highly idiosyncratic ur-women. She is a sensual woman who shares a hard, meagre, and dangerous life (they are a barnstorming team of stunt fliers) with two men and her son by one of them, she does not know which. She is a fecund (at the end of the novel she is pregnant again) but ambiguously feminine type. Like many Faulkner women, she is tough and hard superficially in order to survive and cover a basic sentimentality that is invariably fatal when indulged. Laverne's vulnerability comes from in fact loving one of her men. He is, of course, killed in a stunt, using a defective plane in an attempt to get extra money to cover the birth of the new child. He is the pilot, and so the team is left without means. Laverne must, therefore, give up her son to the parents of the dead "husband," and be cut off from him forever. Here her toughness serves her, and she is able to give him up, suppressing the destructive tendency to indulge sentimentality and keep the child. The child turns out to be the true son of his father in that, like his father, he is obviously a future pilot, and like his father he will give up easy and artificial prospects to embrace a natural life rhythm. And by the end, the drama of the stunt flying team has given moral knowledge to the skeptical newspaper reporter who brackets the novel's main action; and the "grandfather" who doubts his grandson is his grandson is given signs that at least spiritually he is. The novel, then, celebrates the life urge and the spiritual survival of man.

The plot quite candidly denies the existential authority of conventional morality. Monogamy, motherhood, fidelity, thrift, cleanliness in thought, deed, and word—all of the standard moral sentimentalities are simply ignored. All the values antithetic to these triumph, in the sense that they provide the context within which life goes on. The stunt-flying team in its unorthodox, pitiful, and naturalistic way becomes the symbol of the courage, honor, hope, pride, compassion, pity, and sacrifice of which Faulkner speaks in his acceptance speech. The "glory" of man is that he finds a way to survive; he may pay, but he also prevails. At plot's end, the dead pilot's son stands defiantly with his toy plane in hand and his clothes ready to run away as his father before him. Laverne, a new baby in her womb, moves on with her remaining man to the life she chooses to live in the way she chooses to live it. And the skeptical, morally aloof newspaper reporter has been persuaded of a fundamental human dignity and the need to honor it. This vision of the dignity of life for life's sake is pornographically fortified.

The pornographic image comes on the eve of Shumann's death. He is going to make a probably suicidal flight in a defective plane to get a stake for the new child. This is his sentimental mistake, but also of course it is the virtue that defines him. But Laverne makes the fatal sentimentality clear as they lie in bed: she accuses him of knowing that the plane may kill him, and he responds,

> "I guess I can land it, all right."
> "You're lying," she said. "We got along before."
> "Because we had to. This time we don't have to."
> "But it's seven months yet."
> "Yair. Just seven months. And one more meet, and the only ship we have with a shot engine and two wrenched longerons."
> "You bastard," she said in a tense rigid whisper. "You rotten pilot, you bastard rotten pilot. . . ." Her hand shot out and snatched the cigarette from him; he felt his own fingers wrench and bend and then saw the red coal twinkle and arc across the dark and strike the invisible floor. . . . now the hard hand struck his cheek, clutching and scrabbling about his jaw and throat and shoulder until he caught it and held it, wrenching and jerking.
> "You bastard rotten, you rotten—" she panted.
> "All right," he said. "Steady, now. . . . All right, now . . . You want to take your pants off?"
> "They're already off."

This scene sets up the pornographic image. It articulates Laverne's fury at death and existential defeat—"You bastard rotten pilot." Then the narrative returns to a previous scene in which she has exhibited this same vital fury. Faulkner presents it pornographically in order to underscore the symbolic defiance of mortality that Laverne's sexual passion celebrates. It is the occasion of her first parachute jump:

> He sat in the back cockpit with the aeroplane in position holding the wing up under her weight, gesturing her on out toward the wingtip, almost angrily, when he saw her leave the strut and with that blind and completely irrational expression of protest and wild denial on her face, the hem of the skirt whipping out of the parachute harness about her loins, climb, not back into the front seat she had left but . . . scrambling and sprawling into the cockpit . . . astride his legs and facing him.
>
> In the same instant of realizing (as with one hand she ripped her skirt hem free of the safetywire with which they had fastened it bloomerfashion between her legs) and she was clawing blindly and furiously not at the belt across his thighs but at the fly of his trousers, he realized that she had on no undergarment, pants. . . . So he tried to fight her off for a while, but he had to fly the aeroplane, keep it in position over the field, and besides . . . he soon had two opponents; he was outnumbered, he now bore in his own lap, between himself and her wild and frenzied body, the perennially undefeated, the victorious. It was some blind instinct out of the long swoon while he waited for his backbone's fluid marrow to congeal again that he remembered to roll the aeroplane toward the wing to which the parachute case was attached because the next that he remembered was the belt catching him across the legs as, looking out he saw the parachute floating between him and the ground, and looking down he saw the bereaved, the upthrust, the stalk: the annealed rapacious heartshaped crimson bud.

The pornographic fantasy involved here is clear enough, but at this point Laverne's sexuality takes on also a figural dimension. Her very physicality figures a procreative triumph over death—now with Shumann, later with some other. Life is all. She figures too the demi-urge. When she jumps, harnessed and without pants, her skirt up to her shoulders, she triggers the life fury of the crowd below. They go mad and maul her when she lands, until the police rescue and arrest her. Shumann sees the mind of the mob in one of the younger police officers, "a man besotted and satiated by his triumphs over abased human flesh . . . seeing now and without forewarning the ultimate shape of his jaded desires fall upon him out of the sky, not merely naked but clothed in the very traditional symbology—the ruined dress with which she was trying wildly to cover her loins, and the parachute harness—of female bondage." Later Shumann sees in another madman's face the same "terror and wild protest against bereavement" that Shumann had see in Laverne's own face as she looked at him in the plane before her jump. The man screams, "I'll pay you! I'll pay her! I'll pay either of you! Name it! Let me . . . her once and you can cut me if you want." Laverne's sexuality, then, figures the full gamut of human vitality, its power and fear, its desire and frustration. She is infinite sexuality. Where Shumann's phallus, after orgasm, is "bereaved," Laverne takes on the whole universe with her sex. The screaming man, too, will be "bereaved." But not Laverne; she is the figural life energy that survives and prevails. As pornographic image she punctuates the vision with which Faulkner probes moral ambiguity and prospects for the Blakean marriage of heaven and hell.

*The Hamlet* is a much more complex novel, but it too explores the moral ambivalence of human vitality. Central to the novel is the emergence of the Snopes family from the Calibanic Mink Snopes to the phlegmatic machinations of Flem Snopes. The Snopes family, like Laverne's stunt-flying team, figures the brute crouch from which man pulls himself to something like his full height. But Faulkner makes it clear that even in his brutishness there is the faint preview of human "glory."

Sexuality has great importance in the novel, but its most distinctively pornographic character is in the ironic romance of Mink Snopes. Mink is murderous, animalistic, greedy, and ominously pervasive. But, minklike as he is, he is nevertheless a man, and his moral being is an analogue of at least one dimension of all moral being. His pornographic romance defines both the animal and spiritual potentials of man. It is in every way a moral inversion of chivalric romance and its correlative moral idealism. The virtuous knight is an animalistic tramp. The lady fair is a promiscuous lesbian on horseback who surrounds herself with sadomasochistic paraphernalia—razors with which her eunuchs cut her hair, the "big rangy, well-kept horse" she rides, a quadroon procurer, and so forth. Purity is the theme of romance, but the lady—who selects her studs from among the work force of her father's lumber camp—is tupped by "the nameless, the identical, highwayman, murderer, thief." There is even an ironic virgin worship, of which Mink is celebrant: "He had been bred by generations to believe invincibly that to every man, whatever his past actions, whatever depths he might have reached, there was reserved one virgin, at least, for him to marry; one maidenhead, if only for him to deflower and destroy." But even this demonic union, fitted out with all the trappings of pornography, has offspring and becomes part of the domestic culture. And not only does it survive, but for a time at least it even prevails, when Mink bushwhacks a man who has impounded his half-wild, unfenced cattle.

Yet the metaphorical point of the pornographic parody of ideal love is summed up in this judgment by Mink's wife: "I've had a hundred men, but I never had a wasp before. That stuff comes out of you is rank poison.

It's too hot. It burns itself and my seed both up. It'll never make a kid." There is danger in this man's very being. The same frustration, indefatigability, energy, and failure that makes us sympathize with him, also threatens our humanity. He is a killer, by will and by nature. He pornographically figures the brute in us that cannot transcend itself. He is the Caliban attracted, not to the beautiful Miranda, to the tradition of his humane glory, but to the female counterpart of himself—abortive and perverted.

In *Pylon* pornography imagistically enforces an ironic moral counterargument to anemic conventions of good and evil. In *The Hamlet* pornography metaphors the bestial backdrop against which man's moral image must always be projected. In both novels pornography functions negatively. In *Pylon* it negates a sentimental morality; in *The Hamlet* it negates moral idealism. Faulkner is quite consciously using sexuality as figural enforcement of moral statement. His consciousness is verified, I think, by the fact that in such a novel as *Light in August*, where there are both pornographic and allegorical sexuality, he avoids pornography in the development of Lena Grove, whose character constitutes the novel's final comic affirmation. In this sense of profound affirmation, the other two novels are not comic. At most they accept life rather than affirm it. And their pornographic naturalism prefigures or prophesies the deep well of moral contradiction—fire and ice—that is the heritage of human nature. In *Light in August* there is some pornographic treatment of the affair between Joe Christmas and Joanna Burden, but it is altogether transcended by the allegorical treatment of Lena. Lena is alpha and omega; she begins the novel and she ends it. Like Laverne, she is fecund, but unlike Laverne, she is untainted. There is that touch of the holy virgin about her which she maintains to the end, when she denies the comforts of the bed to Byron Bunch. Here, by Faulkner's conscious denial of pornographic treatment, she becomes an allegorical statement of both transcendent fertility and that humanly sullied purity which alone is available to the good man. Comic transcendence, for Faulkner, takes the allegorical route that is traditional to the literature of transcendental statement. But his naturalistic statements, perhaps his most morally profound for their capacity to make judgments without passing judgment, are highly suggestive examples of the artistic possibilities for using sexuality to explore moral actuality.

The polarities of religious eroticism and sexual naturalism confirm the centrality of archetypal sexuality's moral meaning—both in the acts of and the impulse toward sex. The imagery of sex has a coherent significance comparable to that of pastoral nature imagery. Indeed, the pastoral itself was the model for the verses of John of the Cross. Where the pastoral image as a statement of the good derives from transcendental morality, the sexual image as moral statement derives from naturalistic morality. Early pornography, such as *Fanny Hill*, affected a kind of pastoral quality in its stylistic presentation of sex. But as naturalism became increasingly available to the imagination, pornography developed its own dissident identity as a moral phenomenon. Thus in Sade sexuality becomes a complete morality and metaphysics—a world view.

Such a view is not comprehensive, limited as it is by polemics and special pleading. More balanced imaginations have used sexuality in less hyperbolic ways, however crucially they may conceive it as a sign of cause of human behavior and the natural order. Faulkner, of course, is one of these. But the pervasiveness of sexuality in imaginative confrontations with both the behavioral and mythical order of things testifies to the morality of sexual being and consequently of pornography, the literature about sexual being. For artists, pornography is a figural device that enables them to visualize their perception of sexual causality in human and even cosmic nature. For the audience, pornography provides the imagery with which to be instructed in the artist's vision of moral possibility. For both artist and audience, then, pornography can be a rhetorical agency of moral understanding.

# 5

# An Unspeakably Tragic Ethos

## TOWARD PROLIFERATING UNCERTAINTIES

I have been arguing that pornography has the potential for both moral and mythic knowledge. It seems fitting therefore to examine the relationship between pornography and tragedy, that literature which traditionally articulates the most profound problems of both morality and mythology. The predominant motifs of tragedy are war and violence, both analogues of the myth of animality. Plato in fact suggests that the art of war was mythically given to man to put him at parity with the rest of animal nature. Later, he says, the concepts of "shame" and "right" were given man to counteract his animal character and permit social organization. And the act of sex, throughout the history of both erotic and pornographic literature, has been figuratively depicted as an act of war. Sex and violence, as symbols of great passion, are in the logic of symbolism unequivocally connected with tragedy. This chapter will explore some of the artistic potential of that relationship. We must first look at some aesthetic history, and then at pornography's place in the aesthetic movement toward a naturalistic ethos.

First, there is the significance of tragedy's transition from what it was to what it is. Tragedy has been traditionally regarded as the highest mode of Western wisdom literature, and if we are skeptical about the possibilities of modern tragedy, it is perhaps only because we are skeptical about the nature of modern wisdom. But for classical cultures wisdom was, if no less difficult than now of application, at least capable of confident articulation. And tragedy was its way, providing formulation and reflection of the highest levels of cultural imagination. It shaped, as well as being shaped by, the cultural ethos. It gave coherent formulation to religion, myth, and ethics.

Socrates' objection to the tragedians was precisely that their formulations of such wisdom were not only erroneous but far too influential. As things worked out, Greek popular culture obviously thought Homer was closer to wisdom than was Socrates, and accordingly dispatched him as a troublemaker. Aristophanes and the Athenian people, as Hegel so brilliantly notes in *The Philosophy of History*, recognized in Socratic thought a revolutionary threat to the celebrated "middle way," in other words to the fundamental complaisancy, coherence, and clarity of the mythic formulations of Greek law and order. Hegel sums up that pivotal moment in tragic moral history:

> He taught that man has to discover and recognize in himself what is the Right and Good, and that this Right and Good is in its nature universal. Socrates is celebrated as a Teacher of Morality, but we should rather call him the *Inventor of Morality*. The Greeks had a *customary* morality; but Socrates undertook to teach them what moral virtues, duties, etc. were. The moral man is not he who merely wills and does that which is right—not the merely innocent man—but he who has the consciousness of what he is doing.
>
> Socrates—in assigning to insight, to conviction, the determination of men's actions—posited the Individual as capable of a final moral decision, in contraposition to Country and to Customary Morality, and thus made himself an Oracle, in the Greek sense. He said that he had a *δάιμόνιον* within him, which counselled him what to do, and revealed to him what was advantageous to his friends. The rise of the inner world of Subjectivity was the rupture with the existing Reality.

But the Athenians learned, or at least we learned form their demise, as a college freshman once put it, "mental health is better than art." Freud and modern psychology are the somewhat belated vindication of Socrates' insistence on self-knowledge. This knowledge—that, as Milton said, the mind is its own place, creating, as Milton could not say, heaven and hell—is that which modern tragedy has been pressing on its audience.

Tragedy deals with man in the clutches of the dark powers, those beyond human ken and control, and it is the most profound of our mythic sensibilities for that reason, that it wants to help us accommodate ourselves to what is unknown but always with us. The ethos of tragedy is therefore essential to an exploration of the intimidating forces of which we are ignorant but to which we are subject; and in so doing, as Aristotle says of its effects, it relieves us of personal fear by uniting us with humanity, and thereby also makes possible the compassion necessary for human understanding and survival.

To serve the needs and wants, then, of human personality, tragedy developed as an art of religious mythology, relating man to the cosmic forces, which it represented as gods modeled on a frequently compromised but nonetheless ideal human scale. Tragedy in effect humanized the cosmic forces by putting them, however reverentially, into the context of human motivation, that humans might understand their ethical significance by analogy. Thus, by construction of mythic form and substance, humans themselves became the creator of what it was they sought to know. They created an art form to represent their religious ethos, honing their will to meet the cosmic necessities they imagined, as well as the ones they knew. But it is important to remember that the vehicle by which humans understood their relation to themselves and nature was the product of their own making. Thus it is logical that, as understanding evolves, so too will the art form that most closely reflects that understanding. The history of tragedy's transition to modernity is essentially the history of the transition from a religious ethos to a naturalistic one.

The main theme of tragedy is that man lives in the circumference of necessity and that knowledge of it is the crux of human survival. The difficulty, as Plato saw, was that knowledge of the ethics of that necessity was as much obscured by the tragic myth as it was clarified. Specifically he objected to the implicit approval of the passions in tragedy, to the tragedians' acquiesence in the power of passion. Tragedians were persuasive imagists but imperfect philosophers. Caught between the roles of formulator and reflector, poets too brilliantly perpetuated mythic misconceptions—especially of passion as the principal heroic virtue. Thus men, inspired to emulate the heroes, were provided the wrong paradigm for imitation. To counteract the passions, Plato proposed an environment—his Republic—in which men could get in harmony with their rational natures and thus avoid the tragic consequences of overwhelming passion. But, as even he realized, this was a utopian project unlikely to be realized—precisely because men are more passionate than rational. The tragedians may have given bad moral example by their representation of passion as ethical catalyst, but they were nevertheless telling an existential truth. Plato wanted to expand the existential potential of ethics by making men more conscious of the mythical (or decadent) basis of their values. Knowing the force of myth in formulating man's knowledge, he wanted to expand the moral archetypes on which myths are based to include rational analysis. He wanted, in other words, to improve the conscious values of Athenian culture by expanding the ethical basis of the mythic unconscious—represented by poetry, especially tragedy—from which they were derived. And it is on the pivot of this conflict—between, in effect, the conscious and unconscious self—that the transition from classical to modern tragedy begins.

Hegel, in *The Philosophy of Fine Art*, describes the problem:

> In this sense the Greek nation has also, in the representation of its gods, made its spirit visible to the perceptions and the imaginative consciousness, and bestowed on them by means of art a determinate existence, which is entirely conformable with their true content. By virtue of this homogeneous form, which is alike consistent with the fundamental notion of Greek art and Greek mythology, art became in Greece the highest expression for the Absolute, and Greek religion is the religion of art itself, whereas romantic art, which appeared later, although it is undoubtedly art, suggests a more exalted form of consciousness than art is in a position to supply.
>
> In establishing the position, as we have just done, on the one hand, that essentially free individuality is the content of classical art, and, on the other, that a like freedom is the equally requisite determinant of the form, we have already assumed that the entire blending of both together, however much it may be presented in the immediate form, is nevertheless no original unity such as Nature's, but is necessarily an *artificial* association made possible by the subject spirit. Classical art, in so far as its content and its form is spontaneity, originates in the freedom of the Spirit that is clear to itself. And for this reason also we may say that in the *third* place the artist occupies a position different from that of his predecessors.

Schiller, as we have noted earlier, says that the difference between the classical and the sentimental or modern sensibility is essentially that, while classical men felt themselves of necessity in the rhythm of nature, modern men have found themselves increasingly out of touch with it. This alienation is natural enough. Electricity alone, for example, would have been sufficient, allowing humans to no longer regulate their activities by the sun, thus revolutionizing both labor and leisure. Once science and technology start their growth, the changes in people's behavior compound geometrically. Coordinately with greater knowledge of the universe and its provision of leisure time came increasing "scientific" knowledge of the self. The modern mind has become less dependent on nature and more on itself.

After a long look at himself and the nature of things, the moderns have become existentialist. Being out of touch with an ideal, they see little of the heroic in themselves, little analogy between themselves and the gods. Thus, little nobility, much failure. Or, more accurately, more absurdity. For all their knowledge, vast areas of ignorance. But now their failures are measured against their existential potential rather than divine necessity. The sky's the limit, but in reaching modern man keeps losing his footing. Going to the moon, he slips on the banana peels of poverty and starvation and war. Thus he is pathetic, pathetic by virtue of his failure to deliver on the large existential potential promised by science and "democracy." Humans have great ethical promise, but are victimized by the dark powers still lurking in the soul, the dark powers of ignorance within that continually frustrate knowledge. Thus they are perhaps more tragic than their ancestors because they have greater ethical expectations.

In the classical tragic ethos, as Hegel suggests, the audience always knew what its hero should do—as with Oedipus—or at least knew the alternatives clearly—as with Antigone. It was therefore purged by a moral and ethical knowledge the mythical coherence and clarity of which made the audience superior to the hero. His failure reenforced their sense of justice. But in the modern tragic ethos the audience shares the (anti-)hero's confusion. It does not know any more than he what he should do. Thus the audience—as, for example, in *Waiting for Godot*—is not superior to the protagonists, but rather shares their lack of wisdom. What *is* there to do? With no mythic pantheon of gods to depend on, for either wrath or benevolence, with nothing in fact to depend on but himself, man is left to his own pathetic devices. Predictable as things are, the uncertainty principle reigns. Classical tragedy elevated its audience to an ideal ethos that promised deliverance from the dark powers. Modern tragedy, dispossessed of a common belief, simply appeals to the compassion necessary for us to stay in the trenches and slog it out.

The tragic tradition, from which the Greeks gained their moral and ethical confidence, was a tradition of affirmation, not interrogation. Socrates was the victim of a cultural antagonism that plagues us yet today, between a philosophical inquiry into the nature of reality and the cultural affirmation of its mythic configurations. But Socrates, the Socratic role, lives on in a way that Sophocles does not. Cocteau and others have, perhaps as a political ruse, tried to bring him back. But there is a universe of difference between *The Infernal Machine* and *Oedipus Rex*. The large issues—man and morality—may be the same. But the specific differences of moral vision and ethical responsibility are vast: Sophocles' Oedipus affirms the justice inherent in a system of necessity that Cocteau's Oedipus probes and connives against.

Probing and conniving are almost paradigmatic characteristics of the modern imagination. In this sense perhaps Marlowe's *Dr. Faustus* is the first modern tragedy, rooted though it is in medieval and classical conventions. For it shows man willful and unrepentent in his probing and conniving against God, the ultimate synthesis of cosmic forces.

Faust, in going to hell unrepentent, the taste of Helen on his lips, marks the end of man's fear, not only of damnation, but of knowledge. For knowledge, the devil's doing, brings him that sweetness and power in life the experience of which is worth the everlasting death that man, as man, has always secretly suspected to be his fate anyway. Right there, or nearabouts, is the beginning of the death of God. It is, at any rate, a sign of the end of the domination of classical tragic motifs. Faust is no idealized hero endowed with stupendous passion like Achilles or Medea, he is a bookish man, a cloistered scholar who desires merely to know and experience the world.

But it took the modern imagination a while to find itself and escape its religious trappings. The eighteenth century was the time of its most discernible realization, in the development of what Schiller called "sentimental" and Hegel sometimes "romantic" and sometimes "symbolic" art. By the eighteenth century large cracks had appeared in the monolith of religious mythologizing, aided and abetted by the new philosophy represented in such figures as Kant, Hume, and Descartes. The religious order was waning, the secular coming on. Naturally the influence of religion on literature diminished, changed character. Its role became less dogmatic and more implicit. Whereas, in the case of English literature, Spenser and Milton had felt compelled to wrestle with religious dogma; Sterne and Richardson attempted to probe its ethos, discover and isolate those qualities in it that could articulate the good life. This shift in emphasis also had to do, as we have observed earlier, with the democratizing of the arts. As literature (the novel, for example) was increasingly made for a middle class or "common" audience, it naturally opted for a popular ethic. As its education was limited, so too was the new audience's understanding and appreciation of the refinements of religious dogma and philosophical disquisition. But literature, as usual, not only formulated and reflected the cultural imagination, it was as well the mediator between the common man and philosophy and religion. And it fused two of the most complementary concepts, Christian charity and philosophical sentiment, modified them and made them the basis for a democratic ethos.

The great comic paradigm of this ethos is Sterne's *Tristram Shandy*. Two great tragic paradigms are Richardson's *Clarissa* and Sade's *Justine*. We shall shortly look at Sade in some detail. For the moment some general observations on the sentimental tragic mode must suffice to indicate the transition such works signify in the movement of tragedy toward modernity, obscenity, and a naturalistic ethos. Sade's treatment of the sentimental tragedy is parodic, which is to say that he uses that convention to make another, more ironic, statement. But Richardson's use of the motif is real, that is, it reflects in itself a moral vision. In the classical imagination calamity fit into a pattern of more or less coherent cause and effect. Not so with sentimental tragedy. Suffering, for the Romantic (and probably for the modern) mind, is present—because, as we have observed, its archetype, death, is always present—but it is undefined logically. It exists in nature, but its causes are not formally located. It is to be found at the sign of necessity, on Pathos Street. And the effect of suffering is highly unformal; it is in fact pretty sloppy. "Virtuous" people do a lot of it because suffering, in the sentimental ethos, is the sign of their virtue. "Bad" people cause it, though they can become virtuous by recanting, usually on their deathbed or in a letter discovered after their death. Tragedy here, unlike its classical antecedents, exists without the framework of a coherent ethos. Thus, because there is no dialectical cause, tragedy focuses on effect—suffering. Both sentimental and modern tragedy, denied a clear knowledge of cause—denied, that is, a formal sense of what is tragic—have necessarily to represent tragic pathos as the universal imperative.

There are, of course, better and worse resolutions of this dilemma. The sentimental one tends to be rather weak. Richardson demonstrates its weakness, Sade demonically attacked the sentimental. Clarissa, Richardson's tragic protagonist, is the prototypical sentimental hero. Lovelace is the prototypical villain. Clarissa, all virtuous sentiments and "delicacy," is wooed and won (her tragic flaw) by Lovelace, all lace and frippery, without a decent respect for work, without sentiments of conscience (except of course touchingly at his demise). She is made, somewhat lasciviously in fact, to suffer, and then, because she is so steadfastly virtuous (she says, on her deathbed, "It is good for me that I was afflicted!" . . . and "Do you, sir, tell your friend [Lovelace] that I forgive him!—And I pray to God to forgive him!"), she is allowed pathetically to die. Lovelace also dies pathetically, from the avenging sword of Clarissa's cousin, after announcing that his death is expiation. There are causes for suffering here, but they are ethically trivial. Aside from the bourgeois Christian judgments implicit in Richardson's portrait of Lovelace, including Lovelace's somewhat anemic satanism, Lovelace as tragic cause is just undifferentiated badness. Richardson is not, in fact, really interested in causality at all. He is interested in the spectacle of suffering, the tragedy of which will be suffused with Christian salvation. In his postscript to the novel, Richardson explains his purpose:

> He [a third-person reference to himself as author] was resolved . . . to attempt something that never yet had been done. He considered that the tragic poets have as seldom made their heroes true objects of pity . . . and still more rarely have made them in their deaths look forward to a *future hope*. . . . The Author . . . is therefore well justified by the *Christian system*, in deferring to extricate suffering virtue to the time in which it will meet with the *completion* of its reward.

It is an index of the popular sentimental mind that Richardson is here defending himself against charges that his killing off Clarissa violated "poetic justice," a popular poetic doctrine apparently conceived for the preservation of happy endings. The point is that, to justify his plot, Richardson felt obliged to pull all stops. In defense of unhappy endings he enlists the support of Aristotle, Horace, Addison, Steele, Rapin, and the Psalms. Tame and sentimental as he seems now, in his time Richardson was leading his audience toward a tragic sensibility based in what he thought was a naturalistic, although highly Christian, ethos:

> And after all, what is the *poetical justice* so much contended for by some, as the generality of writers have managed it, but another sort of dispensation than that with which God, by revelation teaches us. He has thought fit to exercise mankind: whom placing here only in a state of probation, he hath so intermingled good and evil, as to necessitate us to look forward for a more equal dispensation of both.

But, bold as Richardson may have been for his time, and audience, his morality is too simple and categorical, too dependent on the spectacle of suffering (which, had he read his Aristotle a bit more vigorously, he might have known), to provide the foundation for a significant tragic ethos.

Although mythically profound, the psychic basis of the ethos of sentimentality is inadequate for anyone not sharing its faith in feeling as the ultimately potent moral force. This moral sense works in a comic vision like Sterne's because in it all things—suffering included—are absurd. Calamity in Sterne's vision is the (decadent) invention of humans' preposterous ratiocination. Sterne simply refuses to take it seriously. Men, for example Walter or Toby Shandy, act absurdly and absurd things happen to them. But, his ethos insists, if people would consult their humane feelings, the model for which is Christian charity, they would recognize their absurdity and in so doing escape the morbidity of the indomitable human ego. But suffering is never ultimate in a comic vision; in tragic vision it is always ultimate. So a tragic vision must have an ethos that accounts for the mind's capacity to make a hell of heaven and a heaven of hell. It must, in other words, either have access to a common, stylized morality, as the Athenians did, or it must have a naturalistic ethos to accommodate the full range of human vagary.

The classical tragedian found his material in a mythology to which there was general cultural assent; thus society enforced the substantive themes and the form of his art. Hegel sums up the necessary conditions for a classical art thus: "The content must for the classic artist be presented him as something *already there* . . . as a thing essentially positive, as belief, popular opinion, or as an actual event either of myth or tradition." The sentimental imagination, the beginning of modern imagination, did not have access to an essentially positive public ethos, either naturalistic or mythic. Christian mythology, unlike classical mythology, was ethereal and allegorical. And the efforts of Aquinas and Dante to stabilize interpretation did not help.

But the aesthetics of sentimentality were an approach to the naturalistic needs of a modern ethos. Even *Clarissa,* rooted as it is in an eighteenth-century bourgeois sensibility, gives some indication of what was to come—Clarissa's helpless fascination with Lovelace, perhaps as much with his evil as his charm, and Lovelace's demonism as well as his moral ambivalence (culminating in his "expiation") are a kind of prologue to the Dionysiac preoccupations of the modern imagination. For the modern tragedian is most into probing the paradoxes and contradictions that undermine the vestigial ethos that obliges us to act on it as if it were static and final when in fact it is still evolving and incomplete. To do that he must explore the naturalistic contradictions and paradoxes of the human mind that are a vital part in shaping a modern ethos. The sentimental poetic was neither quite fish nor fully fowl. It has classical impulses without classical content.

Hegel, with uncharacteristic succinctness, sums up the problem of a modern aesthetics in evolution:

> Symbolic art remains the captive of its travail to bring to birth and make clear its form to its own vision, and this embodiment is itself only the original form, that is, on the one side Being in the immediate guise of Nature, and on the other the ideal abstraction of the universal, unity, conversion, change, becoming, origination, and passing away. In this original form of the artistic process, however, art does not come to its rightful possessions. Consequently, these representations of symbolic art, which should be expositions of content, remain still themselves riddles and problems, and merely testify to the struggle after clarity and the effort of Spirit, which on and on seeks to discover without obtaining the rest and repose of discovery.

For all his perceptiveness on aesthetic transition, Hegel's view here is very much the product of the classicism in which he was so well schooled. His analysis of aesthetic history is for that very reason richly suggestive for any attempt at articulating a sense of modern aesthetics. His notion, for example, of art's "rightful possessions" presupposes that there is an ideal to be discovered and that, supposing an ideal, it can and should be formulated in art. Neither supposition is modern; both make art's personal and cultural roles finite and closed; art always knows what it should be doing.

But modern art, like modern culture, is in the process of discovery, sometimes finding new things, sometimes interpreting old things. Its main drift is neither celebration, as with classical art, nor lamentation, as with sentimental art, but analytic naturalism, trying to find out what is "really" there. Its reality premise is, as Hegel understood, subjective (the moral and metaphysical analogy of relativity), but in it the working out of subjectivity is not so cohesive as Hegel and his time had supposed. If subjectivity is real, as Hegel agrees it is, then reality must be as fragmented as subjectivity makes it. Thus finding out what is "really" there will not necessarily lead to the comforts of a univocally ordered sense of nature. In any event, whether there is or is not an ideal yet to be discovered, modern art is in the position of being necessarily experimental and open—that is, engaged in the process of discovery. Its uneasy forms and themes are therefore quite "natural." In this sense, according to even a Hegelian view of aesthetic history, an ethically experimental and open art is in fact the mainstream of the modern artistic tradition.

The cultural role of modern tragedy, therefore, is complex to an unprecedented degree. It must somehow fashion an objective image of life—of man and nature—out of a subjective theory of personal reality and a corresponding relativity in nature. It must, in other words, help formulate a convincing collective ethos out of the fragmented and disharmonious experience of its culture. It must give form to what is formless, make comprehensible what is incomprehensible. Unlike classical or sentimental tragedy, it has no persuasive mythology to draw on. Being analytic and naturalistic, it finds itself in fact suspicious of mythology, tending more to parody of its humanistic fruitlessness, as Beckett does in *Waiting for Godot,* or satirizing its vicious absurdity, as Camus does in *The Stranger,* or exploring its pathological destructiveness, as Nabokov does in *Lolita,* or demonstrating its futility and wrongheadedness, as Arthur Miller does in *The Death of a Salesman.* Myth and the urge to mythologize are treated ironically in modern tragedy because of their tendency to obscure moral reality and thereby render impossible the formulation of the only kind of ethos, a naturalistic ethos, in which the modern mind can feel some ethical confidence. The role of modern tragedy, then, is Socratic rather than Sophoclean. It rejects mythologizing because that clouds the perception of reality, coercing men to ignorance of their individual and collective natures, leading to ethical impotence and disaster.

The moral imperative of modern tragedy is that, although men do not have a universal talisman, they do have the capacity to recognize cause and effect. In ethical relativism, each individual act is ultimate, for which the actor must hold himself responsible. He cannot defer responsibility to death and the justice of divinity. He can be responsible only for what he knows, and, whereas he cannot know divine justice, he can know the ethical implications of his own actions. Knowledge, above all self-knowledge, is the key to this subjective ethos. Not only must humans have hindsight about the ethical implications of their acts, they must work to understand the psyche, its motivations and vagaries, its sickness as well as its health, for they act under the influence of their total being. And if they are to have power over themselves, they must know the forces with which they have to contend. Clear perceptions of reality are therefore crucial.

Like Socrates, however, modern tragedians know that no perception is clear; no perception, therefore, is final. Consciousness is an open-ended and ongoing work, imperative for the moral knowledge for which all men are responsible. So modern tragedy is a gadfly to the consciousness, reminding us that a failure of consciousness, where we hold our fates in our own hands, is fatal. And reminding us, also, that our perceptions are vulnerable, that our conscious vigilance is ethically necessary, and that failure to distinguish the real from the chimerical is, potentially at least, a moral failure. In *Death of a Salesman,* for example, Willy Loman, an archetypal modern protagonist, destroys his sons, himself, and his wife through a failure of consciousness. He fails to recognize that the ethos to which he subscribes and which he imposes on his sons—the ethos of being well-liked to achieve the myth of "success"—is not only in itself destructive of humanity but, ironically, does not even work for his own ends.

Nabokov's *Lolita,* as we have observed in an earlier chapter, makes consciousness a collective cultural responsibility. The novel depicts a telescoping of tragic "demons." Humbert is Lolita's demon; Quilty is Humbert's demon; and Humbert's life story is society's demon. This last, especially, is what Humbert in his trial wants to establish with his audience, the "ladies and gentlemen of the jury." Humbert is purged from Lolita by her pregnancy, the "normal" product of relations with her young husband. The purgation is not soon enough, however, to prevent the dissipation of Lolita's vitality by the age of seventeen, part of the novel's tragic pathos. Quilty is purged from Humbert when Humbert murders him. But Humbert cannot be purged from the culture. That is the point of his defense. There being no question of his guilt and execution, he argues for the consciousness of the whole culture—New World and Old—to recognize his existence and the demons that are part of our nature. These tragedies, like most modern ones, are an attempt to articulate the naturalistic paradoxes out of which human conduct springs and to generate thereby the knowledge and compassion necessary for the formulation of an adequate ethos. If the modern ethos, as Foucault noted, has been confronted with the proliferation of perversities, it is hardly paradoxical that modern literature, especially in the twentieth century, should address itself to those shadows that can cloud our minds.

## VIA THE SADISTIC SUBLIME

The evolution of tragic sensibility from a religious to a naturalistic ethos means that our most profound western literary mode has effected a fundamental transition. Its change signifies an equally important change in our total cultural sensibility. I want to argue, now, that pornography has had a role in that development and to examine something of what its role has been. In a previous chapter we analyzed the hypothesis of decadence and its influence on a poetics of obscenity. Now to get at pornography's relationship to a naturalistic ethos, I use as example perhaps the world's most celebrated pervert/practitioner of obscene poetics, the Marquis de Sade. Because he is so enigmatic and fascinating a figure, one is tempted to fuse his literary and personal histories in an attempt to assess the meaning of the Sade charisma. But that work has been done already by Simone de Beauvoir in her magnificent long essay, "Must We Burn de Sade?" Sade himself is at once a myth and a reality in our cultural imagination, and our long-standing repression of his works and revulsion at his name tell us much. For most of us he is the archetypal "sadist," the model for a disease. There is probably enough "sadism" in his biography at least partly to justify that. But the real models for that character of imagination we exorcise with the label "disease" are much more the literary documents of his imagination than the conduct of his life. In many ways his life is more interesting than his work, but without his extraordinary writings Sade would be a historical curiosity rather than a rich index of subcultural psychology and life. He is, however, important not only to psychology but to the development of literature and philosophy as well. He is not, as some of his enthusiasts claim, a great novelist, a great philosopher, or a great psychologist. But he is a prodigious figure in our cultural history nonetheless. Both as myth and reality, he looms peripherally but inescapably on the path to cultural modernity. And the key to Sade's meaning for us is in his literary remains.

Quite rightly, Simone de Beauvoir says Sade is most significant as a moralist. But, because his moral vision is "decadent" and often contradictory, we can get at his morality more clearly if we consider the artistic medium through which it is articulated. Sade's artistic quality is vitiated by his compulsive personal apologetics—that is, his need to defend his personal behavior and his need to attack society nearly always overpower those personally disinterested perceptions necessary to artistic integrity and universality. But it must be remembered, first, that Sade did nearly all of his writing in prison (it is significant to his political thinking that, as Jean Paulhan has noted, he was imprisoned at various times by all the varieties of French government under which he lived—monarchy, Republic, Consulate, and Empire), and, secondly, that the mythic force and durability of Sade-ism come from the very personality with which he represents his imagination. He is, then, an extraordinary artist, and we do ourselves disservice to dismiss his vision because we deprecate his manner. His vision is so present, so much larger than questions of art, that we are obliged to work through the obstacles presented by his artistic form.

Nor is the problem one of aesthetic simplicity or naivete. Although one detects these in his work, the works themselves are constructed with a peculiar complexity and sophistication of perception, so much so that we have only recently arrived at the aesthetic and moral attitudes necessary to comprehend what he was up to. Far too much so for his time, his aesthetic is distinctly modern. The key is decadence and its characteristic dialectical inversion of morality.

We shall return to that. Now let us look briefly at Sade's ideas about fiction, the form most important to the presentation of his morality. In "Idées sur les Romans," which prefaced a collection of his stories, Sade reveals conventional enough notions of fiction, but not only are the conventions he prefers significant but also those few original perceptions on the nature of fiction with which the essay is spotted. Here, for example, is his designation of the basis of fiction: "Man is subject to two weaknesses which pervade his existence and characterize it. Everywhere he needs to pray, everywhere he needs to *love,* and those are the bases of all novels. . . . Since man *prayed* and *loved* everywhere . . . there were novels, that is to say, works of fiction which sometimes depicted the fabulous objects of his worship, sometimes the more real ones of his love."

Sade's own fictive motives start in these needs, but they are, in characteristic decadent fashion, inverted. Prayer is secularized in Sade's fiction to celebration, and its object is demons rather than gods. Love is best translated in Sade to mean passion, and is thus rendered exclusively mundane and naturalistic. His fiction is in effect a celebration of the demonic passions, to what end, we shall see further on. Nor, in appreciating Sade, can one overlook the fact that man's needs are weaknesses, and that weakness is the basis of fiction. For Sade, fiction was a dialectical vehicle for exploring the weaknesses of man and society, and its most ambitious end is analysis and refutation of the mythic superstitions by which man's weaknesses become idols of the mind. This anthropological notion of fictive utility also informs his theory of fiction's origin and evolution.

> Let us not be in any doubt about this: it was in the countries which first recognized the Gods that novels found their source, and consequently in Egypt, the undeniable cradle of all cults. Men had hardly *suspected* the existence of immortal beings before they made them act and speak; from then onwards we see metamorphoses, fables, parables, novels; in fact we see works of fiction as soon as fiction seizes upon the mind of men. We see fabulous books as soon as there is any question of fancies: when nations, led first by the priests, after having been sacrificed for their fantastic divinities, finally took up arms for their king or their country, the homage offered to heroism counterbalances that of superstition. Not only are the heroes, and very wisely, put in the place of the Gods, but songs praise the sons of Mars just as they had

> celebrated those of heaven. The narrator embellishes the great actions of their lives, or weary of feeding upon them, creates characters who resemble them . . . who surpass them, and before long new novels appear, doubtless more probable, and created much more for man than those that only celebrated phantoms.

Sade's sense of aesthetic history is acute, recognizing that fiction at an early time had moved from a religious to a naturalistic function. In noting that fiction has taken on an increasingly humanistic character, he rightly observes that it must deal more precisely in probability, that is to say it must give a more accurate accounting of cause and effect, an accounting as little confused as possible by phantoms. Sade's interpretation of the history and function of fiction, then, was precociously responsive to the development of naturalism. It was, of course, his own peculiar version, rooted in his idea of the authenticity of the senses. In Sade's dialectical apparatus naturalistic sensuality is the center of epistemology. Man can escape deceptive phantoms of the mind—"virtue," for instance—only by knowledge of the real meaning of the sensual. And fiction, in which that sensuality can be depicted in all its force, imaged working against the ineffectuality (in which its falseness is revealed) of virtue, fiction is the form through which that knowledge can be revealed.

What good he asks rhetorically, are novels? "They are good for painting you just as you are, vain individuals, who would like to escape the pen because you fear its effects. The novel being, if it is possible to define it thus, *the portrait of age-long customs*, is as essential as history to the philosopher who will understand man." The philosopher must deal with man's actions, as man "makes himself seen," whereas the novelist "pierces his innermost thoughts." But Sade clearly wants to fuse the philosophic and fictive roles to get at "the most essential knowledge that is demanded," which is the "understanding of the heart of man." Yet the novelist has over the philosopher the further advantage that according to even the most classical of artistic "rules," he can, indeed he must as an artist, see and represent nature without the prism of dialectical predisposition. For a true perception of nature must take in all her variables and apparent contradictions to account for everything, high and low:

> Nature, more bizarre than the moralists depict her to us, escapes at every moment from the confines that those gentlemen would like to prescribe for her. Uniform in her plans, irregular in her effects, her ever-stirring womb resembles the crater of some volcano from which in turn are cast up either precious stones which serve man's luxury or balls of fire which destroy him; magnificent when she peoples the earth with many an Antonius and a Titus, frightful when she vomits up an Andronicus or a Nero, but always sublime, always majestic, always worthy of our studies, our pens and our respectful

> admiration, because her designs are unknown to us, because, slaves as we are to her caprices and her needs, it is never upon what we are made to suffer that we should regulate our feelings for her, but upon her grandeur and her might, whatever their results may be.

The role of art, being so attuned to nature, is to further the progress of this enlightenment. The artist, being the freest of seers, being obliged to nothing but his perceptions, must extend the range and evolution of all men's perceptions:

> As minds become corrupted and a nation grows old, by virtue of the fact that nature is studied more and analyzed better, that prejudices are better destroyed, it is necessary to get to know them further. This law is the same for all the arts. It is only by advancing that they become perfected, they only arrive at their goal by means of trying. Doubtless it was not necessary to go so far in those frightful times of ignorance when, crushed beneath the iron yoke of religion, those who wished to appraise them were punished with death, and the Inquisition's faggots were the rewards of talent. But in our present state, let us always set forth from this principle, when man has weighed up all the checks, when with an audacious glance he measures up his barriers, when with the example of the Titans he dares to lift his bold hand against the Heavens, and, armed with his passions as the former were with the coals of Vesuvius, he no longer fears to declare war on those who formerly made him tremble, when even his delinquencies seem no more to him than errors justified by his studies, then should one not speak to him with the same force that he himself employs in his behavior? The man of the eighteenth century, in short, is he then the man of the eleventh?

The end of art, then, in Sade's poetics is knowledge, knowledge of nature purged of the defensive machinery imposed on it by man's ambition and vanity, the weaknesses of his mind. On one level of vocabulary Sade's aesthetic rings with the peal of conventional eighteenth-century attitudes. But on a deeper level—the level at which nature means *what is* rather than *what is theorized about*, the level at which nature is experienced and represented as experienced, the level at which natural history is described in terms of its changes rather than its constancy—at this analytical level of understanding Sade is in profound disagreement with his time. Simone de Beauvoir points out, for example, that Sade not only refuted the traditional theists but also the deists. Sade, like some of the deists, knew that nature was not simply good. "But what distinguishes him from his predecessors," she says, "is the fact that they, after exposing the evil of nature, set up, in opposition to it, a morality which derived from God and society. . . ." But Sade, having, as we have just seen, a strict, almost Longinian confidence in nature's sublimity, was prepared to follow her ethos through no matter what paradoxes of experience. His faith in nature is religiously absolute, and the logical manipulations by which he shores up that faith throughout his works are themselves worthy of a Jesuit. This profound faith in nature and Sade's often casuistic efforts to fashion an ethos out of it, in all its complexity and contradiction, define the recurring motifs through which he so extensively anticipated and influenced the development of a naturalistic ethos.

Sade's theory of fiction tells us that to understand the human heart and nature an artist must have both misfortune and extensive travel. Travel, of course, will inform us of ethical relativity; we will discover that different societies manifest different—sometimes antithetical—moral values. But misfortune is the central thesis of Sade's ethical vision. The plot of *Justine* is designed, however hyperbolically, to demonstrate that good or bad fortune as commensurate with good or evil character is a decadent invention of man (in *Justine* the good perish, the bad prosper), and nature is without intrinsic concern for man's affairs. He is here obviously refuting the simplistic Christian ethic that good behavior will bring good fortune. At any rate, making misfortune central to fictive epistemology means that tragedy is the paradigmatic mode of his aesthetic. Furthermore, Sade greatly admired Richardson, especially *Clarissa.*

> It is Richardson and Fielding who have taught us that only the profound study of the heart of man, that veritable labyrinth of nature, can inspire the novelist, whose work must make us see man not only for what he is or what he shows of himself (that is the duty of the historian), but for what he may become, for what he may be made by the modifications of vice and the blows of passion. It is necessary therefore to know them all and to employ them all if you wish to work this field. We learnt also that it is not always by making virtue triumph that interest is maintained. It is quite certainly necessary to aim at this as far as possible, but this rule, existing neither in nature nor in Aristotle, but being one to which we would wish that all men subjected themselves for the sake of our happiness, is by no means at all essential in the novel, and is not even one that must compel interest. For when virtue triumphs, things being what they should be, our tears dry up before they begin to flow; but if after the severest afflictions we at last see virtue crushed down by vice, our souls cannot escape harrowing, and the work, having moved us exceedingly, having, as Diderot said, "steeped our hearts throughout in blood," must indubitably evoke interest, which is the only surety of fame.
>
> Let us ask this question: if after twelve or fifteen volumes the immortal Richardson had ended *virtuously* by converting Lovelace, and making him marry Clarissa *quietly*, would we, reading this novel taken in the revised fashion, have shed the delicious tears that it draws from every sensitive creature? Therefore we must grapple with nature when working in this sphere, with the heart of man, the most remarkable of all his works, and not virtue at all, because virtue, however beautiful and necessary, is never-

theless but one of the moods of this astonishing heart, the profound study of which is so necessary to the novelist, and every twist of which the novel, that faithful mirror of this heart, must necessarily plot.

Sade's appreciation of *Clarissa* and his own aesthetic and moral vision suggest that his highest fictive model is the sentimental tragedy. *Justine* is, for example, clearly modeled on the example of *Clarissa,* and it is the single work that perhaps most comprehensively presents Sade's moral vision. But the fundamental differences between his vision and Richardson's explain why Sade, in using the mode of sentimental tragedy, had to parody it. For Sade was neither sentimentalist nor Christian. It is true that there is a kind of decadent theme in *Clarissa.* Her family, acting according to what they think are the facts, and acting on what they therefore suppose to be an ethical good, are in fact mistaken both about the facts of Clarissa's liaison with Lovelace and the ethic upon which they act. A cloudy perception of the facts, therefore, forces them to cause evil by doing what they assume is good. But the ethical force of this theme is vitiated by the sentimental tone of the novel and its concern to balance bad with good. Richardson's aesthetic is a synthesis of Christian sentimentalism, bourgeois ethics, and popular fiction forms. It is able, as we said earlier, to deal convincingly only with moral effects. Sade had a much stronger dialectical impulse, a much greater faith in nature, and total indifference to (if not contempt for) popular moral opinion. And Sade's aesthetic is symbolic, partly in Hegel's sense of that term and partly in Arthur Symon's later sense. But what that meant for Sade was that he could be more reductive than Richardson in representing a true image of human life. Richardson, being a popular writer, was obliged to represent life as his audience expected it, though there was some dispute about what it expected, as we have seen. The checks and balances of his characterization and plot are in the democratic tradition. Sade, writing for himself, obliged to his vision alone, was concerned only to give himself full rein in depicting his demonically microscopic image of moral reality. His image of life represents exclusively his private vision. And the audacious insistence that this image, private as it is, is universally true signifies the symbolic character of his tragic sense. This being so, he had to parody a form that required philosophical assumptions so radically different from his own.

Although both Sade and Richardson explore the misfortunes to which virtue is subject, Richardson's purpose was to celebrate virtue's ultimate triumph over evil, while Sade's purpose is to demonstrate that good and evil form an ineluctable rhythm in nature that remains indifferent to and unaffected by the passage through it of decadent "virtue." Richardson, in short, was enforcing the myth of sentimentality, Sade was deconstructing the logic of that popular mythology. Richardson's novel is, of course, a much better work of "art" than Sade's. But it is not Sade's artistic quality that is significant; what is significant is his dialectical restructuring of the myth of sentimentality. Richardson reforms human "perversity" (Sade would call it "diversity") by making Lovelace in effect repent his persecutions of Clarissa. Christian grace, thus, exorcises human perversity. No matter how pathetically potent it may be, it need not therefore be accounted for by the cultural ethos. Perversity, in sentimentalized Aristotelian fashion, is purged by the pathos of its effects. But Sade knew better. Not being a Christian, and seeing that much of the world (including Christendom) was not Christian, and seeing that the way of the world was much more warlike than benevolent (Sade admired Hobbes), whatever Christian gloss it might assume, Sade knew that Christian sentiment was incapable of establishing justice. He knew from the warlike state of nature that men act more from their fears and self-protectiveness than from charity, and they construct their social institutions accordingly. Thus he knew that the mythology of the establishment ethos must necessarily suppress what he understood to be natural justice—the condition in which all men are free to realize their particular "natural organization," however perverse it might be. Our difficulty in perceiving the ethical viability of Sade's work comes from failing to see that each of his works is a tactical step toward the realization of his more comprehensive moral strategy, arguing for the completely tolerant ethos that he thought would reflect and help establish a state of natural justice.

This failure is compounded by the fact that the political analogue of his tolerant ethos is anarchy, and, responding as Sade knew we must, our fear of anarchy intimidates our understanding, and so we categorically reject his ethic. The failure, of course, is not all ours. Sade is a prodigiously inadequate novelist, and his own need to refute and reject his audience, to confuse it by invoking its blindnesses so skillfully (and furiously) as to dazzle it with its own sightlessness, indicates his own very real failure to communicate. Toward humanity he was highly ambivalent. He professes concern for human beings (in *The New Justine* he says, "To falsify such basic truths, regardless of their consequences, reveals a fundamental lack of concern for human beings"), and in his own conduct, although it was pretty erratic, he was charitable. When, as a judge just before the Terror, he had opportunity to revenge himself on the mother-in-law he despised, he did not. And he in fact resigned his position rather than pronounce judgments of execution, appealing that such judgments were "inhumane." But toward society, that is, toward the collective abstraction of institutions, he was hostile. And, having been imprisoned by four different kinds of social government, he was not without reason. Whatever the causes, which are not our concern here, the failure at communication is as much Sade's doing as our own. But we shall serve only our ignorance if, at this date, we allow that failure to perpetuate itself.

Sade was propagandist for an ethos still nearly inaccessible to us, although now that his work is more completely available we can see something of his dialectical strategy. *Justince,* as we have observed, is central, adding the dimension of tragedy to what might otherwise be dismissed, as it has often been, as simply perverse. Sade is perverse, of course. But not simply so; as a writer perversity is his stock in trade. The persistent motif through all his work is his defense of perversity as a natural phenomenon. His point is not, as it is so frequently mistaken, that perversity is good, merely that it is and in such quantity that its naturalness is undeniable. If, then, one is to know nature and act according to natural justice—that is, according to an ethos of tolerance—he must know the range of moral diversity under heaven. To confuse the desire for moral unity and coherence, that is, for a univocal idealistic good, with its actuality is, for Sade, necessarily to displace natural justice. "The very masterpiece of philosophy," he says at the beginning of *Justine,*

> would be to develop the means Providence employs to arrive at the ends she designs for man, and from this construction to deduce some rules of conduct acquainting this wretched two-footed individual with the manner wherein he must proceed along life's thorny way, forewarned of the strange caprices of that fatality denominated by twenty different titles, and all unavailingly, for it has not yet been scanned nor defined.

Here is the plan of not only *Justine,* but of all Sade's work—forewarning of strange caprices and a fatality not yet scanned or defined. *Justine,* perhaps not a masterpiece of philosophy, nevertheless is designed to explore those rules of conduct on which life operates, rules sentimentally supposed to reflect Providential benevolence. But, as one of Justine's many persecutors tells her,

> Become better acquainted with your Providence, my child, and be convinced that as soon as it places us in a situation where evil becomes necessary, and while at the same time Providence leaves us the possibility of doing evil, this evil harmonizes quite as well with the decrees of Providence as does good, and Providence gains as much by the one as by the other; the state in which she has created us is equality: he who disturbs the balance is no more guilty than he who seeks to re-establish it: both act in accordance with received impulses, both have to obey those impulses and enjoy them.

"Providence" is not what is usually supposed; it is rather a balance of good and evil; more accurately, a composite of interacting forces to which we apply the labels of "good" or "evil." Therefore one cannot be guilty of violating nature, only of violating man's hypotheses about nature. More important, the dynamic rhythms of nature in which "good" and "evil" contend constitute a state of natural justice. In fact, given the ethos of society, plagued by such decadent idols of the mind as "virtue," Sade proposes that "evil" will more often than not overpower "good," being more attuned to the machinations of what Darwin was to call natural selection. Justine is the heroine whose misfortunes articulate the fate of virtue in a world where the fittest survive best.

Justine sums up her 350 pages of misfortune thus:

> During my childhood I meet a usurer. He seeks to induce me to commit a theft; I refuse; he becomes rich. I fall among a band of thieves; I escape from them with a man whose life I save; by way of thanks he rapes me. I reach the property of an aristocratic debauché who has me set upon and torn by his dogs for not having wanted to poison his aunt. From there I go to the home of a murderous and incestuous surgeon whom I strive to keep from doing a horrible deed: the butcher brands me as a criminal; he doubtless consummates his atrocities and makes his fortune, while I am obliged to beg for my bread. I wish to have the sacraments made available to me; I wish fervently to implore the Supreme Being from whom somehow I have received so many ills, and the august tribunal, at which I hope to find purification in our most holy mysteries, becomes the bloody theater of my ignominy: The monster who abuses and plunders me is elevated to his order's highest honors and I fall back into the appalling abyss of misery. I attempt to preserve a woman from her husband's fury; the cruel one wishes to put me to death by draining away my blood drop by drop. I wish to relieve a poor woman; she robs me. I give aid to a man whom adversaries have struck down and left unconscious; the thankless creature makes me turn a wheel like an animal; he hangs me for his pleasure's sake; all fortune's blessings accrue to him, and I come within an ace of dying on the gallows for having been compelled to work for him. An unworthy woman seeks to seduce me for a new crime, a second time I lose the little I own in order to rescue her victim's treasure. A gentleman, a kind spirit, wishes to compensate me for all my sufferings by the offer of his hand, he dies in my arms before being able to do anything for me. I risk my life in a fire in order to snatch a child, who does not belong to me, from the flames; the infant's mother launches legal proceedings against me. I fall into my most mortal enemy's hands; she wishes to carry me off by force and take me to a man whose passion is to cut off heads: If I avoid that villain's sword, it is so that I can trip and fall under Themis'. I implore the protection of a man whose life and fortune I once saved. I dare expect gratitude from him; he lures me to his house, he submits me to horrors, and there I find the iniquitous judge upon whom my case depends; both abuse me, both outrage me, both accelerate my doom; fortune overwhelms them with favors, I hasten on to death.

What fleshes out her history of course are the elaborately detailed pornographic descriptions of abuse to which she is put. We shall come back to that as we look into the tragic ethos of *Justine.*

The narrative structure of the novel introduces two sisters, Justine and Juliette, who are at an early age bereft of family and economic means of survival. Justine is a "virtuous" girl of sensibility and delicacy; Juliette is a pragmatist. She suggests that, being young and pretty, they make their way through the expedient of marketing their only commodities. Justine naturally declines so indelicate a life. They go their separate ways. Juliette, augmenting youth and beauty with guile, murder, and libertinage, makes her way handsomely, becoming a rich and powerful Lady. Justine, augmenting delicacy with innocence and good will, undergoes the horrors summarized above. When next the two meet—the occasion of Justine's narrative—Justine is on her way to execution, Juliette is lounging through the countryside. They meet, Justine tells her story, is recognized as the long-separated sister, her pardon is secured through Juliette's influence, and she retires to Juliette's country estate, where, what else, she is struck by lightning ("The lightning entered her right breast, found the heart, and after having consumed her chest and face, burst out through her belly. The miserable thing was hideous to look upon . . . "). Juliette is moved by this "appalling stroke" to forfeit her fortune and become a Carmelite nun. The novel ends with a conventionally cursory but significant overture to "Providence": "May you be convinced with [Juliette], that true happiness is to be found nowhere but in Virtue's womb, and that if, in keeping with designs it is not for us to fathom, God permits that it be persecuted on Earth, it is so that Virtue may be compensated by Heaven's most dazzling rewards."

Such is the history of Justine. The "moral" of virtue's misfortunes is that it had best be its own reward to be compensated only in the hereafter, because on earth its reward is problematic. Systematically, as Justine's summary suggests, virtue is corrupted or destroyed while vice marches prosperously on. That is the ethical dialectic of the novel. But its tragic ethos is far more sophisticated than that simplistic opposition. For the novel's moral vitality exists in the symbolic action of its pornography. The sentimental ethos which its use of the format of the sentimental tragedy invokes becomes the foil in which the naturalistic diamond is set. Richardson's straight use of the form was to reinforce belief in the idealistic sentimental mythos—that virtue is real, vice a sensual chimera. Sade demonstrates, through the pornographically vivid imagery of sensuality, that vice is also real, more real in the workings of the world than virtue. And he who would deduce the rules of conduct by which humans may realistically proceed along life's way—they, that is, who would construct a true ethos—had best know this. Virtue, by which Sade designates the myth of sentimentality, must be left to heaven. What a person can know, though it is obscured by the desire for heaven, is nature. And if the ethos is to reflect *nature's* justice, rather than a sentimental myth of it, that ethos must be responsive to humans' full complexity of motives rather than their sentimental evasion via sublimation of human nature to a mythically configured moral idealism.

On earth, in the life we know as humans, misfortune has authenticity. Like pain and pleasure, its reality can be felt. Pathos is real, not the transcendental sign of a better life to come. The sentimental artist invokes vicarious emotions. When, for example, Richardson describes Clarissa's rape, the description is decorous, mythic; one's response therefore is removed to the impersonal level. We have only an analogous fear, which is to say that we can imagine what such a scene would be like. But Sade wants his audience to experience real feelings, not analogous, artistic ones. The pathos of Justine's life is merely philosophical; it tells us something about the abstract relation of man to nature. It takes on human meaning—has, that is, the shock of recognition—only when it is experienced in the context of authentic feeling, the revulsion and desire one authentically feels in confronting Sade's descriptions of sexual abuse, first from *Justine*:

> I remove my mistress' simar, and when she was naked conducted her to her husband who had already taken his place in a large armchair: as part of the ritual she perched upon this armchair and herself presented to his kisses that favorite part over which he had made such a to-do with me and which, regardless of person or sex, seemed to affect him in the same way.
>
> "And now spread them, Madame," the Count said brutally.
>
> And for a long time he rollicked about with what he enjoyed the sight of; he had it assume various positions, he opened it, he snapped it shut; with tongue and fingertip he tickled the narrow aperture; and soon carried away by his passions' ferocity, he plucked up a pinch of flesh, squeezed it, scratched it. Immediately he produced a small wound he fastened his mouth to the spot. I held his unhappy victim during these preliminaries, the two boys, completely naked, toiled upon him in relays; now one, now the other knelt between Gernande's thighs and employed his mouth to excite him. It was then I noticed, not without astonishment, that this giant, this species of monster whose aspect alone was enough to strike terror, was howbeit barely a man; the most meager, the most minuscule excrescence of flesh or, to make a juster comparison, what one might find in a child of three was all one discovered upon this so very enormous and otherwise so corpulent individual; but its sensations were not for that the less keen and each pleasurable vibration was as a spasmodic attack. After this prologue he stretched out upon a couch and wanted his wife, seated astride his chest, to keep him, by means of suckings, the same service he had just received from the youthful Ganymedes who were simultaneously, one to the left, one to the right, being excited by him; my hands meanwhile worked upon his behind: I titillated it,

I polluted it in every sense; this phase of activities lasted more than a quarter of an hour but, producing no results, had to be given up for another; upon her husband's instructions I stretched the Countess upon a chaise longue: she lay on her back, her legs spread as wide as possible. The sight of what she exposed put her husband in a kind of rage, he dwelt upon the perspective . . . his eyes blaze, he curses; like one crazed he leaps upon his wife, with his scalpel pricks her in several places, but these were all superficial gashes, a drop or two of blood, no more, seeped from each. These minor cruelties came to an end at last; others began.

He seizes her ferociously, places her as I was placed, arms suspended by two black straps; mine is the task of securing the bands; he inspects the knots: finding them too loose, he tightens them, "So that," he says, "the blood will spurt out under greater pressure"; he feels the veins, and lances them, on each arm, at almost the same moment. Blood leaps far: he is in an ecstacy; and adjusting himself so that he has a clear view of these two fountains, he has me kneel between his legs so I can suck him; he does as much for first one and then the other of his little friends, incessantly eyeing the jets of blood which inflame him. For my part, certain the instant at which the hoped for crisis occurs will bring a conclusion to the Countess' torments, I bring all my efforts to bear upon precipitating this *dénouement*, and I become, as, Madame, you observe, I become a whore from kindness, a libertine through virtue. The much-awaited moment arrives at last; I am not familiar with its dangers or violence, for the last time it had taken place I had been unconscious. . . . Oh, Madame! what extravagance! Gernande remained delirious for ten minutes, flailing his arms, staggering, reeling like one falling in a fit of epilepsy, and uttering screams which must have been audible for a league around; his oaths were excessive; lashing out at everyone at hand, his strugglings were dreadful. The two little ones are sent tumbling head over heels; he wishes to fly at his wife, I restrain him. I pump the last drop from him, his need of me makes him respect me; at last I bring him to his senses by ridding him of that fiery liquid, whose heat, whose viscosity, and above all whose abundance puts him in such a frenzy I believe he is going to expire; seven or eight tablespoons would scarcely have contained the discharge, and the thickest gruel would hardly give a notion of its consistency. . . .

Then from *Philosophy in the Bedroom*:

MADAME DE MISTIVAL, *screaming like a banshee*—Aië! aië! aië!

DOLMANCÉ, *driving the needle deep into her flesh*—Silence, bitch! or I'll make a hash of your buttocks. . . . Eugénie, frig me. . . .

EUGÉNIE—Willingly, but upon condition you prick her more energetically, for, you must admit, you are proceeding with strange forbearance. *(She frigs him.)*

MADAME DE SAINT-ANGE—Work upon those two great cheeks for me!

DOLMANCÉ—Patience, I'll soon have her carved like a shank of beef; Eugénie, you are forgetting your lessons: you capped my prick!

EUGÉNIE—'Tis because this bitch's sufferings are inflaming my imagination to the point I no longer know exactly what I am doing.

DOLMANCÉ—Sweet fucking God! I'm beginning to go out of my mind! Saint-Ange, have Augustin bugger you in front of my eyes while your brother flies into your cunt, and above all dress me a panorama of asses: the picture will finish me. *(He stabs Madame de Mistival's buttocks while the posture he has called for is arranged.)* Here, Mamma dear, take this . . . and again that! . . . *(He drives his needle into at least twenty places.)*

MADAME DE MISTIVAL—Oh pardon me, Monsieur, I beg your pardon a thousand times over . . . you are killing me. . . .

DOLMANCÉ, *wild with pleasure*—I should like to . . . 'tis an age since I have had such an erection; never would I have thought it possible after so many consecutive ejaculations.

MADAME DE SAINT-ANGE, *executing the called-for attitude*—Are we as we should be, Dolmancé?

DOLMANCÉ—Augustin, turn a little to the right; I don't see enough ass; have him lean forward: I must see the hole.

EUGÉNIE—Ah, fuck! Look at the bugger bleed!

DOLMANCÉ—Rather a good deal of blood, isn't there? Well, are the rest of you ready? As for myself, one minute more and I'll spray life's very balm upon the wounds I have just opened.

MADAME DE SAINT-ANGE—Yes, my heart, yes . . . I am coming . . . we arrive at the end at the same time. . . .

DOLMANCÉ, *who has finished his task, does nothing but increase his stabbing of the victim's buttocks as he discharges*—Ah triple bloody fucking God! . . . my sperm flows . . . 'tis lost, by bleeding little Jesus! . . . Eugénie, direct it upon the flanks I have just mutilated . . . oh fuck! fuck! 'tis done . . . over . . . I've no more . . . oh, why must weakness succeed passions so alive? . . .

MADAME DE SAINT-ANGE—Fuck! fuck me, brother, I discharge! . . . *(To Augustin:)* Stir yourself, great fucking-john! Don't you know that it is when I come that you've got to sink your tool deepest into my ass? . . . Ah, sacred name of God! how sweet it is, thus to be fucked by two men . . . *The group disperses.)*

And from *The One Hundred Twenty Days of Sodom*:

> He is bound hand and foot, as if he were a wild beast, and he is dressed in a tiger's skin. When thus readied, he is excited, irritated, whipped, beaten, his ass is frigged; opposite him is a plump young girl, nude and tied by her feet to the floor, by her neck to the ceiling, in such a manner she cannot stir. When the roué is all asweat, his captors free him, he leaps upon the girl, bites her everywhere and above all her clitoris and her nipples which, usually, he manages to remove with his teeth. He roars and cries like a ferocious animal, and discharges while shrieking. The girl must shit, he eats her turd upon the floor.

An artist, like Richardson, would manipulate our feelings, that we might have them more piquantly. Clarissa's rape is elaborately prepared for, and happens more in the anticipation than in the event. She herself is drugged and feels nothing. And when she dies, she dies of so abstract a thing as shame. But Sade is not really interested in art or exquisitely conceived emotions. He wants a thump in the gut. Revulsion and desire. He wants us to feel those passions that make life tragic. If we will not be revolted at the perhaps subliminal knowledge we have of viciousness in our daily conduct—as he knows we will not be, having practiced and disguised it for so long that we are blind to it—maybe we will be revolted at his pornographic descriptions, and, if not at those, then he will so describe them that we will be sexually aroused. If we are able to suppress that, we must certainly be revolted at the desire we have had to suppress. Or, at their brutality, we will feel fear. We will, by God, feel something; and in the feeling know those passions that motivate people in the conduct of their tragic lives.

This is why pornography is so crucial to Sade's tragic vision. He not only had a spontaneous kinship with it, but pornographic rhetoric was, he knew, the one kind capable of generating a real effect. And it was the one kind of rhetoric able to elicit both revulsion and desire, the precise passions upon which Sade's tragic ethos turns. Father Clement, one of Justine's persecutors, after a prolonged flagellation scene (". . . the whip's long and supple strands, penetrating [the vagina] with much more facility than could withes or ferules, leave deep traces of his rage. . . . His eyes glitter, foam flecks his lips. . . . The villain brings us to blood. . . . The blows are redoubled. The unhappy Armande receives one upon the breast which staggers her, this last horror determines his ecstasy. . . ."), tells Justine:

> One never tries of this mania notwithstanding the fact it is a very pale image of what one should really like to do; ah, dear girl! you have no idea to what lengths this depravity leads us, you cannot imagine the drunkenness into which it plunges us, the violent commotion in the electrical fluid which results from the irritation produced by the suffering of the object that serves our passions; how one is needled by its agonies! The desire to increase them . . . 'tis, I know, the reef upon which the fantasy is doomed to wreck, but is this peril to be dreaded by him who cares not a damn for anything?

Clement, like all of Sade's spokesmen for perversity, may be hyperbolic in fictive representation (Sade's conclusion apologizes for the "perhaps too heavy brushstrokes" in his portrayal of life), but he argues a truth that subsequent psychology has demonstrated about all human nature, a truth that explains the orgies of the Roman Coliseum, the French Terror, the Nazi experiments, the Japanese Rape of Nanking, the American atrocities at My Lai, not to mention the civilization-long history of pornography itself. Practiced to the extremes of Sade's characters, or perhaps in Sade's own life, sadism is doubtless a derangement, but referring to its power in human imagination, Clement's perception is unerring. Nor, as Sade knew, is it totally buried in the "normal" imagination. Its normal manifestation is in such social institutions as the public execution, reaching a maniacal pitch in the Terror, repeating itself at Buchenwald, the search and destroy missions in Vietnam, on and on. "One never tires of this mania notwithstanding the fact that it is a very pale image of what one should really like to do." Pain, pleasure, and sex: Sade knew the myth of animality well. He knew how it felt, boiling as it was within him. He saw others feeling it, acting on it, and denying it—with myths of sentimentality, idealism, civilization, what have you. And he wanted to confront us with an image of ourselves that could not fail to revolt us, and in the very revulsion arouse desire. He wanted humans to see themselves face to face.

This is not a sick vision of man. It is rather a vision of man's sickness; but normal enough for all of that, as Freud later saw. And natural; Clement goes on:

> Will it never be understood that there is no variety of taste, however bizarre, however outlandish, however criminal it may be supposed, which does not derive directly from and depend upon the kind of organization we have individually received from Nature? . . . Have we the power to remake ourselves? Can we become other than what we are? Would you demand the same thing from someone born a cripple? And is this inconformity of our tastes anything in the moral sphere but what the ill-made man's imperfection is in the physical?

As Schiller said, at about the same time, the modern imagination is a sickness seeking health, restoration to classical nature. But, says Sade, that idealist nature is a delusion. Nature is instead a sublimely indifferent vortex of contradictions. Hapless human being is willy-nilly in its crucible. The dynamics of this condition are the movements by which tragic life is defined. Sade's vision is the vision of one of the few men in literary history who have actually believed in tragedy as the truest statement of human life. The state of nature, for him, is a state of tragedy, filled with pain and ending indifferently in destruction. And the tragedy is compounded by human pleasure in pain and destruction, making them all the more inescapable. We aspire to them, both the giving and the getting. We nurture them, as Clement says, in our fantasies, even though the fantasies themselves are doomed, incapable of their own realization, spurring us on to further rhythms of pain and pleasure. The mind is indeed its own place and, as Sade knew, it controls us. Our tragedy is its power.

The ethos of such a vision, a vision of absolute tragedy, cannot be transcendental. We cannot be relieved of what is inescapable. The act of love, says the saint, is on the arm. Indeed, all acts are on the arm. Man became man when he was made flesh. Before that, he was an idea. The mind then can act only through the flesh. The body is inescapable. Thus Sade, like all morally serious pornographers, makes the flesh the figural sign of the tragic rhythms of pain and pleasure. Thus, too, the flesh symbolizes the spirit. As the flesh is raped, tortured, destroyed, so symbolically is the human spirit.

Clement, one of Sade's most profound fictive spokesmen, is not accidentally a wolf in shepherd's clothing. False priest that he is, he is the answer to his own question, of whether we have the power to remake ourselves. The answer is no, and so to survive we adopt disguises, assuming the signs of Virtue to mask the workings of Vice. The idealistic prejudices of human morality preclude an honest representation of human nature. Given the choice of criminality or hypocrisy, we will naturally choose hypocrisy. Hypocrisy, therefore, is the gearwheel of social action in Sade's vision. Society, like Clement, masks its true nature behind the formal guise of Virtue, constructing false values and institutions designed to perpetuate the hypocrisy and thus keep true human nature underground. When it pops up, as it persists in doing, it is simply rendered criminal by virtue of its honesty. Society, like Clement, keeps the sacrament of Hypocrisy, and thereby the human spirit is defiled. How figuratively appropriate to such a theme that Justine's flesh should systematically be defiled by the priest and his social analogues—the aristocrats, the shopkeepers, the doctors, the judges—the good citizens. Social prejudice and superstition, the bases of the myth of sentimentality, are, in Sade's vision, defilements of nature. And that relationship can best be articulated in the pornographic depiction of innocence debased by the canny guardians of hypocrisy.

Hypocrisy is of course rooted in egoism. And egoism is the root of Sade's theory of man and, as well, of his pornographic representation of human nature. Clement observes that, "If egoism is Nature's fundamental commandment, it is very surely most of all during our lubricious delights that this celestial Mother desires us to be most absolutely under its rule." Pleasure, then, takes one into the self, and its intensity corresponds proportionally to the degree that nothing interferes with selfishness. Somebody else's pleasure, that of the sex partner, is an interference and diminishes one's own. Therefore it is expendable. Indeed, Clement continues, somebody else's pain may heighten one's own sense of pleasure, and he proposes therefore an ethic of pain and cruelty to restore a natural balanced upset by the myth of sentimentality:

> The more the deed seems appalling to us, the more it is in contradiction with our manners and customs, the more it runs headlong against restraints and shatters them, the more it conflicts with social conventions and affronts them, the more it clashes with what we mistake for Nature's laws, then the

> more, on the contrary, it is useful to the same Nature. It is never but by way of crimes that she regains possession of the rights Virtue incessantly steals away from her.

Again, we must remember to interpret Clement, as we must interpret all Sade's spokesmen for perversity, in the figural context of symbolic hyperbole. Sade did not expect that his audience would conclude, with Clement, that "the vaster the crime, the better it will serve Nature." Clement's ethic, after all, is perverse. And Sade did not intend to argue that perversity is good, only that it is. At another point, for example, Clement observes, by way of a Sadean modification, that, "The man endowed with uncommon tastes is sick." The ethic of cruelty is not an ethic to be emulated; but it is an ethic that the world knows and uses, and it indisputably exists in nature. It articulates nature's tragic rhythms. Justine says of the man who subscribes to such an ethic of cruelty, "But the man you describe is a monster." Clement replies, "The man I describe is in tune with Nature." Justine's response is more ironic than she knows, "He is a savage beast." Yes, Clement allows, savagery is elemental to nature. "Say what you will," says Justine, "I shall never accept this destructive lubricity." "Because," says Clement, "you are afraid of becoming its object—there you have it: egoism." And, of course, for Sade's dialectical purposes, he does have her. Characteristically, an ethic is the product of one's desires and fears. An ethic of abstinence, then, such as a fundamentalist Christian ethic, is not necessarily or naturally better than an ethic of indulgence. It is the product of weakness, the inability to indulge. Here is Clement's explanation of Christian ethics:

> The doctrine of brotherly love is a fiction we owe to Christianity and not to Nature; the exponent of the Nazarene's cult, tormented, wretched, and consequently in an enfeebled state that prompted him to cry out for tolerance and compassion, had no choice but to allege this fabulous relationship between one person and another, by gaining acceptance for the notion he was able to save his life.

Even "virtuous" docility, then, has its naturalistic cause, egoistic fear. But, of course, Clement's arguments are, as we have noted, purposely exaggerated to emphasize the naturalistic basis of even the most exalted idealism. What Sade is after here, as elsewhere, is the recognition that an ethos not rooted in nature, and not taking account of those passions that are undeniably in nature, must be false and designed to serve, again, the social sacrament of hypocrisy.

But the flesh is inescapable, the starting point of all sensation, the proof that man is alive. And Sade of all men knew man's need to feel alive. Moreover, he knew that if man did not feel, he was dead, ambulatory but in decay. Zombies with political power are dangerous, for their moral imagination is unreal; dissociated from sensation, they administer pain and death abstractly, under the guise of political, or social, or some other kind of chimerical necessity. Zombies with political power are dehumanized, and so are the institutions they conceive and administer. Sade saw it in the Terror, and he resigned his role in the revolution, at considerable risk to his own life, because he would not do what was "inhumane"—kill human beings in cold blood. A rational modification of the demonic hyperbole of Sade's ethos of pain and pleasure (which is what Sade expected of his readers, knowing, as he said, that few of them would manage it) tells us not only that pain and destruction are tragically inevitable facts of life, but that pleasure and temporal happiness are also possible. But only if we honor the flesh; if we honor its sensations for what they are, an index of human capacity for life.

Clement offers a demonically brilliant exegesis of this capacity:

> Voluptuous emotion is nothing but a kind of vibration produced in our soul by shocks that the imagination, inflamed by the remembrance of a lubricious object, registers upon our senses, either through this object's presence, or better still by this object's being exposed to that particular kind of irritation that most profoundly stirs us; thus, our voluptuous transport—this indescribable convulsive needling that drives us wild, that lifts us to the highest pitch of happiness at which man is able to arrive—is never ignited save by two causes: either by the perception in the object we use of a real or imaginary beauty, the beauty in which we delight the most, or by the sight of that object undergoing the strongest possible sensation; now, there is no more lively sensation than that of pain; its impressions are certain and dependable, they never deceive as may those of the pleasure women perpetually feign and almost never experience; and, furthermore, how much self-confidence, youth, vigor, health are not needed in order to be sure of producing this dubious and hardly very satisfying impression of pleasure in a woman. To produce the painful impression, on the contrary, requires no virtues at all. The more defects a man may have, the older he is, the less lovable, the more resounding his success. With what regards the objective, it will be far more certainly attained since we are establishing the fact that one never better touches, I wish to say, that one never better irritates one's senses than when the greatest possible impression has been produced in the employed object, by no matter what devices; therefore, he who will cause the most tumultuous impression to be born in a woman, he who will most thoroughly convulse this woman's entire frame, very decidedly will have managed to procure himself the heaviest possible dose of voluptuousness, because the shock resultant upon us by the impressions others experience, which shock in turn is necessitated by the impression we have of those others, will necessarily be more vigorous if the impression these others receive be painful, than if the impression they receive be sweet and mild; and it follows that the volup-

> tuous egoist, who is persuaded his pleasures will be keen only insofar as they are entire, will therefore impose, when he has it in his power to do so, the strongest possible dose of pain upon the employed object, fully certain that what by way of voluptuous pleasure he extracts will be his only by dint of the very lively impression he has produced.

We must read this, of course, with an eye to Sade's dialectical determination to make the worse appear the better cause, to the end of forcing men simply to recognize its reality, its power in the lives of men. Clement is not only a fictive example of social hypocrisy, he represents also the desperation of humans to feel alive within the confines of moral prejudice. Like nearly all of Sade's pornographic "heroes," Clement is impotent without the application of gross and violent stimulants. Having been cut off from sensation by its suppression in moral idealism, it can only be realized through the excessive modes of "irritation" that Sade so tirelessly invents and describes. And it is pertinent that Sade here echoes Edmund Burke and David Hume. His polemic may be perverse, but it is not altogether marginal to the discourse of its time.

Assuming, like Clement, the mantle of Virtue, the social animal becomes increasingly social and decreasingly animal. He becomes, in other words, an abstraction defined by the context in which he lives, rather than what is intrinsically his passion. Soon the guise becomes second nature, satisfying his political needs, perhaps, but violating psychic ones in the process, obscuring and suppressing the animal dimension of human nature. But the body is inescapable. Animal nature, willy-nilly, manifests itself. The more it is suppressed, the more devious it becomes. It wages a guerrilla war with public sentimental nature. Rendered impotent, threatened with extinction, it slashes out in a desperate and devious fury, asserting its life violently because it is left no other means. Having been outlawed, it plays the outlaw's role.

But, being animal, it will have its pleasure. And the sign of pleasure, like that of love, is on the arm. Animal vitality, then, asserts itself through voluptuousness, the pleasure of the body, "the strongest possible sensation." Thus, again, since "one never better irritates one's senses than when the greatest possible impression has been produced . . . , he who will most thoroughly convulse this woman's entire frame, very decidedly will have managed to procure himself the heaviest possible dose of voluptuousness." And because woman's pleasure, still more than man's, has been vitiated by the sentimentalities of Virtue, because women more even than men have been superstitiously dissociated from their bodies, the agency of convulsion, perversely, is pain. Thus the ethic of cruelty, is at once hyperbole and truth. It is the truth that Sade indefatigably expounds, the terrible, tragic, insatiable human rhythm of pleasure and pain.

Pornography, then, the hyperbolic representation of the pleasure-pain syndrome in the sexual life of man, is Sade's rhetoric of naturalism. It represents the entrapment of being inside its skin and the volcano of its fevered brain. But it is more than rhetoric, too; for the rhetoric is itself an assault on the sensibilities of the audience, a symbolic confrontation between Sade and his fellow man. "I am about to put forward some major ideas," Sade says in "Yet Another Effort, Frenchman, if You Would Become Republicans." "If not all of them please, surely a few will; in some sort, then, I shall have contributed to the progress of our age, and shall be content." This parenthetical essay in *Philosophy in the Bedroom* presents Sade's political naturalism. He lays out here, with clear self-consciousness and social purpose, the metaphysics of republicanism, the form of government in which he thought personal freedom and idiosyncrasy would be maximized. But even here, in direct philosophical disquisition, he wanted his argument bracketed by pornographic authenticity, the reality of the senses substantiating abstract ideas. "Yet Another Effort" articulates the necessity for republicanism to extend the revolution to religion and manners, but, again not accidentally, it is presented in the middle of a dialogue pornographically attacking chastity, simple heterosexuality, and motherhood. It ends with the debauched "ingénue" professing hatred for her mother, assisting at her torture and sodomizing, and sewing up her mother's vagina, "so that you'll give me no more little brothers and sisters." This is the hyperbolic ethic of cruelty. Here again is Sade's demonic dialectic at work, not simply informing or persuading, but assaulting his audience with the self-consciously fluid juxtaposition of rhetorical and real arguments: "If not all of them please, surely a few will."

Sade knew how little his pornographic naturalism would please, and that was its utility, for he wanted to "convulse" society's "entire frame." Perhaps he was serving his own voluptuousness, but his larger purposes and his vision are astute, committed to a finally healthy evolution of morality and manners:

> In this age, when we are convinced that morals must be the basis of religion, and not religion of morals, we need a body of beliefs in keeping with our customs and habits, something that would be their necessary consequence, and that could, by lifting up the spirit, maintain it perpetually at the high level of this precious liberty, which today the spirit has made its unique idol.

Sade is speaking to the French Revolution, at once the greatest and most terrifying in history. He knew its terror first-hand. But he also knew its greatness, its humanistic spirit. He saw the revolution as one of the great cyclic events in the establishment of natural justice, the rhythmic recurrence of the "have nots" wrenching power and authority from the "haves." And, as with the sensual body, so with the body politic, the agency of convulsion is pain, the shock of recognition. Spirit, for Sade, was not a mystical infusion. It was the manifestation of the strongest of passions, the desire for personal liberty: thus his pornographic analogy between the body personal and the body politic. Religion, because it institutionalizes the idols of superstition and prejudice that paralyze man's mind and body, was Sade's primary enemy; he warns the revolution that if it does not solidify its work by abolishing religion,

> Before ten years are out—utilizing the Christian religion, its superstitions, its prejudices—your priests, their pledges notwithstanding and though despoiled of their riches, are sure to reassert their empire over the souls they shall have undermined and captured; they shall restore the monarchy, because the power of kings has always reinforced that of the church; and your republican edifice, its foundations eaten away, will collapse. . . .
>
> Be persuaded that . . . people, a good deal wiser than you suppose them, once rid of tyranny's irons, will soon also be rid of superstition's. You are afraid of the people unrestrained—how ridiculous! Ah, believe me, citizens, the man not to be checked by the material sword of justice will hardly be halted by the moral fear of hell's torments, at which he has laughed since childhood; in a word, many crimes have been committed as a consequence of your theism, but never has it prevented a single one.

The people unrestrained. Responsive to the rhythms of their bodies, the rhythms of nature, that is the positive dimension of Sade's political and moral ethos. It will not preclude the tragic, but it will maximize the pleasure and temporal happiness that are available. And he was wise enough to know the need, given human savagery, for education:

> Frenchmen, only strike the initial blows; your State education will then see to the rest. Get promptly to the task of training the youth, it must be among your most important concerns; *above all, build their education upon a sound ethical basis*, the ethical basis that was so neglected in your religious education. Rather than fatigue your children's young organs with deific stupidities, replace them with excellent social principles; instead of teaching them futile prayers which, by the time they are sixteen, they will glory in having forgotten, let them be instructed in their duties toward society; train them to cherish the virtues you scarcely ever mentioned in former times and which, without your religious fables, are sufficient for their individual happiness; make them sense that this happiness consists in rendering others as fortunate as we desire to be ourselves. If you repose these truths upon Christian chimeras, as you so foolishly used too, scarcely will your pupils have detected the absurd futility of its foundations than they will overthrow the entire edifice, and they will become bandits for the simple reason they

> believe the religion they have toppled forbids them to be bandits. On the other hand, if you make them sense the necessity of virtue, uniquely because their happiness depends upon it, egoism will turn them into honest people, and this law which dictates their behavior to men will always be the surest, the soundest of all.

Sade at his best, at his least bedeviled, knew the revolutionary need for construction. And he had, at his best, a humanistic faith in the human capacity to achieve at least so much happiness as is available. And he knew, for better or worse, that the body is inescapable. And he knew that a true ethos would have to account for its rhythms—its desire for pain and pleasure, its desire for liberty, its desire to feel its own vitality.

Nor, regardless of his rhetorical ethic of cruelty, did Sade contradict the principle of maximal freedom even when it came to enforcing the abolition of religion:

> I do not, however, propose either massacres or expulsions. Such dreadful things have no place in the enlightened mind. No, do not assassinate at all, do not expel at all; these are royal atrocities, or the brigands' who imitate kings; it is not at all by acting as they that you will force men to look with horror upon them who practiced those crimes. Let us reserve the employment of force for the idols; ridicule alone will suffice for those who serve them. Julian's sarcasm wrought greater damage to Christianity than all Nero's tortures.

Liberty, political and moral liberty, is Sade's theme, liberty rooted in a naturalistic ethic. Thus libertinage, a freely pornographic life style, is his symbol of the free life. It is, as he acknowledges, an exaggerated statement. But he knew to whom he was talking, and that they were few and perhaps some way off in time. He knew he was bound to be misunderstood, that his vision authentically presented would have to be incomprehensible to minds molded by the very sentimentality he refuted:

> Let no one say that by my writings I seek to blunt the remorse in evildoers' hearts, that my humane ethics are wicked because they augment those same evildoers' penchant for crime. I wish formally to certify here and now that I have none of these perverse intentions; I set forth the ideas that, since the age when I first began to reason, have identified themselves in me, and to whose expression and realization the infamous despotism of tyrants has been opposed for uncounted centuries. . . . I address myself only to people capable of hearing me out, and they will read me without any danger.

Sade knew that somewhere, sometime there was an audience capable of handling his extravagantly obscene manner. And he knew that this audience would be able to assimilate his vision and give it its proper relation to that progress of enlightenment to which he so feverishly wanted to contribute.

His philosophical, logical, and stylistic lapses result from his furious need, in prison, to write and exorcise the fantasies his sensual deprivation manufactured in his brain. They are nonetheless faults. His fury diminished his art, but it also made possible the writing out of his vision. Sade's faulty work exhibits the difficulty of articulating the myth of animality. No pornography before or since has had his significance or vitality, because no serious writer has worked so exclusively in the genre. Perhaps one needs to be as possessed as Sade was to do it, or as persecuted. If mad Ireland hurt Yeats into poetry, surely mad humanity hurt Sade into pornography. In spite of the infamy of his life, as Simone de Beauvoir suggests, Sade's Humbertian eroticism reached its truest dimension in literature. In life it was merely criminal. His vision fastened on the fundamental inconsistency in the morality of Western culture—that economic rape is legal while sexual rape is not. Sade simply raped the logic of that fact and forced the dialectic to its logical conclusion, one way or the other.

Sade's own mythic battle with the forces of civilization recalls the mythic battle between the Titans and the new Greek gods. The old gods, Prometheus for example, showed how to use the powers of nature, as Prometheus gave the gift of fire. The new gods, for example Apollo, the god of wisdom, introduced spiritual values. As the new subdued the old, spirituality prevailed over nature. Sade's writing is a parable of the old gods; in him the natural powers raise their heads again, and find their celebrant. In this parable, Sade saw that the new gods—and their analogue, the Judeo-Christian God—had gone berserk. In their zeal to bring man the benefits of the new message, they suppressed his ineluctable animal origins, the natural roots from which detachment is fatal. So, in the pornographic myth of animality, Sade reminded us of the inescapable facts of our nature. He reminded us that the old gods may be subdued but not destroyed. Sade's pornography tells us that the old gods live and that, however much they be forced underground, they have powerful sway still in the processes of human being.

# 6

# The Anarchy Connection

## REGENERATION AND ORGIASTIC BEING

In raising the spectre of the mythic battle between the old and the new gods, Sade invokes the concomitant spirit of moral anarchy—the humanistic equivalent of both natural and religious rhythms of death and resurrection. Moral anarchy means simply the denial of any univocal ethical authority, and it follows quite logically from a naturalistic ethos, especially as represented in the aesthetic of pornography for which Sade's argument is paradigmatic. Anarchy in this sense, then, is positive, depending not only on a sustained interrogation of moral assumptions but also on the capacity of the human mind to progressively reintegrate itself in the face of a continuously expanding knowledge of nature and the resulting moral ambiguity.

In this sense Sade saw the French Revolution as a naturally anarchical event at once destroying an anachronistic order and preparing for the birth of a new one. His arguments against religion and conventional morality in *Philosophy in the Bedroom* show his awareness that the Revolution in his time had left the French strung out between the monolithic morality represented by the Church, on the one hand, and the relativistic subjective ethos of naturalism, on the other. He was rightly afraid that this unresolved antagonism would vitiate the positive possibilities of moral anarchy by a mindlessly confused focus on revolutionary destruction. The murderous destructiveness of the Terror confirmed his fear. Consequently he urged, as we have seen, the Revolution to complete the cycle it had begun by recognizing the constructive anarchy implicit in a thoroughly naturalistic ethos.

Although Sade's own ideas on this are not sufficiently systematic or complete to make it clear, his choice of an obscene dialectic to illustrate the constructiveness of moral anarchy has religious and symbolic support. To see this, we can refer briefly to the sacred orgiastic traditions modern anthropologists have discovered to be endemic in both primitive and civilized societies. Sade's own use of the orgy, most elaborately sustained in his *One Hundred and Twenty Days of Sodom*, is of course vehemently profane. But his conception of the orgy derives, nevertheless, from the sacred communal sexuality of agricultural societies. And there is of course a tendency of the sacred orgiastic rituals to profane themselves as time and cultural evolution dissociate them from their religious origins. But, sacred or profane, the orgiastic tradition is rooted in the anarchic impulse to destroy the old to make way for the new.

The orgy seems to have originated as part of what Mircea Eliade calls, in *Patterns in Comparative Religion*, the "seasonal ritual drama" of fertility:

> Unbounded sexual frenzy on earth corresponds to the union of the divine couple. As young couples re-enact that sacred marriage on the ploughed fields, all the forces of the community are supposed to increase to their highest point. . . . Men cannot do better than imitate the example of the gods, particularly if the prosperity of the whole world and, above all, the course of animal and vegetable life, depends on their doing so. Their excesses fulfil a definite and useful role in the economy of the sacred. They break down the barriers between man, society, nature and the gods; they help force life and the seeds of things to move from one level to another, from one zone of reality to the rest. What was emptied of substance is replenished; what was shattered into fragments becomes one again; what was in isolation merges into the great womb of all things. The orgy sets flowing the sacred energy of life.

The orgiastic impulse, then, is clearly religious, symbolically serving to bring man, natural powers, and the cosmos into the harmony necessary for the preservation of life.

The orgy is at once agricultural and mythic, inducing not only productive and reproductive generation but also a unity of human spirit. On the human level the orgy is magic, a talismanic metaphysics, a symbolic synthesis of the myth of animality and the myth of love. In the orgy man is his own husbandman; he recognizes the natural analogy between himself and his crops, his flocks. He augments his animal state with spiritual hope and recognition of forces larger than himself, to which he is subject. And the orgy signifies that he knows these forces are simultaneously within him and without, psychic and cosmic. The orgy therefore serves to unify humanity with itself by synthesis with natural rhythms. Significantly, we see in the orgy a more comprehensive morality than our quotidian ethic permits; so, in honor of that higher morality, and to remind ourselves of ultimate responsibility to it, the orgy is the ritual drama through which we violate our petty ethic in order to harmonize with the cosmos. Eliade observes of the Holi Indian vegetation rites that "All decency was forgotten, for the matter was far more serious than mere respect for norms and customs; it was a question of ensuring that life should go on." The celebrants, men and children, paraded through the streets, and when they saw a woman, either on the street or through a window, "tradition required them to hurl the most appalling obscenities and insults." It is of course this verbal aspect of the orgiastic ritual drama that is of particular interest to the cultural meaning of pornography, and we shall come back to it.

Orgiastic regeneration also had a specifically social dimension. Eliade comments that not only is the orgy important to agricultural mystique but that it is also "a way of expressing the life of the community as a whole." He cites the orgiastic rationale of an Indian sect, that through the year men and women accumulated and harbored vicious impulses; the orgy satisfied these and so restored the equilibrium of community life. Thus, again, the quotidian ethic, usually reflected in civil laws, is violated with cultural sanction in order to harmonize with the higher natural law. In such situations, animality, by virtue of social acknowledgment, is harnessed to serve rather than bedevil the individual and society. Scholars of such divergent background as J. J. Meyer, a cultural anthropologist, and E. K. Chambers, a literary historian, have noted the pagan New Year saturnalias common in medieval European churches, which survive still in some places. Although the Church naturally tried to suppress these practices, they tended rather to be absorbed into Christian New Year celebrations, where they survive now in such muted forms as mummers and the like. But in their early orgiastic vitality these traditions were anarchical, reversing the usual order of things, overturning normative relations—both in sexual behavior, where debauch became the norm, and in administrative hierarchy, where custodians became priests and priests custodians, and so on—to the end of regenerating community life. Thus the cycles of community life were regarded as analogues to those of natural life.

Eliade sums up the intent of the sacred communal orgy thus:

> Like seeds that lose their shape in the great underground merging, disintegrating and becoming something different (germination), so men lose their individuality in the orgy, combining into a single living unity. They effect thus a total fusion of emotions in which neither "form" nor "law" is observed. . . . And further, by bringing back the mythical chaos that existed before the creation, the orgy makes it possible for creation to be repeated. For a time man goes back to the amorphous, nocturnal state of chaos that he may be reborn, more vigorous than ever in his daylight self. Like immersion in water, the orgy destroys creation while at the same time regenerating it; man hopes, by identifying himself with formless, pre-cosmic existence, to return to himself restored and regenerated, in a word, "a new man."

In the orgy, then, mankind merged with its mythic past, the processes of nature, and with its own natural impulses to transgress social restrictions and harmonize symbolically with a naturalistic ethos. The orgy was a sacred act, attempting, as Eliade says, to renew the sacred act of creation annually, to sustain a communal sense of the ubiquitous presence of sacred time and life.

The rhythm of the orgy, then, like that of moral anarchy, is the rhythm of death and regeneration, destroying creation while at the same time regenerating it. It signifies man's unity with nature. However, that unity requires the disordering of social authority, for society is constructed to protect man from nature and therefore stands between him and it. The orgy, in its various manifestations, did precisely this in dissolving the normal order of society. Slave and master, king and subject, whore and lady, priest and janitor, all hierarchical structures were toppled, reversed. Eliade, again, sums up the object of orgiastic anarchy:

> Licence is let loose, all commands are violated, all contraries are brought together, and all this is simply to effect the dissolution of the world—of which the community is a copy—and restore the primeval *illud tempus* which is obviously the mythical moment of the *beginning* (chaos) and the end (flood or *ekpyrosis*, apocalypse).

The orgy is not only consciously hypersexual, it is conscious disorder, the denial of any univocal ethical authority. The ultimate moral authority is natural energy, the symbolic representation of which is sexual license, both verbal and physical. The subordination of all things to that is thus represented in the orgy. But it is not simply a purge of disorder; it is, with each repetition, the beginning of a new order modeled on creation, which is to say closer to nature than the social order permits. Orgiastic chaos is a way of exorcising social decadence and revitalizing human cognizance of natural self, the cell around which can grow the body of a naturalistic ethos.

Keeping in mind the verbal role of obscenity in the sacred orgy, we may see pornography as a kind of profane descendant of the orgy. The orgy flourished in either "primitive" (that is, non-urban and non-industrial) or non-Christian cultures. As Western culture became urban and Christian, ritual fertility dramas dropped the sexual orgy and masked its anarchy in allegory. Inasmuch as cultural norms forbad acting out the ritual, it is reasonable to regard pornography as the symbolic acting out (in Kenneth Burke's sense) of the ritual orgy, and at its most artistically ambitious the searching after unity with nature.

In *Love's Body*, Norman O. Brown postulates an erotic symbolism that configures a new consciousness, of "an erotic sense of reality." This suggests how close the modern erotic imagination is in its concerns to those of the orgy. Brown reminds us of Freud's observation that "symbolism is on the track of a former identity, a lost unity." Brown goes on to say that, "It is the erotic sense of reality that discovers the inadequacy of fraternity, or brotherhood. . . . We must be either far more deeply unified, or not at all. The true form of unification . . . is: 'we are all members of one body.'" He notes, with Freud, that, "The tendency of the sexual instinct is to restore an earlier state of things, an earlier state of unity," and goes on to say that modern egoism, with its emphasis on individuation, has broken with "the Dionysian, or drunken, principle of union, or communion, between man and man and between man and nature. The integration of the psyche is the integration of the human race, and the integration of the work with which we are inseparably connected." Brown is here describing, though at a highly sublimated level, the principle of the sexual orgy. The level of sublimation tells us something of how removed the modern erotic imagination is from its orgiastic ancestors. Nevertheless, its basic concern, as represented in such theorists as Freud and Brown or in such pornographers as Sade or D. H. Lawrence or Jean Genet, is much the same—the regenerative possibilities of moral anarchy.

The regenerative conception of orgy is complicated somewhat by Georges Bataille's erotic theory in *Eroticism*, primarily because his perspective is existential rather than holistic. Where Freud and Brown postulate a lost unity and a restorative function for the sexual instinct, Bataille sees an ontological conundrum and an anguished dialectical function for eroticism. Human being is suspended between the "continuity" of nature—birth, prodigality and, especially, death—and the "discontinuity" of individual consciousness—social order, economy, and especially work. Discontinuous being is characterized by the rationality necessary to sustain body heat and is contradicted by the violence of nature's continuum. Birth wrenches each separate consciousness into being, just as death wrenches away its distinctness. Each distinct, and thereby discontinuous, existence thus begins and ends in violence and in the interim is obliged to mediate between nature's violence, necessary to generate the life cycle, and human rationality. But even as nature is violent so is it continuous, and death configures the agency of return from discontinuous to continuous being, for which human consciousness subliminally yearns. While the social response to this ontological tension is to make rationality pre-eminent in the work to maintain life, it also must accommodate violence, especially in its erotic forms, because it too has claim on life. To promote productive order, society imposes taboos to restrain sexual energy, which is always prodigal in nature and the extreme state of which is the orgy. But, since compression of sexual energy must have an equal and opposite reaction, society allows for this by instituting a matrix of *transgressions*.

The taboo in fact requires the transgression. As the exception proves the rule, so the violation confirms the efficacy of the taboo. On the other hand, transgression must be regulated. Where the frenzied Maenads of myth were supposed to devour their young, for example, in fact socially their rites were restricted to its ritual enactment by members of Dionysian cults; similarly with the Saturnalia and other festivals, where licentiousness was confined in time. "Elemental violence," Bataille says, "kindles every manifestation of eroticism. In essence, the domain of eroticism is the domain of violence, of violation." Thus the triad of eroticism, taboo, and transgression is the key to mediating the contradiction between the demands of social rationality and those of natural violence. With all three aspects of eroticism—physical, emotional, and religious—"the concern is to substitute for the individual isolated discontinuity a feeling of profound continuity." Since continuity implies death, and death is the final assertion of nature's violence on the individual consciousness, death and violence are integral to the erotic imagination. "What does physical eroticism signify if not a violation of the very being of its practitioners?—a violation bordering on death, bordering on murder?" says Bataille. "The whole business of eroticism is to destroy the self-contained character of the participators as they are in their normal lives."

So eroticism is more than its physicality; in its extreme orgiastic form, "It is a religious effusion first and foremost . . . the disorder of lost beings who oppose no further resistance to the frantic proliferation of life." Its religious character makes it atavistic, evoking the age of sacrificial rites, where "the female partner in eroticism was seen as the victim, the male as the sacrificer, both during the consummation losing themselves in the continuity established by the first destructive act." While eroticism is ultimately "the sexual activity of a conscious being," it functions at a subliminal level. And the deep well of its imagination overflows with death and violence, the primary signs of the ontological agon of human being.

The matrix of taboo and transgression therefore weaves eroticism together with death and violence. As taboo requires its own violation, and violation is the essence of eroticism, the erotic imagination necessarily associates sexuality with the ultimate violation, death. Hence transgression is the functional pivot, the required pique, of erotic activity in Bataille's theory. Eroticism transcends animal sexuality precisely because it carries the consciousness of transgression. Further, while the taboo represents the profane world of productive social order, the transgression represents the sacred world that temporarily up-ends order in orgiastic celebration of the divine violence of generation. Transgression is the imperative assertion of the sacred force behind the social order. Under its aegis humankind at once revels in and agonizes over the irreconcilable separateness of discontinuous and continuous being. The orgy, then, is the manifestation of the human awareness of its predicament, yearning for a continuity impossible to individual being, and its sexual frenzy is an attempt to burst the self-contained bounds of being and connect with the divine continuousness. Eroticism is not only an acting out of resistance to humanity's restricted order of ontology, its dependence on transgression means that it is also a flirtation with death. Indeed, for Bataille it is rather more a courtship; as he says, "The final sense of eroticism is death."

However, despite its awesome fascination, seldom do we follow eroticism to its ultimate sense: The rules of transgression forbid this. To go beyond the limits is to cancel awareness of the act of transgression, which is to revert from eroticism to non-conscious animal liberty. Transgression of sexual taboos is an "accord with animal nature," but it is not animal sexuality. It functions within the implicit awareness of the power of the thing transgressed, and it requires consciousness of itself. Hence, for practical purposes transgression is a figural phenomenon, simultaneously reminding human beings of its limits and their urge to exceed the limits. Obviously its particular preoccupation is excess, a symbolic evocation of nature's sexual prodigality as opposed to society's sexual economy. Its literary manifestation is hyperbole, and pornography abounds with transgression of taboos: incest, inter-racial sex, promiscuity, nymphomania. . . . In Bataille's context, the most telling of these categories is the debauched Catholic priest, who of course is at zenith in Sade's fictions. Sade's priests are not merely susceptible, errant religious leaders, like Hawthorne's Dimmesdale, they are malevolent inversions of the human and divine norms alike. They completely invert good and evil, and preach the justice of the inversion. Their religious facade, rather more ironic than anthropological in Sade's deployment, nonetheless underscores the dialectic of profane and sacred that Bataille describes. "Profanation," he says, "is the same as transgression": "Humanity implies the taboos, and in eroticism it and they are transgressed. Humanity is transgressed, profaned and besmirched. The greater the beauty, the more it is befouled." In pornography, the literature of eroticism, transgression with all its spoliation and profanity functions to invoke the natural religious violence of sexuality and at the same time, if not purge, at least appease its energy.

As in tragedy, however, the instigation of violence and transgression is primary. Certainly this is the case in Bataille's most famous novel, *Story of the Eye.* Although first published in 1928, nearly thirty years before his *Eroticism,* it clearly illustrates the theory of the later book. It is sometimes characterized as surrealist pornography, perhaps because like surrealism it cultivates an aesthetic response of stupefaction. But, while it may bridge surrealism and French existentialism, its assumptions are more distinctly existentialist than surrealist. It is not so much concerned with disorienting perception as it is with existentially validating the perception of humanity's horrifying erotic brinksmanship with violence and death. In *Eroticism* Bataille shows some impatience with those who think that sexual taboos are merely vestigial impediments (just as he thinks that apologists for Sade diminish the force of his ideas):

> I must . . . make plain the futility of the common contention that sexual taboos are nothing but prejudice and it is high time we were rid of them. The embarrassment and shame that go hand in hand with a strong feeling of pleasure are supposed to be simply proofs of stupidity. We might just as well say that we ought to make a clean sweep of the whole business and get back to animal habits of eating anything and ignoring filth and excrement: just as though our whole humanity did not spring from the reaction of horror followed by fascination linked with sensitiveness and intelligence.

Without taboo there is no transgression, and without transgression there is no consciousness of the horror endemic to erotic existence. If eroticism is subordinate to work as a human problem, it is nonetheless "the problem of problems. In that he is an erotic animal, man is a problem for himself. Eroticism is the problematic part of ourselves. . . . Of all problems, eroticism is the most mysterious, the most general, and the least straightforward." To dismiss a part of the problem is to exorcise rather than confront the labyrinth of existential reality. The truth itself is orgiastic, excessive, and does not accommodate our logics. It in fact obliges our logic to accommodate excess.

Accordingly, *Story of the Eye* is quintessentially orgiastic. It begins in the mindless genital urges of its adolescent protagonists and proceeds toward a truth at once horrifying and fascinating as their sexual energies take on the erotic consciousness of transgression in increasingly outrageous manifestations. The first-person narrator and his companion, Simone, are the young protagonists. Their erotic *bildungsroman* begins with a pun. Simone, eyeing a cat's milk saucer and, observing that "Milk is for the pussy," sits in the saucer, which incites the two of them to masturbate. Although they are sexually precocious, not to say obsessive, and there is a plethora of sexual activity, the two of them do not actually copulate until more than halfway through the novel. The narrator notes, in regard to their deferred coupling, that transgression supercedes physicality in eroticism; "We did not lack modesty—on the contrary—but something urgently drove us to defy modesty together as immodestly as possible." That is, they are not simply responding to genital impulse, they are exquisitely conscious of the modesty taboo and their violation of it. Just as sitting in a milk saucer is an unconventional form of seduction, so they systematically avoid conventions. When the narrator inadvertently makes a normal overture, Simone replies, "You're totally insane, little man . . . I'm not interested—here, in a bed like this, like a housewife and mother! I'll only do it with Marcelle!" Only orgiastic conditions will serve. In eroticism normal standards are reversed, and sanity means excess. They are at once contemporary and atavistic erotic beings for whom sex is a quirky, even deadly, ritual theater of transgression and disorder.

Their real pleasure comes from drawing others into the protagonists' gravitational field—to which of course the others are susceptible, being latent erotic beings themselves—and inducing them to violate themselves, i.e., transgress their social definition of self. Marcelle, their modest young friend, is their principal target, and their traduction of her takes up the first half of the novel. "The purest and most poignant" of their friends, Marcelle's disintegration is instructive in the matter of consciousness. Discovering the protagonists on the seashore in a bizarre embrace where the narrator is trying to pee into Simone, Marcelle is introduced to orgy by accident. Reduced to sobs befitting her purity by the scene, Marcelle is promptly stripped and assaulted by the pair. As it does consistently throughout the novel, nature punctuates sexuality, here providing a thunderstorm to whip the trio into "brutal frenzy" and "utter violence." The befouling of Marcelle's purity is underscored by the accommodating elements: "Simone had found a mud puddle, and was smearing herself wildly: She was jerking off with the earth and coming violently, whipped by the downpour, my head locked between her soil-covered legs, her face wallowing in the puddle, where she was brutally churning Marcelle's cunt . . . yanking the thigh, forcing it open." But being brutal and natural, as distinct from conscious, this action is too much animal sexuality to be eroticism, at least for Marcelle, whose modesty has been trampled only by force.

The protagonists manipulate Marcelle into another orgy with some other friends under the guise of a tea party. But champagne is served instead, and soon the group is lured into lewdness. Marcelle hangs back, but is dissuaded from leaving by the promise that no one will touch her. When Simone goes into a fit, begging one of the boys to "Piss on me. . . . Piss on my cunt," Marcelle is curiously suborned, asking to be stripped and closing herself in an antique wardrobe in order to masturbate in isolation. The orgy gathers force around her, cuts from broken glass adding blood to the sperm, urine, and vomit resulting from "a brutal onslaught on cunts and cocks." Meanwhile Marcelle masturbates, urinates (invariably sex is associated with urine or excrement), and sobs, until the bloodied narrator opens the wardrobe door on a scene of total debauchery and Marcelle goes over the edge into hysteria. Now, having participated by consent rather than force, Marcelle would seem to have entered eroticism. But in fact she has tried to "cheat" (as Bataille calls such behavior in *Eroticism*); by closeting herself she has attempted to evade modesty rather than defy it. Transgressing while at the same time suppressing awareness of the transgression, she has cancelled eroticism's restorative power and is left with only horror and shame. This is compounded by her isolation from her fellow beings, contradictory to the orgiastic principle; their Dionysiac communion has lifted them momentarily beyond discontinuous to continuous being, thus purging their violence (Simone, for example, lies "sleeping tranquilly . . . her hand still on her beaver, her pacified face almost smiling"), while Marcelle's aroused violence has risen to her head and disordered her brain, her discontinuous individuality even more pronounced than before. Eroticism is not to be entered into lightly. And, what's worse, it is the nature of the being to enter into it.

Marcelle is carried off to a sanitarium amid "a jeremiad of howls that grew more and more inhuman." The furor has of course attracted neighbors and parents, and the narrator flings open the door, he and Simone alone exulting in the delirium and chaos of resulting threats, shrieks and recriminations. They have indeed effected a nearly immaculate transgression—although that achievement is yet in the wings—and have defied modesty as immodestly as possible. Nor are they yet through with Marcelle. She has become their erotic imperative, and they arrange her escape from the sanitarium. Marcelle herself has made peace with violence by taking permanent leave from objective reality, insanity presumably offering a fortress to her purity. But purity itself, as noted in the wardrobe scene, is a cheat, and eroticism is essentially subjective, so insanity is mere temporizing with the ineluctable ontological problem. Sure enough, when she is returned to the room with the wardrobe a surge of deranged associations overload her circuits, and she destroys herself by hanging. Hers is the "normal" person's failure to come to terms with the dialectical function of eroticism. Naturally unable to avoid eroticism, neither is she able to let it negotiate the paradoxical coincidence of sacred and profane (i.e., continuous and discontinuous, violent and rational, natural and social) being. Thus she becomes the latter-day analogue, in her unmediated horror and shame, of the victim of orgiastic rites, as opposed to their participants.

So what are normal folks to do? That, perhaps disconcertingly, is not Bataille's address to the problem. His approach is to this ultimate dilemma of being, which obviously compounds daily ethical concerns. Such facile answers as eliminating taboos, on the one hand, or making them totally comprehensive, on the other, are chimerical because they fail to account for the nature of eroticism as central to problematic human existence. Bataille is rather more concerned to articulate the authenticity of the problem. *Eroticism* is his anthropological and philosophical exposition of it; *Story of the Eye* is his artistic and hyperbolic projection of it. Marcelle's failure registers one response, and the protagonists' exaltation registers another. Both are extreme to the point of being allegorical representations of Bataille's analysis in *Eroticism*. The narrator and Simone prevail in the same sense that eroticism prevails. But if they are exaggerations, their extravagance provides perspective on the dynamics of eroticism and being. Transgression being pivotal, they probe its furthest reaches.

Projecting his inverted values onto the cosmos, the narrator says,

> To others, the universe seems decent because decent people have gelded eyes. That is why they fear lewdness. They are never frightened by the crowing of a rooster or when strolling under a starry heaven. In general, people savor the "pleasures of the flesh" only on condition that they be insipid.
>
> But as of then, no doubt existed for me. I did not care for what is known as "pleasures of the flesh" because they really are insipid; I cared only for what is classified as "dirty." On the other hand, I was not even satisfied with the usual debauchery, because the only thing it dirties is debauchery itself, while, in some way or other, anything sublime and perfectly pure is left intact by it. My kind of debauchery soils not only my body and my thoughts, but also anything I may conceive in its course, that is to say, the vast starry universe, which merely serves as a backdrop.

Since one cannot survive the acme of eroticism, which would burst the bounds of being, the narrator here smacks of metaphysical bravado. But one *can* piss on conventional bounds, a bravado closer to the bone.

The narrator's desire to defile the universe, in the spirit of Lautréamont's *Maldoror*, and illustrative of Bataille's theory of transgression as at once celebrating and befouling nature by way of purging its violent claims, is made more humanistically threatening by his and Simone's response to Marcelle's death. It inspires their first actual intercourse, as if her corpse were the altar of their erotic consummation. As Simone is still a virgin—itself an irony of consequence, given their concupiscent excesses—their sex is painful, which energizes their pleasure. Further, Simone desecrates the continuity to which Marcelle has sacrificed herself by urinating on her face, the eyes still open. Finally, the narrator explicates the existentially absurd state of things. Marcelle, having entered death's continuity, has in fact emphasized the discontinuity of human existence, reminding the protagonists all the more of their individual "isolation." They are, as the narrator says elsewhere, "beyond hope and despair," left disinterestedly in a disinterested existence, "very remote from anything we touched, in a world where gestures have no carrying power, like voices in a space that is absolutely soundless." Remote indeed, as remote as erotic possession is from a common standard.

So paradoxical is eroticism, however, that the fact that you can't get there from here, to continuous from discontinuous being, and survive serves only to spur their orgiastic indulgence in greater transgressions. Their culminating rite is the sacrilegious debauch and strangulation of a priest in his sacristy. In Marcelle's case purity victimizes itself; in the priest's case the church is sacrificed to the obscene, and the irony is that religion is obtuse to the erotic nature of the religious. The priest, for example, mistakenly thinks that his submission to Simone's ministrations makes her and her cohorts furious at his hypocrisy, which of course totally trivializes the issue. What is at issue is his passivity in the face of eroticism. One of two courses would save him: a resounding enforcement of the sexual taboo, or embrace of its transgression. While his erection indicates he has energy enough, his trivializing perception indicates he does not have understanding enough. Proving irrelevant to religious ecstasy, the church is sacrificed to orgiastic frenzy. In the process the host and wine are desecrated and rededicated, from body and blood to sperm and urine. The priest is strangled in such a way that he is forced to ejaculate into Simone at his death. And then his eye is plucked out, rolled about the bodies of the madly coupling protagonists, and is at last stuffed into Simone's vagina as she succumbs to a final "urinary spasm," and thus the immaculate transgression is effected.

Throughout the novel an elaborate symbolism is developed connecting sex and urine, eggs and turds, eggs and eyes. Bataille himself provides a kind of explication of the symbolism in an addendum to the novel called "Coincidences." But the meaning of the symbols is probably less significant than the fact that Bataille offers autobiographical data for their origins. After explaining how one incident from his youth worked itself into what he calls "this partly imaginary tale," he says, "I was very astonished at having unknowingly substituted a perfectly obscene image for a vision apparently devoid of any sexual implication." In general this seems to have been the pattern, that sexually neutral experiences became narratively transformed "as soon as I gave myself over to lewd dreams." He says that such associations reside in a psychic well where, especially, obscene images coincide, "i.e., the most scandalous, precisely those on which the conscious floats indefinitely, unable to endure them without an explosion or aberration." That is, a more or less normal associational mechanism can produce aberrant collages when put to the service of lewd dreams as in the *Story of the Eye*. In terms of the erotic theory his tale illustrates, his exposure of the process suggests that apparently aberrant associations are in fact the norm.

Bataille offers himself as the evidence that rational experience is transformed into violence under the aegis of eroticism, which is always with us whether or not we are conscious of this process. In other words, while rationality may prescribe the social standard, erotic aberrance is an existential fact of life from the standpoint of the psyche. In making this premise persuasive in both erotic theory and pornographic practice, Bataille's influence has been profound. His theory provided both anthropological and ontological bases for the function of orgiastic inversion. His practice has established that pornography itself is an extension of atavistic orgiastic consciousness, and that its objectionable transgressions are the very justification of its being. If his example has been important to existential writers, it has been even more so to subsequent writers in that tradition—most notably Pauline Réage, William Burroughs, and Jean Genet—who have specifically evoked obscene and pornographic anarchy as regenerative and dialectical possibilities.

## WHERE STRAIGHT AND GAY CONVERGE

Pornographic anarchy reaches its most comprehensive and sustained development in Bataille and Genet. But it is used to greater or lesser degree by many of the most significant modern and contemporary writers. It proliferates, for better or worse, in the hundreds of minor writers. D. H. Lawrence, of course, was one of the first not only to use it, but to attempt constructing a social and moral dialectic from it. It is at its most pornographic, that is, its most sexually exclusive, in *Lady Chatterley's Lover*. There he articulates sexual anarchy, the refutation of what is humanly divisive. Of Mellors, Lady Chatterley's lover, Lawrence says:

> And he realized as he went in to her that this was the thing he had to do, to come into tender touch, without losing his pride or his dignity or his integrity as a man. After all, if she had money and means, and he had none, he should be too proud and honorable to hold back his tenderness from her on that account. "I stand for the touch of bodily awareness between human beings," he said to himself, "and the touch of tenderness. And she is my mate. And it is a battle against the money, and the machine, and the insentient ideal monkeyishness of the world."

Lawrence and Genet are antithetical on many grounds, but on the necessity and moral viability of sexuality they are one. It is there, in the spiritual orgy, that the straight and queer worlds can recognize a common humanity. Lawrence, like Genet, celebrates the regeneration of orgy:

> In the short summer night she learnt so much. She would have thought a woman would have died of shame. Instead of which, the shame died. Shame, which is fear: the deep organic shame, the old, old physical fear which crouches in the bodily roots of us, and can only be chased away by the sensual fire, at last it was roused up and routed by the phallic hunt of the man, and she came to the very heart of the jungle of herself. She felt, now, she had come to the real bedrock of her nature, and was essentially shameless. She was her sensual self, naked and unashamed. She felt a triumph, almost a vainglory. So! That was how it was! That was life! That was how oneself really was! There was nothing left to disguise or be ashamed of. She shared her ultimate nakedness with a man, another being.

Lawrence develops these themes more subtly and comprehensively in other novels, *The Rainbow* and *Women in Love*, for instance, and they are his major themes. But *Lady Chatterley's Lover* was specifically intended as a work of confrontation, a disruption, a declaration of orgiastic anarchy. It was a work to clear the air, so that the works of his more comprehensive vision, and the works of others as well, might breathe the better.

Genet is the quintessential anarchist, more "dangerous" than Sade because less mad, more dangerous because, unlike the self-destructive Sade, he is existentially, homicidally free from his own indomitable ego, more dangerous therefore because he is free to see into the cauldron of social and private self, to sing, celebrating its obscene reality. In *The Thief's Journal*, commenting on a beggarly sojourn in Andalusia, he says:

> I dared not even notice the beauty of that part of the world—unless it were to look for the secret of that beauty, the imposture behind it, of which one will be a victim if he trusts it. By rejecting it, I discovered poetry.

The very basis of Genet's aesthetic is anarchic, rejecting beauty as imposture, dangerous to him who becomes its victim. Which is to say that to respond to beauty is to respond to idealism, and to make idealism your metaphysic is to make believe—make believe that reality is the good, the true, and the beautiful. Genet counters. Plumb the depths of your desires, storm the heavens, and steal the fires. Like Sade, Genet has been made a criminal—bastard, thief, murderer, homosexual—and, like Edmund, he cries, "Now gods, stand up for bastards." What gods will do so? The shadow knows; speaking directly to us, the solid citizens, Genet says:

> It seemed to me to be definitely settled that I was to dwell in shame, . . . I

> made up my mind to live with my head bowed and to pursue my destiny toward darkness, in an opposite direction to yours, and to exploit the underside of your beauty.

What gods? The dark gods living on the underside of beauty. And, ironically, Genet's destiny has been well served by his commitment to the obscene, to the underarm of idealistic reality. For the genius of his vision he was pardoned and his life sentence commuted. He tells us in *The Thief's Journal* that "I am writing this book in an elegant hotel in one of the most fashionable cities in the world, where I am rich. . . ." Not only is he rich, he regrets not being able to flaunt his riches before the poor with "more ostentation and insolence." Here of course he surpasses Sade again in anarchical example. Not only does crime pay, but one need not even be humble or repentant about it. And what more convincing proof of the truth of Genet's vision than that we will handsomely subsidize his trip to the nether world. We want a report that badly. Being the archetypal con-man, Genet must have known all along—even hopelessly imprisoned, writing *Our Lady of the Flowers* on the paper sheets he was to make bags of—through all that he must have known how hungry we were for what he knew. And knowing that, his faith in his destiny must have been reinforced. So, too, his faith in the obscene backside of beauty. Like Moses, Genet saw God's hinder parts and lived profitably to tell the tale. Genet, unlike Sade or Al Capone, who were too hysterically anarchists, is the living proof of the social viability of moral anarchy.

Moral inversion and orgy are the *sine qua non* of Genet's dialectic. *Our Lady of the Flowers* begins with a catalogue of public enemies, three murderers and a traitor; the list is punctuated by Genet's dedication: "And it is in honor of their crimes that I am writing my book." Murder bespeaks, he says, their secret and future glory. The criminal, in Genet, is sanctified, the more so as his crime is more debased, degrading, and profitless. For then his life articulates the "motiveless malignancy" of humanity and he becomes an example of man's dark reality, an upside-down saint.

*The Thief's Journal* begins:

> Convicts' garb is striped pink and white. Though it was at my heart's bidding that I chose the universe wherein I delight, I at least have the power of finding therein the many meanings I wish to find: *there is a close relationship between flowers and convicts.* The fragility and delicacy of the former are of the same nature as the brutal insensitivity of the latter. Should I have to portray a convict—or a criminal—I shall so bedeck him with flowers that, as he disappears beneath them, he will himself become a flower, a gigantic and new one.

*Fleurs de mal:* A single unity, humanity, devised and represented from the antipodes of fragility and brutality, delicacy and insensitivity. Genet's passion to synthesize moral antitheses, to reveal "the man in the god," is at one with the orgiastic passion. Like Freud or Bataille or Brown or the pagan naturalisms before them, Genet sees the fusion of man and god, man and nature, man and man in erotic reality; and his linking criminality with sexuality brilliantly illuminates a dehumanizing cultural association inherited from sentimental idealism:

> Men doomed to evil possess the manly virtues. Of their own volition, or owing to an accident which has been chosen for them, they plunge lucidly and without complaining into a reproachful, ignominious element, like that into which love, if it is profound, hurls human beings. Erotic play discloses a nameless world which is revealed by the nocturnal language of lovers. Such language is not written down. It is whispered into the ear at night in a hoarse voice. At dawn it is forgotten. Repudiating the virtues of your world, criminals hopelessly agree to organize a forbidden universe. They agree to live in it. The air there is nauseating: They can breathe it. But—criminals are remote from you—as in love, they turn away and turn me away from the world and its laws. Theirs smells of sweat, sperm, and blood. In short, to my body and my thirsty soul it offers devotion.

Love, as the Greeks knew from Medea, Clytemnestra, Antigone, can make men outlaws. Sex, the sign of love, can also, as Christ and Augustine and Sade knew. This mythic dichotomy between man's private and public order, rooted in anarchical antithesis, is the heart of Genet's vision. Genet, outlawed by his terrible loves—love of men, criminals, evil, obscenity—says of *The Thief's Journal* that it is "a song of love," that his life was preparation for "erotic adventures," and that of what he has to tell "only this book of love will be real." Love and sexuality, then, the love of evil and homosexuality, are Genet's reality. *The Thief's Journal* (does the title recall Christ's fellows in crucifixion?) is Genet's anarchical Bible. He brings a new testament of love and squalor, refuting the singular authority of beauty with a vision of its underside. Evil, he says, be thou my good. And he seeks, from us, the consecration of his perverse law, the old testament: "my book, which has become my genesis, contains—should contain—the commandments which I cannot transgress."

What better vehicle for this mission of moral anarchy than orgiastic celebration. He turns the moral universe on its ear to show *all* of what is there. If he can persuade us of a sanctity in the underworld, persuade us that a man may reject all our prejudices, live in a world we consign to madness, embrace what we find repulsive, if he can do all this and still persuade us that he is in touch with reality, then we must acknowledge more dimensions of reality than we suspected. This is precisely what he attempts in *Our Lady of the Flowers*. It is the inspired word, inspired by his vision of public enemies transformed to saints by the creative energy, the orgiastic regeneration, achieved in his nightly prison-cell masturbation fantasies. The criminals whose crimes his book honors—Weidmann, Angel Sun, Pilorge—are made over into the saints of Genet's black liturgy. They are given appropriately allegorical names: Divine, Our Lady of the Flowers. Naturally the protagonists are men in moral drag, emphasizing the moral inversion of Genet's dialectic. Nightly Genet masturbates. He mimes the creation. From the mud of earth ("Made of mud and mist," he says in *The Thief's Journal*, "Stilitano was indeed a divinity to whom I could sacrifice myself"), he creates his perverse universe:

> At night I love them, and my love endows them with life. During the day I go about my petty concerns. I am the housekeeper, watchful lest a bread crumb or a speck of ash fall on the floor. But at night! Fear of the guard who may suddenly flick on the light and stick his head through the grating compels me to take sordid precautions lest the rustling of the sheets draw attention to my pleasure; but though my gesture may be less noble, by becoming secret it heightens my pleasure. I dawdle. Beneath the sheet, my right hand stops to caress the absent face, and then the whole body, of the outlaw I have chosen for that evening's delight. The left hand closes, then arranges its fingers in the form of a hollow organ which tries to resist, then offers itself, opens up, and a vigorous body, a wardrobe, emerges from the wall, advances, and falls upon me, crushes me against my straw mattress, which has already been stained by more than a hundred prisoners, while I think of the happiness into which I sink at a time when God and His angels exist.

And having made his world of mud and mist, Genet saw that it was good: "It was a good thing that I raised egoistic masturbation to the dignity of a cult!" The isolation of his cell is repeated in the egoistic isolation of masturbation. He creates the world that society had made available to him—night after night. Being a criminal, having his being in crime, having no other being than crime, he naturally generates a criminal world. He creates the world of sweat, sperm, and blood, and in the creation, a creation drawn from his descent into that underworld, he testifies to its reality. And not only to its reality, but, in the anarchy of his vision, he argues for its sublimity. "I wanted," he says in *The Thief's Journal*, "to affirm it in its exact sordidness, and the most sordid signs became for me signs of grandeur." In that solitary world, sordid and obscene, he finds love. Through the orgy of masturbation he regenerates his life; through it he makes communion with man, with nature, with cosmic spirit. He affirms it with the life material at his disposal, affirms it deliberately with the materials the normal world negates. And in so doing he existentially refutes the univocal authority of normality. And, he reminds us, marvelling that we take such trouble to keep him in his cell ("My good, my gentle friend, my cell! My sweet retreat, mine alone, I love you so!"), we are his accomplices, for he, a prisoner in prison, is subsidized in the maintenance of his world by society. We help him cultivate the anarchy of his antipathetic reality. He knows what we want. He does his part.

He shares with us his orgiastic vision, complete with real sexuality, figural sexuality, ritual sexuality. And, like the archetypal orgy, sexuality is magic; Genet's sperm and pornographic fantasy fertilize his otherwise barren world. Through them he comes to love his cell, the prison, his isolation, and above all the criminality that is their catalyst. As in the orgy, in Genet's onanistic vision all things are inverted. Having been born and grown up a criminal, first a bastard, then a thief, he recreates the furtive sexuality he has known—masturbation and homosexuality. Nor, if such chroniclers as Stephen Spender are to be believed, is the juvenile penal colony appreciably different in this respect from the British public school and its counterparts elsewhere. But real sexuality is not sufficient, and he needs to expand it, interpret it in the context of natural and social forces. Again, his world, expanded now to include more unequivocally our own, provides the model. The common denominator of imprisoning and warring societies is power. Orgiastic power is the power of growth and procreation; but war and imprisonment are barren, and this is total anarchy after all, the underside of normality. Thus the barrenness of homosex and masturbation are raised to a figural level, articulating the ironic barrenness, criminality, and violence of the larger frame of reality:

> Darling is a giant whose curved feet cover half the globe as he stands with his legs apart in baggy, sky-blue silk underpants. He rams it in. So hard and calmly that anuses and vaginas slip onto his member like rings on a finger. He rams it in. So hard and calmly that his virility, observed by the heavens, has the penetrating force of the battalions of blond warriors who on June 14, 1940, buggered us soberly and seriously, though their eyes were elsewhere as they marched in the dust and sun. But they are the image of only the tensed, buttressed Darling. Their granite prevents them from being slithering pimps.

Police, both as sexual and official objects, naturally fascinate the thief: "Criminals and the police are the most virile emanation of this world. You cast a veil over them. They are your shameful parts, which, however, I call, as you do, noble parts." But the Germans of *der Führer* (Genet's characters, conversely, pray to "Our Mother who art in Heaven"), like their latter-day counterparts in Russia and America, certified on the transfigural scale the nobility of crime; they ripped off the veil we try now with decadent discretion to replace:

> It was no longer a social institution but a sacred power, acting directly upon my soul and troubling me. Only the German police, in Hitler's time, succeeded in being both Police and Crime. This masterly synthesis of oppo-

> sites, this block of truth, was frightful, charged with a magnetism that will continue to perturb us for a long, long time.

The inversion, thus, of heaven and hell, or rather its synthesis. Our history feeds with such blocks of truth the orgiastic anarchy of Genet's morality. In full pornographic truth, the lion and the lamb lie together. Finally, then, the orgy becomes ritual, a celebration of the obscenely sacred anarchy of sexual energy:

> I close my eyes. Divine and Darling . . . Darling's penis is in itself all of Darling: the object of her pure luxury, an object of pure luxury. If Divine is willing to see in her man anything other than a hot, purplish member, it is because she can follow its stiffness, which extends to the anus, and can sense that it goes farther into his body, that it is this very body of Darling erect and terminating in a pale, tired face. . . .
>
> I close my eyes beneath the lice-infested blankets. Divine has opened the fly and arranged this mysterious area of her man. Has beribboned the bush and penis, stuck flowers into the buttonholes of the fly. . . . The result is that to Divine, Darling is only the magnificent delegation on earth, the physical expression, in short, the symbol of a being (perhaps God), of an idea that remains in heaven.

Genet closes his eyes. He masturbates. He conjures. He invokes his dark reality. Denied, reviled, and hid away, he creates a "beautiful" life out of obscenity. He worships, and his worship unveils the aesthetic potential of shame. A life reduced to shame finds there the stuff not only of survival but of affirmation. And the transfiguration of our shame is the anarchic refutation of our idealistic nobility.

For Genet all things are charged with the eroticism and inversion of orgy. He tells us, in *The Thief's Journal,* that the "pursuit of traitors and treason was only one of the forms of eroticism." Likewise his pursuit of theft, murder, fraud, crime of any sort. Crime destroys the illusion of purity and righteousness, and prepares him for acceptance of himself in all his shame. With the strength of that acceptance he is empowered to construct an ethos. That ethos is at once antisocial and authentic. Its very existential authenticity calls in question the wisdom of the normal ethos that expends its energy denying the natural authenticity and even, witness the murderous virtuousness of democracy in Asia, the efficaciousness of evil. To enforce our consciousness of that paradox Genet turns crime into a sacrament—his books, remember, should contain "the commandments which I cannot transgress." He builds an ethos on those commandments of evil:

> The theft I had committed became in my eyes a very hard, very pure, almost luminous act, which only the diamond can symbolize. I had, in achieving it,

> destroyed once again—and I thought to myself once and for all—the dear bonds of brotherhood.
>
> "After that, after this crime, what kind of moral perfection can I hope for?"
>
> As the theft was indestructible, I decided to make it the origin of a state of moral perfection.
>
> "It's cowardly, weak, dirty, low . . . (I shall define it only with words expressing shame). None of the elements composing it leaves me a chance to magnify it. Yet I do not deny this most monstrous of my sons. I want to fill the world with its loathsome progeny."

This ethos becomes the basis for sanctification of Divine and Our Lady. To fill the world with such progeny is to fill the world with the consciousness of evil's vitality, and with the consciousness that, although evil may be repented, it cannot be undone. An evil act, like any other, is discrete, eternal. There is here of course the refutation of Christian grace, a concept, latterly distorted by sentimentalism, whereby evil is exorcised, the consequence of which is that its vitality is denied.

But Genet knows, as many of the Christian fathers knew, that evil is vital, that it exists simultaneously with good, and that it is an indelible fact of human life. Any true ethos, then, must acknowledge and genuinely cope with its reality. Our Lady's orgiastic sanctification comes about when he strangles an old man, a friend, to commit theft. After doing so, he cannot find the money and, as he is about to leave, he accidentally knocks over a vase, "The vase falls down and twenty thousand francs scatter graciously at his feet." God's grace indeed works in strange ways. Genet's life and dialectic tell us that crime pays. Evil has vitality. After the murder, itself an orgiastic creation of Genet's onanistic dream, "the murderer's hand seeks his penis, which is erect. He strokes it through the sheet, gently at first, with the lightness of a fluttering bird, then grips it, squeezes it hard; finally he discharges into the toothless mouth of the strangled old man." Then he falls asleep. To dream, of course, is to regenerate: the destruction of the old to regenerate the new.

Divine's sanctification is still more perverse. He unscrews a railing so that a child will fall to its death. After watching the fall, he gently scoops together the mangled remains, respectful of the means of his beatitude. "Divine's goodness was dead. For: 'What good would it do me to be a thousand times good now? How could this inexpiable crime ever be redeemed?'" The irretrievable act is irretrievable. The straight world, the world of sentimental comedy, denies humanistic value by making its violation redeemable, and thus its morality denies its ethics. The queer world knows better. What is done is never undone by metaphysical magic. Thus Genet's plot refutes the authority of a deceptively casuistic ethos. Evil has vitality. He articulates our moral absurdity with the image of orgy working out in human life. And we are reminded that his perverse fantasies have their origin in real life, the lives of his honored public enemies.

And he knows that we need and want such reminders of our own dark reality. Our Lady's murder trail is reminiscent of that in Camus' *The Stranger*. Our Lady's defense advocate, representing the sentimental ethic of redemption, pleads for rehabilitation. He invokes poverty, hardship, Our Lady's youth. But Our Lady has more mythic sensibility than that: "Ah no, not the Corrida, it ain't worth it. I'd rather croak right away." And when Our Lady is asked what he has to say in his own defense, this is the scene Genet describes:

> The old tramp who was his cellmate . . . had prepared a few suitable words for him to say to the Court. He looked for them but was unable to find them. The phrase "I didn't do it on purpose" took shape on his lips. . . . Nobody would have been surprised. Everyone expected the worse. . . . He had to be natural. To be natural, at that moment, was to be theatrical, but his maladroitness saved him from ridicule and lopped off his head. He was truly great. He said:
>
> "The old guy was washed up. He couldn't even get a hard-on."

Luckily, for Our Lady's beatitude if not his survival, the jury too recognizes his mythic meaning. "The Court felt that it had to sanctify this young man." The defense attorney and the judge, committed to their sentimental justice, nevertheless cannot prevent Our Lady's sainthood. The jurymen, his peers, know that they live in him, that they must honor his evil as their own, that they must canonize it by executing him. Unlike the official guardians of sentimentality, they can perceive the necessary truth of moral anarchy.

At the end of *Our Lady of the Flowers* Genet tells us that the hearing for his pardon looms on the morrow. He considers the meaning of freedom.

> Free, in other words, exiled among the living, I have made myself a soul to fit my dwelling. My cell is so sweet. Free: to drink wine, to smoke, to see ordinary people. And tomorrow, what will the jury be like? I have anticipated the stiffest possible sentence it can inflict. I have prepared myself for it with great care, for I have chosen my horoscope (according to what I can read of it from past events) as a figure of fatality. Now that I can obey it, my grief is less great. It is annihilated in the face of the irremediable. It is my hopelessness, and what will be, will be. I have given up my desires. I too am "already far beyond that" (Weidmann). Let me therefore live between these walls for a man's lifetime. Who will be judged tomorrow? Some stranger bearing a

> name that was once my name. I can continue to die, until my death, amidst all these widowers. Lamp, washbasin, regulations, broom. And the straw mattress, my spouse.

He affirms here the reality he has pictured for us; he asserts its irremedial authenticity. The judgment of society is too late to free him. It is irrelevant to his being. To free him is to rather postulate another being. Genet is after all Our Lady, and like him/her he knows his mythic utility to mankind. And he knows that his life metaphors, hyperbolically but nonetheless authentically, our own. Life consists in each man being exiled to himself. Throughout Genet's work is the emphasis on solitude and isolation, the inviolability and persistence of the imagination to formulate its own reality. Prison figures the human condition. To be free is merely to exchange one mode of exile for another. To be released from his cell is simply to have access to different materials for his construction of reality. Criminal or citizen, the pattern is the same. Faced with the possibility of a new life, he continues to affirm the values of the old life. He will not renounce that truth. To do so would be to deny the authenticity of the underworld, to deny his own being, to forfeit the mythic significance that he knows perfectly well he has. And, as it turns out, we know it as well. After all, we honor it. Sartre calls him "Saint Genet," not because he embraces a new faith but because, faced with burning at the stake of liberty, he still insists on the truth of his awful vision. That, precisely, is his mission.

Genet's homosexual obscenity, then, seeks to inform us of man's spiritual determination to be at one with himself and his environment, whatever its degradation or hopelessness. The spirit of orgy he sees in man is in fact spiritual. Isolated, man must love himself. And, as the act of love is on the arm, he masturbates. If a man has only the company of other men, he must love them—homosexually. How he manifests his need and determination to love is of petty consequence. Genet's books—all of them thief's journals—are books of love, and they document the insistence of man to tear down what stands between him and it. Heterosexuality is an accident of time, place, opportunity. Its normality cannot and will not stand between man and love. Genet tears down its monolithic imperatives to regenerate himself, to make life possible in his peculiar circumstances. In so doing he discovers a reality he had not hoped for. He finds life in the environs of death. With wonder he tells us that, depraved, shameful, and evil as he and his fellow criminals may be, they are alive. And the very vitality of their being testifies to the authentic moral reality of their mode of life.

The moral object of modern literature is the same as that of the whole history of literature, to represent reality according to the philosophical possibilities of its representation at a given time in history. It is no accident that pornography began to appear in significant quantity at about the time that materialistic philosophy was developing, in the eighteenth century. But formal aesthetics tends to lag behind both philosophical speculation and poetic practice. At roughly the same time that neoclassical aesthetics was declaring that "the first Almighty Cause/Acts not by partial but by general laws," John Cleland was writing *Fanny Hill* and Defoe had already written *Moll Flanders,* both of them books about aberrant life, that is, depicting "partial" laws in operation. And the philosophers too were referring man to nature rather than the "first Almighty Cause."

As the materialist possibilities of representing nature opened up, literature assimilated them. Pornography, being one of those possibilities, began to develop accordingly, began to take itself more seriously. What was fun for Casanova and profit for Cleland became philosophical necessity for Sade. In the development of materialism pornography became the logical genre for the extreme affirmation of the myth of animality. As materialism gained the authority necessary to challenge idealism, pornography became a phenomenological vehicle of refutation, howevermuch underground. In our time, finally, it has emerged and has become more distinctly a principal agent of moral confrontation.

The essential quality of all pornography, its orgiastic anarchy, began in serious or artistic pornography to take on moral significance. It became, to greater or lesser degree, a phenomenological statement of naturalism documenting the existence of animal energy as a positive rather than negative force. Like the orgy, it seeks now to reunite us with the mythic sacredness of creative energy most recognizable in our sexuality. This refutes the main line of Western philosophy, which, since Plato, has emphasized reason as an echo of divine harmony, and which has feared and suppressed the passions as disruptive. Pornography, being the literature of orgiastic sexuality, is particularly suited for the confrontation with idealism, especially in its latter-day deterioration into sentimentalism. For sentimentalism is an attempt to idealize the passions and thereby deny the natural and moral significance of their physicality, and often to deny their physicality altogether. By denying the passions to the point of ignoring their physical and moral viability, idealism has become morally vestigial. It recommends an ethos that is based on only half of human nature. The murderous chaos of contemporary world culture is evidence of how that ethos is failing us. Obscenity has become, therefore, the rhetoric of attack on this ethos. Its physicality is disruptive, disruptive of the serene ontological assumptions and moral categories that Bataille and Genet challenge. The insistent, loin-shaking beat of its physicality refutes the human authority of sentimental idealism. As that beat urges us to dance, we are forced, in our dancing, to acknowledge its viability.

# 7

# Comic Catharsis

## AMIABLE ANARCHY

Tragedy, in exploring cosmic myths, has the cultural function of defining the range of moral possibilities. However symbolically, anarchistic literature politicizes the moral imagination and informs it of the mythic rhythm of death and rebirth; its emphasis, as we have seen, is on the destruction of the old, from the ashes of which the new can be regenerated. Comedy represents the spirit of the new. Synthesizing the tragic and anarchic visions, it traditionally augments them with the celebratory confidence that, through regeneration, the golden age can be restored. As Northrop Frye points out in his essay, "The Argument of Comedy," tragedy and comedy grew out of the same ritual and each presents merely a different focus on the cycle of life and death, and each is therefore contained in the other: "For in the ritual the tragic story has a comic sequel. Divine men do not die: they die and rise again. The ritual pattern behind the catharsis of comedy is the resurrection that follows the death, the epiphany or manifestation of the risen hero." Tragedy, in this sense, is "uncompleted comedy," and comedy, being about life—whatever the extent of its affirmation—contains within itself the potential of tragedy.

Moral anarchy tells us that we must exert our own energy to effect the passing from destruction to a New Jerusalem. Hope being endemic to human nature, we tend to think of the comic as the higher vision. And perhaps philosophically it is. But in its artistic representation, especially for the modern imagination, comedy is most persuasive—which is perhaps to say instructive—when put in the morally realistic context of tragic potential. Thus, much of what is called "black humor" (and its attendant obscenity) derives from the recognition that the truest fiction requires fusion of the tragic and the comic. Wisdom consists in knowing that cosmically neither happiness, the condition of comedy, nor pathos, the condition of tragedy, is final. But man learns slowly, and, as the biblical lessons of the Flood and threat of the Fire Next Time attest, man seems best to learn of the good life through the pedagogy of destruction. To understand the connection between comedy and pornography, therefore, we do well to begin by considering this tension in the argument of comedy.

Satire, standing between comedy and tragedy, synthesizes the concerns of both, although its resolutions tend to be comic. Frye says that "Old" or Aristophanic comedy was essentially passé before Aristophanes died. Perhaps, but the satiric dimension of Aristophanes, the serio-comic spirit which frequently takes for its subject topical morality—such as, for example, the war with Sparta—has never died, and it has in modern comedy become something very like a paradigm. Whereas "New Comedy" developed into elaborate plotting of confused romantic situations which would eventually resolve themselves happily, as in *A Midsummer Night's Dream*, "Old Comedy" developed into such mythic critique and affirmation as *The Tempest*. There not only is the State righted, true love triumphant, moral generosity manifest, but nature and the elements are restored to proper order. *A Midsummer Night's Dream* may make us feel happy, but *The Tempest* gives us happiness with an ethical basis. Prospero provides us with a vision of moral possibility and a happiness with not only personal but social and even cosmic significance. Its comic affirmation develops out of potential tragedy: Prospero might very well have been the hero of a vengeance tragedy. The comedy, in fact, depends on Prospero's overcoming tragic passion. When he gives up power—magic—he surrenders to the human virtues of love and charity. In so doing, he restores man and nature to equilibrium. He provides, therefore, the comic moral model, the man who knows himself well enough to escape the destructiveness of passion and who knows the necessity of cosmic balance. Thus the most ethically instructive comedy is that which is morally naturalistic rather than fantastic or sentimental. It is that sort which advises us that happiness is accessible as a consequence of moral action based on moral knowledge. Ethical comedy presents humanity emerging positively, however bedraggled, from the necessary confrontation with tragic destructiveness.

Prospero, a moral anarchist, turns things on their ear in order to prepare for their ultimate righting. In this way *The Tempest* represents a kind of paradigmatic structure for ethical comedy. The force of its comic affirmation comes from its potential tragedy. But the tragedy is modified to anarchy and prepares its world for a moral regeneration, the resolution of which is comic. Anarchy, then, is central. It tells us that, if anyone does, we have the power to make, at least proximately, our own happiness. Such a premise is, in the sense that we have been discussing it, naturalistic. Naturalism is of course at the heart of pornographic comedy. The prodigious erect phalluses of Aristophanes' *Lysistrata* have been more recently unsheathed in an Off Off Broadway production of Ronald Tavel's *Indira Ghandi,* indicating how the history of comedy has been and continues to be not only naturalistic but pornographic. As in tragedy, the comic use of obscenity is to explore the potential of an existential ethos.

When, in the Preface to his *Memoirs,* Casanova says, "Man is free; yet we must not suppose that he is at liberty to do everything he pleases, for he becomes a slave the moment he allows his actions to be ruled by passion," he underscores the essential theme of ethical comedy. For comedy characteristically presents the myth of enslavement overcome. *A Funny Thing Happened on the Way to the Forum,* a modern musical pastiche from Plautus, exemplifies this fact, on a parodic level. The slave becomes master, although, as is often the case in this sort of comedy, when he gets too big for his britches he gets his comeuppance and order is restored. In more profound naturalistic treatments of the theme, such as Joyce's *Ulysses* or Lawrence's *The Rainbow,* man works through his "enslavement" to the passions to reach a knowledge and love of himself and thus achieve, or at least approach, moral freedom. Casanova's *Memoirs* are a kind of comic biographical novel, a comedy of manners; largely erotic manners, for much of their interest centers on Casanova's extensive sex life (love life, if you prefer, although it is sexually explicit even in the decorousness of its style). From the comfort of his well-provided "retirement," he says of his adventures that:

> They are the follies inherent to youth; I make sport of them, and, if you are kind, you will not yourself refuse them a good-natured smile. You will be amused when you see that I have more than once deceived, without the slightest qualm of conscience, both knaves and fools. As to the deceit perpetrated upon women, let it pass, for, when love is in the way, men and women as a general rule dupe each other. But on the score of fools, it is a very different matter . . . for fools generally are insolent and so self-conceited that they challenge wit. We avenge intellect when we dupe a fool, and it is a victory not to be despised. . . .

Casanova invokes the virtues of eighteenth-century gentility, the dispassionate exercise of intelligence. In the "reasonable life" Casanova, like his century, saw human dignity and freedom from "enslavement." Be not too passionate in judgment; be not too passionate in love; do not suffer fools gladly. Accepting the world and its mores, indeed using them so brilliantly to his advantage, he is the comic answer to Sade.

Casanova is complacent in the face of life, recognizing his own responsibility for its conduct:

> As for myself, I always willingly acknowledge my own self as the principal cause of every good or evil which may befall me; therefore I have always found myself capable of being my own pupil, and ready to love my teacher.

He is, however, also naturalistic in his sense of fortune:

> I have often met with happiness after some imprudent step which ought to have brought ruin upon me, and . . . dire misfortune has befallen me in consequence of actions prompted by the most cautious wisdom.

He recognizes that accident and chance rather than moral deserts describe the pattern of human affairs. But such things do not sway him from his pragmatic poise or his orthodox Christian faith. He is at peace with the world, free from the obsessive "enslavement" of a Sade. He is a comic hero, picaresquely wandering through life's good fortune and vicissitudes with perfect tranquility. Nor, to maintain that posture, does he deny the "ugly" or the "obscene." He professes not only a liking for strong tasting and smelling food but also for body odors and the like; "I have always," he says, "found the odour of my beloved ones exceedingly pleasant":

> "What depraved tastes!" some people will exclaim. "Are you not ashamed to confess such inclinations without blushing?" Dear critics, you make me laugh heartily! Thanks to my coarse tastes, I believe myself happier than other men, because I am convinced that they enhance my enjoyment. Happy are those who know how to obtain pleasures without injury to anyone; insane are those who fancy that the Almighty can enjoy the sufferings, the pains, the fasts and abstinences which they offer to Him as a sacrifice, and that His love is granted only to those who tax themselves so foolishly. God can demand from His creatures only the practice of virtues the seed of which He has sown in their soul, and all He has given unto us has been intended for our happiness: self-love, thirst for praise, emulation, strength, courage, and a power of which nothing can deprive us—the power of self-destruction if, after due calculation, whether false or just, we unfortunately reckon death to be advantageous. This is the strongest proof of our moral freedom so much attacked by sophists. Yet this power of self-destruction is repugnant to nature and has been rightly opposed by every religion.

Casanova is, then, the most amiable of anarchists, arguing by word and deed for man's liberation from all enslavement, even life itself if it should be so construed. He is a prototype of naturalistic comedy, intent, like Bacon, on liberating us from idols of the mind, knowing that such idolatry makes us slaves. And, being a rational sensualist, he articulates the smiling dimensions of existential naturalism for the balanced mind capable of turning all things to the ultimate in humanistic pleasure—the canny enjoyment of what life does have to offer. "The really virtuous," he says, "are those who can practice virtue without the slightest trouble; such persons are always full of toleration; and it is to them that my *Memoirs* are addressed." Because his is a pragmatically comprehensive and highly social vision, an eighteenth-century handbook on how to succeed in life without working up a sweat, Casanova presents in his *Memoirs* a kind of sentimental or soft-core pornographic version of Cleland's hard-core pornographic comedy, *Fanny Hill*. Cleland presents an exclusively sexual and non-social ethic of happiness. Casanova augments Cleland's sexuality with aristocratic sociability, in effect advising men to learn the ropes and let life work for them. He is, however, more than the original Playboy, for his *Memoirs* mark an important step toward naturalistic erotic comedy.

## HIGH AFFIRMATION AND THE LOWDOWN TRUTH

Henry Miller is the democratic extension of Casanova's pornographic comedy. In a 1966 interview, Miller said that he thought he had made the erotic novel meaningful to "the man on the street." Casanova retired to the patronage of a Count's castle. Miller retired to a solid middle-class neighborhood in Los Angeles. So goes history. But, although Miller is probably not yet as accessible to the man on the street as he had hoped, he is a popular writer, and his significance, especially to pornographic comedy, is immense. His work combines the relaxed intellectual graciousness of Casanova and the demonic Sadean insistence on the complete animalistic "truth." Miller's is ethical comedy, concerned at once with representing the possibility of the common man emerging from life's destructiveness, usually in the form of social convention, with his head bloody but unbowed, and representing human energy, often taking the Dionysian form of sexual activity, as a mode of affirmation. Unlike Genet or Lawrence, Miller is not dialectically oriented. His comic vision is rather figural than logical. Using his own life to figure the possibilities of freedom and happiness he becomes himself the comic hero, documenting the viability of liberation from bourgeois enslavement with his own, perhaps partly fantasized, life.

*The Rosy Crucifixion*, a trilogy consisting of *Sexus, Plexus,* and *Nexus,* depicts Miller working through his own personal anarchy—an analogue and effect of the destructiveness of the American environment—eventually to free himself and leave the country for a new life. The plot of the trilogy constitutes a comic exorcism of bourgeois enslavement to profit, self, and the varieties—from sex to fraud—of moral debauch. It is, in other words, an exorcism of the living death Miller finds in American culture. The concluding sequence of events in *Nexus* shows him routing the enemy. The day before he is to leave for Europe he is walking the streets of New York, and he has a reminiscent vision of death. After reading to his grandfather, he dreams, he looks through a smokehouse fence and sees "Rows and rows of stiff, blackened fish. . . . They're hanging by the gills, these rigid, frightened fish." He asks his grandfather why dead things are always so stiff: "Because there's no joy in them anymore." Joy, in Miller, is the vehicle of life, and his vision of American culture shows him its deadness:

> By day the graveyard of senseless sweat and toil; by night the cemetery of love and despair. And these creatures who had so faithfully learned to run, to beg, to sell themselves and their fellow men, to dance like bears or perform like trained poodles, ever and always belying their own nature, these same wretched creatures broke down now and then, wept like fountains of misery, crawled like snakes, uttered sounds which only wounded animals are thought to emit.

Miller is escaping that death, and to do it he needs a final liturgical gesture, the exorcism of the symbol of death, the exorcism of the Yankee Dollar. Conveniently, a panhandler asks him for a dime. Miller offers him a dollar instead. The panhandler, among the living dead, unliberated even by his poverty, is suspicious. "All I need is a quarter . . . two bits. That'll do. And I'll thank you kindly." Miller offers him up to five dollars, "Five's the maximum." But the panhandler only wants two bits. When Miller hands it to him, he drops it and it rolls into the gutter. Miller tells him to let it stay there, for "the other fellow." Miller gives him another. The panhandler asks, Can he not have the other one too? Miller counters, giving him a dollar bill:

> Imagine, if you can, that it's tomorrow and that you're passing the same spot, wondering who'll give you a dime. I won't be here, you see. I'll be on the *Île de France*. Now then, your throat's parched and all that, and who comes along but a well-dressed guy with nothing to do—like me—and he flops down . . . right here on this same bench. Now what do you do? You go up to him, same as always, and you say—"Spare a dime, mister?" And he'll shake his head. No! Now then, here's the surprise, here's the thought I had for you. Don't run away with your tail between your legs. Stand firm and smile . . . a kindly smile. Then say: "Mister, I was only joking. I don't need no dime. Here's a buck for you, and may God protect you always!" *See?* Won't that be jolly?

The panhandler panics, running off waving the bill, shouting, "You crazy bugger! You dirty cocksucker! Piss on you, you goon!" Thus the power of the dollar is exorcised. "There you are," Miller muses to himself, "Couldn't take a little joke." Even the panhandlers are zombies, programmed for the usual. Everyone knows his miserable place. Miller, to build anew, destroys the confidence of that place. And, naturally, for his efforts he is condemned as mad. But he, at any rate, is ready for the new life. If humor and joy are "crazy," if palsied panhandlers are part of the mortuary establishment, it's damn well time to get out.

The way out is not easy. Given the psychic and social representiveness of the life we define for ourselves, it takes heroic action and persistence to reach the point of freedom. Miller, as comic hero, has two keys to human joy that seem imperative to making it. He is at once a con-man and a sex artist. Both of these qualities become figural antitheses of establishmentarianism. They are the anarchic means the comic hero has of weakening the cultural stranglehold. And it is clearly imperative to break that hold if one is to get free. Characteristically, the con-man manifests the free-enterprise virtue of wanting to get rich. Only his means, being vaguely criminal, are objectionable. His ends are laudable, in a capitalist context. He mirrors the capitalistic ethos. Which is why, in the criminal code, he is the aristocrat of criminals.

But Miller's use of the motif contradicts the ethos from which it derives. He does not want to get rich. His con-artistry is used to make life accessible to himself. The figural implication is that we should all have the access to life that the rich have—the access to good food, good wine, good women, good homes, security—without having to suffer the spiritual corruption, the surrender to living death, necessary to getting and spending within a capitalistic ethos. As with Casanova, when Miller cons men out of their money to give himself or someone else vitality (he as often cons for someone else's benefit as for his own), he strikes a blow against folly, the folly of materialism, and for life. This is rather simply illustrated when, in an episode in *Nexus,* he and a friend con a speakeasy out of an extravagant evening by paying the bill with a check to which they sign the name of a rich friend who died the day before. This episode not only pools the straight and underground worlds in their common corruption, it celebrates con-artistry as the proper weapon of the true moral anarchist. For not only does he give himself joy but turns as well the decay of the culture against itself.

But the con-game has a larger and more fundamental significance. Even an ethos where fraud is the norm has something to teach us. There is a metaphysics of fraud; the decadent notion that reality is what we say it is, that it is distorted by the medium of its articulation, has also a positive character. If reality is largely a product of consciousness, then a "better" consciousness will make a better reality, both psychically and morally. Reality, then, is a con-game, a game in which, when the rules become oppressive, we can change them, make them accord more truly with our needs.

Miller discovers this metaphysic when, in *Sexus*, he undertakes the role of analyst with a doctor friend who himself aspires to be an analyst. At first the doctor introduces Miller to some of his patients as a psychoanalyst, and Miller "treats" them, although he has no formal training. The patients are pleased with his services, and show improvement. It works so well that the doctor himself decides to become Miller's patient. Miller plays the role strictly, and sustains it. In doing so, he discovers the metaphysics of fraud and the moral freedom that is its corollary.

He discovers that everyone, with infinite time and patience, could be saved. The art of healing, which he learns through his con-artistry, comes to this:

> *Everybody becomes a healer the moment he forgets about himself.* The sickness which we see everywhere, the bitterness and disgust which life inspires in so many of us, is only the reflection of the sickness which we carry within us. Prophylactics will never secure us against the world disease, because we bear the world within.

This moral recognition is the ultimate moral anarchy, bringing with it the possibility of regeneration and the triumph of a new life. Bearing in ourselves moral and psychic reality, we have the power to shape a new life. "We must," says Miller, "die as egos and be born again in the swarm, not separate and self-hypnotized, but individual and related." We must, then, reject an ethos of false self-denial, the effect of which is to force the ego underground for its gratification. We must discover the processes of life and have confidence in their efficacy, their ability to direct us in keeping with our nature. This is the theme of the naturalistic comic ethos, that nature in its full complexity is the only way out. Miller says,

> The way of life is toward fulfillment, however, wherever it may lead. . . . And so the analyst says "Adapt yourself!" He does not mean, as some wish to think—adapt yourself to this rotten state of affairs! He means: adapt yourself to life! *Become an adept!*

And one must learn to do it well. It is a beginning to recognize the moral potential of fraud, the utility of the con-game. And to do that one must have confidence in the ability to redefine reality. Miller offers God as an existential example, for God is, after all, the ultimate comic hero:

> We are all guilty of crime, the great crime of not living life to the full. But we are all potentially free. We can stop thinking of what we have failed to do

> and do whatever lies within our power. What these powers that are in us may be no one has truly dared to imagine. That they are infinite we will realize the day we admit to ourselves that imagination is everything. Imagination is the voice of daring. If there is anything God-like about God it is that. He dared to imagine everything.

Imagination is the basis of the con-game. It provides the context, the reason and meaning, for conning one's way to freedom, to life. God is the archetype and the example. One can do no better than to imitate him. Miller's ethos, therefore, advises us to imagine more than the prison we already know: "The prisoner is not the one who has committed a crime, but the one who clings to his crime and lives it over and over." Imagine the way out, the way to freedom. This is Miller's moral imperative, *sine qua non*.

Equally important to his exorcism of enslavement is Miller's use of sexuality. For if the body is, as the Christian fathers teach, a prison, it is the more so if we imprison ourselves within it in our own minds; if, in other words, we follow an ethos that inspires fear, suspicion, and compulsive privateness about the body, as we have done, then the body becomes more than ever a prison. Miller bursts these bonds, and in so doing extends sexuality to configure the way of shattering so humanly destructive an idol of the mind. Sexual freedom signifies a human freedom to be human, the freedom to take pleasure in being a human animal. The process of being human is everything, and to deny a part of that process is to deny it all. This theme is exemplified in the story of Maude, Miller's first wife, in *Sexus*. As the novel opens Miller is already alienated from her and has just discovered Mona, his second wife, with whom he has a tortuous relationship throughout the trilogy. He is alienated from Maude because she is alienated from herself. Her jealousy, pettiness, and morose self-indulgence are incompatible with Miller's restless, large-spirited need to live.

After he has left her to live with Mona, he takes Maude and his daughter on an outing to the country. While there, Miller fondles Maude, not averse, although they are divorced, to giving and getting sexual affection. Maude poutingly puts him off, playing out her dehumanized role flatly. Later, however, back at her house, after they have been caught in a rainstorm and soaked so that they take off their clothes to dry them out, she engages Miller in what turns out to be an orgy. It begins thus:

> I'm standing in front of the big mirror admiring my quivering cock when Maude trips in. She's as frisky as a hare and all decked out in tulle and mousseline. She seems not at all frightened by what she sees in the mirror. She comes over and stands beside me. "Open it up!" I urge. "Are you hungry?" she says, undoing herself leisurely. I turn her around and press her to me. She raises a leg to let me get it in. We look at each other in the mirror.

> She's fascinated. I pull the wrap up over her ass so that she can have a better look. I lift her up and she twines her legs around me. "Yes, do it," she begs. "Fuck me! Fuck me!" Suddenly she untwines her legs, unhitches. She grabs the big arm chair and turns it around, resting her hands on the back of it. Her ass is stuck out invitingly. She doesn't wait for me to put it in—she grabs it and places it herself, watching all the time through the mirror. I push it back and forth slowly, holding my skirts up like a bedraggled hussy. She likes to see it coming out—how far will it come before it falls out. She reaches under with one hand and plays with my balls. She's completely unleashed now, as brazen as a pot. I withdraw as far as I can without letting it slip out and she rolls her ass around, sinking down on it now and then and clutching it with a feathery beak. Finally she's had enough of that. She wants to lie down on the floor and put her legs around my neck. "Get it in all the way," she begs. "Don't be afraid of hurting me. . . . I want it. I want you to do everything." I got it in so deep it felt as though I were buried in a bed of mussels. She was quivering and slithering in every ream. I bent over and sucked her breasts; the nipples were taut as nails. Suddenly she pulled my head down and began to bite me wildly—lips, ears, cheeks, neck. "You want it, don't you?" she hissed. "You want it, you want it. . . ." Her lips twisted obscenely. "You want it . . . you want it!" And she fairly lifted herself off the floor in her abandon. Then a groan, a spasm, a wild, tortured look as if her face were under a mirror pounded by a hammer. "Don't take it out yet," she grunted. She lay there, her legs still slung around my neck, and the little flag inside her began twitching and fluttering. "God," she said, "I can't stop it!" My prick was still firm. It hung obedient on her wet lips, as though receiving the sacrament from a lascivious angel. She came again, like an accordeon collapsing in a bag of milk. I got hornier and hornier. I pulled her legs down and lay them flat alongside my own. "Now don't move, damn you," I said. "I'm going to give it to you straight." Slowly and furiously I moved in and out. "Ah, ah . . . Oh!" she hissed, sucking her breath in. I kept it up like a Juggernaut. Moloch fucking a piece of bombazine. Organza Friganza. The bolero in straight jabs. Her eyes were going wild; she looked like an elephant walking the ball. All she needed was a trunk to trumpet with. It was a fuck to a standstill. I fell on top of her and chewed her lips to a frazzle.

The sexuality of this scene is uncompromised. It is pure sexuality, unmitigated with pretence to love. But it has an almost miraculous regenerating effect on Maude, who has heretofore been spiteful, vicious, and mean. Miller asks her if she hates him still. She answers, "I don't hate anyone. I'm sorry it's turned out the way it has. Now I'll have to share you . . . with her." As she goes about fixing them something to eat, Miller notices, "She looked a thousand times better than I had ever seen her look. She was like a bright voracious animal. . . . Jesus, it was quite wonderful. It was like getting to know one another all over again." Maude recognizes the difference herself. Their sexuality takes on more affection as they play erotically. Maude asks if it was her fault that they had not done this before. "Was I such a squeamish creature?"

Then, as if consciously consecrating her new humanity, her regeneration, she turns the affair more formally into an orgy, bringing down a girl friend from upstairs. "I want to celebrate," she says. They light candles, drink wine, play music, and dance. It is a Dionysian orgy. As their sexuality becomes more involved, Maude's humanity expands. "Maude looked on with a pleasant smile of satisfaction. I leaned forward and kissed Elsie's cunt. 'It's wonderful not to be jealous any more,' said Maude very simply." They arrange themselves in an elaborately entwined sexual trinity. Miller brings both the women and himself to a climax. Maude says, "I've never been so happy." And so it goes. Maude is given a new life through the specific agency of sexuality. Following Miller's rule of thumb, she becomes a healer of herself, when she forgets about herself, when she releases herself from the prison of her body. Through sexual orgy she takes on a richer personality and humanity.

But, though sexuality is consistently a figure of liberation in Miller's work, it does not exist in isolation, however purely physical his scenes. For the trick is not to be enslaved, either, to sexuality if one is going to achieve human liberation. "The moment you stop having a good time, you grow melancholy. You don't regulate your life—you let your cunt do it for you. You're at the mercy of a stiff prick. . . ." The good, the human, life requires something far more complex than sex, even though free and joyous sex are signs. One must have the desire to live, what Miller calls "hunger." Life requires going after even more than gratification. Hunger is the naturalistic counterpart of transcendental sublimation:

> Food is poison to the spirit. Food doesn't satisfy hunger, nor drink thirst. Food, sexual or otherwise, is only satisfying to the appetites. Hunger is something else. Nobody can satisfy hunger. Hunger is the soul's barometer. Ecstasy is the norm. Serenity is the freedom from weather conditions—the permanent climate of the stratosphere. That's where we're all headed . . . towards the stratosphere.

This is hunger for life, living, the avoidance of the great crime of not living life to the full. Hunger is a product, not of the belly, but of the imagination. When Maude gets hungry, she comes to life. It is so throughout Miller's work. His hunger is what makes him the comic hero. It is what sets him apart from other men.

Sex, being a complete act, cannot satisfy hunger, of course. Rather, it feeds hunger. It is a symbol of the serenity available to men: Elsie, the third person of the orgiastic trinity, says in the throes of orgasm, "This is heaven." It is not; but it is the figural basis by which we might believe in heaven. It is also the source of the most intense physical feeling, by which we may know that we are and want to be alive. "Nobody," says Miller, "is altogether dead." Wherever he goes, he sees people trying to come alive, too often failing. Sex, being available to all men, a part of the processes of life, becomes therefore the way, the Tao. Its value to the body is that it certifies the possibility of life. Its value to the soul is that it feeds hunger, the will to live.

Miller, then, is the comic celebrant of the myth of animality. A naturalist, a kind of latter-day deistic naturalist, he embraces the positiveness of what is, professing love for all things under the sun, excepting work and flies. "Of course," he says, "I don't feel that way every day—but I'd like to. And I do when I'm normal, when I'm myself. Everybody does, if given a chance. It's the natural state of the heart . . . but . . . we terrorize ourselves." Get free, then, free from terror. Liberate body and soul from the system, by fraud if necessary, since that's the pattern established by the system. "Woof, woof, woof, woof," is how Miller ends *Plexus* and begins *Nexus*. It is the cry of the animal in us trying to get free, to help us get free from ourselves, from the great, morose, depressed mind-rape perpetrated on humanity by its vestigial institutions. "I know," says Miller, "that underneath the mess everything is marvelous. I'm sure of it. I know it because I feel so marvelous myself most of the time. And when I feel that way everybody seems marvelous . . . everybody and everything. . . . That's what I want to write about. . . . " That is his comic message. If we can get in touch with ourselves, really in touch, as in the act of sex, then perhaps we can route the downhead meanies and find the joy endemic to life.

Miller approaches life-joy, in sex as in all things, with heroic capacities. There is, consequently, in his work a defiance; you, he tells the establishment, may detour me, you may slow me down, you may depress me occasionally, but you will never defeat me. All of his work radiates the confidence of his vision. There is something of the superman about him. And it does not matter much whether the Miller of life is the same as the Miller of the novels. Whoever he is, we feel in him the triumph of the comic hero.

But, for that very reason, there is also something austere and unapproachable about him. We may acknowledge his truth; we may even use him as an ideal—as to large extent the Beats and the Hippies have done—but the fusion of fiction and fact in his work make it at once too life-like and too much larger than life for most of us. We do not have the heroic capacity, by and large, to say, as he does at the beginning of *Tropic of Cancer*, "I have no money, no resources, no hopes. I am the happiest man alive." Somehow, when Merseult, in Camus' *The Stranger*, comes to the same recognition in a work that is unequivocally fictive, we are better able to assimilate it. Perhaps we are embarrassed at our personal timidity. Perhaps we are afraid of failing at life, precisely Miller's point. Perhaps we do not have the genius he has demonstrated for defying the cultural mores and emerging, after all, on top. As with Casanova and Genet, and as ironic as it may be, Miller's life has paid off, in coin. In short, there is something too challenging in Miller, too direct. His ethos is somehow too much like Elsie's orgasm, it's heaven. To adopt it we would have to immerse ourselves completely in his, for most of us, inaccessible comic world. To translate his ethos we need a more fictive context, a context into which we might ease ourselves more obliquely. This is not to say that Miller is not hugely valuable; it is only to say that we also need other, perhaps less heroic, perspectives on the comic ethos he represents.

Lawrence and Joyce, for all their "artistic" complexity, are more easily assimilable into "normal" human morality. Yet they represent an ethos essentially similar to Miller's. They too celebrate the life force as the means of our emergence from the enslavement imposed by the ignorance and denial of human animality. And sexuality, especially with Lawrence, is their figure of liberation. Lawrence, in his essay "A Propos *Lady Chatterley's Lover*," says:

> The greatest need of man is the renewal forever of the complete rhythm of life and death, the rhythm of the sun's year, the body's year of a lifetime, and the greater year of the stars, the soul's year of immortality. This is our need, our imperative need. It is a need of the mind and soul, body, spirit and sex: all. . . .
>
> It means a return to ancient forms. But we shall have to create these forms again. . . . We have to go back, a long way, before the idealist conceptions began, before Plato, before the tragic idea of life arose, to get on our feet again. For the gospel of salvation through the Ideals and escape from the body coincided with the tragic conception of human life. Salvation and tragedy are the same thing, and they are now both beside the point. . . .
>
> Now we have to re-establish the great relationships which the grand idealists, with their underlying pessimism, their belief that life is nothing but futile conflict, to be avoided even unto death, destroyed for us. . . . The Christian religion lost, in Protestantism finally, the togetherness with the universe, the togetherness of the body, the sex, the emotions, the passions, with the earth and sun and stars.
>
> But relationship is threefold. First, there is the relation to the living universe. Then comes the relation of man to woman. Then comes the relation of man to man. And each is a blood-relationship, not mere spirit or mind. We have abstracted the universe. . . . So that all three great relationships are bodiless, dead.

Here, in brief, is the essential argument of this book. Lawrence wrote *Lady Chatterley's Lover* specifically to articulate in fiction this theme. Although it contains the tragic potential of paralysis and death, it is finally a comic theme, affirming the possibility of life's triumph over death, and its symbol is the sexual and emotional liaison of Lady Chatterley with her gamekeeper.

The theme takes on a more archetypally mythic character in *The Rainbow*, where three generations of a family wrestle with it. In that novel Lawrence explores the Jungian implications of love and sex, and, in the novel's final image, celebrates the liberation of the third generation. Through the novel a dialectical tension is developed between the female *anima*, which Lawrence sees characterized by the impulse to vision and spirit, and the male *animus*, which he sees trapped into work and pragmatism, and resistant therefore to spiritual vision. In this psycho-mythic sense, all humankind is hermaphroditic. Two generations are subdued by the *animus*, but Ursula, of the third generation, works her way through the suppression by male domination and reaches the apocalyptic vision by affirming her option for life. The apocalypse begins when she takes her lover, in a desperate and demonic consummation, beneath the light of a full moon. The emotional failure of their lovemaking signifies the failure of their relationship. Later, thinking she is pregnant, Ursula goes for a walk in the country to decide if she should marry her lover. She is caught in a thunderstorm in a pasture, where a herd of horses is made wild by the storm. The scene takes on the mythic quality of Lear's madness on the heath. The threat of the horses, a time-honored erotic symbol, takes on a distinctly masculine and sexual character: "She knew the heaviness in her heart. It was the weight of the horses. But she would circumvent them. She would bear the weight steadily, and so escape." But the horses draw nearer and cut her off,

> The horses had burst before her. In a sort of lightning of knowledge their movement travelled through her, the quiver and strain and thrust of their powerful flanks, as they burst before her and drew on, beyond.
>
> . . . She was aware of their breasts gripped, clenched narrow in a hold that never relaxed, she was aware of their red nostrils flaming with long endurance, and of their haunches, so rounded, so massive, pressing, pressing, pressing to burst the grip upon their breasts, pressing forever till they went mad, running against the walls of time, and never bursting free. Their great haunches were smoothed and darkened with rain. But the darkness and wetness of rain could not put out the hard, urgent, massive fire that was locked within these flanks, never, never.

She has then a clearly orgasmic image, "Like circles of lightning came the flash of hoofs from out of the powerful flanks." And the flanks of the horses, as if with one purpose, "were up against her." But she escapes, and in so doing she is liberated from their power and terror: "They were almost pathetic, now. Her will alone carried her, till, trembling, she climbed the fence. . . . " This apocalyptic experience helps her interpret her relationship to her lover:

> Must she belong to him? . . . Something compelled her, and yet it was not real. Always the ache, the ache of unreality, of her belonging to Skrebensky. . . . Why must she be bound, aching and cramped with the bondage, to Skrebensky's world? . . . Anton and Anton's world, not the Anton she possessed, but the Anton she did not possess, that which was owned by some other influence, by the world.

She struggles with this tension, until she sees herself as a natural object, "the naked, clear kernel thrusting forth the clear, powerful shoot, and the world was a bygone winter." She is a natural thing, with her own power of being, not dependent on what is clearly seen to be the conventionally crippling enslavement of marriage, the forfeiture of self demanded by the world. "The kernel was free and naked and striving to take new root, to create a new knowledge of Eternity in the flux of Time. And the kernel was the only reality; the rest was cast off into oblivion." The child, then, need not be a prison gate. Nothing need be a prison gate. Through her sexual being, in all its complexity, she comes to a knowledge of the freedom of choice she has as a human being. And her choice is confirmed by the final apocalyptic vision, that of the rainbow, in which, as in herself, there is a new cosmic architecture, a communion of relationships—of man to nature, of man to woman, of man to man.

Lawrence's sexual dialectic is at once epistemological and metaphysical. There are, he says, many ways of knowing and many kinds of knowledge. "But the two ways of knowing, for man, are knowing in terms of apartness, which is mental, rational, scientific, and knowing in terms of togetherness, which is religious and poetic." Metaphysically, reality confronts unreality at the level of individual consciousness of self and the possibilities self has for communion with the other and with nature. Lawrence's now much sentimentalized concept of "togetherness," then, is the key. So sexuality is its natural and spontaneous field. Highly ritualistic and figural as it is, its physicality is emphasized in *Lady Chatterley's Lover*; its racial myth is emphasized in *The Rainbow*. Other works, such as *Women in Love* and *Sons and Lovers*, continue the exploration of the sexual myth.

*Lady Chatterley* was intended not only as an exploration of Lawrence's basic theme, but also as a wedge into public resistance to that theme as a serious poetic statement. He wanted, in effect, to exorcise the whole concept of "pornography" by a direct and healthy representation of sexuality. His hostility to masturbation and homosexuality is well known. He despised them as he despised "pornography," because all of them, he thought, contributed to making sex "secret" and "dirty." As such, they separated man from his body, from the rhythms of nature. Their "dirt" makes for fear and rejection; their "secrecy" makes for isolation, the separation of man from nature and himself.

Nor is his dialectic harmlessly stratospheric. He saw political consequences from such isolation and fear.

> The sense of isolation, followed by the sense of menace and of fear, is bound to arise as the feeling of oneness and community with our fellow-men declines, and the feeling of individualism and personality, which is existence in isolation, increases. The so-called "cultured" classes are the first to develop "personality" and individualism, and the first to fall into this state of unconscious menace and fear. The working-classes retain the old blood-warmth of oneness and togetherness some decades longer. Then they lose it too. And then class-consciousness becomes rampant, and class-hate. Class-hate and class-consciousness are only a sign that the old togetherness, the old blood-warmth has collapsed, and every man is really aware of himself in apartness. Then we have these hostile groupings of men for the sake of opposition, strife. Civil strife becomes a necessary condition of self-assertion.

Thus, Lawrentian pornography, in both its physical and mythic configurations, is designed to affirm human community. It is a comic vision that transcends Henry Miller's defiance. It lives at a figural level that permits us to absorb and learn from it without being made to feel inadequate to its ethos. While its imaginative challenge may be greater than Miller's, its personal challenge is not so great. It enfolds us, and we feel a part of its morality even as we fail it. And we are thereby the more liberated from our failure.

Liberation from failure is even more pronounced in Joyce. *Ulysses*, for example, is finally a comedy of failure. Certainly Leopold Bloom, Joyce's comic answer to the Homeric Ulysses, is a "failure" in may ways, as a businessman, as a husband, as a father, as a lover. Molly Bloom's partly affectionate, partly contemptuous diminutive, "Poldy," indicates something of his failure at achieving dignity. Molly herself is only slightly less a failure. Although professionally and sexually successful, she too is a failure as a wife and mother. Nor is Blazes Boylan, Molly's lover, much more successful. He cuckolds Bloom, and ridicules him in the bars, and has the appearance of typically florid, loquacious, Irish masculine success. But even as lover he is something of a failure, for all his virility: Molly, in her soliloquy, says of him, "he must have come 3 or 4 times with that tremendous big red brute of a thing he has I thought the vein or whatever the dickens they call it was going to burst . . . it like iron or some kind of a thick crowbar standing all the time he must have eaten oysters I think a few dozen . . . no I never in all my life felt anyone had one the size of that to make you feel full up." He fails to earn more than Molly's amazement, and even with that she concludes, by way of comparison, "but I don't know Poldy has more spunk in him." And being, in spite of her promiscuity, a profoundly religious person, Molly is contemptuous of Boylan's arrogance: "he says your soul you have no soul inside only grey matter because he doesn't know what it is to have one." Human failure, then, is one of the basic themes in *Ulysses*.

Like Lawrence, Joyce sees the dichotomy of the masculine and feminine worlds represented by the tension between materialism and spirituality. Unlike Lawrence, and here is where Joyce's celebrated genius in creating point of view is significant, he does not impose a dialectical reality on the feminine *anima*. Nor, through ritual or myth, does he sublimate the naturalism of that point of view. It may be possible, with Molly lying in bed recounting her erotic life, to find in her a mythic earth-mother figure. But that seems to be fetching pretty far. Joyce goes to some trouble to make her consciousness distinct and personal rather than archetypal. And if, as it has been suggested, her soliloquy is an extended masturbation fantasy, then that reduces the likelihood of her archetypicality still more. Earth-mothers do not masturbate. Unlike human beings, they do not have such neurotic needs. Molly is above all a human being, with all the weaknesses, needs, and failures of human beings. But she also has the spiritual dignity of humanity at its best. She is, in that sense, the most comprehensive kind of feminist, conscious of the need and superiority of femaleness in the world,

> I dont care what anybody says itd be much better for the world to be governed by the women in it you wouldnt see women going and killing one another and slaughtering when do you ever see women rolling around drunk like they do or gambling every penny they have and losing it on horses yes because a woman whatever she does she knows where to stop sure they wouldnt be in the world at all only for us they dont know what it is to be a woman and a mother how could they where would they all of them be if they hadnt all a mother to look after them.

These are clichés, yet coming from the mind of a woman who is also conscious of herself as an adultress, and conscious of her sexuality and its indulgence, and conscious also of masculine sexuality and its vagaries and conscious, through all, of human spiritual dignity, the clichés take on profound meaning. Above all they exemplify the spiritual generosity necessary to love not only humankind but oneself.

Spiritual generosity in the face of human failure is the crux of Joyce's comic vision, and Molly is its spokesperson. One thinks of its antithesis in the terrifying, obscene, and spiritually mean retreat sermon Joyce describes in *A Portrait of the Artist as a Young Man*. Molly, conversely, affirms everything human. The word "yes" recurs throughout her soliloquy like a liturgical incantation. "Yes," she begins, "because he never did a thing like that before as ask to get his breakfast in bed," and we know she is affirming Bloom, her "Poldy." She affirms Bloom not simply because, after ten years of impotence, he asserts himself as a man, but because that assertion confirms what she has perceived in him through all of his indignity and depravity, the presence of spiritual generosity and self-consciousness in the best epistemological sense. Bloom, unlike Boylan, has been on an odyssey in search of himself. Potentially, at least, he finds the image of that self when he befriends Stephen Dedalus, in whom he finds an analogue to his dead son, Rudy. Bloom, like Ulysses, has at last come home to his "faithful" Penelope. And Molly affirms even that sad relationship, her infidelity and his impotence; she affirms it by finding a way for them to "make it," however abnormal it may have to be:

> Its all his own fault if Im an adulteress . . . if thats all the harm ever we did in this vale of tears God knows its not much doesnt everybody only they hide it I suppose thats what a woman is supposed to be there for or He wouldnt have made us the way He did so attractive to men then if he wants to kiss my bottom Ill drag open my drawers and bulge it right out in his face as large as life he can stick his tongue 7 miles up my hole . . . Ill let him do it off me behind provided he doesn't smear all my good drawers O I suppose that cant be helped . . . I know every turn in him Ill tighten my bottom well and let out a few smutty words smellrump or lick my shit or the first mad thing comes in my head . . .

Shortly after this passage, Molly begins the crescendo of affirmation with which the novel and her soliloquy end. She too, like Lawrence's Ursula, has a vision of apocalypse. But rather than co-joining earth and sky as the rainbow does, Molly's vision is altogether earthy, a reminiscence of Bloom's proposal of marriage. In the remembering, punctuated with the rhythmic incantation of "yes," she affirms what happened then and all that has happened since:

> I gave him the bit of seedcake out of my mouth and it was leapyear like now yes 16 years ago my God after that long kiss I near lost my breath yes he said I was a flower of the mountain yes so we are flowers all a womans body yes that was one true thing he said in his life and the sun shines for you today yes that was why I liked him because I saw he understood or felt what a woman is . . . and then I asked him with my eyes to ask again yes and then he asked me would I yes to say yes my mountain flower and first I put my arms around him yes and drew him down to me so he could feel my breasts all perfume yes and his heart was going like mad and yes I said yes I will Yes.

And so the novel ends, with existential celebration, regretting nothing. Bloom's "triumph" derives from his moral hermaphroditism, his fusion of the masculine and feminine worlds; he may only be a man, but he strives, however bunglingly, to be more. And Molly, the voice of Joyce's comic ethos, honors both Bloom and herself as existential models. What we are is what one can expect—"doesn't everybody only they hide it"—and we must love ourselves and one another nonetheless, in all the failure of our nature. We find some beauty, as Joyce says we must, in the very grossness of earth

We have been considering pornographic rhetoric in the structure of high or philosophical comedy. It also has a role in satire. There too it works to exorcise mental idols. Sex itself, or fear of sex, has become a bogey. It has become, in fact, almost a cultural mania. Popular magazines, newspapers, and books are filled with sexual advice columns and articles. Schools are badgered by proponents and opponents of sex education. The relation between sexuality and society has itself reached something like burlesque proportions. This does not mean that the problem is not serious. It is. But the hysteria it causes is frequently pretty funny. Satirical pornography has picked up this mood, and uses it to mock the seriousness with which we regard sex, and because of which we tend to be controlled by it. The popular media, such as *Playboy*, and the recent pornography tabloids, have particular fun with it.

The cultural need to have some fun with sex, and relieve the oppressiveness of our preoccupation with it, made Terry Southern's and Mason Hoffenberg's *Candy*, which might otherwise have been an amusing trifle, an international sensation. The conception of the novel, the sexual adventures into which a simple, beautiful, ingénue is thrust by her innocence, offers marvellous possibilities for satirical allegory. The movie version seems to have pursued them even more imaginatively, if in less physiological detail. What the novel ridicules is the notion that something so natural and ubiquitous as sex is reasonably compatible with moral and religious traditions of innocence as a moral virtue and as well the sentimental idealism that is its philosophical basis. Candy Christian, motivated by the great sentimental ideals of self-sacrifice and good deeds, of as she puts it (in the words of Professor Mephisto, her great teacher of contemporary ethics, who turns out, alas, to be a lascivious queer and lecher *extraordinaire*), the "privilege and duty of giving oneself fully to those who have great need," has her succulent honey pot plundered by one needy (rhymes with greedy) dipper after another. The burlesque opportunities are obvious enough, and the novel exploits them well. What is ridiculous, our sublimation of natural impulses to transcendental virtues, is covered with ridicule. Nature and absurdity prevail. The idea is to exorcise the sullenness of sexual preoccupations and put them, through humor, into a reasonable perspective. For, as Lawrence's Ursula and Miller's Maude discover, carnal knowledge is not the end of the world, it is a new beginning.

Comedy overrides the anxiety caused by the myth of animality by turning that myth to irony, playing off reason and passion against one another. Man's passions are ridiculed, and thus cut to size, because they are finally so puny. Joyce's Bloom is a puny hero with puny, abortive passions. In presenting him as a modern hero, Joyce is at once banishing the mythology of heroics as morally useful for a modern ethos and telling us that the existential condition, however quotidian, has moral reality.

Philip Roth continues the tradition of *schlep* as hero in *Portnoy's Complaint*. While the mythic heroes are moved to rape by their passions, Portnoy, the *schlep* hero, can only get it up for masturbation. Portnoy's complaint, "a disorder in which strongly felt ethical and altruistic impulses are perpetually warring with extreme sexual longings, often of a perverse nature," is the logical conclusion of the cultural ethos against which Sade, Miller, and Lawrence raged. Man is made impotent by being put out of touch with his body. The narrative framework of the novel, in which Portnoy talks out his complaint to a mythical analyst (much the same way that Humbert talks out his defense to the mythical jury in *Lolita*), suggests the pathological consequences of levitating sex from the loins to the head.

Superficially, *Portnoy's Complaint* is the longest Jewish mother joke in history. But, like all such jokes, it taps into a much larger issue, the conflict between the new and the old, death and regeneration. It is therefore natural that the novel's chief figure is the malfunction of the organ and the imagination of regeneration. Portnoy's story, simply put, is that the compulsive care of his Jewish parents has given him a mania for masturbation. From self-abuse he expands to self-indulgence ("While all the other sons have been carrying forward the family name, what he has been doing is—chasing cunt. And *shikse* cunt, to boot. Chasing it, sniffing it, lapping it, *shtupping* it, but above all, *thinking about it*"); from that to perversity (three in a bed); and finally in Israel, where other Jews find new life and potency, to impotence, as he tries to seduce a kibbutz girl, thus:

> Licked her earholes, sucked at her unwashed neck, sank my teeth into the coiled braids of hair . . . and then, even as resistance may actually have begun to recede under my assault, I rolled off of her and came to rest, defeated, against the wall—on my back. "It's no good," I said, "I can't get a hard-on in this place."

In short, Portnoy is sexually ridiculous: "'Then,' I pleaded, as she began to drag me by her powerful leg across toward the door, 'at least let me eat your pussy. I know I can still do that'." And sexually ridiculous is humanly ridiculous.

The ostensible cause of the absurdity is the anal compulsiveness of the Jewish mother. More profoundly, however, it is the moral alienation of man from his body, enforced by the cultural emphasis of "success" and "cleanliness." It gets to Portnoy's father as constipation; he is an insurance agent, so much so that he cannot even let go of his waste. It gets to Portnoy in his compulsive masturbation. It is summed up in his cunt-chasing, "but above all, *thinking about it.*" The separation of mind and body, the separation of man from himself, from the rhythms of nature, as Lawrence lamented, diminishes being to self-mockery. When Portnoy sings "Impotent in Israel" to the tune of "Lullaby in Birdland," the kibbutz girl asks, "Another joke?" "And another," Portnoy replies, "and another. Why disclaim my life?" Roth, then, satirizes the ethos of impotence by making it a joke. A sick joke, but a joke nonetheless, because finally all there is to do is laugh at yourself, maybe a little hysterically, when you have been reduced to parody.

Roth lands on the Jewish mother and the culture whose values she represents as the causes of human life being so reduced, so wasted. But they are only the agencies. The real causality is in the ethos that denies the viability of nature. The symbolic Jewish mother, with all her cooking and housecleaning, manages to make her son impotent and her husband constipated. She fouls up the mechanisms of nature. The culture and values she represents, then, are an antidote to nature, stopping it up, distorting it, killing life. Portnoy's complaint, a disorder in which the mind and body are at war, is a satiric statement of the theme of ethical disorder that runs through pornographic comedy. Comic pornography prescribes an enema, and if they can sell the script to the movies, just as the tube goes in, the camera eye will move in for a close-up of the anal aperture in good working order. It's messy, but a thing like that, believe it or not, can be good for the soul.

# 8

# Women and Pornorotica

## ASSERTING SEXUAL AUTONOMY

Such feminist critics as Andrea Dworkin and Susan Griffin so conceive pornography that it is necessarily vicious in itself and in its effects. Their definitions, being polemical, do not usefully address the aesthetic function of pornography. Moreover, neither Dworkin nor Griffin acknowledge, let alone credit, the considerable body of pornographically inclined work (whether or not it would fit their notions of "pornography") by women published since 1974. These include Nancy Friday's *My Secret Garden* and *Forbidden Flowers,* Erica Jong's *Fear of Flying* and *How to Save Your Own Life,* Anaïs Nin's *Delta of Venus,* Edith Wharton's posthumous "Beatrice Palmato," and such sociological documents as *The Hite Report,* that indicate a greater female use of auto-eroticism, sexual fantasy, and even pornography than had heretofore been supposed. Their response to this development seems to be summed up in Dworkin's one-liner on Anaïs Nin, that she "tried to conform to the rules of the pornography-for-fast-money game, but dripped sensibility helplessly and foolishly." For Dworkin, "arguments about the real gender of authors of pornography [e.g. whether *Story of O* was in fact written by a woman, as is contended] are meaningless, since the goal is to please the male consumer whose tastes are entirely predictable, existing as they do within the limited framework of male sexual values and ideas."

Dworkin and Griffin have, however, alerted us to the assumptions and dangers inherent in pornography, and they are right in their reminder that historically pornography has been delineated by men and male preoccupations. In that context an obvious question poses itself, does pornography have the epistemological and aesthetic potential for the writing by women that I have been arguing it has in the writing of men? *Story of O* would suggest that it does, but since that novel's authorship is uncertain, its feminine character is equivocal, quite apart from Dworkin's dubious assumption that women cannot articulate themselves as women on the subject. Alix Kates Shulman contends that not only can women so articulate themselves, and do so in pornography, but that they should and will, because pornography is a valuable vehicle of psychic and social exploration. Her position is reflected in the Feminists Against Censorship Taskforce (FACT) brief opposing the Dworkin/MacKinnon anti-pornography ordinance; among its signatories are several other prominent feminist writers. The FACT brief makes the point that,

> Even pornography which is problematic for women can be experienced as affirming of women's desires and of women's equality. . . .
>
> The range of feminist imagination and expression in the realm of sexuality has barely begun to find voice. Women need the freedom and the socially recognized space to appropriate for themselves the robustness of what traditionally has been male language. . . . [We] fear that as more women's writing and art on sexual themes emerges which is unladylike, unfeminine, aggressive, power-charged, pushy, vulgar, urgent, confident, and intense, the traditional foes of women's attempts to step out of their "proper place" will find an effective tool of repression in the . . . ordinance.

In short, there is now developing a feminist voice that finds pornography a viable genre for probing the nature of sexuality, how it functions and how it relates to the general situation of women and society.

In 1974 female pornography came out of the closet in the United States. Prior to that women had published pornography in disguise. The English translation of *Story of O* appeared in 1965 (the original French edition in 1954), but its pseudonymous authorship continues to make its feminine character speculative, although recent scholarship, e.g., Michael Perkins' *The Secret Record*, identifies the literary critic Dominique Aury as its author. Similarly with Harriet Daimler's pornographic novels of the 1960s: Daimler was a pseudonym for Iris Owens, and her books were published only in "dirty book" format by Olympic Press and North Hollywood and were regarded as commercial smut for the male market. The poet Diane di Prima's *Memoirs of a Beatnik* (Olympia Press, 1969) bore her name but was also generally relegated to the same category. But in 1974 the poet Erica Jong published *Fear of Flying* and Nancy Friday *My Secret Garden*, both of which became best sellers and so successful that each writer published sequels. The only woman before them to so successfully present sexual fiction to a general readership was Jacqueline Susann, who began her soft-core pornographic career in 1966 with *Valley of the Dolls*. Jong and Friday were far more direct; Jong's main metaphor was "the zipless fuck," a fantasy her heroine pursues en route to her psychic independence, and Friday offered three hundred-plus pages of women's real-life sexual fantasies. Public acceptance of the motif of female sexuality cultivated the ground for other "pornographic" works by women, both fictional and sociological. Perhaps the most prominent of the latter sort was Shere Hite's *The Hite Report* in 1976.

Hite's report was in fact the more comprehensive sequel to her 1974 volume *Sexual Honesty by Women for Women*. It is a report on how 3,000 women aged 14 to 78 described their physical and emotional sexuality and an analysis of the data that sometimes reads like a manifesto of female sexual independence:

> There is no reason why physical intimacy with men . . . should always consist of "foreplay" followed by intercourse and male orgasm; and there is no reason why intercourse must always be a part of heterosexual sex. Sex is intimate physical contact for pleasure, to share pleasure with another person (or just alone). You can have sex to orgasm, or not to orgasm, genital sex, or just physical intimacy—whatever seems right to you. There is never any reason to think the "goal" must be intercourse, and to try to make what you feel fit into that context. There is no standard of sexual performance "out there," against which you must measure yourself; you aren't ruled by "hormones" or "biology." You are free to explore and discover your own sexuality, to learn or unlearn anything you want, and to make physical relations with other people, of either sex, anything you like.

Though it is not my purpose here to discuss this study generally, it is pertinent to note its significance for the female pornographic imagination. Perhaps foremost is its demonstration that female sexuality is as libidinous as male sexuality. The corollary to this is that the traditionally imperative association of female sex with married love, or even love itself, is *contra naturam* and has been imposed for cultural and economic purposes, principally the social stability supposedly derived from monogamy. Hite, as the above citation suggests, construes the data to mean that women not only can and do enjoy sex in and for itself but should continue to explore the possibilities for sexual gratification. In this respect, the association between masturbation and orgasm is particularly important. More than eighty percent of Hite's test group reported reaching orgasm via masturbation, whereas about thirty percent reported reaching orgasm via intercourse. Moreover, Hite says that ninety-five percent of those women who reach orgasm by masturbation do so "in just a few minutes . . . easily and regularly, whenever they wanted," thus refuting the assumption that orgasm is unimportant to female sexuality and that women neither need nor necessarily want it. Hite's data also argue that female orgasm is overwhelmingly clitoral rather than vaginal, and she contends, with scientific support, that the female orgasm has no reproductive function.

Hite's findings document that the female impulse, to sexual gratification is not a misty emotionalism but is as physical and as strongly "animalistic" as its male counterpart. The mystery of women's elusive sexual response appears to be no mystery at all, but a relatively lucid problem in clitoral mechanics. The validation of the clitoris has transformed the sexual image of women. The preponderance of clitoral orgasms by masturbation is an index of the female sexual will to pleasure. It is also an index of sexual autonomy. Men have always assumed their sexual autonomy, just as they assumed that their pleasure ought to be sufficient for women. Hence, the traditional pornographic image of the woman "no better than she should be," meaning really that she should be always available. If not, force is acceptable, because force can be a piquant re-confirmation of male sexual autonomy. That is, forcing the unavailable woman metaphorically validates the male's autonomous right to female availability. Inconveniently, this ignores sensibility, the fact that occasionally a man notices a distinct absence of pleasure in his woman. And it would appear, from Hite's data, that he has no better than a thirty percent chance of satisfying her, which is to say he has a seventy percent chance of keeping company with a frustrated and unhappy woman. She may educate him, and if he is a good pupil the odds for their mutual pleasure will go up, though Hite's report suggests that they are not likely to go as high as eighty percent and that he is not so very likely to be a good pupil on a sustained basis. Or she may discover that her best chances for sexual pleasure are masturbation, that she doesn't need him. If she nevertheless wants him this will not solve her problem. But the solution of it will have now shifted from him to her as she recognizes that she has options. At this point she will have discovered her sexual autonomy.

Men have always known that they could reach pleasure through masturbation. Men have also known, however, that a woman's body was more satisfying, partly because the body provided a more complex physical pleasure but perhaps more so that the consciousness within that body, willing or no, reflected and thus stimulated their own consciousness of their autonomy. When women assume their own autonomy they no longer reflect passively. They also recognize that they do not need men for pleasure because most of the time men's bodies do not reciprocate the maximum pleasure that their bodies provide men. At this point, which is increasingly the current situation, the autonomous genders are in a dialectical relationship. While men have always asserted their dialectical terms, women have only recently begun to figure out what their terms are. For better or worse, men have frequently put their terms pornographically. At their worst, they are vengeful and vicious. Sade is generally seen in this light, although I have earlier said how I think Sade transcends his viciousness. At their best, or at least more benign, these terms are often self-serving. Joyce and Faulkner, for example, make Molly Bloom and Lena Grove succorers and redeemers of man's failures. Occasionally someone like Lawrence recognizes the dialectic for what it is and attempts to present both the male and female terms. But he is after all a man, and however admirable it may be for him to recognize the contradictions, it is not reasonable to suppose he or his fellows can resolve them. The resolution requires the participation of women. As they continue to discover their terms, many of them specifically or even exclusively sexual, as in *The Hite Report,* they have also begun to put them pornographically. Women, too, have been obliged to assert their own myth of animality in order to explore it.

At about the time of Hite's report, Nancy Friday fulfilled a similar function in *My Secret Garden,* but her focus was on the pornographic imagination in women's sexual fantasies. Just as Hite had to confront a retrograde masculine myth of feminine nature, so did Friday. Hite encountered what she called "the glorification of intercourse," the myth that the naturally feminine woman should either experience orgasm from vaginal penetration or do without, and that clitoral stimulation, as in masturbation, was an unnatural act. Friday encountered the problem as a psychological conundrum, which she ironically sums up in the masculine plaint, "Why fantasize when you have me?" Again, the supposition is that even as the penis should be sufficient in lieu of orgasm, so should it be in lieu of an autonomous psyche. On the one hand, that question—the sociological representativeness of which Friday documents from her correspondents as well as from her own experience—reflects an obvious male anxiety. For example, Friday recounts how she once lost a lover by responding during sex to his question, "Tell me what you are thinking?" She was having a rather elaborate fantasy about being fucked by a stranger at a football game during a big play: Her lover couldn't take the competition. On the other hand, the question puts the burden of an answer on women, the short version of which might well be the mountain climber's, "Because it's there." But a thing's being so impenetrably *there,* as Sartre revealed, can be a problem. Men were threatened, and women responded accordingly. To threaten your man, especially in the sexual arena, has always evoked the dread image of the castrating woman. In any event, since it has been supposed that natural women don't need orgasms, would it not be even more unnatural for them to have sexual fantasies?

What is surprising about Friday's report is the degree to which it is not surprising. Why do women fantasize? For reasons one might expect, reasons rather similar to those of men. Some fantasize as compensation for an unsatisfactory sex life. The reasons for unsatisfactory sex lives are manifold and at this point fairly well researched and widely published; Friday's correspondents represent a more or less common spectrum. The most frequent reason, however, is for sexual enhancement, even when one's sex life is satisfactory or better. Friday characterizes it as a form of foreplay—simple arousal, overcoming inhibitions, constructing approval contexts, taking the initiative, etc. Friday's own sense of the most comprehensive reason is exploration:

> a psychic need for a more complete exploration of everything that was kept from [women] as girls, of everything that conceivably could be thought sexual. . . . For women, sex is still the infinite and inexhaustible variable, the one way she can unravel the mystery of what it is to be and feel a woman.

But whether for compensation, pleasure, or imaginative research, women's sexual fantasies seem connected to their autonomy. For those more evolved, it is a confirmation; for those less so, a mode of recognition. In any event, to acknowledge one's fantasies—whether it is telling one's lover or neighbor or publishing them in a book—is for women not only to assert their sexual will but to help present their terms for the continuing sexual dialectic.

In this regard it is again surprising that the character of women's sexual fantasies is no more surprising than it is. One function of feminist commentary has been to heighten the awareness of contradictions between the genders. The resultant sense of polarity has led us to suppose that when women had their say about sex we would have a very different picture than men have given. But insofar as Friday's correspondents reflect the range of women's fantasies, the gestalt is not significantly different from the range of fantasies reflected in men's pornography. Variations on submissiveness, for example, are the most frequently recurring motifs. And in general the sixteen "rooms" Friday posits as the composition of "the house of fantasy" reflect standard pornographic themes: anonymous seductions or rapes, exhibitionism, masochism, nymphomania, incest, bestiality, super-potent blacks, prostitution, etc. One explanation might well be what feminists have contended, that women have been so thoroughly defined by male terms that even their fantasies manifest them. Friday believes that "In time . . . women would go far beyond the obvious, building new wings beyond the Domination Room, finding new roles for the staff to play in addition to the Big Black Bully." Hite, while she observes tendencies in the individuation of stereotypical motifs that indicate a tension out of which a more specifically feminine range of fantasies might develop, suggests that women tend toward the stereotypical in order to evade the intimate psychological implications of fantasy. Even in this, however, there is not a great distinction from men. For it is just as likely that men, by resorting to their own standardized pornography, equally evade the intimate implications of their fantasies. But literary men, e.g. Genet or Burroughs, have incorporated their pornographic impulses into their larger imaginative concerns, and male literary pornography has evolved beyond its simplistic, hard-core base. There is every indication that women are doing likewise. The significance of Friday's books for pornography, then, is not so much what kind of fantasies they catalogue, nor how they might be interpreted, but that they document the fact that women do have fantasies and that the fantasies are, at whatever tentative stage of evolution they may be, as potent a source for exploring the myth of animality, its aesthetic and social assimilation, as are the fantasies of men.

Nonetheless, there is the as yet undetermined association between fantasy violence and real violence, all the more complex because the concept of fantasy itself is extremely fluid in psychoanalytic theory, occurring generally in theories of libido development. In Freud it tends to be associated with dream patterns and repression of infantile sexuality, the likely source of its popular connection with wish fulfillment. Fantasies for Freud (e.g., in "A Child Is Being Beaten") reveal unconscious or lost Oedipal anxieties, rooted in early stages of libido development. Thus, in regard to women, they may be the key to why an analysand has failed to progress from "infantile" clitoral to "truly feminine" vaginal sexuality, i.e., why she is "frigid." Wish fulfillment may become a problem, for example, if the woman has been arrested at the penis-envy phase, in which she is neurotically preoccupied with her clitoris, the female analogue of the penis. But here we might recall Karen Horney's cautionary note *(New Ways in Psychoanalysis)*, that Freud's methodology must be applied according to the individuality of the case and without obsessive allegiance to Freud's ubiquitous sexual thesis; thus, every dream of a woman slicing up a sausage does not necessarily mean the dreamer desires to mutilate her brother or father any more than every rape fantasy necessarily means that the fantasizer wants to be raped. According to Horney, even where a positive correlation may be established, it is frequently the case that the dream itself is fulfillment of the wish, whereupon the wish itself becomes a form of dream and introduces a new set of psychic dynamics.

The objection to the Freudian model, as has been much observed, is its thesis-ridden assumptions about the omnipotence of sexual causality and the nature of female sexuality. The extreme of this thesis can be seen in Marie Bonaparte *(Female Sexuality)*, who follows the Freudian fantasy premise and posits an "essential feminine masochism" based on the notion that only the vaginal orgasm certifies "the functionally adapted, evolved and adult woman." In this context, at least without Horney's caveat, many fantasies in Friday's *My Secret Garden* might well be construed in terms of subconscious wish fulfillment. Indeed, when Bonaparte says, "Beating, in fact, is an act preliminary to penetration, to effraction. One knocks at a door before entering. One shakes, if necessary, the lock or key," it is clear that the Freudian theory of fantasy and related psychophenomena has culminated in metaphor, a metaphor that has kept its own door closed until quite recently.

The problem this has posed for analytic practice becomes apparent in Theodor Reik *(Of Love and Lust)*, a man who is generally commonsensical about sex. But when it comes to determining the function of sexual fantasy (in 1957), his Freudian normative predispositions are at odds with his clinical experience. For example, he somewhat contradictorily says that men who fantasize before, or presumably during, sex are "perverted," although, "It is not unusual for a [presumably normal] man to call up the phantasy of a certain situation in order to become excited" when with a partner who is insufficiently inspiring. By his account of treating sexual dysfunction in women, it appears that the use of sexual fantasy as a therapy was successful about half of the time. But he is nonetheless inclined to think that fantasies "are harmful to the emotional health," although his particular example is the case of a psychotic personality who substituted other fantasy men for her real lover over a sustained period of years and finally succumbed to a "nervous breakdown." For milder neurotic cases it seems that fantasy therapy was beneficial. What is clear is that Reik himself is largely bemused by the whole phenomenon, so much so that when he addresses Freud's famous question, "What does a woman want?" he suggests that Nietzsche's Zarathustra has given the answer: "All in woman is an enigma, and all in woman has a single solution. It is called pregnancy." Doubtless even Freud hoped for a better answer than keeping women pregnant and barefoot, but when Reik's clinical experience conflicts with the conventional wisdom, he retreats discreetly to what's expected.

Luckily, however, there is Horney's common sense to modify Freudian excess. And there is Jung, who also broke with Freud on the sexual imperative. For Jung, fantasies are of course associated with dreams but also more comprehensively with myth and religion, which provide a yet more complex dynamic joining the personal and collective unconscious. Regressive fantasies may dredge up "slime from the depths . . . or inconvenient and objectionable animal tendencies," while progressive ones may generate "germs of new life and vital possibilities for the future" ("On Psychic Energy"). Since regression serves individuation, whereas progression serves adaptation to environment, each complements the other in coordinating the personal and collective myth. Here dreams and fantasies are like signposts of the psyche's progress in negotiating between the ego and the unconscious, signs of the continuing process of individuation. In this context, where concern with fantasy is more interested in the transformation or development of the psyche than with its pathological variants, wish fulfillment is a relatively insignificant concept. That is, Jung seems more attentive to the holistic function of fantasy than to its neurotic character. He also distinguishes between fantasies unconsciously emerging and those consciously invented.

Pursuing this distinction, and relating it to Jung's sense of the evolution of science from magic and the alchemical arts, M. Esther Harding *(Psychic Energy)* contends that healthy individuation in transforming the libido to constructive energy can only be achieved by trained psychoanalytic or accidentally intuitive "art." However, she seems to feel that fantasy is often inclined to regression and that a "slothful preoccupation with phantasy" will cut the flow of one's libido and arrest psychic development. Still, the way in is the way out; for one must then use "will" and "art" to probe the psyche; "The phantasy or dream images found there will surely give the clue to the difficulty." In Harding's application of Jungian theory, then, she is of two minds about fantasy function, that it can be a regressive seduction into itself and that it can be the guidon for finding the way out of the psychic morass. In its latter and positive function she makes the analogue with creative art, which serves the communal or holistic purpose of articulating archetypes, both sexual and otherwise, and casting them into forms comprehensible to their time. "The genuine artist," she says, "will portray not only his own inner condition but also the unconscious psyche of his time."

Psychological theories, then, project a correspondence between fantasy and the unconscious but do not tell us much about any but aberrant behavior. The Jungian approach is fruitful in the context of pornography because it suggests a useful analogy between fantasy and art. The kind of fantasy represented in *My Secret Garden* is by and large what Jung understood as consciously invented fantasy, although the content of any given fantasy, or any given work of art for that matter, may well be beyond its author's total control or comprehension. The fantasy component of art has been acknowledged, whether or not approved, throughout the history of aesthetics and art criticism. Even idealist aesthetics, which preferred art's ennobling function, accommodated the fancifully ugly and grotesque if it supported the proper moral perspective. Materialist aesthetics, on the other hand, have held that "truth" is ennobling whatever "objectionable animal tendencies," to use Jung's phrase, might be dredged up by its revelations.

Pornography is obviously in the materialist tradition, probing as it does the myth of animality. By the mid 1970s Shere Hite and Nancy Friday had put an approach to the female perspective toward that myth squarely on the table. They had demonstrated that women were sexually active, that they were seeking pleasure as much if not more than maternity, and that they indulged a vigorous fantasy life in this pursuit. On the popular front this was received not only as news but also as a declaration of rights. But however it was received, it demonstrated that female nature had the capacity for pornographic imagination.

## DEFINITION AND DIALECTIC

We turn now to pornographic fiction by women. Women's soft-core pornography is, like that of men, sentimental, and ranges from culturally conservative to reactionary; it has a distinctly feminine perspective, however much that might be disputed by some feminists, but its conservatism inclines at its maximum to confirm women's traditional roles and at its minimum to be dubious in assessing the transformation of them. Women's hard-core pornography is more problematic, in that there is very little of it, and what there is has been produced under contrapuntal auspices. What might be called the old pornography—represented here by Anaïs Nin and Diane di Prima—was written for men and reflects the conventions of male pornography, although it adds a feminine dimension that has been largely ignored. The new pornography—represented here by three recent anthologies—is self-consciously feminist and seeks to explore specifically female, if not feminist, sexual attitudes. In this context I will discuss the much debated difference between "erotica" and "pornography."

Women's literary pornography is aesthetically similar to that of men. Both probe sexuality's psychic and cultural implications so as to serve epistemological functions. The four primary instances discussed here happen to be in a "realistic" style, although writers who use pornography more incidentally, such as Marge Piercy or Joanna Russ, show that women have used the motif in experimental and futuristic forms. What does distinguish women's literary pornography from that of men, at least for the present, is its address to feminist dialectic. Women novelists, like their sociologist and sexologist counterparts, are concerned with finding female definitions of feminine nature and differentiating them from traditional masculine definitions. Correlatively, they're also concerned to examine the social contradictions inherently derived from traditional concepts of "feminine nature." Pornography is a new tool for women, and its pertinence to sexual nature, identity, and roles encourages its current focus. Its future, as some feminist writers anticipate and current experiments suggest, will likely be more divergent. Obviously not all female pornography is feminist in outlook. But those who contend that no pornography can be feminist, or even female, are either using a subjectively polemical definition of the term or are ignoring the evidence produced by women writers past and present.

### *Soft-Core Sentiments*

What is true is that women's soft-core pornography tends to counterpoint feminist concerns. Sentiment is the staple of women's soft-core pornography, just as in that written by men. The theme of power prevails for men, while love is the prevailing motif for women, although obviously there is a good deal of overlap in both directions. This form of pornography is particularly appropriate for popular literature, which tends to cast life in the mold of sentimental melodrama, while being sufficiently responsive to modern relativity to represent good and evil somewhat less categorically than its earlier nineteenth-century versions. The main business of the modern form is to acculturate the passions. While sex is represented more or less explicitly on occasion, it functions more as a general motivational presence and frequently as a sign of thematic poignance and implication. When love is the theme, sex is of course the field on which it is proved. Currently women are much concerned with the relationship between female sexuality and love, and this is naturally enough being exploited in popular literature. The Harlequin series of romances is a good instance, "because," as its back covers proclaim, "no one touches the heart of a woman quite like Harlequin!" Or at least the hearts of some women, since Harlequin books tend to oppose feminist ranks in the famous battle between the sexes. It is not so much that they don't represent independent women as that they don't approve of women being too independent, which means that deep down women should recognize their traditional rootedness to men. Charlotte Lamb's version of *The Sex War* (1983) is a case in point. In it the function of sex is to invalidate the feminist dialectic by confirming that old sentimental favorite, the status quo. The "sex war" is a chimera; men are simply doing their job, and women are too hung up in competition née jealousy née frigidity to properly understand that their accommodation of men as they are has a mutual payoff. Naturally, the bigger the payoff, the better.

But after all Harlequin books are a quick read for a cheap thrill; one can find dozens of them in the free bin at any local used book store. Not so with the heavyweights of the genre, such as Jacqueline Susann. It is probably not accidental that Lamb's featherweight version of the sex war uses a business backdrop, for in modern popular literature sex and cash frequently validate one another—sex renders cash natural, while cash civilizes sex. Susann's first novel, *Valley of the Dolls,* addressed this nexus so adroitly as to become a standard for the genre. Moreover, it was a tremendous commercial success itself. A bestseller, it then was made into a movie spectacular. The movie has not survived so well as the novel, although it did inspire at least one pornographic parody, *Beyond the Valley of the Dolls.* Significantly *Valley of the Dolls* appeared (1966) a year after Helen Gurley Brown had been hired to transform *Cosmopolitan* magazine from a bland journal of housewifery to a sexily chic baedeker of feminine "careersma" (an apt coinage for our age by the critic Gerald Graff). Not only did Brown, author of her own bestselling *Sex and the Single Girl,* provide cover puffery for the novel, but *Cosmopolitan* ran a condensation of it in June 1966.

Susann and Brown seem to be cut from the same bolt, both skillful exploiters of the tension women face in trying to reconcile feminine roles with professional careers, the ground on which much feminist argument still takes its stand. That they were exploiters rather than stateswomen is suggested in the fundamental contradiction between their positions. Brown's stance in *Cosmopolitan* was that women could and should reconcile femininity with careers, advice she gave with a blithe cheeriness. Susann's plot, however, quite explicitly traces the destructive consequences of attempting this reconciliation. In the great forum of ideas this merely presents differing perspectives, but insofar as the forum becomes a marketplace, it would seem to offer the buyer two opposing remedies. That buyers bought both in great numbers may imply a schizophrenia on the subject but most certainly indicates a fascination with it.

That the jury is still out, indicated by the fate of the Equal Rights Amendment, makes *Valley of the Dolls* all the more intriguing. Essentially it is a melodrama of two American dreams—marriage and show business success—in conflict, although it provides ready extrapolation to the more generalized conflict between marriage and careers. Behind this of course lurks the still more generalized anxiety that the burgeoning feminist aspirations of the mid-1960s threatened social and cultural stability. Susann's plot exploits this anxiety maximally and ultimately confirms it. Set in the glamorous world of show business, the action is more or less evenly distributed between New York and Hollywood, in such showplaces as the Persian Room, El Morocco, Copacabana, the offices of show biz moguls, stage play rehearsals, movie and television studios, and bedrooms, where we are treated to exploratory sex, frustrated sex, manipulative sex, desperate sex, and ecstatic sex, as well as conspicuous consumption of seconal, dexedrine, and benzedrine (the "dolls" of the title), and suicide. The general metaphorical conception is that a woman's struggle to the top of Mount Success is a bitch, and then she dies—or sustains herself on the dolls. It appears that benign success is possible for a man (one of them manages it), if he forfeits his claim to love, marriage, and family. Not so for women, who are unable to separate themselves, just as Freud contends, from their maternal instincts, or at least the natural analogue of those instincts, their sexual/emotional need of a man.

Thus Susann, like Lamb after her, promotes that old sentimental favorite, the status quo. But unlike Lamb, Susann offers no exit. If the conflict between marriage and career is destructive, so is each one as an alternative in itself. Female careerists are frustrated and mean-spirited solipsists, and so are wives, who bear the further onus of being trivial and dull. That there is no redeeming hero on the horizon, let alone in the nick of time at the railroad track, is perhaps what saves *Valley* from being at least a traditional melodrama. It is melodrama, in that the characters and their fates are sentimentalized cardboard types, but it is "tragic" melodrama, in that the destructiveness for women is open-ended and continuing. Susann acknowledges that women have an existential problem, but the solutions of competition with men on the treadmill of worldly success or indulging a Barbie Doll ethos are equal dilemmas. To this extent even latter-day feminists might acknowledge a feminist content in Susann's otherwise exploitative plot.

### *Interrogation of Nature and Bourgeois Liberation*

By the mid-1960s, as the success of *Valley of the Dolls* and *Cosmopolitan* indicated, there was clearly an audience, and market, for soft-core pornography by and about women. But the validation of explicit sexuality required the sentimental cover of an association with the search for love and marriage, and the dovetailing of that, for better or worse, with careersma. The motif continues in popular literature, as evidenced by Harlequin's *The Sex War*.

The logic of the love/marriage imperative is a cultural mythification of the energy of love. That domesticated myth is in turn an attempt to harness the energies of passion. The concept of passion has burdened theories of female nature since classical times. Women have been credited with being the source of passionate implosion or explosion, and either way the consequences were bad. Sex goes with passion, of course, just as passion goes with love. But the thorny realities of those associations were acculturated by normative myths. Freud's giant step in disentangling sexuality from love and passion was somewhat checked by his and his generation's predisposition under social pressure to fall back on myth. The recent push of Kinsey, Masters and Johnson, Hite, Friday, and others toward hard data has doubtless been hampered by residual mythologies, but it has demonstrated that sexuality has a reality distinct from the myths of love and passion, however much it may be part of an ecosystem with them. Serious female writers, feminists in particular, use pornography and eroticism to investigate both the nature of sexuality and its relation to the emotional and social mythologies that house it.

One of the first to confront the problem was Radclyffe Hall, whose 1928 novel about lesbianism, *The Well of Loneliness*, is a classic if for no other reason than its intensive treatment of the subject. Although its theme is almost exclusively sexual, this is developed in terms of its protagonist's vain search for normal life and love, denied because of her "inverted" sexuality, as Hall terms it. So it is an erotic rather than a pornographic work, but it is notable here because its attitude toward sexuality is characteristic of much feminist fiction that is pornographic. Its decorous erotic tone is in part due to its time, a period when women did not publish their sympathies with lesbianism, let alone do so with explicit description. But its tone is probably more a function of its author's purpose, to make a case for the normality of "inverts," if only society would accommodate them. In addition to this polemical purpose, there is an exploratory one, an inquiry into how a "freak of nature" might live a sane, productive life, and to what extent she could morally indulge her sexuality and love in a heterosexual world.

Even its polemic, however, poses questions. While it is made pointedly clear, for example, that the protagonist's sexuality is not genetically based, there is the suggestion that her parents' strong prenatal desire for a boy has had a determining effect on her mannish predispositions. Objectively, this seems like an eighteenth-century Shandyan fancy, but as the plot develops, the concept of "normality" is in fact characterized as anachronistic, one in which "aberrations" are categorically disappeared. So the protagonist's inversion, a product of nature, is only perceived to be unnatural by a benighted cultural ethos. In all other respects than her inverted sexuality, she is normal, in fact a talented contributor to the commonweal—as a writer in civilian life and a valued ambulance driver in World War I. The protagonist strives for a lesbian monogamy that is made analogous to heterosexual marriage, as another means of validating lesbianism's niche in nature.

While contemporary feminists have critically scrutinized the myths of love and marriage, Hall's choice in 1928 was to fit lesbianism into the prevailing mythology. To be perceived as unnatural is in fact to be rendered unnatural and thus denied a normal life. The weaker inverts turn decadent, wrapping themselves in the shroud of their assigned nature. The protagonist's strength preserves her from that cynicism, but without it she is preyed upon by hope of a normal life. While this tension provides the novel's pathos, more important, it questions both the reality of "the state of nature" and the cultural causes for this perception of the "natural."

The interrogative approach to assumptions about nature, especially about the nature of women, characterizes much feminist pornographic literature.

In 1974—the year both Shere Hite's preliminary report, *Sexual Honesty*, and Nancy Friday's *My Secret Garden* were published—Erica Jong's *Fear of Flying* became a bestseller. Its concurrence with those books was pertinent in that it explores the correspondence between sexual fantasy and sexual reality, thus bringing the pornographic imagination to bear on the nature of women by asking "What does a woman want?" for herself and from sex and marriage. Freud's famous question is evoked not only by the book's title, which alludes to the common dream of flying that Freud construed to signify "nothing but the longing for the ability of sexual accomplishment . . . an early infantile wish," but also by the protagonist's confrontation with her wants, which takes the form of a choice between two men, both psychoanalysts, and is frequently punctuated by remembrances of things past psychoanalysts have said to compound the difficulty of her knowing herself.

The story line is quite simple, based on the eternal triangle. Isadora Wing, the protagonist, flies with her husband, psychoanalyst Bennett Wing, to a psychoanalytic convention in Vienna (where Freud taught until he fled the Nazis), at which she meets an English analyst, Adrian Goodlove (the names of course parody the plot), with whom she immediately falls in love. She leaves her husband and wings it around Europe with Goodlove, but discovers that neither his sexuality nor his love are up to snuff. Deserted by Goodlove, broke and bedraggled, she tracks Bennett down in London and is tentatively reunited with him. Isadora is an aspiring writer in whose craw is stuck a lifetime of analysis. So complete is her Freudian typicality that she's even married an analyst, an unimaginative anal compulsive to boot, one who can't do anything from taking a leak to making a baby without first consulting its unconscious meaning. Nevertheless, he's good in bed, although that does not diminish her guiding light, her fantasy of "the Zipless Fuck."

The Zipless Fuck, under the symbolic umbrella of "flying," is the novel's central metaphor, its vehicle for investigating the powers of sexuality. It is the logical extension of "Growing up female in America":

> What a liability! You grew up with your ears full of cosmetic ads, love songs, advice columns, whoreoscopes, Hollywood gossip, and moral dilemmas on the level of TV soap operas. . . . What all the ads and whoreoscopes seemed to imply was that if only you were narcissistic enough, if only you took proper care of your smells, your hair, your boobs, your eyelashes, your armpits, your crotch, your stars, your scars, and your choice of Scotch in bars—you would meet a beautiful, powerful, potent, and rich man who would satisfy every longing, fill every hole, make your heart skip a beat (or

> stand still), make you misty, and fly you to the moon (preferably on gossamer wings), where you would live totally satisfied forever.

Reality is not only beside the point, it is an intrusion on the cultural mythology. The culture, in short, breeds a woman better equipped to indulge fantasy than address reality. Hence, the Zipless Fuck, not just sex but "a platonic ideal," so transcendent that all impediments to communion disappear, "Zippers fell away like rose petals" and "Your whole soul flowed out through your tongue and into the mouth of your lover." And of course the fantasy supplies a "passion" that reality deflates, the transcendent passion that we've already noted as a sentimentalizing agent so functional in the mythology of feminine nature. The fantasy has three requirements: that she not get to know her lover well, which would of course introduce the deflation of reality, that therefore the encounter be brief, and better yet that it be altogether anonymous. As the Kronhausens have noted, these are standard aspects of hard-core pornography, although here their purpose is not to induce orgasm but to get beyond the "ulterior motives" of sexual politics; as Isadora says, "The zipless fuck is the purest thing there is. And is rarer than the unicorn. And I have never had one." So Isadora is primed for her encounter with Goodlove.

Goodlove is the antithesis of Bennett Wing, the free-flowing Laingian to Bennett's constipated Freudian. Isadora promptly recognizes in him the long-sought object of her fantasy. But things are not what they seem, in either direction. Adrian is more impotent than not, and even when he's not he isn't particularly good. But what he lacks in starch he compensates for with brainy fertility, and Isadora falls in love with him precisely for the contradictions, "His limp prick penetrated where a stiff one would never have reached." Ordinarily, reversing the masculine commonplace, she likes men's bodies and their "silky" pricks but not their "hopelessly befuddled" minds or "intolerable" ideas. But, free flowing bzazz notwithstanding, Goodlove is after all a man, and his intolerable ideas will out. One of these is a "typical Laingian" idealization of madness as the source of poetic creativity. Corollaries to madness are irresponsibility and lack of commitment. Goodlove steadfastly refuses to commit himself to loving Isadora, which probably should be a warning. But, dazzled by a Platonism even more platonic than she had anticipated, she can't quite give up the ideal that her fantasy has become.

Still, the longer she's with him the more she realizes that his apparent free spirit masks a half-baked Laingian existentialism that is at bottom an intolerably cruel indifference. That is, his reality has intruded on her fantasy. This purges her fantasy and permits her a new look at reality: If Goodlove's indifference is an inadequate ethos, so too is the dependence she has heretofore indulged—dependence on analysts, dependence on her husband, dependence on her fantasy ideal. Her recognition of what independent being means had come from what she calls—in an argument with a reactionary professor about "permissiveness" in democracy—"constructive permissiveness," i.e., giving herself the freedom and independence to live out the failure of her fantasy. Upon its ruins she builds a new, materialist rather than idealist, relation to reality. She returns to her husband not because she ought to or needs to but because she chooses to, just as thereafter she can choose to stay or go.

*Fear of Flying*, then, turns pornographic fantasy back on itself as a form of narcissistic idealism that tantalizes the culture. And, somewhat like Plato, Jong envisions a split female psyche, between its craving for an ideal passion and the human necessity to survive the daily round. That the two are not compatible in Jong's view is evidenced by Isadora's long unhappy history with analysis, for analysis continually refers the quotidian back to the unconscious, based on mythic and ideal sources. Particularly in an age of technology, when flying is commonplace, Freud's interpretation of the dream of flying can only be a mythic construction predicated in the desire to explain the psyche by linking it with the ideal. To try out the idea, as Isadora does, is to refute its authority, that is to take it from the realm of ideas to that of the daily round, in her case the proving ground of sexuality. Once the incompatibility between ideal and actual is clear, as it is to Isadora by novel's end, then the choice becomes an index of independence and sanity. Thus pornographic imagination is the agency of both philosophical and personal discovery.

The discovery and its process also have social implications, which have a polemical function in *Fear of Flying*. Social convention prescribes a passive social role for women, but this is in contradiction to the active fantasy life generated, for example, by advertising of the sort we have noted Jong evoking early in the novel. An active fantasy life is sooner or later likely to result in action, and the data on extramarital and premarital sex indicate that Isadora's is hardly an aberrant case. But Jong's plot goes a step farther and makes "constructive permissiveness," heretofore known as promiscuity, ethically viable. It might be too much to say that Jong becomes an advocate; however the implication is strong that any given woman (men are assumed to be granted license already) would have to put fantasy on trial to discover, like Isadora, its invalidity. Otherwise one would simply be subscribing to yet another idea. But this may be carrying philosophical ramifications beyond the plot's requirements. In any event, Jong unequivocally casts women in a sexual light conventionally reserved for men. Women have pornographic fantasies, they are promiscuous, they see men as sex objects, and men even have their own form of frigidity, impotence.

All of this also has obvious implications for the institution of marriage, primarily in terms of the passion/love/marriage nexus. Once love is removed from the mythology of passion and defined by the tentativeness of quotidian choice, as it is in *Fear of Flying*, then the foundation of marriage is rendered rather dubious as a social institution. Divorce statistics suggest this negation is already under way, but statistics don't make an ethos. Jong is exploring an ethos of infidelity and divorce, i.e. an ethos of relativity.

This promised to become clearer in Jong's 1978 sequel, *How to Save Your Own Life*. The narcissism that victimized Isadora in *Fear of Flying* was culturally induced at the expense of healthy ego development. By the end of that novel she has the foundation for a healthy ego, which liberates her from reductive narcissism. This ego is the basis of the ethos proposed in the later work. How you save your own life is by keeping faith with yourself. This makes fidelity a dialectical relation between the self and the other. *How to Save Your Own Life* features the return of the eternal triangle with one Josh Ace taking Goodlove's place in the continuing saga of Isadora's right to life without Bennett. But the ethical problem is unfortunately reduced to melodrama when Isadora discovers that Bennett—who "had always played saint while he cast [Isadora] in the role of sinner" because of her Goodlove affair—himself had had an affair at an earlier crucial point in their marriage and had thus broken faith with her. This takes Isadora off the hook, but it also effectively shelves the ethical question. In fact Jong gives herself another chance to engage it when she introduces Isadora into a lesbian relationship, which makes the triangle consist of Josh, Isadora, and Rosanna, the lesbian. But here again, when Rosanna breaks faith with Isadora by keeping Josh's letters from her and thereby manipulating her away from Josh into her own waiting lesbian arms, the ethical issue is shelved, or at best trivialized.

It is worth noting, nevertheless, that Henry Miller (cast as Kurt Hammer, once again exemplifying Jong's relentless search for the parodic name) is credited as the inspiration for the enlightened egoism of the novel's ethos. But the ethos itself remains vague and is superseded by a form of popular psychology that focuses on relieving people of the burden of guilt. Sex and fantasy seem intended to serve the same dialectical function they have in *Fear of Flying*, but when the pertinent ethical issues are subordinated to flaccid psychology they lose their signifying edge. Nevertheless, if Jong failed to resolve the ethics of her plot, these two novels do form a contemporary *bildungsroman* exploding the conventional mythology of passive feminine sexuality. They also demonstrate that the pornographic imagination can have a vital function in feminist fiction that is prospecting for a viable concept of female nature.

### *Mining the Hard-Core*

Jong's novels, and their popularity, contributed a fictional perspective to the general literary renaissance of female sexuality in the mid-1970s.

Perhaps it was this fictive and sexological eruption, generally under a feminist aegis, that encouraged Anaïs Nin to publish *Delta of Venus* in 1976. This collection of stories and vignettes, presented as "erotica," had actually been written in the early 1940s. The pieces had been originally commissioned as hard-core pornography, and at their least ambitious they are more or less that. But at their most ambitious they are serious literature, if not altogether realized. A year earlier, in 1975, Edith Wharton had posthumously contributed to the female pornography boom when R. W. B. Lewis' biography of her included an appendix, for the first time publishing Wharton's "Beatrice Palmato" fragment. Wharton's accompanying outline of the work, probably written in 1935, indicates that the fragment was to be part of a story or novella, but the fragment itself is unequivocally pornographic. It was becoming clear that women writers had been more involved in pornographic production than had been previously supposed.

That was, however, no news to the poet Diane di Prima, who had published a pornographic novel with Olympia Press in 1969 under the title *Memoirs of a Beatnik*. Unlike her two famous predecessors di Prima was writing both for a masculine market and for a publisher's series that had a prominent pornographic tradition, and one that included several other women among its authors (see Michael Perkins, *The Secret Record*, especially Chapters 4 and 9). Before turning to Nin it will be useful to note how a contemporary writer made use of hard-core pornographic material.

As with Henry Miller's work, di Prima's *Memoirs* seems to be part autobiography and part fiction. Likewise, insofar as the autobiography is credible, di Prima's sexual activity is as relentlessly gargantuan as Miller's. In Miller's work free and abundant sexuality signifies a free and abundant person; it has an analogous although less programmatic function in *Memoirs*. In a book of otherwise casual and unself-conscious style, sexuality is calculated, with at least one eye toward the requirements of the pornographic series for which it was intended. The story picks up di Prima in late adolescence, takes her into college, from which she departs after a year or so, through a two- or three-year period in the mid-1950s spent beatnik fashion in communal pads, and deposits her, pregnant, on the threshold of her adult life as a poet. Along the way she encounters, and describes in pornographic detail, all of the predictable sexual liaisons—heterosexual, lesbian, homosexual, group—though there is a minimum of autoeroticism and no bestiality. Sex is depicted as the casually youthful expression of free spirits and is generally beneficent.

Even exceptions prove the rule. When she is raped by her girlfriend's father—whose family is wracked by various sexual repressions and perversions—the rape itself is minimalized, and essentially serves as a Juvenalian satire on the sick sexuality and unhealthy spiritual life of the American family; similarly with modeling for commercial pornography, to which she is driven by financial exigency. She finds an integrity in hard-core pornography that makes it far less "obscene" than the titillation of soft-core. These negatives provide such dialectical edge as there is to di Prima's otherwise blithely beatific sexual ethic. Although the book never works hard enough to really break a sweat, its working hypothesis is that sex without psychopathic games and manipulations promotes fellow-feeling and communal spirit. This laissez-faire bohemianism obviously predates contemporary feminist attitudes toward pornography. But it does have in common with some contemporary feminism the desentimentalizing of sexuality. Or, more precisely, if it risks sentimentalizing sex as the sign of the free-spirited possibilities for the community of non-acquisitive humankind, it desentimentalizes its imperative association with love and marriage. Aside from a schoolgirl lesbian crush, love rears its hoary romantic head only once. And although she describes sex with her lover as more transcendent than it is elsewhere in the novel, she dispatches both love and lover without a backward glance.

Marriage to di Prima is obviously for squares. Love makes out like a bee bumbling from blossom to blossom and is not to be taken too seriously. Toward novel's end, as di Prima and her merry band of beatniks feel the call of the wild waning in favor of the more mature responsibilities of their various arts and sciences, di Prima decides to punctuate this new spirit by having a child. She selects the father according to his genetic and karmic character and sends him innocently into the sunset, suggesting that if love is vulnerable to how the wind blows, making babies is an act of will. Meanwhile, after her budding poetic craft has been given benediction by Allen Ginsberg and seminal baptism by Jack Kerouac, di Prima ends the novel with a kid and a career and embarks on the first day of the rest of her life with nothing more sentimental than a wink and a grin.

The wink doubtless comes from di Prima's consciousness of making a few bucks by writing for a notorious pornographic publisher. This, and the fact that as a novel *Memoirs of a Beatnik* is at best cursory, seriously qualify the book's thematic weight. Still, once the book gets beyond its first three absolutely cynical chapters it exhibits an ironic disinterestedness in its crassest pornographic aspects that suggests at least a minimum of di Prima's imagination is at work. Only a committed professional pornographer could altogether expunge her imaginative sensibilities, and di Prima, as a writer, is at most an incidental pornographer. And there are signs, as we've noted, of a sexual ethic that is not in itself necessarily either sexist or cynical, as we might expect from a book written solely to induce male orgasms.

Similarly with Anaïs Nin, who notes in her preface to *Delta of Venus* that,

> Here in the erotica I was writing to entertain, under pressure from a client who wanted me "to leave out the poetry," I believed that my style was derived from a reading of men's works. For this reason I long felt that I had compromised my feminine self. I put the erotica aside. Rereading it these many years later, I see that my own voice was not completely suppressed. In numerous passages I was intuitively using a woman's language, seeing sexual experience from a woman's point of view. I finally decided to release the erotica for publication because it shows the beginning efforts of a woman in a world that had been the domain of men.

Nin's "beginning efforts" were not the work of a novice writer—she had been seriously writing for more than a decade—but neither were they the work of an established author. Composed in 1940-41, they predate the publication of the main body of her fictional work, which did not begin to appear until 1944 and reached a peak in the late 1950s, in this respect, they are relatively early work. Moreover, given the lifelong passion for the aesthetic life and its integrity that she records in her *Diaries,* it is quite natural that she would be indignant at a patron who demanded pornography without "poetry." Her *Diary* entries about this patron and his commission (several of which are included as the preface to *Delta*) are explicit in their contempt. They are also explicit in declaring the parodic cynicism with which these stories were conceived. However, in their very protest they also document Nin's resistance to the terms of the commission, to denying her poetic sensibility. So it is not surprising that later in her life, with her writing career in perspective, she should perceive what she must have felt all along, that her "own voice was not completely suppressed." Neither is it unusual that this earlier work, born as it was in such a salacious context, would be tentative and uneven in its manifestation of her voice. Nonetheless, her voice does assert itself, as she says, in numerous passages, and in at least one story—the longest and most complex in the collection—her voice so molds pornography to her larger imaginative preoccupations as to be dominant.

One indication that this was likely to happen comes in a *Diary* passage where Nin characterizes her anonymous patron as sexually neurotic: "Clinical sex, deprived of all the warmth of love—the orchestration of all the senses . . . all the euphoric accompaniments, background music, moods, atmosphere, variations—forced him to resort to literary aphrodisiacs." In response to his continuing insistence on more sex and less poetry, she notes, "I began to write tongue-in-cheek, to become outlandish, inventive, and so exaggerated that I thought he would realize I was caricaturing sexuality." In the context of an entry from several years later—"While neurosis rules, all life becomes a symbolic play"—one sees the ironic twist operating within Nin's compliance with her client's demands. At the same time as she feeds her patron's symbolic play, she counterpoints it with one of her own. For if his neurotic need is for an aphrodisiac, her own slightly neurotic fantasy (stimulated by her need for money to support an "irresponsible" entourage) is that he will come to his senses and become a true patron rewarding her for her genuine poetic talents, as she also notes in her *Diary*: "Wasn't the old man tired of pornography? Wouldn't a miracle take place? I began to imagine him saying: 'Give me everything she writes, I want it all, I like all of it. I will send her a big present, a big check for all the writing she has done'." Thus, her counterpoint is calculated, not altogether unconsciously, to awaken him to a more comprehensive imagination. A frontal approach would be sexual caricature, which she executes blatantly in "Pierre," one of the later stories in *Delta of Venus.*

The story opens with necrophilia. Pierre happens upon a man pulling the nude body of a drowned woman from the river. While the other goes to fetch the police, Pierre becomes enamored of the corpse and proceeds to foreplay and " as he began to penetrate her, water flowed from between her legs, as if he were making love to a naiad." He has some difficulty in reaching a climax, as one might imagine, which he achieves only when he hears the man returning with the police. Nin's *Diary* unfortunately does not tell us whether her patron regarded the naiad detail as an aphrodisiac or as poetry, or whether he got the symbolic "play" between corpses and pornography. But the story pushes on to voyeurism and an incipient Oedipal preoccupation, and Nin then gets seriously "outlandish." Pierre's wife has a health complication that precludes sex and children. They adopt two children, naturally two sexually ripe teenagers. The boy is a bit of a prude, but the girl is "dark and vivid," and her natural mother had been a hooker to boot. In the orphanage they had been "inseparable . . . as close as a brother and sister." The boy doesn't know how to take her post-pubescence, but Pierre does. Father and daughter get it on, in detail and at length. Pierre is feeling pretty cocky, but the boy is somewhat sullen, particularly after inadvertently seeing sister and father at play. Meanwhile the daughter, who is perfectly happy with her father's ministrations (although ignorant of his necrophiliac past), has a yen for someone her own age, namely her brother. By ingenious strategem she gets her brother to perk up, and everybody lives happily ever after.

It seems almost impossible that Nin's patron could fail to get the hyperbolical message, but perhaps he was more amused than chagrined by pornography's connection to the incestuous and the dead. In fact, from internal evidence in the stories (Pierre appears in earlier stories before he gets one of his own), as well as its distinct lack of subtlety, it appears that this story is a fairly late act in Nin's continuing symbolic drama with her employer, as if she had reached a pique of impatience with his dogged singlemindedness. Rather earlier on in their dialogue (her *Diary* places it in

December of 1941, and it is the first story in the collection) Nin had been more coy, although considerably more ominous, with "The Hungarian Adventurer." He is a man whose formidable charm and style have earned him the nickname of the Baron. His vocation is charming women out of their pants and fortunes, which he does so winningly and with such sexual expertise that they never complain even when he moves abruptly on to new horizons, as he invariably does. However, his pornographic lifestyle has a severe aftereffect. Down the pike of life the Baron develops a modest taste for little girls, which takes a kinkier turn for the worse when his two teenage daughters come to live with him. The plot thickens to counterpoint the pornography as the Baron becomes obsessed with sex, this pathology stripping him of charm, reason, and restraint. The culmination comes when, having debauched his daughters and driven off his latest wife, the fevered Baron pokes his lollypop into his sleeping son's mouth. This is the last straw, and everyone deserts "the now frenzied, aging Baron." Apparently her patron identified more with the pornography than with the Baron's fate, because he passed word to her that he was "pleased," but that she should "Concentrate on sex. Leave out the poetry."

Nin's *Diary* is never quite precise about what the patron means by "poetry." She does contrast his taste for the "clinical" with her own for the "euphoric," but it is not clear what that might mean in any given passage. When Nin, for example, says of an exotic Brazilian dancer and prostitute that "her sex was like a giant hothouse flower," is the flower simile "poetry"? Or when that same lady kneels before a customer and takes "his penis in her jeweled hands" are the jewels an unnecessary fancy? Certainly such prototypically clinical sexologists as Masters and Johnson do not refer to their subjects' organs as flowers or their digits as bejeweled. If this is what the patron meant, Nin does not seem to have paid much attention; her descriptive style is fairly "literary" throughout. If by "poetry" he meant elaborate rendering of situation, character, and plot, she met him halfway. Sometimes her characters and their situations are the essence of simplicity, but at others they are complex. But either way sexual obsession is a recurring motif in *The Delta of Venus*, usually providing plot causality. Preoccupation with sex, i.e. isolating it from the fuller context of being, causes neurotic enslavement to a symbolic role in a play from which there is no exit to a free life.

In some part this theme is a function of her running argument with the patron. But it was an argument that obliged her to readdress her concept of human sexuality, a subject which had intrigued her at least since her "unprofessional study" of D. H. Lawrence in 1931. It was also an important dimension of her relationship to Henry Miller, under whose aegis she first took up the pornographic commission. In her *Diary* for December 1941, she finally writes a letter to the patron, in which she notes,

> Sex loses all its power and magic when it becomes explicit, mechanical, overdone, when it becomes a mechanistic obsession. It becomes a bore. You have taught us more than anyone I know how wrong it is not to mix it with emotion, hunger, desire, lust, whims, caprices, personal ties, deeper relationships that change its color, flavor rhythms, intensities. . . . Sex does not thrive on monotony. Without feeling, inventions, moods, no surprises in bed. Sex must be mixed with tears, laughter, words, promises, scenes, jealousy, envy, all the spices of fear, foreign travel, new faces, novels, stories, dreams, fantasies, music, dancing, opium, wine.

Curiously, Nin seems not to have noticed, in her hostility to the patron, that in fact the pornographic stories he had been buying *did* include every item she notes as essential to sex, his disclaimers of "poetry" notwithstanding. It would seem that, just as she had been playing a game with him by counterpointing his pornography with her own poetic touches, he had been playing a game with her. It was certainly obvious to him as the stories kept coming in that the more he protested her poetic touches the more wily she became in putting them in. The result, from his point of view, was some of the best pornography in the history of the genre. This did not of course reduce Nin's frustration. But her complaint was not quite what she thought it was at the time. It did not involve sex per se, as she had articulated it; it involved the synthesis of sex with being. Moreover, there was another problem, which she had described in a *Diary* entry for February 1941:

> I had a feeling that Pandora's box contained the mysteries of woman's sensuality, so different from man's and for which man's language was inadequate. The language of sex had yet to be invented. The language of the senses was yet to be explored. D. H. Lawrence began to give instinct a language, he tried to escape the clinical, the scientific, which only captures what the body feels.

Not only was the language of sex in general as yet uninvented, but what progress had been made was by men. Women, whose sexuality she supposed was quite different, had no sexual language at all. So what language was she writing in? She couldn't be sure, as she noted retrospectively years later in 1976, "I long felt that I had compromised my feminine self." But this problem, like the other, was not quite what she described. It really was not about language and style but rather about perception. She supposed that her perception of women's sexuality had been warped by masculine assumptions in general and her patron's demands in particular. There doubtless was this warp, but it was not so comprehensive as she then thought. As she noted, again, when she published *Delta* in 1976, "In numerous passages I was intuitively using a woman's language, seeing sexual experience from a woman's point of view." And in "Elena" that point of view distinctly transcends the limitations of the pornographic genre to assert itself, exploring the function of obsession in the synthesis of sexuality and being.

At 64 pages, "Elena" is both the longest and most aesthetically realized story in *Delta of Venus*. In general Nin's fictional works are comparatively short, and "Elena" is somewhat longer than *House of Incest* (1936, 1958), her first sustained book-length work, and it is a little over half the length of *Collages*, her last novel. So it represents a serious investment of time and energy. This was doubtless due in part to the fact that the patron was paying her a dollar a typescript page. But it unequivocally challenges his admonitions to "cut the poetry." It is not a great story—although it will likely stand as one of the great pornographic stories—but it is a serious story, giving coherence to the psychosexual perceptions that miscellaneously pop up in the other stories. It also manifests the principal recurring motif of her mature fiction, the exploration of "inner space," as she later phrased it. And it evoked the persistent themes of her *Diary*—identity and liberation of the self, femininity in that context, neurosis, love and its dynamics, the aesthetic life. Moreover, it reflects the basic tension in her life; as she noted in the fourth volume of her *Diary*, "What ought to be and not what is interests me. . . . In between, an all-consuming loneliness." Elena experiences this loneliness, the interior isolation of one who probes what she is in relation to what she "ought" to be. The probe transpires in her relationship with Pierre (whose later story, as we've seen, Nin turned to sexual caricature). Because this is a love affair, Elena, whose point of view dominates, seeks the nature of both her self and the other, another recurring theme in Nin's later work, and in so doing lifts the lid of that "Pandora's box" of "woman's sensuality" that Nin cites in her *Diary*.

Elena is a writer whose aestheticized experience has not tapped her sensuality, which Nin makes analogous to the capacity for a vital life by comparing Elena with D. H. Lawrence's Lady Chatterley, "It was the submerged woman of Lawrence's book that lay coiled within her, at last exposed, sensitized, prepared as if by a multitude of caresses for the arrival of *someone*." But in fact Nin takes Elena into realms of inner space that make Connie Chatterley resemble Marian the Librarian. This was obviously the function of the pornographic mode she wore like an albatross, but it freed her to invent a language for exploring "the mysteries of woman's sensuality," as she would not otherwise have done. If she took a handoff from Lawrence, once she had the ball she ran with it on her own. She even adroitly negates some of Lawrence's turf. Pierre, for example, is a professional revolutionary, and when he meets Elena he is on the lam and she is on vacation in the Swiss Alps. Thus close to nature in Lawrentian terms, and removed from responsibilities, they have an idyllic and passionate romance. But unlike Mellor's cottage, where Lady Chatterley and her lover discover the vital essence among the birds and the bees, it is a fool's paradise. Elena and Pierre cannot discover the hard-core realities of life and love among the Homo sapiens until they return to Paris. And then it's possible only when Pierre gives up his politics.

When his next assignment comes in the Alps, Pierre leaves Elena, saying, "I am not in love with any woman. . . . I am in love with my work. With you I was in great danger. . . . I forgot my work." But later, when he returns to her in Paris, Elena's anxiety about the work/love contradiction prevents her orgasms, signifying the unresolved tension. Perceiving the problem, Pierre tells her that he is "struggling" to prove to himself that he was really a "café revolutionist" under the illusion that he was an activist; once this can be proved, an imminent prospect, then he "can stay and be free." One can see the origin of this problem in Nin's *Diary* and its development in her later work. In her *Diary* of the 1940s, she remarks the contradiction between politics and the intense emotional life she felt was the root of reality. Certainly the politics of World War II, which drove her from her career in Europe to uneasy exile in New York, disrupted her reality as it altered that of millions of others. And the politics of the mid-1950s McCarthy era was almost equally nightmarish. A certain solipsism in this view notwithstanding, it is at least understandable that Nin associated politics with "what is" and love with "what ought to be." For her, reality was in the "ought to be," and in "Elena," as in her later work, she straightened out the reality/illusion nexus by simply exorcising the validity of politics. One may or may not approve her metaphysics, but it is clear that "Elena" reflects Nin's profoundest concerns.

Elena and Pierre, then, cannot address the reality of love until Pierre dispels the illusion of politics and work. Here again the pornographic mode ironically served Nin's vision, for hard-core pornography—unlike soft-core—does not permit its fantasy to be intruded upon by the mundane. Dagwood always has time for a voluptuous tumble with Blondie before he has to catch the bus. In "Elena," politics and work, even Elena's writing, do not rear their ugly heads again. This does not mean easy sailing, sexual or psychic; it means rather that they can get down to their real human business of trying to synthesize their whole beings. This is not quite the exercise in irreality it might seem if one is skeptical about its pornographic context. Nin was an intense student of psychology and a lay analyst. Her perception was that neurosis caused problems in the work-a-day world and not the other way around. So the real business of life was to attend to the pathology of inner space, and then the rest would fall into coherent perspective. While Elena is temporarily released when Pierre gets his priorities in order, the archetypal anxiety returns to keep her in the frigid zone. Now the exploration of self and other begins in earnest.

Elena's frigidity comes from her mistrust of the other. The question of durability—whether Pierre would once again not be there—is answered only to stimulate the next existential question of what his thereness, his being, means and whether or how it will intrude on her own. As he becomes obsessed with lighting her fire, for example, she sees that his "struggle to always obtain an orgasm from her [is] destructive" of her reality and their love. Why does he need her orgasm? Does she need it? Does their love need it? His preoccupation with their sexuality, which she associates with a kind of masculine depravity, finally does what he hopes, lifts the lid on her sensuality. Naturally it gets out of control.

From this point Elena follows the lead of its possibilities, simultaneously exploring herself and fearing what she finds. It leads her to indulge it with others, revealing a capacity for promiscuity that she had not suspected. If passion is one with love, as she had supposed, does the capacity for several passions mean an equally broad capacity for love? What, then, is love? She has a liaison with a notoriously mannish lesbian, in whom she sees and admires her *animus*, her masculine other. Through her she meets Bijou, the whore, with whom Pierre has earlier had an affair. She is jealous, but the very jealousy inspires a sense of identification. Bijou is also her other, her animal and voluptuous self as distinct from her rational or poetic self. Similarly, she and Bijou are contrapuntal feminine myths, "Bijou, the sex organ walking undisguised" and "Elena . . . the opposite of the whore, a woman who poetized and dramatized love . . . made of another substance . . . created by a legend." Here Nin compares three types of women to put Elena, the archetypal woman, in perspective.

> Elena . . . would have liked to change places with Bijou, for the many times when men grew tired of courting and wanted sex without it, bestial and direct. Elena pined to be raped anew each day, without regard for her feelings; Bijou pined to be idealized. Leila [the lesbian] alone was satisfied to be born free of man's tyranny, to be free of man. But she did not realize that imitating man was not being free of him.

Nin's comment on Leila establishes the essential heterosexuality behind Nin's sexual theme. Leila's *animus* is admirable, but she lacks *anima*. In consequence she is drawn to weak women in a futile attempt to compensate. This recognition frees Elena from Leila's spell.

Now Elena has become obsessed with her sexuality and ponders the thesis that Nin more or less tentatively projects throughout the volume, that to separate sexuality from love—i.e., to indulge the pornographic imagination, especially in women—is to awaken a maniacal sleeping giant:

> Elena now understood why some Spanish husbands refused to initiate their wives to all the possibilities of lovemaking—to avoid the risk of awakening

> in them an insatiable passion. Instead of being contented, calmed by Pierre's love, she had become more vulnerable. The more she desired Pierre, the greater her hunger for other loves. It seemed to her that she had little interest in the rooting of love, in its fixity. She wanted only the moment of passion from everyone. . . . She wanted to be burnt. She thought to herself, I talk almost like a saint, to burn for love—for no mystic love, but for a ravaging sensual meeting. Pierre has awakened in me a woman I did not know, an insatiable woman.

This premise, which accepts the mythic synthesis of love and sex as well as the implicit double standard, runs counter to the more contemporary feminist thinking we have earlier noted. Partly it is another instance of her rebuke of the patron, but more so it reflects that she is of an older generation and an older European culture. Nonetheless, she herself is obviously uneasy with it and presents it tentatively, in her awareness that women did not have an adequate language for expressing their sexuality. Still, by the end of her life she recognized that history was taking its course and that she, willy-nilly, had been a part of it. So, for the record, she put it on the table. Be that as it may, Elena rejects lesbianism as an option and returns to heterosexuality. She tries Jean, a sculptor who has been courting her. Significantly, their sex is described, in contrast to the animality of the lesbian triad, in more high-flown terms of "being" and "essence" and "beauty," as if to confirm the organic rightness of heterosexuality. But by now it is becoming clear to Elena that her obsessive sexuality is a kind of fantasia, an illusory aphrodisiac that is already losing its appeal as she recognizes its threat to her real commitment to love and Pierre.

Yet there is another obstacle, the masculine *animus* Elena discovered in herself with Leila. Has it diminished her female *anima*? Her encounter with a homosexual friend of long standing assures her it has not. He is attracted to her masculinity, the illusion of which he maintains by focusing on her ass, rather like that of a boy. But when he enters her he is unequivocally in a woman, and he wilts in the heat of reality. Elena's self thus confirmed, she has now only to reconcile herself with the other, Pierre. In her vague attraction to the brutish appearance of workers she recognizes that she has cast both Pierre and herself in stereotypical roles—he as a primitive brutal force, she as a woman in need of violation. This clouds their relationship in fantasy. She must come to him as a free being and allow him his free being. Their free beings, like Sartre's stone, are sometimes so undeniably there that they are mutually nauseating, mutually abrasive, mutually negating. But recognition of this reality permits a merger, and after all they manage to come together. Thus, while "Elena" is a distinctly pornographic story, it is also a story manifesting the concerns of Nin's later work. In the context of sexual awakening as a causality, Nin takes Elena systematically through an exploration of her own inner spaces, as they relate to the nature of love and sanity as well as sexuality. Elena, somewhat like Jong's Isadora, plumbs the depths of pornographic fantasy in order to recognize its obsessive invalidity, which purges its hold on her. Free of the distracting idols of the self, she can come to terms with the other; i.e., she can synthesize her being and is thus enabled to find a love that is simultaneously at peace with and transcendent over sexuality. Moreover, as is the case with much contemporary feminist fiction, Nin dissocated love and sex to explore their respective dynamics and their relation to holistic being. In this regard, despite her own skepticism, she anticipates the contemporary use of pornography as an epistemological tool for the investigation of female nature.

Near the end of Edith Wharton's life, when she wrote "Beatrice Palmato," it would appear that she was somewhat more bemused even than Nin about the harmonious prospects for love and sex. Perhaps this is because in her own life, especially in her marriage, love and sex seem not to have happily coincided. Her marriage seems to have been bereft of both. Toward the end of the marriage, when she was 46, she had a three-year affair documented in R. W. B. Lewis' *Edith Wharton, A Biography*. But that seems in the end to have been characterized more by intense sexuality than durable love. After that and her subsequent divorce she seems to have settled into literary production and the life of a grand literary lady in France, projecting at least the public image of high propriety, until her early seventies, when Lewis detects "a new mood of sensuality" in her life. This, however, was essentially literary. She developed a taste for what she called Colette's "pornography *à la vente*," although she regarded the erotic aspects of Joyce's *Ulysses* as "silly." In fact Lewis speculates that Wharton composed her "Beatrice Palmato" fragment in part "to demonstrate that she could do much better than James Joyce at this kind of writing, and that, as against Joyce, Lawrence, and other male observers of female sensuality, she could give a truly accurate portrayal of a woman's sexual response." Nonetheless, she wrote only an outline sketch of the plot and one pornographic scene.

Perhaps at the age of 73 she did not have the energy to take up the challenge. It seems just as likely, however, since she continued to write practically up to the moment of her death two years later in 1937, that her rather literary approach to its incest theme did not finally satisfy her. Lewis notes that in her later years her admiration for "too carefully wrought fiction" in the Jamesian mode declined. And her outline suggests that "Beatrice Palmato" was conceived more along the lines of a Jamesian *tour de force*, with the incest somewhat mistily implicit until it is revealed in retrospect as the source of more or less predictable psychic fallout, than as a very direct address to its subject. The outline also suggests that Wharton would have focused, as she did in much of her major fiction, on the effects of repressed passion and sensuality rather than passion and sensuality themselves. Not so with the fragment, which provides a different perspective. It presents a pornographically explicit consummation between father and daughter, including detailed descriptions of cunnilingus and fellatio. Moreover, it emphasizes what is only obliquely alluded to in the outline, the contrast between the father's sexual courtliness and elegance and the crudeness of the daughter's husband. Further, the fragment would seem to be placed in the middle of the story and essentially features the daughter's point of view, while Wharton's outline suspends the revelation of incest until the end and from the point of view of the daughter's brother. Lewis speculates sensibly that Wharton could not possibly have expected to include the scene in any version of the story published at that time. If the scene neither fits Wharton's scheme for the story nor could have been published in any event, there is the obvious question of why she wrote it.

There are various speculations, but none adequately account for the fact that she so conspicuously kept both the fragment and the outline among those papers designated for her biographers. If for no other reason than that it accounts for the fragment's emphasis on contrapuntal kinds of sexuality, Lewis' autobiographical hypothesis is perhaps most suggestive. The theme of incest had appeared in earlier work, and she had projected a narrative about Lizzie Borden that was to feature it; also, themes around parent-child relationships were prominent in her earlier work, to which incest has an obvious association. She was, further, interested in how other writers—both precursors and contemporaries—had dealt with incest, so her attention to the subject was at once organic and competitive. At this period of her life her renewed perception of sensuality seems to have coincided with a retrospective attitude. As she looked back she would have recollected her unhappy sex life with her husband and compared it with the ecstatic sex life she had enjoyed with her lover. Lewis goes out on a limb when he speculates that she had reached a point "where she could finally acknowledge and give fantasy form to the strong physical attraction she had once felt for her own father, the consciousness of which she had buried deep for many decades," but the fragment's specificity lends credibility. Speculation becomes yet more intriguing when one factors her relationship with her mother into the situation. Lewis recounts, presumably from Wharton's journal, her interview with her mother about sex and marriage shortly before her own marriage. "I'm afraid Mamma," she said, "I want to know what will happen to me," revealing what was possibly a greater than normal anxiety even for that time (1885, when she was 24). Her mother, who had nothing more useful to tell her than that she surely must have noticed from pictures and statues that men were "made differently from women," put an abrupt end to the conversation by saying,

"You can't be as stupid as you pretend." Wharton would later observe that her mother's failure to provide even basic sexual information "did more than anything else to falsify and misdirect my whole life." She continued to feel that familial obtuseness about sexuality contained "the seeds of tragedy."

"Beatrice Palmato" plays out the tragedy with a peculiarly ironic twist. The rather obliquely mysterious outline implies that Beatrice's father has debauched her older sister, resulting in her sister's suicide and her mother's subsequent madness. Her mother dies in an asylum, after she has tried to kill her husband, and thereafter it seems that Beatrice begins her sexual liaison with her father, possibly at the age of 12. The liaison, apparently vital to Beatrice's spirits, continues when she marries a kindly but dull—i.e., gentrified rather than aesthetically sophisticated—man. She has a boy and then a girl, although the girl's paternity is in question, as it turns out.

Beatrice's father dies, according to the outline, and the story begins to recycle itself, at least in Beatrice's eyes. Her husband "adores" the girl, and Beatrice develops "a morbid jealousy," which of course her husband cannot fathom. One day, returning from a week's journey, he hugs the girl and kisses her as Beatrice appears demanding that he put the child down and how he dare kiss her. Her husband, dullard though he is, suddenly has the perception of "some profound moral perversion of which he had always been afraid to face the thought. . . . He looks at her with his honest eyes, and says, "'Why shouldn't I kiss my child?' and she gives him back a look in which terror, humiliation, remorseful tenderness, and the awful realization of what she has unwittingly betrayed, mingle in one supreme appeal and avowal." Whereupon she runs upstairs and shoots herself.

The outline of the story ends when Beatrice's brother, a sagacious young man who seems to know the score (having been "adored" by his mother and disliked by his father), has with Beatrice's husband "a long talk together—about Mr. Palmato," Beatrice's father. Here is familial sexual instruction with Oedipal vengeance. Obviously these tragically falsified and misdirected lives have no specific connection to Wharton's life. Lewis does, however, suggest that Wharton's sympathetic treatment of Beatrice's husband in the outline reflects her benign retrospection on her own husband, who was a bust as both a man and a lover but was also victimized, as it were, by having married in over his head.

But if the outline treats Wharton's possible surrogate for her husband generously, the fragment quite distinctly does not. The father's courtly ministrations to his daughter, which are taking place a week after her wedding night, are interrupted by their reflections on that "cruel experience," one that "has to come once in all women's lives." Since the fragment emphasizes that they have been so sporting themselves for some time past, they can't be talking about her loss of virginity. So they must refer to sex with a "stranger." Much is made of their own intimacy, and its "swooning sweetness" is contrasted to the cruelty of the other. But, given its destructive consequences in the outline, this can hardly be advocating incestuous intimacy. And the emphatic incestuousness discourages analogy to a more generic intimacy. Finally, the incompleteness and non-complementarity of outline and fragment baffle interpretation, and one can only speculate biographically. Perhaps she was trying her hand in competition with Joyce. Perhaps she was inspecting some now obscure connection to her mother's failure. Perhaps she was identifying her one-time lover with her father. Perhaps she was exploring her failed relationship with her ex-husband. Perhaps she was simply interested in incest as a literary motif, and it became the occasion for her to experiment with pornographic prose or depict her view of female passion. Or perhaps her reminiscence took her back twenty-five years to her lover, who had had a quasi-incestuous affair with a cousin raised as his sister. And perhaps, given the apparent absence of a grand passion in the intervening years, she had concluded that sexual love was at best unlikely and at worse tragically impossible.

In any event, what is clear is that she wrote it, that it is pornographic, and that she preserved it. Given her rigorous literary standards, she would not have supposed that so slight a piece would have literary significance in itself. So it would seem that she wanted posterity to know that sexuality was not beyond her ken (she also preserved her detailed journal of her extramarital affair), her talents, or her sense of aesthetic appropriateness. In any event, given that it is meticulously composed and obviously no afterthought, "Beatrice Palmato" indicates that Edith Wharton had at least addressed the potential of pornography for her work.

### *Class Analysis and the Pornorotica Debate*

While Nin took up the theme of incest, her approach was significantly different from that of current feminism. In Nin's pornography, incest subordinately punctuates her preoccupation with sexual obsession. In her later work, most notably *House of Incest*, it is a symbolic image of the dialectic of "inner space"—between the self and other, passive and active, male and female, idol and whore, sanity and madness. Incest is of course a standard hard-core pornographic motif, reflecting the human fascination with taboos. We've noted Diane di Prima's use of it, although she is uncharacteristic of the hard-core genre in that she makes incest a sign of an unhealthy psyche. Her ideological treatment of incest is similar to the symbolic treatments by Nin and Edith Wharton—none of the three are much concerned with incest as a victimizing phenomenon. Contemporary feminism, on the other hand, sees incest as a psychosociological sign of the class war between the genders, with women as victims of the oppressive patriarchal class. But there is a curious parallel between Nin's and Wharton's depiction of the incestuous father and that of some contemporary accounts (see, for example, *The Family Secret*, 1984, an autobiographical account of incest by "Eleanore Hill"). While the fathers are malicious, driven men, they are also intelligent and charming. This may be only coincidental, but it may also be an analogue for women of what the *femme fatale* is for men. Men (as both fathers and patriarchy?) are at once attractive and dangerous, as in the traditional image of the attractive Satan. Whatever the significance of this characterization of men—which would seem to represent their ambivalent antagonistic role toward women—it manifests itself in women's fiction and autobiography alike.

It recurs, for example, in Alix Kates Shulman's *On the Stroll* (1981) and Linda Lovelace's *Ordeal* (1980). Lovelace recounts how she was dragooned into prostitution and the porn film trade by a man whose charming facade masked a criminally perverse personality. I will address her book in a later chapter, and for now note only its similarity in male characterization to other women's works. Shulman's is a novel based on two prominent sociological phenomena, the prostitute/pimp relationship and the life of "bag ladies." It is consciously pornographic in the sense that it presents prostitution, a traditional aspect of the genre, and explicit sexual description as well. Its two protagonists are Robin—a teenage runaway who comes to New York City, where a pimp named Prince adroitly takes her under his wing and manipulates her into prostitution—and Owl, an increasingly senile woman whose paranoia prompts her to keep her pitiful possessions in shopping bags which she totes around in her life on the street. Their stories are separate though analogous in one important respect, as described in an interview by Shulman:

> I was trying to explore some of the extreme consequences for women living in a society where they are marginal, unless they are under the protection of men. That whole prostitute/pimp relationship is in some ways a reflection of the dependency relationship between men and women in the straight world. And, of course, the bag lady . . . is without the protection of a man, and she—like many bag ladies I know, actually—was once under the protection of a man. And as soon as she left that protection—and that protection, of course, in itself carried a very high price—but as soon as she lost it, she became one of the toss-aways of our culture.

Robin has run away from an alcoholic mother and overbearing father only to deliver herself to an even more self-destructive dependency on Prince, who skillfully applies his single-minded street savvy about women to her seduction. He wins her confidence both by understanding her antagonism to her father (and her fear of being caught by juvenile authorities and returned to him) and by being attentively "loving" in bed, hence his charm and her gratitude. Then, manipulating both his charm and her gratitude, i.e., asserting both paternalism and exploitation, he turns her out on the street.

What holds Robin to Prince for as long as it does, about a year, is analogous to the "Stockholm Syndrome," where captives identify with their captors. Partly Prince has mesmerized her by a wily alternation of kindness and force, and partly she is paralyzed by a lack of options. For example, Prince buys her attractive clothes and houses her comfortably as if they were a normal couple, at the same time he forces her to give him each night's take (calculated at about 15 minutes per trick) under penalty of a beating. Similarly, as her inexperience mistakes her gratitude for love, he offers her "love" and sympathetic treatment (e.g., each night he massages her and runs a bath for her) at the same time he intimidates her into staying on the street, the velvet glove over the iron fist further facilitated by the ruse that she need only do it until they can get on their feet. Although she does not know it, these are, of course, standard and well-documented pimping techniques. Still, it is not force exactly that holds her. Prince's contrapuntal treatment, in concert with her own psychic needs and vulnerability, keeps her sufficiently off balance that she clings, despite her increasing awareness of her bind, to the prospect of his "love." When, for example, he has to go out of town for a couple of days, rather than embrace the opportunity for escape, she begs him to stay, more fearful of losing him than energized to free herself:

> Deep inside, Robin felt herself stirring. She moved her fingers to his cock. If she could make him happy, would he stay with her? She had no other power. She ran her tongue along the back of his cock, feeling the heat of her own loving, and up over the mushroom's ridge. She slid her lips slowly down over it. When his fingers tensed on her neck in a sign, she began to move her mouth slowly up and down, like a buoy in calm waters, feeling the delicate skin of him against her tongue and throat.

Her need for a pacifier is precisely what makes her vulnerable. Prince manipulates and exploits sex, knowing that Robin associates sex and love. So strong is her association that it transcends the obvious contradiction of her prostitution. In the end Prince miscalculates the tenuousness of a love so working against itself. His cynicism makes him suppose that it will hold her until she hardens into a pro. But it doesn't and she doesn't. Here the sexual motif melds into the thematic heart of Robin's story. Commercial sex, Robin learns, is at best an indifferent business transaction that belies her pimp's professions of love and at worst sick and dangerous—

clients with sadistic predilections, the occasional murder of a hooker, busts by the vice squad. As for its function in society, or at least the GNP, one of her more experienced colleagues tells Robin:

> I'm telling you, the biggest racket of all is the government. Why do you think there are laws against hooking? . . . They want to take their cut. Because think about it: Doctors and nurses do some of the same kind of work we do. . . . Really. . . . Ever hear of sex therapists? . . . Or take dancers and actresses and strippers. What's the difference between our work and theirs? . . . Just who touches their dick? Well, what about wives and girl friends, then? You think they don't do it for the money? . . . Talk about pimping—the government is the biggest pimp of all, busting us, fining us, then sending us back out to work. That's why they're after our pimps, they're their competition. Well, it stinks. . . . And it's probably unconstitutional, too.

The argument is somewhat reductive, but then Robin's colleague makes no claim to intellectual finesse. Nonetheless, she does identify a social contradiction, one to which many contemporary feminists point as signifying a double standard. Moreover, a prominent real life prostitute, Margot St. James, has in fact made a less reductive argument along these same lines for legalizing prostitution (see *Rolling Stock*, no. 7, 1984). Shulman may have appointed a crude spokeswoman to articulate a crude contradiction, but it is, at any rate, an issue raised seriously by "libbers," as she has Prince contemptuously refer to them.

Robin is not a libber, and insofar as she understands the issue it is in personal rather than theoretical terms. Prostitution forces her to recognize the contradiction in her own life with Prince. The reader, however, perceives at once the situation of prostitution and its analogy to the domestic context of male/female relationships, which is underscored by the inclusion of "wives and girl friends" in the indictment by Robin's colleague. Behind this is the notion of telescoping dependency. A dependency on sex, as manifest in Robin, is the sign of dependency on a man. Thus there is a significant difference between good sex and healthy sex. Robin's sex with Prince is good, in the sense that it is mutually gratifying, but it is unhealthy because it is based on her dependency and his manipulation. That Prince manipulates Robin for profit rather than pleasure is only a slight twist on the more normal familial situation, in that a now standard feminist analysis of housewifery—including sex—is that it can and should be subject to a financial calculus. So Robin—and by analogy women in general—must purge herself of dependency to become a free agent.

Here Shulman's analysis is similar to Erica Jong's, although by posing the problem to a less sophisticated and self-conscious protagonist her resolution takes on a more populist, even Hogarthian, flavor and a far less optimistic resolution. Jong's Isadora Wing is highly educated and self-consciously introspective, an intellectual. Shulman's Robin—although so "marginal" as to be subproletarian, i.e., hers is socially unacknowledged work—is more socially typical. She goes to the College of Hard Knocks, and she gets no summer vacation in Europe. Isadora's fantasy of the Zipless Fuck is highly organized and so articulate that it carries its own critique. So hers is the comparatively straightforward problem of comparing the fantasy with reality in order to exorcise it. Robin is never even aware that she has a fantasy or that there is a myth of love. So she is maneuvered by "material circumstances" and has no awareness whatsoever of her situation or its dynamics.

Only when the contradiction has her flat on her back in thrall does she even recognize that there is a problem. And then she fights back instinctively, not consciously. Even when she finally gets herself sufficiently together to leave Prince, she carries her dependence with her. She takes it to the apartment of a young student who, not knowing her trade, has become infatuated with her. She would become dependent on him, exchanging household services and sex for her keep, but he doesn't want either a "wife" or a dependent and gets her a job as a live-in domestic for a New York family. Once again material circumstances are the moving force rather than conscious choice. Similarly with the new job, which provides another perspective on the family motif.

This theme begins with Robin's parents, an economically struggling family in which the father's self-absorbed and heavyhanded attempt to keep hearth and home together drive her mother to drink. It develops as we have noted, with Robin's liaison to Prince. Prince's history, in turn, adds the dimension of his cynicism: his mother, impregnated and deserted, sustained the illusion that the "husband" who never existed is waiting for her; and later, when Prince returned from the military to his own wife and child, his wife "treated him like a meal ticket, a trick. . . . For the family, she said." Owl's family history is equally disastrous. Deserted by both father and husband, in her senility she covets little mementos of the former and wages a continuing battle with the latter for the soul of their daughter, who has, with her own obtusely "happy family," rejected Owl in any event. Having more or less covered all the class possibilities, Shulman gives the modern family its *coup de grace* when Robin strikes out with the upper middle class family. The wife overworks her, the kids are insufferably spoiled brats, and the husband, whose business takes him in whatever direction the wife's social activities do not take her, climbs into Robin's bed. The family does not fare well in this plot.

The economic-psychosexual analysis cited earlier has specific application to Robin's relations with Prince but seems to spill over on the others as well. That model suggests that if a woman is dependent, as with Robin's mother, she obliterates herself with drink or some other analogue. If she is independent, as with Owl (and Robin, potentially), she winds up an outcast. If she is somewhere in between but without focus, as with the upper middle class wife, she maintains only the facade of a family. The other side of this thematic coin is seen in Prince's ex-wife, who has carried the economic-sexual hypothesis to a cynical extreme in treating her man like a "meal ticket, a trick." As for men, they are in general no-account, so given how things are there's no accounting for them.

The family, then, is the charnel house of consciousness for both men and women but most especially for women, on whose situation the plot focuses. In fact the two most active consciousnesses, those of Prince and Owl, reveal the bottom line of that situation. Prince's consciousness is cynical, a product of his own family history and his reading of social institutions that reward only adroit manipulation. Shulman makes it clear that he has been jacked around by these institutions—for which the family and its pimp/prostitute analogue are the metaphorical paradigms—as much as a woman might be, but his birthright membership in the male club, albeit at a low level, provides him the defense of a cynical strategy. When he has finally lost Robin he simply dusts himself off and prepares to meet the next bus in from the provinces, which will invariably have another Robin disembarking. His benighted consciousness may serve to keep him in his place, but that after all is a place; it also serves, therefore, to make him loyal to the system that gives him a place, however low and static his caste may be. And it serves to make him an implacable antagonist to women. Owl recognizes that antagonism for what it is, but her marginal social status has so battered her consciousness that she is no longer coherent. Still, even with her incoherence—where she confuses Robin with her daughter, suggesting a survival bonding among women—she is obsessed with leaving a legacy. At the crucial moment, when she and Robin are cornered in an abandoned building by Prince, she gives Robin her savings, about $200, and manages to obstruct Prince long enough with her heretofore useless and pathetic bags for Robin to get away. This is a desperately obsessive act, not a consciously strategic one, but it is nevertheless a symbolic legacy of liberation from the older to the younger generation of women. But its very obsessiveness signifies a battered, inchoate groping toward consciousness. Robin takes the legacy. It's enough to get her a bus ticket to sunny California, with a little left over. Yet her future does not promise much in the way of conscious strategy. She has youth going for her, and presumably she won't be suckered by another pimp. She has the instinct to run, but she has not exhibited much consciousness, largely reacting to exigencies as they arise. Her immediate objectives are to bathe in the Pacific and possibly find an elusive friend who may be in Hollywood. That Shulman evokes the celluloid California of fantasy, rather than, say, the mythic California of westering optimism, seems deliberate. For if her view of women makes them historically analogous to that pre-conscious state of the early settlers, like the Donner Party, ill-equipped and vaguely in search of a new life, women are after all emerging into a pre-formed culture. Unlike Jong's Isadora Wing, most of them are no more equipped to soar above it than the Donner Party was equipped to soar over the Sierra Nevadas. Unlike the educated avant-garde that Isadora represents, most of them cannot afford to dabble in the media's pornographic fantasy because they are still mired in a much more unsavory relationship with their pimps. Shulman's vision does not invalidate Jong's, nor is it necessarily pessimistic. It is, though, a reminder that the lumpen proletariat of women, as it were, is still in Conestoga wagons, and the luxury of flight, let alone fear of it, is a sign of progress that they haven't yet experienced.

Shulman's caveat is well taken, since most writers address their worlds from a position of relative advantage. And most writers who work with the pornographic imagination attempt to integrate sexuality with their view of the world's complexities. Jong, writing self-consciously as a middle class artist, puts sexuality in a middle class context and proffers individualistic middle class resolutions to its problems. Radclyffe Hall, writing self-consciously as an upper class British artist, put the problems of lesbianism in that context, although she did attempt more or less successfully to complement that perspective with a tragic subplot about a lower class lesbian couple, and posits no resolutions for either class. Diane di Prima, writing self-consciously and perhaps cynically as a Beat bohemian, places her sexuality beyond the bounds of class structure, so that the problems of sex and love are mythical beasts and therefore require no resolutions. Shulman—having written with middle class self-consciousness about the psychic consequences of middle class sociosexual fantasy in her earlier *Memoirs of an Ex-Prom Queen*—in *On the Stroll* writes unself-consciously (i.e., as an observer rather than a participant, as distinct from Polly Adler or Xaviera Hollander, who write self-consciously as participants in prostitution) about two castes of outcast people. That these two castes are not a significant part of her readership, which is largely middle class, suggests that she is attempting to integrate an outcast perspective into middle class consciousness. In this context, since the novel's sociosexual agon manifest in its prostitute/pimp calculus is rather more compelling than its resolution, the implicit resolution would seem to be the consciousness of consciousness. Thus Shulman has introduced class consciousness, i.e., a specifically, if low-profile, leftist political component, into the development of female pornography in fiction. For the most part this development has taken place in the more rarefied ontological dialectic contrasting prospective female terms for female nature and the traditional male characterization of it. Shulman's addition of a political ground gives the dialectic a more comprehensive material base.

But in general women's pornographic writing is more preoccupied with female ontology than with class analysis. To some extent the reasons for this can be seen in the attempt of some feminists to distinguish pornography from erotica. Although earlier enunciated in Gloria Steinem's "Erotica and Pornography" (*Ms.*, November 1978), the premises of debate about this issue are effectively explicated in the Dworkin/MacKinnon antipornography ordinance and the FACT brief opposing it, both cited earlier. Pornography was perceived pejoratively because it was conceived by men for men and necessarily was degrading to women because it depicted them as sex objects and dissociated sex from emotional ties. When it became clear that women were writing sexually explicit literature it became inconvenient to call that "pornography" as well, because it confused the discourse attempting to differentiate men's and women's approaches to the subject. "Erotica" was a convenient term traditionally associating love and sex, which was presumed to be an association characteristic of women and uncharacteristic of men. It followed that erotica, informed by a female perspective, would not degrade women, that it represented, in other words, the proper conception of female nature.

But, such opponents as Shulman and her FACT colleagues argued, not only was the determination of what was degrading to women too subjective for reliable analysis, but the emerging data about female sexuality challenged *a priori* assumptions about female nature. Hence the distinction between pornography and erotica was arbitrary. As we have seen, the biological literature on women's sexual response has dissociated orgasm from love, the vagina, and the penis. Similarly with the data on fantasy, which also dissociates female sexual imagination from love. Certainly, as we have seen, women's contemporary sexual fiction has made a concerted effort to dissociate the two, partly as a means to better explore their dynamics and partly as a means to refute the perennial typecasting of woman as wife. The data are obviously not definitive about feminine nature, but they do challenge *a priori* assumptions and indicate that the subject is open to continued exploration. The debate itself indicates that within the larger male/female dialectic there is an internal female one. And there is a logic that would give ontology priority. If woman is an animal of sex before she is an animal of society, then the imperative is to determine the nature of her sex prior to that of society. Shulman qualifies this: sex and its social circumstance are equally material to woman's nature, and to dissociate them is not only to invite mistaken assumptions but also a political division among women. If the debate about female nature in relation to pornography signifies division, it is one within the educated middle class majority of feminists. Fights over abortion and the ERA, on the other hand, signify a division more along class lines, with the educated middle class tending to the affirmative and the religiously oriented middle and working class tending to the negative. Behind this division, also, are very different assumptions about the proper nature of women.

*Radical Perverts and Pornorotic Pleasures*

When it comes to variations on the nature of women, the "lesbian/feminist S/M organization" SAMOIS profoundly complicated the issue in 1981 with the publication of its anthology, *Coming to Power*. In the context of a collection of essays, fictions, and graphics on sado-masochistic fantasies and practices, the SAMOIS credo presents its challenge to heterosexuals, lesbians, and feminists alike:

> We believe that S/M must be consensual, mutual, and safe. S/M can exist as part of a healthy and positive lifestyle. Many approaches to S/M are possible. However, its basic dynamic is an eroticised exchange of power negotiated between two or more sexual partners. We believe that sadomasochists are an oppressed sexual minority. . . . We believe that S/M can and should be consistent with the principles of feminism. As feminists, we oppose all forms of social hierarchy based on gender. As radical perverts, we oppose all social hierarchies based on sexual preference.

The primary confrontation with received opinion is its premise that women are and can be sado-masochistic. As its emphasis on consensuality indicates, its sado-masochism is essentially ritualistic in both fantasy and practice. This is not to say that the pleasure-pain nexus isn't actualized but rather that it is controlled in a symbolic theater where power relations are imaginatively explored, particularly in terms of dominance ("top") and submissiveness ("bottom"). SAMOIS seems to use the term "eroticism" in reference to S/M acts and "pornography" in reference to writings about them, although its fictions sometimes incline more to the erotic—emphasizing S/M and love—and sometimes more to the pornographic—emphasizing S/M and sexuality. In the sense that "pornography" is not used as a necessarily pejorative term, the SAMOIS writers appear to align themselves with the feminist left. In any event, their sense of embattlement within feminism is reflected in this joke, anthologized from "Aunt Sadie's" column in the SAMOIS newsletter:

> Riddle: How many S/M dykes does it take to change a light bulb?
> Answer: Two—one bottom to do it and one top to tell her what to do.
> Riddle: How many anti-S/M feminists does it take to screw in a light bulb?
> Answer: At least four. One to handle the bulb, one to critique the word "screw," one to lend professional credentials to the operation, and one to find common ground with the utility company.

The tone of the book ranges from such low wit to simple lyrical expostulations on S/M to accomplished narrative and high seriousness. While much of the writing is clearly occasional, at least one writer projects a collection of "pornographic short stories," and there are several notable essayists. Apart from the pleasures of S/M, the most recurrent motif is the validation of them as feminist.

Since S/M features both violence and subordination, and is generally regarded as aberrant behavior, to legitimate its female nature requires some serious suasion. The most direct address to this is in the power theme. Susan Farr, in "The Art of Discipline: Creating Erotic Dramas of Play and Power," states the function of power thus:

> Power is not an invention of men, to be wished out of existence in a new women's society. Power is the capacity to make things happen—power is energy—and we would do well to know as much as we can about it. . . . So far, I can identify two analytically distinct but emotionally and physically interconnected functions of discipline for us. One function has to do with play—with playacting, with sexual foreplay, with imaginative rituals, with scary dramas of pleading and relief. The other is something about power—about dominance and submission, about anger and its expression, about distance and intimacy, about aggression.

There is an iconoclastic similarity between lesbian sadism and Sade's own variety. For Sade the icon to be demolished was Christianity's benevolent nature that was supposed to succor the virtuous weak. Sade's premise was that nature operated by power rather than benevolence, that sentimental theories of virtue masked this fact, which was exploited by men, and consequently women were victimized by their association with powerlessness. The icon for S/M lesbians is the supposition that power is a malicious invention of men, rather than a force to which both men and women are subject. For them, as for Sade, power is neither good nor bad but an existential reality. Moreover, it is a force that manifests itself in the microcosm of sexuality. It follows that to observe its dynamics on the sexual stage will provide useful knowledge: hence, their theory of play, of the dramas of aggression. S/M lesbians acknowledge it as a vital force in erotic life, rehearse it in the relatively safe theater of lesbian relationships, and explore it imaginatively in pornographic fantasies. For both Sade and the S/M lesbians, then, power is the source of the contradictions that comprise the dialectic by which nature can be more analytically investigated.

There is also, however, a significant difference. Sade's dialectic requires that the "good" woman be invariably victimized by the sentimental weakness that defines her goodness. Like Sade, S/M lesbians evoke the contradiction between received opinion and the force of nature, but unlike him they empower the "bottom," or passive woman, and she in turn empowers the "top" by consenting to play her role. Sade's victims never experience pleasure, but lesbian bottoms do. In Sade's time Sacher-Masoch had not yet arrived to articulate the pleasures of submission, which in any event would not have suited Sade's purposes. He wanted to demonstrate that pleasure was rooted in power rather than in virtue, and that the historic situation of power was that it flowed only from top to bottom. The feminists, acknowledging both the pleasure and potency of power, want to explore it in terms of its reciprocal dynamics. Thus, when bottoms choose to relinquish power, they bring the potential of its reciprocal dynamics to social consciousness. Conscious and consensual submission, here, is not weakness—and certainly not sentimentality—but demonstration of a cyclic rather than one-directional flow of power. Lesbian S/M pornography, in this sense, contributes a more complex perspective on the nature of power to feminist dialogue.

Complications, of course, are not necessarily persuasive. Feminist skeptics, particularly from the right, charge that S/M is a male syndrome and is consequently dubious if not impossible as a feminist enterprise. This is the same critique that is brought against pornography, and one's position toward it will likely depend on whether one agrees that women cannot truly participate as women in either S/M or pornography. The SAMOIS fictionists are at the very least persuasive that at least they feel a positive value in both phenomena. Without exception, they celebrate the sexually energizing character of S/M. In one sense the very existence of this literature testifies to its validity for at least some women, and the question of whether they are normal or aberrant or brainwashed by male preoccupations seems moot. The SAMOIS writers themselves clearly feel that their sexual disposition and its fantasies are at once female and natural. Moreover, they contend that S/M not only contributes to feminist cultural analysis but that it also cultivates personal discovery. In the context of S/M's delicate balance of pleasure and pain and its essential dominance/submission dialectic, the SAMOIS writers claim that it generates an atmosphere of psychic trust and emotional sensitivity in the face of vulnerability. If the SAMOIS approach seems to make sexual relations extremely programmatic, its writers counter that sexuality is already programmed by the culture and that their minority report serves to reveal contradictions and promote interrogation. If, for example, both parties to an S/M relationship can manifest mutual consideration in the framework of its characteristic aggressiveness, then we discover that aggression can exist in dialogue with more benign human traits. To polemicize aggression as an aberrant masculine vice is to mystify its workings as a human energy that is not after all gender specific.

The more modest SAMOIS fictions tend simply to assert the benevolent effects of S/M. Crystal Bailey's "Girl Gang," for instance, is essentially a description of a lesbian gang bang, but its conclusion attempts to provide a transcendence: "We were her [the "victim's"] servants then. Blankets were brought, a pillow, and very slowly, bringing ourselves down too, we rubbed her, offering soothing caresses along this woman's body who had opened so far for us. We love one another for sharing together. We began to sing a soft lullaby: 'We have traveled a long way into places we had not known. We found pleasure there, we went together, we came on home'." While these sentiments may be admirable (and programmatic), coming as they do rather abruptly from a narrator who has heretofore been intent only upon conveying the heat of S/M pornographic energies, they are fictionally unpersuasive. This of course is one of the problems of missionary fiction.

But the more sophisticated narratives play with the inherent ironies of S/M aggressiveness and convincingly integrate them with both pornographic description and the SAMOIS ethos. Pat Califia's "Jessie" is an instance. Its narrator is a highly self-conscious, witty, and perceptive bottom who tells of her night with Jessie, a notorious top. The story is persuasive largely because its point of view adroitly keeps erotic activity, psychic dynamics, and social ironies in shifting perspective. The conclusion, for example, subtly punctuates the difference between pornographic fantasy and daily life. The morning after their strenuous indulgence of fantasy, the submissive narrator almost imperceptibly switches roles with the dominant Jessie, who cooks breakfast and does the dishes. Moreover, both acknowledge that they don't want a "24-hour-a-day S/M relationship." As Jessie puts it, "Kicking ass is hard work." Thus, sensitized to mutual needs, they maintain a rational balance between the pornographic fantasy essential to their erotic life and the quotidian demands of two independent personalities. At its best, then, lesbian S/M pornography has an effective ritual function, exploring the cyclical prospects of power relationships and purging the tensions endemic to the alternating current of power dynamics.

While the SAMOIS writers produce unabashed pornography, two 1984 anthologies of female writing are rather more equivocal about their distinction between pornography and erotica. Both bill themselves as erotica, and both consciously take on the project of producing sexual writing specifically appealing to women. In this respect, with the important proviso of their assumption that such a literature will be different from that of men, both aspire to establish the characteristics of a female genre analogous to hard-core pornography. *Ladies Home Erotica,* conceived by The Kensington Ladies' Erotica Society, whose members have published their work pseudonymously, acknowledges having but "one rule: no victims." Obviously this negative convention rejects lesbian S/M premises and is conceived in relation to the feminist charge that male pornography features the victimization of women. That the FACT brief has refuted this characterization of male pornography is not altogether pertinent here, since the anthology was published prior to those feminist findings and clearly reflects prior assumptions. That they are assumptions is confirmed by the Ladies' claim to research that consisted essentially of "a dutiful look at Anaïs Nin, Henry Miller, and Nancy Friday and even . . . at the technicolored vaginas and the muscled playboys of *Penthouse, Chic,* and *Playgirl.* We were not amused!" To have hit on those particular sources—as compared, say, to *Story of O* or *Hustler*—for evidence of victimization of women suggests that the Ladies were using a polemical definition of the term. But, while the general drift of the anthology is borne on a polemical assertion of benign feminine sexual imagination, the Kensington Ladies are not, on the evidence of their fictive tone, unqualifiedly polemical. In fact, one suspects that they *were* amused by Nin, Miller, et al., since their attitude toward sex is unflappably good humored and holistic.

These qualities don't necessarily make for vital literature, erotic or otherwise, but the Ladies profess to having been more interested in their communal address to the feminine sexual imagination than in the production of writing, which came " as a kind of afterthought." This is not to say that the writing is bad, only that it reflects the group sessions out of which it came, sessions in which they "confided . . . sexual fantasies like pajama-clad schoolgirls." They appear, for example, to be about equally interested in cuisine, both *haute* and *bourgeois,* and cuckoldry. The latter reflects their Chaucerian wit and the former their feminist integration of sex and quotidian life. They frequently punctuate their stories with recipes, and for them the texture of sex seems to be creamier than "Lilah's Chocolate Fondue." And their feminism they wear as lightly as the chiffon of their generation ("an improbable group of women over forty"). The Kensington Ladies are not plagued by Nin's obsession with sexual obsession, nor by Edith Wharton's anxious memories of sexual ignorance, nor Radclyffe Hall's tortured sense of homosexuality, nor Jong's preoccupation with sexual neurosis, nor Shulman's class analysis. If anything, they're a bit like Diane di Prima, tossing off sexual problems with a wink and a grin.

Partly this is of course a function of the genre they are trying to create, which is to evoke sexual pleasure, after all, not obstacles. But it is as much a consequence of the somewhat abstract character of their mission, what they call their "experiment," the illustration of the premise that women's sexual imaginations are civilized and just. The Kensington Ladies themselves certainly appear to be so, and if this is an essential component of female nature they have demonstrated it. Their writings, however, read like genteel literary exercises: In addition to the little Chaucerian ironies, there are fictive twists reminiscent of Colette and O. Henry, verse in the mold of Dorothy Parker, parodies of gothic tales and murder mysteries and domestic vignettes. In this respect their condescension to Anaïs Nin and Nancy Friday is ironic. Nin, who wrote unequivocal pornography, assumed that it was antagonistic to women's natural synthesis of love and sex; Friday, who collected sexual fantasies in the manner of an anthropologist, recorded attitudes in women that challenge Nin's assumed synthesis. Whatever the state of that debate, however, both Nin and Friday took the emotional intensity of sexual imagination quite seriously. The Kensington Ladies, though, have opted to transcend the debate altogether, and in so doing their writing fails to assert a gut level response to sexuality. It is cerebral, stylized and witty. In keeping with its general gentility, comparatively little attention is given to sexual description, and its language is rather decorous and even breathless, like that one might find in *Cosmopolitan* or the Harlequin romances. In this sense it is perhaps appropriately designated erotica, not because sex is necessarily in syncopation with love or the higher emotions, which it isn't, but because sex is treated more as a bauble than as an experience. Still, the book's vice is also its virtue, and if it does not so clearly define its genre as it perhaps had hoped, its "Address to a Penis Owner" is nonetheless a useful manifesto for its future:

> We are not anti-penis. . . . We do appreciate a lusty penis when it knows its place. . . . If it knows a trick or two, so much the better. A well-behaved penis is indeed woman's best friend, but we object to those mindless penises that indiscriminately push their way in and out of our folds like sewing machines. . . .

No more mechanical sex, the Ladies say, for either men or women. If they have established no other guidon for their genre, they have established that, and done so with a good measure of fellow feeling.

Lonnie Barbach, editor of *Pleasures*, also has a distinct consciousness that the female erotica in her anthology will "by its very nature be more appealing to women than the erotica written by men." That she attributes erotica to men, as distinct from pornography, and that she includes John Cleland's *Fanny Hill* in that category, somewhat blurs the differentiation between the two concepts. Apparently she prefers "erotica" as a term because it is less offensive and distracting rather than because she conceives a programmatic difference between erotica and pornography. In any event, the narratives in her collection are of both types, according to traditional conceptions. Susan Griffin's "Viyella," for example, is the story of a lesbian love affair in which sex is altogether subordinate to the dynamics of love and its failure. The language of her sexual description, moreover, is impressionistic and figurative, referring, for instance, to "the red canal between her soft thighs." Her story is consciously conceived as erotic in the traditional sense. Carol Conn's "A Few Words on Turning Thirty in Marin County, California," on the other hand, is just as consciously conceived as pornography. Given a birthday gift of a night with two male "geishas," a woman enters a pornographic paradise where she is fucked, fed, bathed, and otherwise sexually stimulated by her two attendants. It is a fantasy of sexual power, the sign of which is that she is gratified without even an inclination to reciprocate the pleasure. Her language is direct: "men . . . bathing their faces in cunt juices," or they "worship my pussy," or one's "cock . . . sliding gracefully in and out, in and out of my cunt." Sex, in short, is the beginning and the end, and love isn't even in the vocabulary.

Barbach's contributors are all professional writers commissioned by her to write up "real experiences" rather than fiction. She asserts with a straight face that they do so, although many of her contributors pretty clearly have tongue in cheek. Barbach acknowledges that "fantasy and reality often become thoroughly intertwined in a sexual experience," but after all it makes little difference. Narratives, autobiographical or fictive, are structured as stories. These stories exhibit as wide a range of narrative sophistication and complexity as they do a range of thematic focus. Unlike the Kensington Ladies, these writers have no common sensibility. One thing that emerges from these stories is that the sexual motif serves women writers in ways as various as it does men. In terms of pornography, the variations suggest that the sexual imagination of women is not so divergent from that of men as is supposed, confirming what Nancy Friday's collection of fantasies implied. Women are sexually predatory ("The Moon over SoHo," anonymous), enjoy an anonymous "quickie" ("A Very Special Dance" by Carol Conn), indulge infidelities ("Women Who Love Men Who Love Horses" by Susan Block), counterpoint their boredom with fantasies ("The Fifty-Minute Hour: Between the Minutes," anonymous), get off on group sex and voyeurism ("Morning Light" by Beth Tashery Shannon), relate to cars as sex symbols ("Truckin'" by Brooke Newman), patronize prostitutes (" A Few Words on Turning Thirty in Marin County, California" by Conn), see men as "sex objects" ("Picasso" by Mary Beth Crain). In short, there are not so many surprises emerging from women's pornography as had been predicted. What is clear is that women do have a pornographic as well as an erotic imagination and that they use it to explore and articulate their experience. Time will tell if the feminine genre evolves in some unique direction. Its present state suggests that, so far as sexuality is the battleground, the genders are more complementary than the war between the sexes would indicate.

In sum, there is clearly a body of work that can be characterized as female pornography. To call it a tradition at this point would be premature. But the pornorotic works of such earlier writers as Radclyffe Hall and Edith Wharton suggest that pornography has had a longer history in women's literature than has been supposed. Moreover, this body of work shows signs of a structure. Soft-core pornography is generally conservative, cautioning women against radical change, although—as Susann's *Valley of the Dolls* shows—not necessarily confirming traditional female roles. Even hard-core pornography produced under masculine auspices reflects on the situation of women. If di Prima's bohemianism scorns bourgeois hangups over love, sex and marriage, Nin's psychosexuality invites women to explore their interiors and refute masculine dissociation of sensibility. Pornography produced under feminist auspices on the one hand confirms Nin's sensibility hypothesis and on the other asserts an unequivocally animal sexuality in women. Both modes thus participate, at least marginally, in the feminist dialectic that is the principal focus of literary pornography. That dialectic has both an ontological address to the nature of female being and a political address to power relations between and within the genders. Ontology and politics are obviously connected, in that traditional definitions of the passive, nurturing woman confirm traditional power ratios.

While women are skeptical of their nurturing assignment, however, they do contend that they are more emotionally holistic than men. But this carries the correlative burden of monogamy, the danger of which is that it promotes dependency on the emotional and sexual need for a man. Thus sexuality provides the logic and lexicon for solving the contradictions of the situation. One option proposed is lesbianism, which transcends the problem but apparently is not a satisfactory resolution for most women. The other is to work through the problem by investigating whether or not women are by nature sexually and therefore socially passive and dependent, at which point pornography becomes the laboratory. Pornography implies promiscuity, and promiscuity implies a possible independence, after the traditional model of men. So much of the fictive experimentation attempts to come to terms with this phenomenon. But, while writers explore promiscuity for its potential, thus dissociating sex and love, they tend to find it ultimately unsatisfactory as a resolution. This is clearly the case with the works of Nin, Jong, and Shulman. Thus, behind the pornographic experimentation, there hovers the appeal of eroticized sex. Still, Shulman makes this prospect problematic, in both *Memoirs of an Ex-Prom Queen* and *On the Stroll*. And the SAMOIS lesbians, as well as the specifically pornographic contingent of Barbach's contributors, suggest that pornographic sex is both normal and healthy. After all, then, pornography is but one feminist logic for the issue and not a resolution. The contradictions about feminine nature among women and between women and traditional conceptions remain, and the dialectic continues.

In terms of its power ratio component, lesbian S/M challenges even feminist assumptions with its emphasis on what can be learned from exploring the roles of both dominance and submissiveness. While Shulman compounds the ontological with an economic and political analysis, Nin dismisses this approach as beside the psychic point. Di Prima dismisses it with aestheticized bohemianism. Jong does not so much dismiss as transcend it with bourgeois individualism. The Kensington Ladies are too domestically comfortable to bother with it, nor does it seem to occur to Barbach's contributors. But Shulman's analysis renders these incomplete. Private solutions evade the problem's typicality. Women are not just atomized units, some of whom may be sufficiently advantaged to rise above their fix, but also a class oppressed by the male class, as illuminated by her exposition of the prostitute/pimp relationship. Therefore, she implies, the problem is not adequately addressed, let alone resolved, until it is seen as a class problem with class dynamics.

It is clear that feminists do not speak on pornography with one voice. Where conservatives such as Dworkin and Griffin find a *bête noire* to be expunged, centrists such as Jong and leftists such as Shulman find an effective tool for exploring assumptions about the nature of women as well as the social and political dynamics of the female situation. The divergence of addresses from within the ranks of those for whom pornography has aesthetic viability indicates the energy of feminist dialectic; it also confirms that pornography itself has been assigned a distinctive role in the discourse.

# 9

# Unspeakable Spectacle, the Movies

## WHAT TO DO WITH THE BODY

Vatsayana's *Kama Sutra* is to sex what Aristotle's *Poetics* is to drama. Both describe the possibilities of form. Vatsayana says, for example, "When a man, during congress, turns round, and enjoys the woman without leaving her, while she embraces him round the back, it is called the 'turning position,' and is learnt only by practice." Sex, here, is an art complete with its appropriate forms. And, as erotic statuary at such temples as Konark suggests, it is an art that can accommodate an audience. Aristotle thought that spectacle—scenery, actors, and other audio-visual effects—was the least artistic aspect of drama. Greek theater conventionally kept violent and sexual spectacle off stage. Still, in *Lysistrata* Aristophanes got considerable comic mileage from the spectacle of frustrated male tumescence. Even for the Greeks, while spectacle was low art, it nevertheless was art.

Movies, from their inception, have exploited spectacle. It is the *raison d'être* of the camera, which can record, manipulate, and make portable anything—décolletage, mountain ranges, or battlefield panoramas. Cinema technology can render its subject at once intimate and remote in a way no other art form can. In fact the very capacity, and therefore temptation, to exploit spectacle is probably the thorniest problem for film poetics. When the subject is sex, the problem is what to do with the body. Vatsayana suggests that the forms of sex require rehearsal. Pornographic film actress Georgina Spelvin, star of *Devil in Miss Jones*, implies that that is only half the cinematic problem. She recounts her difficulties in doing a troilism scene: "There were a few moments . . . when I was not in character. . . . I was . . . trying to keep the guys turned on and get the insertions completed, and so on. . . . It became a rehearsal and not in character for the camera. I was most concerned with trying to build the tempo . . . feeling the vibrations . . . to get them both to come simultaneously." She seems to have been busier than a one armed mule skinner, but she does reveal aesthetic preoccupations, albeit at the low level of spectacle. The problems of verisimilitude, tempo and character that concerned her are, after all, matters of form. The problem of what to do with the body is indeed complex, and one of the most intriguing developments in the conjunction of obscenity and film poetics has been precisely in the area of form.

The form of the most elementary kind of pornographic movie—what I will call the "smut film"—is largely dictated by the forms of sexual congress itself. Both the economics of the smut film industry and the psychic dynamics of eroticism have contributed to the smut film's more or less mechanistic sexual imagery. For both reasons, as we shall see, the basic smut film maker need not provide more than the spectacle of the body as a sex machine. But sexual spectacle is also an aspect of pornographic films that do have artistic claims.

There are of course contexts in which spectacle itself is poetic. Just as in painting, photography, and other graphic modes, there are poetic landscapes, cityscapes, portraits, nudes, so are there analogues in cinema. In such works spectacle is the object. It becomes an aesthetic problem where it is in relation to some other poetic end, which in narrative film is action, i.e. story and/or plot. A narrative film aspiring to some level of poetry will integrate spectacle and action rather than subordinating the latter. The high artistic aspiration of Nagisa Oshima's pornographic film *In the Realm of the Senses*, for example, is reflected in the fact that its extensive sexual spectacle is integral and subordinate to its tragic plot, whereas the minimal artistic aspiration of Gerard Damiano's *Deep Throat* is reflected in its subordination of plot to sexual spectacle. Nevertheless, vulgar comedy though it is, *Deep Throat* does have a functional plot that is integral to the humor that counterpoints its spectacle. The difference between *Deep Throat* and the standard smut film is that its sexual spectacle, although unequivocally exploited, coexists with a content that challenges its authenticity, an important development in pornographic film to which we will return. For now I want merely to contrast it with the standard smut film, which admits no impediment—other than its own inept production—to the sovereignty or vitality of spectacle. In fact reviewers of these films—in *Screw, Hustler,* and other journals—tend to be particularly critical of their lack of sexual persuasiveness, the degree to which performers do not project authentic spontaneity and zeal. The critics are next most attentive to production quality, especially cinemagraphic values. These elements are of course most pertinent to the essence of the genre, sexual spectacle. As the reviewers, and often the makers and actors, generally agree, upwards of ninety percent of the films are badly made because they are conceived quickly and produced cheaply to exploit the market. Obviously, poetry is no object, not even in rendering spectacle.

What, then, *is* the object? How do such films exploit a market when they do not satisfy even what would appear to be their own basic standards? Part of the answer is that the general market does not really have a coherent constituency beyond gender. There are films for special interests—gays, transvestites, sado-masochists, various pederasties—but although aspects of specialty films overlap, they do not define the genre. Moreover, the audience itself is for the most part critically mute. The development of a critical review network since the early 1970s has induced a slight improvement in the incidence of competence. This has resulted in a relatively small corpus of films—e.g., *Deep Throat, Devil in Miss Jones, Behind the Green Door*—that have a minimal but still sufficient artistic interest to distinguish themselves from the rest of the genre. But the genre continues to be characterized by a high volume of low-grade quickies. Its audience has no identifiable standard of taste and makes few or no demands. It is in fact quite likely that the audience does not know what it likes, either collectively or individually.

Presumably the audience wants to be eroticized. Eroticism, however, is elusive. From Georges Bataille's anthropological perspective, for example, it is inextricably associated with subtly counterpointing archetypes, taboos, and transgressions. Freud describes psychic forces at work, Marx and Engels, social and economic forces. Eroticism is a social and psychic drama for which sexual spectacle is at best only a potential and unpredictable catalyst. And it is, after all, eroticism that brings the audience to these films; the viewer is not a blank tablet passively receiving an impression. Moreover, it is a commonplace of sexological research, borne out by retailers of smut books, magazines, and films, that the functional life of such stimuli is relatively brief; turnover is regular because people require variety but within very narrow parameters. The smut film industry skirts the problem of erotic complexity by settling on slight variations in the common denominator, sexual spectacle. Its object, then, is to feed its audience's fickle appetite a variety of body specimens—since bodies, at this point principally female, are the staple of smut spectacle—while staying within the predictable scenarios that may or may not eroticize its audience but will at least not be distracting from whatever erotic potential a viewer brings along.

The smut film aim is therefore essentially neutral, and produces a spectacle that serves as a pacifier to eroticized expectations. While viewers with particular tastes will want variations in emphasis—more violence or less, more paraphernalia or less, more lesbianism or less—the mainstream scenario accords with a predictable median. It does not attempt anything that might distract from the various fantasy potentials endemic to its audience. The chief function of its spectacle is its license to indulge fantasy and, by inference, sexuality itself. In Bataille's terms the indulgence alone is eroticizing, since it evokes the taboo against sexual indulgence by being a transgression of it. The consciousness of transgression is maintained by the subcultural role and sleazy public image of smut films. The greater the general public disapproval, the greater the eroticizing potential of these films, regardless of their intrinsic quality. That is why such films as *Deep Throat* lose their eroticizing function as they gain popularity. In its heyday, viewing *Deep Throat* conferred a kind of liberal status, and so the pleasure it provided shifted from eroticism to art and possibly even politics. It lost the power of transgression vital to erotic imagination. It also lost its status as a smut film.

The smut film plays a peculiar role and need not upgrade or complicate its spectacle, since it serves its eroticizing function precisely by existing as social marginalia. The industry must be aware of this at some level, if for no other reasons than that it continues to profit without significantly improving its product. Improvement, which would by analogy with *Deep Throat* almost certainly infect it with imagination, would probably threaten the genre. Imagination raises the ante from fantasy license to erotic aesthetics, which is to say philosophy. Russ Meyer's parodic interpretation of sexuality, for example, anticipates *Deep Throat's* comic interpretation, which in turn anticipates tragic interpretations such as *In the Realm of the Senses*. These works exhibit a progressively philosophical integration of sexuality and life, going well beyond the simple function of endorsing and complementing fantasy. So there is an important distinction between the smut film spectacle and that of more artistically ambitious films.

Nonetheless, as spectacle is the *sine qua non* of cinema, it is basic to any pornographic film, whatever its artistic ambitions. The simplicity of smut spectacle invites its viewer to take the images for what they purport to be. Although it is possible for a viewer to imagine that he is surreptitiously watching a private encounter—and indeed viewers may insist on that or some similar fiction—in fact he is watching a performance. His pleasure is voyeuristic but not, strictly speaking, voyeurism, since in general he does not get sexual gratification from watching. What he gets is an invitation to indulge erotic imagination. He may simply subscribe to the scene before him, or he may use it to facilitate his own fantasies, possibly but not necessarily projecting himself into the scene. Whether or not it leads him to genital activity will likely depend on circumstances. But prior to that, in any event, is the invitation to indulge the transgression of the taboo against indulgence which the workaday world imposes.

Yet sexual activity in itself is not transgression, and it or its prospect may not even be eroticizing. Eroticism, as we have seen in Bataille, is more comprehensive, and involves a yearning for a unity inaccessible to human being, a fusion that the orderly world denies him. If sex itself could satisfy this, the viewer would very likely be doing something else. This is not to deny that there are viewers for whom the smut spectacle is preparing for sex, or for whom it is a substitute. But it is to suggest that the dirty old man in the trenchcoat may have a fantasy bigger than he knows. After all, watching images in itself is a rather oblique route to sexual gratification. On the other hand, the images are obscene, a transgression, an invitation to a communion of defiance, a violation of the most sacred of privacies. And privacy symbolizes the very isolation the individual human being yearns to transcend. In terms of transgression, of course, there are better and worse sorts of invitations. For the smut viewer spectacle and transgression are one, if the sexual performance is convincing.

Insofar as they record a specific performance smut films are something like documentaries, and like documentaries they have their element of fiction. They float the dream of sex without a hitch. In actuality one carries one's life, more or less, into sex, and sex is consequently more or less problematic. But sometimes sex is less problematic or even nonproblematic, and in that sense the smut dream is not altogether a fiction. It simply exorcises the problems and paves the way to imagining an eroticized existence, which is not simply sexualized but simultaneously a defiance of society's insistence on rationally productive order. This defiance obviously requires a special energy, symbolized in the potency of sexual spectacle. So the smut viewer wants evidence of real sexual energy, not illusion. One index of this is the smut convention of showing sperm ejaculating from an erect penis (which of course also has to do with sexual politics, the female servicing the male, and is another manifestation of the individual abrasion with social structure; in female-oriented smut, not yet much evident in film, a different set of dynamics is assumed). Without such distinct signs of vitality the smut film diminishes, if not altogether frustrates, its eroticizing function.

Given the nature of cinema, there is always the problem of illusion. Apart from self-conscious gestures toward exposing illusion—e.g., when Tom in *Tom Jones* covers the camera lens with his hat to afford his bare-bosomed lady friend privacy—the convention of narrative film is to induce something akin to "willing suspension of disbelief." There are various ways of approaching the problem. Smut films make cursory overtures to it with their story lines, but do not seriously employ it: As we have noted, they depend on belief rather than on suspension of disbelief. The low comic narrative of *Deep Throat* assumes the suspension of disbelief but parodies it in the absurdity of plot and dialogue, and similarly with Russ Meyer's soft-core pornographic parodies. Avant-garde films may toy with the convention, as Ben Van Meter does in *Poontang Trilogy*, but are generally non-narrative and need not deal with suspension of disbelief, as for instance its irrelevance to the visual lyricism of Stan Brakhage's erotic films. But such artistically advanced pornographic feature films as *In the Realm of the Senses* and Bertolucci's *Last Tango in Paris* employ the convention outright. They also illustrate two opposing approaches to suspension of disbelief in terms of spectacle.

Bertolucci induces it by sustaining a highly pornographic ambience but not showing genitalia on the screen. His plot turns on the causality of pornographic imagination rather than explicit sex, so spectacle would distract from credibility. On the other hand, the resolution of Oshima's plot is emasculation, so genital imagery is integral and imperative to credibility. In parodies, such as those of Van Meter, Damiano, or Meyer, illusion is one of the things parodied, so it ceases to function in its own right. In Brakhage's lyricism, interpretation or perception is the point rather than illusion. But the illusion of pornographic ambience is central to Bertolucci's narrative, and something so ephemeral as ambience very likely would be overpowered by the spectacle of genitalia. Oshima's focus on the sensuality of eroticism makes genital spectacle appropriate to his film's dramatic illusion; moreover, his dramatic conclusion relies on the spectacular illusion of emasculation, for which genital exposure is both a visual and rhythmic anticipation. Thus the illusion/spectacle nexus has a variety of possible dynamics, which are manipulated according to the film maker's purposes.

Pornographic spectacle in a narrative art film is characteristically used to help articulate complications of character and situation. *In the Realm of the Senses*, for example, has the male protagonist's ready erections signify an appetite that has the potential to consume him. At various moments the erection in action may eroticize the viewer, but that happens within a complex plot, whose unfolding places eroticism in a highly problematic context. The viewer's eroticism is controlled by the film maker's structures and directed to the film maker's ends rather than the viewer's. The art film maker anticipates a disinterested viewer, one more or less open to the film maker's imagination or at least without predetermined expectations.

Conversely, with the smut film the viewer expects to be eroticized and anticipates sexual spectacle rather than complicated situation and character. The smut viewer does not want contemplation, he wants to gorge himself on erotic promise. It is imperative that he not be distracted by a connection between "pornotopia" and life. Whether he follows the film's fantasy or drifts into his own, indulgence is the object, not the film maker's vision. Thus, smut spectacle is essentially generic. That a smut scene may be laboriously manipulated to give the illusion of spontaneous continuity is unimportant to the viewer. What the smut film documents, after all, is ritual performance, not sexual reality. One wants to watch Fred Astaire and Ginger Rogers dance, when one wants to watch them dance, not the rehearsals necessary for them to perform, and certainly not the cinematic finessing that further enhances their gracefulness. If one wanted to be dancing that's what one would be doing. Similarly with the smut viewer, if he wanted sex itself, that's what he would be doing. While smut films have an obvious masturbation and foreplay potential, particularly with their availability on home video, these acts by the viewer in themselves do not necessarily provide erotic gratification. Masturbation can gratify animal urges and may express erotic yearning, but eroticism as such is more durable and compelling. It requires, as Bataille describes it, a transcendence of individual isolation that is only satisfied with sexual communion, sex with at least one other person. And to achieve that while simultaneously watching a film is rather more unlikely than it might seem. So a smut film viewer is oriented to eroticizing fantasy while watching a more or less highly stylized sexual actuality.

This use of ritualized sex is also the ground on which one can distinguish a smut film from an art film, in those few cases where the question is pertinent. *Behind the Green Door*, for example, is more artful than most smut films, but is still a smut film. Plot and character serve exclusively to draw the viewer more and more deeply into pornographic fantasy. Such reference as there is to a connection between life and fantasy merely brackets the main action and also serves to enforce fantasy. *Deep Throat*, in some ways less artful than *Behind the Green Door*, nonetheless crosses over into the lower echelons of the art film by virtue of its binary structure, a comic parody of the fantasy it ostensibly exploits. Its viewer is presented with a contradiction between the psychological grip of fantasy and its absurdity, whereas the viewer of *Green Door* is simply encouraged to indulge.

One should note the obvious here, that there is high art and low, good art and bad. *Deep Throat* is definitely low; it may also be bad, but its toying with its subject takes it beyond the category of the smut film, however deeply it is rooted there. But even for films of a higher artistic order there is an irony that goes with pornographic territory, at least in terms of the Romantic concept of art as a spontaneous overflow of imagination. The greater its artistic realization, the greater control it exercises on the viewer. Obscene spectacle has an unpredictable detonation point. It inveterately upstages the other cinematic components. It generates ambivalence. Its function is subversive and subterranean. Wresting the aesthetic from its aggressiveness requires more than customary adroitness. For the smut film, which has only the aim of setting indulgence in motion, any explosion of energy and any direction it takes is sufficient to its purposes. But art films manifest a vision, greater or lesser to be sure, and aim to induce recognition of that vision. An uncontrolled explosion of energy is counterproductive to that end. Thus an art film carefully manipulates obscene spectacle, deploying it in a controlling ecology of images, situations, nuances. Where the smut film turns eroticism loose, swats its hindquarters and lets it run, the art film mounts it, spurs it here, reins it in there, disciplines and directs it through a course. In smut, obscenity may run proud and free, or buck and fart, or simply stop and graze, and the viewer responds according to his or her inclination. The effect of the art film depends on the tension between the rider's discipline and obscenity's natural energy. Obviously there are better and worse riders, just as there are more and less intriguing courses.

The challenge of obscene spectacle makes it all the more compelling that pornography is asserting itself in increasingly sophisticated ways in an increasing number of artistically ambitious films. While one can speak of a smut film genre, the pornographic character of more complex films becomes too diverse for usefully synthetic labels, as the foregoing discussion suggests. As with that of literature, pornography's most probable aesthetic potential in film is as a rhetoric complementing other themes. Still, in the following discussion of films I apply "pornography" to any film in which explicit sexual imagery, themes, and action are in whole or in part of sufficient prominence either to be ends in themselves or constitute a rhetoric toward more complicated ends. I have selected films and film makers that I think are particularly relevant to the development of pornography as an aesthetic motif. My particular interest is in examining the character and potential of this development. While I suggest historical connections—a kind of evolution of the pornographic from the avant-garde cinema of the 1950s and 1960s to the feature films of the 1970s and 1980s—I am not presenting a history of cinematic pornography. Obscenity, eroticism, and pornography did not spring without precedent from the fevered brow of the late 1950s and early 1960s. Still, I think there was a broader community of interest in the aesthetic prospects of obscenity in that period than had existed before.

In American culture there were several reasons for this. World War II had a destabilizing effect on domestic values. The war industry had run round the clock, and the entertainment industry accommodated it, with night spots often running shows for swing and graveyard-shift clientele. High employment circulated currency. Women were brought out of the kitchen and into the work force in unprecedented numbers. The aura of intensity had a reciprocal release of energy that bordered on the orgiastic. In the postwar period there was a reaction to get things back to normal. The repressiveness of the McCarthy era was only the most prominent sign. But it served to sharpen the contradiction between liberal and conservative sensibilities. The arts, which during the war had largely been taken up with promoting patriotism, began to bring contradictions to the surface. Writers such as Chester Himes, James Jones, and Norman Mailer, among others, produced works in which the contradictions ranged from the absurd to the catastrophic, and were characterized by obscenities ranging from the logical to the lascivious. The same population that elected General Eisenhower as President also consumed *The Naked and the Dead,* which assaulted the very military logic and integrity with which Ike was presumably to restore normality. Where conservatives sought to keep the ox well under, as the Buddhists say, liberals sought to let it loose. Moreover, the conservative majority provided rallying points for at least the aesthetic minority by suppressing such books as D. H. Lawrence's *Lady Chatterley's Lover* and Henry Miller's *Tropics* up to the early 1960s. Thus the issue of pornography was joined to the more generalized obscenity that was beginning to be perceived as already in the bourgeois mainstream. The Kinsey Reports not only sharpened the sexual focus but suggested hypocrisy in the mainstream culture. Contradiction and confrontation were in the air, subterranean perhaps, but highly articulate. In fact artists reveled in their underground, offbeat role. The Beat writers became the guides for what was in fact a multigenerational generation.

This was the cultural and aesthetic atmosphere that cultivated the renaissance of what was called "underground" or "experimental" or "avant-garde" film. In some respects, avant-garde film took on the most romanticized image among the arts, probably because it provided the most conspicuous counterpoint to that most aggravating of American institutions, Hollywood. Kenneth Anger's campy and irreverent film, *Scorpio Rising,* became an ensign of the new cinema and, perhaps by association with his earlier homoerotic *Fireworks,* implied an obscene aesthetic. His book *Hollywood Babylon,* confirmed avant-garde paranoia about mainstream mentality. Post-war avant-garde film, like Beat literature, developed in this climate of antagonism to bourgeois normality and adopted obscenity, among other attitudes, as an appropriate mode of confrontation. These attitudes were not in themselves unique, but their synthesis and collective appeal to a generation of artists gave the prospects for obscene poetics a distinct momentum. Feature films, of course, had had a long history of sexual imagery and a long line of sex symbols—Theda Bara, Jean Harlow, Hedy Lamarr, Jane Russell. And this tradition provided material for parody in avant-garde films. Hedy Lamarr's sex-queen status was founded on her performance in *Ecstasy*, an early feature film that broached the pornographic with scenes of nakedness, both titillating and humorous, and with depiction of a female orgasm that shook the light fixtures if it did not make the earth move. There was also the occasional sex "documentary." *Mom and Dad*, for example, was a 1940s film that had a brief but vigorous feature distribution. It was promoted in equal parts as scientific and salacious. In fact it was about reproduction and birth, and nurses were advertised to be in attendance for the faint of heart. Since it was received as a hybrid of the unvarnished truth and obscenity, it served to emphasize cultural schizophrenia on the subject of sex, which of course was grist for the avant-garde mill. The avant-garde tradition itself had more incisive antecedents, for exampLe Bunuel's *Un Chien andalou* and *L'Age d'or* and Webber and Watson's *Lot in Sodom*. These films addressed pornographic aesthetics in that their sexual motifs had a consciousness of obscenity and were integrated with broader psychic and social themes. They were also cinematically adventurous (and still are), thus further counterpointing the bourgeois tepidness of mainstream films. Their influence on avant-garde film was and continues to be significant. Nevertheless, my analysis begins with the 1950s and 1960s because the dynamics of pornography's emergence as an artistic cinematic phenomenon are more clearly discernible in the concentrated assertiveness of the film makers and films of that time.

## THE AVANT-GARDE CINEMA OF SEXUALITY

Because of its energetic exploration of cinematic possibilities, its indifference to popular taste and commercial enterprise, and, therefore, its attempt to adhere to imaginative authenticity, the avant-garde film has had an aesthetic impact far beyond either the volume of its production or the limits of its distribution. Underground though it may have been, its spirit continues to pervade the study and practice of cinema. This ephemeral state makes documentation of its influence speculative at best. Nonetheless, it is there. And when one sees how television advertisements have, after polishing them up, co-opted the techniques of avant-garde films, one recognizes how inadvertently pervasive their influence has been.

Stan Brakhage is among the most aesthetically influential avant-garde film makers, especially among those whose careers began in the 1950s. Early in his career, he briefly flirted with the prospect of becoming an Alfred Hitchcock apprentice and presumably going Hollywood. Significantly, it was the making of an erotic film that caused him to reject that direction and confirm his avant-garde future. When the Hitchcock appointment was offered to him, Brakhage was at work on his film *Flesh of Morning* (1956), which he describes as "a psycho-drama of masturbation." He deferred acceptance in order to finish the film, but in that process he realized that his aesthetic inclinations could not accommodate Hollywood. While *Flesh of Morning* was Brakhage's eighth film, he notes that it was the first in which he "consciously used light to create a tone poem." This emphasis on the poetics of light has become the impressionistic hallmark of Brakhage's subsequent style. He also discovered the appeal of making what he calls a "hermetic film, a completely private film," which he alone wrote, acted in (although an actress also appears), and photographed (via pulleys by which he manipulated the camera while acting). While many of his films have employed actors, the hermetic ambiance persists in Brakhage's intensely lyrical and idiosyncratic imagery, particularly in later works along the lines of *The Text of Light* (1974). In making *Flesh* he also discovered the power of eroticism. "Only the subject of sex," Brakhage says, "would have had the power to get me not only to make a completely private film but also to turn my career away from Hollywood." Yet, at this same time he declined an offer to make smut films because he did not want his work stigmatized by that approach. Thus *Flesh of Morning* signifies both in the development of Brakhage's impressionistic style and that of his perspective on sexuality and the erotic.

In the sense that *Flesh of Morning* reflects a conscious rejection of both mainline Hollywood and conventional smut, while at the same time insisting on the integrity of sexuality's function in human consciousness, it is paradigmatic of an avant-garde address to cinematic sexuality. Not that there was or is a common avant-garde perception of sex; far from it. But Brakhage reflected what was a common concern, and he was among the first of the post-war film makers to challenge cultural duplicity about the role of sex in life and art by demonstrating that pornographic imagery had aesthetic viability. In part, *Flesh of Morning's* masturbation motif may be attributable to the romantic frustrations of Brakhage's youth, but the film's erotic vision has archetypal as well as personal reverberations, particularly in the context of the 1950s. If its erotic yearning is intensely personal, so does it reveal the human spirit's yearning to articulate its sexual nature.

In conception the film is a psychodrama; in execution, however, it transcends clinical implications to become an elegiac supplication to Eros. In narrative or dramatic terms the film presents a young man acting out his sexual anxieties, which culminate in fetishism, the phantasm of a woman, masturbation, and prayer. In this respect it is about isolation and absence, the isolation of the psyche in the absence of love and any communion with what gods there be. In perceptual terms, though, the plot is subordinate to visual apprehension and cumulative tension, the visual cadence of the film inducing in the viewer an emotional empathy that is rationalized by the plot but is not dependent upon it.

The first half of the film focuses on the young man's mounting anxiety, as he is trapped in a sequence of near-hysterical visual perceptions. The camera eye establishes a shifting point of view, sometimes exterior to him and sometimes becoming his interior "eye." The young man's psyche conditions how he sees and consequently how the viewer sees. Seeing is both an act of stress and a continuing aggravation of stress. The reflection of his frame from a chrome coffee pot, for example, is of course distorted, and when he looks outside the brilliant white light all but obliterates the landscape. Ironically, vision not only reflects his anxiety but turns him increasingly inward on himself. He enters his disheveled bedroom. A woman's underclothes are strewn on the floor. He grinds his shoe on them, fondles a stocking, his face tormented. A woman's photograph becomes a phantasm, her very white face against a black dress and background luring him, taunting. He undresses, lies down on the bed. The masturbation scene is intercut with positive and negative images, their alternation providing a fantasy implosion for the viewer. The viewer, having been prepared by the shifting point of view, now visually shares the young man's masturbatory agitation. The alternations of positive and negative light in this climactic scene induce a dialectic of objective and subjective perception in the viewer. The man does ejaculate, for example, but the viewer does not so much see this as apprehend it subliminally, so visually and psychically complex is the rendering of the spectacle. Thus the viewer is not so much observing a sex act as participating in an emotional state.

The last two scenes release the viewer, restoring an objective point of view and reinvoking the plot. The camera looks out the window into a now normal light; children are playing in the street. Children, the natural consequence of love and sex, enforce the theme of isolation and absence and the pathos of masturbation. In the final scene the camera returns to the man on the bed. His hands form a church, as in the child's rhyme of "Here's the Church and Here's the Steeple," while his lips silently mime the "Lord's Prayer." But this scene seems to reach through its Christian framework to invoke an antecedent god, Eros.

In addition to its use of light as a "tone poem," this film's intense privacy and erotic theme laid the foundations for the erotic lyricism that Brakhage developed in subsequent films and which constitutes his distinctive contribution to the development of obscene poetics in contemporary cinema. *Flesh of Morning* is structured by the unfolding of a dramatic situation, but after it Brakhage began turning away from the model of drama and toward the model of the lyric poem. Moreover, it appears that Eros heard his prayer, for two years after *Flesh* he married, an act which provided a logical progression in his erotic vision. Lyricism implies personalness, and Brakhage's is an extraordinarily personal art. *Flesh* left him in an untenable erotic limbo. As he describes it in *Metaphors on Vision* (1963, 1976),

> I can remember when I got married many of my friends who had been waiting for me to transform into a homosexual were bitterly disappointed, frustrated and considered that by their mythos of what the artist was I was completely through. It wasn't all just their personal wants, but it was in respect to the mythos . . . in [Cocteau's] Orpheus . . . where the whole film unreels itself and Orpheus is cast back into the arms of Eurydice, and he himself as poet . . . is completely destroyed.

Brakhage's friends were right to see eroticism's centrality in his art but wrong in supposing that his art should be separate from natural rhythms—birth, life, death. They might have seen it a year before his marriage in his film *Loving* (1957), which depicts a man and a woman making love in a forest. This brief film is meticulously appreciative of the act of love and quite consciously places that act in a natural setting. In fact Brakhage's camera is as attentive to the color, light, and configuration of the forest as it is to the texture, shape, and motion of lovemaking; nature and love in equal parts are lyrically synthesized. The lovers were two close friends of Brakhage, film maker and artist Carolee Schneemann and musician James Tenney, whose relationship Brakhage idealized in life as well as the film. Idealization would be a hopeful alternative to the limbo of *Flesh of Morning*, but it too would be untenable. In many respects Brakhage's personal erotic myth is romantic; it is not, however, naive romanticism. He discovered this in making *Wedlock House: An Intercourse* (1958) a few months after his marriage.

The realities of marriage seem to have made Brakhage recognize the inadequacy of idealized love. During an argument he began shooting footage of his wife Jane's face, holding the camera in one hand and playing light from a lamp over her face with the other, "painting her image" with light. She took the camera and light and did the same to him: "We got glimpses of each other, in flashes of moving light, as if emerging out of long hallways in sheer darkness. All the quarrels we were having at that time became pitched on that visual level." By this point the quarrel obviously had been transformed into a symbolic exploration, an act of literal and figurative seeing. There was also, as they later discovered in editing, subconscious projection. He projected other women into her image—past girl friends, actresses in his films, his mother—and she other men into his—past boy friends and her brother (the poet Jack Collom). These projections do not emerge recognizably as such in the film, but it is informed by the probe and discovery of mutual being that the projection represented, an exorcism of "non-seeing." Of course they were not only quarreling during this period, they were also making love, confirming the "something flowering between us." And Brakhage filmed that too, stationing the camera and letting it run. The structure of *Wedlock House* is a dialectic—the slow-strobe searches and their portraits in light counterpointed by scenes of intercourse projected in negative. The contradiction is transcended at film's end, when the image of Jane's face goes to pure white from which the concluding intercourse scene emerges.

The quotidian is at the center of Brakhage's vision, and at the diurnal center is eroticism, which is to say sex as the touchstone of more complex intercourse flowering up and out into the world. Sex itself is imperative because it *is* imperative. But without love, as in *Flesh of Morning*, sex is alienation and wasted seed (there is a strongly implicit religious strain in much of Brakhage's work). With the prospect of love, as in *Wedlock House*, sex can get one to the brink of life. With the flowering of love, as manifest in the corpus of Brakhage's work, one can see; to a visual artist, seeing is being, and to Brakhage being is erotic. If in itself this perspective is conventional enough, Brakhage has given it aesthetic significance in cinema and the world by virtue of the vivid lyricism with which he has celebrated this vision.

One distinct contribution Brakhage has made to obscene cinematography is his demonstration that explicit sexual spectacle can be treated lyrically. His approach to this problem in both *Flesh of Morning* and *Wedlock House* was to present the sexual scenes in negative. The effect of that reversal is to stylize the image of bodies and give them a spectral appearance. The spectral configures the spiritual, and it is the spiritual root of sexuality upon which Brakhage focuses not only in these films but in all of his erotic works. The aesthetic motive for projecting sex in negative was to oblige the viewer to alter the seeing of sex by having to see into the image. Moreover, the camera eye remains constant, declining to influence or assist the viewer's focus by panning or zooming or changing perspective. So in terms of both light and focus the viewer must necessarily be active in construing the image and cannot simply sit back and absorb sex passively or voyeuristically. The shift from the expected positive image to negative precisely at the moment of sex also tends to levitate the image so that it seems to float in space. The tonality of sexual spectacle becomes songlike, lyrical.

However, Brakhage was mindful of the potential for legal charges of obscenity, and in this respect it is pertinent to note that all of his erotic films up to *Lovemaking* (1968) had difficulties with censorship by film processing labs. This included *Window Water Baby Moving* (1959), a film on childbirth. This is not the place to take up censorship, except to observe that in the 1950s and 1960s it did have some aesthetic ramifications. In the case of *Flesh of Morning* and *Wedlock House*, Brakhage's aesthetic choice to project the sex scenes in negative was at least strongly seconded by his vain hope to avoid censorship problems. Many stylistic decisions by film makers of the time were similarly influenced. This problem is more crucial for film makers than for other kinds of artists. If a typesetter, for example, refuses to set a writer's text, the writer still has the text. If a lab refuses to develop film, the film maker is stymied. In the case of *Window Water Baby Moving*, the Kodak lab threatened to destroy the film until the doctor who delivered the baby requested it and promised that it would only be shown for purposes of childbirth instruction. Suppressions and harassments also had a more general aesthetic effect, which was to confirm avant-garde film makers in their commitment to confronting social myopia and hypocrisy with sexual material.

Brakhage's much acclaimed major work of the 1960s, *Dog Star Man* (1964), provides a unique perspective on the interiority of eroticism. Where the image of sex is spectral in *Flesh of Morning* and *Wedlock House* and romantically earthy in *Loving*, here Brakhage emphasizes its psychic dimension by presenting it via phantasmagorical montage, punctuated by visceral images of a pumping heart. It is as if the evolution of Brakhage's erotic vision required a qualification of his previous representations of sexuality. In *Dog Star Man* the sexual spirit is cast in terms of dream associations, and romanticism is connected to physiology. This would seem to give sex a more material ground, which it does, but its materiality is complicated by the film's central mythopoeic motif. The film is in five parts. The "Prelude" is a dream sequence that in effect prophesies and establishes oneiric format for the rest of the film, which explores the struggle to invent or reinvent the myth of being. The remaining three parts explore the components most integral to the myth—life energies, sexuality, birth and death.

Thus sexuality, which is the specific focus of "Part Three," is part of the process of mythopoeia, inventing a myth for being. Myth implies story, but *Dog Star Man* is not narrative. It is silent and visual (or visionary) and more concerned with revealing the mind's necessity for encountering those felt truths by which one's life may be guided, as by a star. As a truth in Brakhage's pantheon, sex is not vitally felt until it has consciousness of its holistic psychic function, until it is manifest in the soul as well as the body. To illuminate this psychic imperative, Brakhage dissociates body parts. Images are choreographed in a fantasia—now a breast, now a penis, now a dancing torso, now a nipple spurting milk, now a magnification of skin texture. The dream quality is enhanced by superimpositions and intercuts of film that has been painted and scratched to emulate what Brakhage calls "closed-eye vision, what we get when we close our eyes in daylight and watch the moving of shapes and forms through the red pattern of the eyelid." Again, although now from a psychic rather than spectral point of view, the viewer is obliged to see into the images, to construe them and interpret their transformation from animal sexuality to human eroticism. Brakhage likens this to the Victorian inclination for veiled nudity, where the nudity is quite distinctly implicit but must be discovered through the veils and thus seen anew. "I was after an aesthetic revelation," Brakhage says, "as opposed to dirty pictures, which are after all rather easy and witless. Something is left out when you just photograph people fucking. . . . It becomes an absurdity." One thing that is left out is the heart. And Brakhage intercuts the sexual images with the vividly visceral images of a beating heart, this cadence thus emphasizing the vital function of eroticism.

However, while the mythopoeic preoccupation of *Dog Star Man* induced dissociative sexual spectacle for its purposes, the more direct celebration of sexuality in *Lovemaking* (1968) cultivated a correspondingly more direct sexual imagery. In terms of sexual spectacle, this film is perhaps Brakhage's most categorical treatment. The first part features a heterosexual couple, and its photography is more typical of Brakhage's sexual footage than the other parts. Unlike the earlier *Loving*, also in color, this scene was shot indoors. Where the earlier film exploited the natural colors and light of a forest glade, here Brakhage "paints" the couple with light in the manner of *Wedlock House*. The camera, however, does not explore the couple's sexual psyche so much as attend to its sinuous embraces, so that, while we are watching the spectacle of sex, the dominant impression is of sensuous human forms emerging from dark into light, which illuminates skin tones like petals opening under the sun until the image evolves into the yet more brilliant light of overexposure and then back into darkness from which the process recycles itself with variations. The shots are from one to three seconds, and here again the viewer must see into and invent the image. Sexuality is not romanticized, but it is quite consciously lyricized, to be apprehended aesthetically rather than carnally or even psychologically.

The photography and editing are significantly simpler in the following three parts of *Lovemaking*. The second part features a group of dogs going about their daily doggy business, including sex and its consequent litter of pups suckling the mother. The cinemagraphic approach is documentary and straightforward. The dogs' unconscious sex would seem neither to be nor to aspire to eroticism. The third part of the film consists of probably the most graphically intimate footage in the Brakhage canon. It is an interior scene of two homosexual lovers making love, again photographed in documentary fashion. At first they are fully dressed, fondling and kissing in mutual seduction, which continues as they undress. The camera occasionally focuses the viewer on signs of intimacy—the lovers kiss, hold hands, stroke one another's skin—as it also focuses on the male form—a foot, hand, buttocks, chest, face, implying a sensuality more comprehensive than genital orientation. But here neither camera nor lighting lyrically interpret the action; despite intimations from the camera's occasionally shifting focus, it essentially records. Moreover, its primary attention as the tempo of sex builds is on fellatio, and this is the only instance of such sustained and conspicuous genital focus in Brakhage's work. Given Brakhage's sense of the imperative integration of eroticism in the life cycle, it is not surprising that he might be more bemused than lyrical at the spectacle of homosexual love. Nonetheless, his treatment connotes that this is a viable mode of "lovemaking," albeit one that sits somewhat self-consciously in his erotic theory.

The fourth and final part of *Lovemaking* again emphasizes the breadth of Brakhage's erotic sensibility and its function in daily life processes. It documents naked children, ranging in age from three to twelve, at play. They are the Brakhage children and those of a family of close friends. The children, seven or eight in number, had spontaneously disrobed and were playing as children will on a mattress—jumping, tumbling, piling on, having pillow fights, making up a rhythm band and dancing. Touched by their pre-pubescent ebullience, Brakhage filmed their play. Apart from the childrens' nudity and two or three instances of a child tugging or scratching his or her private parts, there is no sexuality per se. In Brakhage's terms the children represent eroticism or lovemaking in the sense that they are children, and thus the signifiers of erotic love, that their bouncing naked butts and bellies reflect a cherubic vitalism, and that they are taking pleasure in their naked beings. Its innocence notwithstanding, this section of the film has occasioned such misunderstanding and consternation as to suggest that Brakhage inadvertently tapped an anxiety about the sexuality of children at once subliminal and sociological. When, for example, the film was shown at the Huntington Hartford Museum in New York City, the outraged museum projectionist refused to project its second showing. And the *New York Times* review characterized it as a child-abuse film. This sort of response, and the prospect of some child pornography promoter using the film as a court test case, prompted Brakhage to remove the film from distribution in 1982.

The difficulty with *Lovemaking* is that it is caught between celebration of eros and exposition of the qualities of love. I suspect, for example, that the reason viewers like the *New York Times* reviewer can misperceive the children sequence is its juxtaposition with the homosexuals, which implies an expository connection between the two scenes. Thus a viewer so disposed can see the children as objects for pederasty. Brakhage's peculiar strength is in the lyrical mode, to which he returned unequivocally in such subsequent erotic films as the *Sexual Meditations* of the early 1970s. Brakhage's primary contribution to pornographic cinematography has been his infusion of lyric sensibility into the treatment of sexuality in general and of sexual spectacle in particular. While his erotic theory of the necessary synthesis of sex with love and the life cycle is in itself more or less conventional, it profoundly informs all of his work and gives it a coherently integral vision that is by and large missing from avant-garde approaches to sexuality. His intense commitment to this age-old truth has also inspired him with the unique visual articulation that has enabled him to "make it new," that is, to revive the mythopoeia of eros in recasting it in a contempory idiom.

While Brakhage was developing his distinctive erotic impressionism, other avant-garde film makers were also taking up the subject of sex. The most prominent centers of this work in the early 1960s were San Francisco and New York, which tended to rather different styles. Jack Smith's *Flaming Creatures* (1963), now an underground classic, is a paradigm for the New York aesthetic. It is certainly the obscene ensign for avant-garde films, so much so that without it the Warhol "factory" films—the zenith of the New York school's productivity and popularity—very likely would not have existed. Its influence permeates *Blow Job* (1964), *Harlot* (1965), *Chelsea Girls* (1966), and most especially *Trash* (1970). Smith's sense of form is baroque, cinematic images rich with Art Nouveau-like configurations and texture, elaborately posed shots that seem often to be almost still compositions. *Flaming Creatures,* although it is not comic, is a parody of a transvestite orgy. But it is an elaborately camp orgy, a transvestite's artificial paradise where any resemblance to living persons is purposely coincidental. But out of its frenzy of dancing about, fake voluptuousness, rape, and sexual carryings on, Smith disciplines his camera to produce a sequence of extraordinary compositions. Formally and thematically the film is fascinated with both aesthetic and moral "decadence." Smith himself has called it "moldy" or "pasty" art. Interpreting these terms, Ronald Tavel, playwright and sometime scenarist for Warhol films, emphasizes their aesthetic complexity:

> "Pasty art" refers to what it suggests—bad art. But bad in a very special sense. It is bad and "moldy" and "pasty" because it involves all that is pitiful and miserable and lost and degraded about people. It encompasses their wretched, deceitful, inherited dreams, the abominable fantasy prisons that follow their twisted childhoods and their doomed, unrequitable groping into a dismal future. The art is pasty because this is not only the subject matter but, properly, its form and method and surface. Smith is one of the least objective artists I know. His brand of creation is convincing and over-

> whelming because he is so inextricably immersed in it. . . . Through his insistent concentration on costumes and ecstatic, exotically placed transvestites, Smith has achieved a comprehension of humanity and its sadly mortal flesh unique in our artistic culture.

Clearly this does not describe stereotypical pornography. It refers rather to a cinema of sexuality, in which the spectacle of "aberrant" sexual forms configures, in the socially paralyzing duality of transvestitism, the human impotence endemic to sexual fantasy. In short, although its rhetoric is pornographic, the impact of *Flaming Creatures* is distinctly asexual.

Nonetheless, *Flaming Creatures* is all flame, although, despite the plenitude of genitalia, sex is given a highly idiosyncratic focus. Sexual parts are disembodied. Smith makes us see the nipple, for example, out of all proportion. It fills the screen, obscures the shape of the breast with its overwhelming presence. Its potential consequences are thus immensely threatening. And, having eradicated scale, he goes on to parody the breast's sexuality: It is prodded, squashed, and flapped until it becomes grotesque, as if at once to invoke and exorcise it, and with it sexuality as well. The effect is compounded by the grainy outdated Army-surplus film Smith used. Not only is the breast grotesque, it is dingy, i.e. "moldy" or "pasty." Likewise the penis, flapped, prodded, and parodied. And the vagina. Disembodied parts, with their associational reverberations intact but separate, become Figures 1, 2, 3 in a baroque anatomy lesson. Smith obliquely satirizes (obliquely because satire is an implication of the film rather than its mode or purpose) the American fantasy of Miss Clean, sexually represented in the Playmate. She too is disembodied, but lord what a difference! How pretty the surface, she says, grazing her belly with a manicured fingertip, how clean. Pigshit, Smith says, and one is right to hear the echo of Artaud; inside there's another world. All those glands *secrete*. And those swirling juices make things happen. Ugliness, grotesquerie, distortion—the tragic mask—are the underside of the coin.

It is its "insistent concentration" on the "comprehension of humanity" in terms of its "sadly mortal flesh" that makes *Flaming Creatures* the obscene touchstone of experimental films. In this respect—as distinct from the film's purely compositional grace—Smith's is what Ezra Pound called a "diagnostic" art, derived from the "cult of ugliness" and manifest in such figures as Villon, Baudelaire, Corbière, and Beardsley. The cult of beauty (where one would locate Brakhage) may be of a higher order, as Plato said. But, Pound reminds us, "the cult of beauty and the delineation of ugliness are not in mutual opposition." The art of cure requires diagnosis. Smith's genius has been to synthesize a diagnostic metaphor with elegantly "beautiful" images.

Pornography has been an important dimension in the experiments of the avant-garde film makers. Traditionally, in graphic art from painting to photography, the body has been rendered static and cosmeticized, according to whichever theory of "beauty" it confirmed. Smith's camera emphasizes naked vulnerability, the body's resilience and its complex aesthetic and moral capacity. Not so grand or symmetrical as the idealized, cosmeticized versions, but considerably more interesting; that is, more authentically human. Apart from his cinematography, the influence of which has been considerable, Smith's contribution to the evolution of obscene cinema was to demonstrate that the body could be used simultaneously as an image in itself and as an existential rhetoric with moral reverberations. By virtue of the movie camera he has gone Beardsley one better. Like Beardsley he has created "beautiful" images of what are conventionally regarded as "ugly" things—orgy, bisexuality, transvestism, decadence—the aesthetic irony of which is punctuated, in the manner of Sade, by an imagery of "real" bodies rendered at once sadly grotesque, morally startling, and compositionally beautiful.

If Smith and the New York aesthetic derive from the demonic insistence of Corbière, Beardsley, and the Symbolists, the San Francisco aesthetic seems to have come from the caprice of surrealist collages and readymades, in the spirit of Marcel Duchamp, Max Ernst, Man Ray, and others. Bruce Conner's *Movie* (1958), *Cosmic Ray* (1961), and *Marilyn Times Five* (1968-1973), Van Meter's *Poontang Trilogy* (1964), and Robert Nelson's *Oh Dem Watermelons* (1965) are good examples. Their contribution to the formal development of cinematic obscenity has been to help establish the montage technique. These films are characterized by rapid-fire image sequences of caprice and good humor. Their vision is not so dense or macabre as Smith's, but they are at the same time more accessible because they do not depend on Lower East Side curiosities, as Smith and Warhol do.

The San Francisco film makers are the sunshine to New York's black light. With montage, they have good fun with the obvious phallic associations—rockets, dirigibles, skyscrapers. And, while Smith goes to school to exotic Grade B Hollywood movies, Conner steals clips from them, which he uses most irreverently. The San Francisco effect, therefore, is much different. It is much more associational and frenetic, whereas Smith and Warhol are more static and design-oriented. The pornographic motif blends rhetorically into general social parody, and the effect is to get a laugh—bitter and ironic finally, but for the moment a laugh. And the guffaw, as, in montage, a dirigible penetrates a naked lady, is not conducive to either Mrs. Grundyism or that more "sophisticated" indignation protesting too loudly that pornography is "a bore." The guffaw, moreover, is liberating, a refusal to take either pornography or life lugubriously, even when, later in the film, the dirigible goes up in flame, in an unpretentiously obvious symbol. Nor do they take pornography seriously as a threat to the social order, nor as what D. H. Lawrence called the "dirty little secret." Nor even as a lyrical revelation. Pornography is something to have fun with, because people are so-o-o serious about it, even one's colleagues in New York.

Rapid-fire montage can be an effective comic technique, which has very likely been its appeal for subsequent film makers in the smut mode, most notably the makers of *Deep Throat*. The appeal is partly commercial. Audiences for smut do not go to a dirty movie expecting to think. And the audience for commercial movies—and one must remember that smut movies, unlike avant-garde ones, are commercial rather than aesthetic ventures—always determines aesthetic parameters. So, if anything other than sex is admitted at all, it is likely to be comic. Moreover, given the simplemindedness of even the more pretentious smut films, montage exploits ready-made humor, simply and efficiently relieving the heavy business of sex without inadvertently activating the audience's brain. This is the dimension of montage that pornographers have picked up from the avant-garde. The frame jump from an erect phallus to a shot of a rocket launch and back again can be made so fast as to break the tense monotony of prolonged voyeurism and still not in fact really distract the audience from sex. Conner and Van Meter, on the other hand, use the technique to integrate sex with a general social absurdity. In *A Movie*, for instance, one sequence begins with a voluptuous blond undressing, jumps to old war film footage of a submarine commander looking through a periscope and firing a torpedo, as the sequence ends with an atomic mushroom cloud from an old newsreel. This sex-power-destruction nexus is a recurring montage motif. Similarly, although without the thematic precision, pornographers have adopted montage both to inject humor (thus minimizing the residual embarrassment one feels as a voyeur) and to integrate sex into the world.

In any event, avant-garde film makers such as Brakhage, Smith, and Conner have influenced the development of a more artistically complex cinema of sexuality. Their interest has been in pornography as a rhetoric rather than an end, which has been precisely their importance. They demonstrated that the pornographic image, which had found a dead end in the stag film, had an untapped cinematic and thematic potential as subsidiary rhetoric for statements of complex aesthetic interest. Perhaps central to their contribution was the parodic explosion of the macho myth upon which the simplistic stag film depends. In *Cosmic Ray*, for instance, Conner masterfully develops the sex-power-destruction montage to at once explore and parody the visual associations—howitzers, rifles, rockets, mushroom clouds, and sexy, naked ladies—inspired by Ray Charles singing "What Did I Do?" He frenetically distorts a female nude, subjecting her elasticized image to overlays of violence and destruction. Thus the connection between sex, violence, and cultural imagination is made, which through "diagnostic" ridicule explodes the high seriousness of the macho myth. This motif in itself opened a whole new perspective on pornography. Once that myth no longer needed to be fed, pornography could be used to explore rather than exploit sexuality, as, for instance, the motif of impotence is explored in Paul Morrisey's and Andy Warhol's *Trash*.

In short, the avant-garde film demonstrated the possibilities of a formally complex pornographic cinema. And that there was an audience for it. Pornographers, in its wake, recognized not only the artistic potential of pornography but also that, with adroit handling, there was a market for pornography wide enough to repay the time and cost of more artistic treatment. To be sure there were many other factors—diminished societal paranoia, more liberal laws and law enforcement, less prosecution, and the Presidential Commission's report on pornography—but these too derived somewhat from the cultural impact of experimental films. Experimental films established a viable precedent for an artistic pornography. One may, for example, see their influence in Saliva Films' presentation of *The Best of the New York Erotic Film Festival* (1972), which became a commercial touring package. The festival films show a variety of influences, but the most predominant are along the Brakhage-Smith-Conner axis.

But the sign of the future can perhaps be seen even more in Andrew Noren's *The Adventures of the Exquisite Corpse* (1967), a film so beguiling to Brakhage that he has called Noren one of the two young film makers he most admires. The film's original title was *Kodak Ghost Poems*, which suggests its formal principles. (The Kodak Company objected to the use of its name.) Noren's surrealist allusion in the new title complements his ghost motif. It also carries an ironic edge that is perhaps more pertinent to the cultural situation of an obscene aesthetics than to the character of the film. *Kodak* alludes to the home-movie manner, the low-budget production, and the distinctively "amateurish" screen image that is frequently cultivated in the experimental film. *Poems* alludes at once to the film's dominant lyricism and its structure, fourteen separate visual "poems" through which winds the unifying motif of a domestic hedonism. And *Ghost* is a bridge joining the cinematic mode to the poetic, where the lyrical center of Noren's vision is manifest in the celluloid "ghosts" of the very people whose lives authenticate that vision—Noren himself, his wife, his child, his friends, even his pets. For there is a haunting quality about Noren's quiet celebration of quotidian sensuality, sex, and eroticism. Or, as Brakhage put it, "Noren leaves, better than anyone else I think, an impression of the track one makes through life."

The film is essentially a series of home movies in which one sees the

Noren circle at play. Making love, bathing, brushing one another's hair, making love, going on outings to the country, sleeping, looking out the window, making love, dressing, undressing, masturbating, making love, getting married, sitting, walking, masturbating, ice skating, picking flowers, eating, making love. One sees the influence of Brakhage in the film's attention to the daily round. Play is its center of vision, and sex is at the center of its play. The film celebrates a gracefully simple hedonism, a sense of pleasure so profound it seems, almost inadvertently, to have simply exorcised displeasure or work.

The effect of this is, ironically, to inform pornographic imagery with a dialectical edge. The contradiction between work and play is sharpened by invoking the humane value of sensible pleasure—the pleasures of the bed, the pleasures of the board, of the family, of friends, in short, of a civilized domestic nature. And the imagistic refrain—it should be noted that the film has no sound track—coordinating these pleasures is pornographic. Eros, in the flesh, is alpha and omega. But however fleshy and pornographic—images, for example, of fellatio, cunnilingus, and masturbation—the focus is on sex as humanistic, neither exploitive nor dehumanizing. So, while pornography is the central metaphor, it flows organically from the life depicted in the film, a life essentially "normal," given its hedonistic basis. There is, consequently, a sense of organic balance in the film's vision, wherein sex is the principal source of joy and pleasure but is thoroughly integrated with other life activities, the whole pleasurable bunch of them resisting what D. H. Lawrence called "the money, and the machine, and the insentient ideal monkeyishness of the world." Pornography, in short, becomes a rhetoric for aesthetic purposes beyond its mere spectacle.

*The Adventures of the Exquisite Corpse*, then, is a film that is at once pornographic and aesthetic, presenting a hedonism in which sexuality is lyrically integrated into a life that, though hyperbolically pleasure-oriented, just might be preferable to the power plays of the status quo. It sharpens, as we have noted, the contradiction between the present and the possible. It is this high comic transfiguration—presenting, as it were, a comedy of pornographic manners—that recommends this film as a model. As Brakhage points out, "What makes it transcend itself is that Noren films only what he loves, and that lovingly." That, after all, is its importance, the synthesis of the myth of animality with the myth of love. It is this synthesis that speaks persuasively, reminding us that animality is a fact of life and love, and that, in a sensible perspective, acknowledgment of animality can energize the pleasure we take in life. Its pornography, like its art, transcends itself and in so doing suggests the formal possibility of the experimental cinema of sexuality. And, as we shall see, those possibilities have been subsequently picked up, not only by such obvious subcultural examples as *Deep Throat* and *Devil in Miss Jones*, but also by the big budget mainstream *Last Tango in Paris,* where the mythic explorations of the experimental underground have been made visually presentable to general audiences.

## HARD-CORE FULL BLOWN

Russ Meyer's films, as I've noted, facilitated the transition of celluloid sex from the avant-garde to pornographic features. Meyer projected pornographic parody through conventional cinematography and demonstrated that pornography had a potential for feature film format and general audiences. His films are playfully soft-core and parody not only prurience but politics, popular culture, racism, and practically anything else that comes into their line of sight. Their spirit is perhaps best exhibited in *Fanny Hill.* Made in 1966, three years after Cleland's classic pornographic novel was given its first modern republication in the United States, the film traded on the celebrity of the book's litigation and prominence. Its joke is that, while its namesake promises explicit if florid eighteenth-century pornography, the movie delivers instead a chaste slapstick costume comedy. If his audience expected Cleland's stylish smut, what it got was Meyer's tongue in cheek. Self-consciously parodying both his source and his audience's expectations from this source material, Meyer's typical humorousness is coyly represented.

A few years later, with *Beyond the Valley of the Dolls* in 1970, Meyer took another swipe at another famous novel, or perhaps it was the movie. But by this point he had established his trademark, the spectacle of heftily endowed women either bare breasted or in provocative décolletage. The film's only connection to its source is its show-business setting and its motif of the decadence that goes with show-biz success. But Susann obviously provided a broader and more contemporary range of social parody than Cleland had. By the time Meyer is through—although in this one he enlisted the help of film critic Roger Ebert to write the screenplay—he has travestied rock and roll, hippie counterculture, racial stereotypes, Shakespeare, transvestites, Hollywood high life, feminism, television, soap operas, horror movies, gays, Nazis, Arthurian legends, Superwoman, romantic love, and of course titillation and pornographic prurience. And just as the parody covers a lot of ground, so does the dialogue range from High Renaissance rhetoric to low current inanity—"It's so gas, man . . . like, I dig man. . . . You're on an ego trip." But perhaps the parodic spirit is best summed up by Harris Allworth, exhausted lover pro tem to Ashley St. Ives, the nymphomaniacal porn queen, who says, "We've made it under water, on horseback, and standing up in a canoe. . . . Would it be weird to just get it on in bed?"

If *Beyond the Valley* is perhaps the high point of Meyer's work—in terms of both comic conception and production quality—*Vixen* (1968) is perhaps more characteristic of his style. Its pace is not so frenetic, but its sense of incongruous absurdity is more thorough, as is its focus on sexual spectacle and motifs. Its opening title background, for example, is the Canadian national anthem accompanying the Canadian flag rippling proudly in the breeze. As the camera then pans the Canadian bush country, a narrative voice-over mimics those travelogue promotion shorts of the 1930s and 1940s, finally locating its hero, the bush pilot who makes the wonders of the wilderness accessible. Just as the viewer is wondering whether there has been some mistake, the plot kicks into gear. While Tom, the heroic if naive bush pilot, is gassing up his Piper Cub and explaining to a lasciviously curious airport attendant that his wife Vixen may be fun-loving and flirtatious but knows "where to draw the line" as a responsible wife, Vixen is out in the woods being mounted by a Mountie. Vixen is just what her name implies, a she-devil in heat. Her kid brother is an oversexed and slightly demented biker with a Black American buddy who is in Canada evading the draft. Vixen, who naturally has hot pants for every genre of homo erectus excepting Blacks, has a yen for her brother. He, being properly scandalized by the prospect of unnatural acts, promotes his buddy, which in turn scandalizes Vixen, who after all knows where to draw the line. In fact she shows just what a vixen she is by calling the Black such names as "Rufus" and "Sambo." This racial conflict later meshes somewhat improbably with the Irish Republican Army and the international Communist conspiracy to resolve the plot.

In the interim, however, the action features Vixen sporting with her husband in bed, in a river with her husband's fishing client, with her husband's client's wife in a cottage, and with her brother, whose scruples are suborned, in the shower where, this being a soft-core movie, Vixen masturbates the gushing shower nozzle. These variations on the theme are punctuated when the brother eggs on the Black to rape Vixen. After a few tense preliminary moments, interruptus is achieved by the arrival of bush pilot Tom with a new client. If probability is but slightly stretched by a Black biker evading the draft on a Yamaha in the North Woods, it gets rather nearer its elastic limit when O'Banion (after Dion, the infamous Chicago gangster?), the new client, turns out to be an IRA operative who has come to British Columbia to skyjack a Piper Cub by way of getting to Cuba. Perhaps it was just this absurdity that most attracted Meyer to the idea of tacking this political apostrophe onto the spectacle of Vixen's gamey life. O'Banion, who has ostensibly hired Tom and Vixen to fly him to San Francisco, confides his plan to Niles, the Black, in a conversation where O'Banion cozies up to Niles on the theme of bourgeois racism and imperialism in Vietnam, which he contrasts to the paradise of Cuban equity and brotherhood. O'Banion, naturally in the tradition of great Irish talkers, is as smooth as a shot of Old Bushmill, and Niles is persuaded to go along. Enroute, however, after O'Banion has pulled a Luger to effect the skyjack, Vixen turns intellectual, undermining Niles's confidence in the benevolence of the international Communist conspiracy. This exchange so exasperates O'Banion that he loses his Gaelic poise, calling Niles a "nigger," which not even Vixen had done, and telling him to shut up. Once it is clear who the common "enemy" is, O'Banion is dispatched by means of a convenient monkey wrench, and Niles is reconciled with Vixen and Tom as "the lesser of two evils." It is not insignificant that while Vixen has not been so reconstructed as to go to bed with Niles, neither has she shown even the slightest inclination to diddle with O'Banion. Thus, so far as redeeming social content is concerned, although Meyer has not solved the problem of racism, he has certainly tarnished the sex appeal of Communism.

One reason for Meyer's popularity was his inclination to throw topical subjects into his parodic sexpot. Much of his humor derives from the preposterous juxtaposition of bare boobs and mock seriousness played with a straight face. The mockery is enforced by Meyer's lack of fussiness about everything but photography, which in general is rather good. The dialogue is consistently inane, occasionally punctuated by sharp wit but usually piling up clichés. The acting is erratic in the extreme, competent performances cheek by jowl with incompetent. Some scenes appear to be unrehearsed and shot but once, as if to tell the viewer, "That's enough, you get the point," while others are quite carefully constructed. Sound tracks may vary from scene to scene, and Meyer seems to cultivate a sort of reedy timbre. He seems, in short, to caricature feature film production as much as he does their themes or prurience itself. Nor did he ever seem to be interested in shifting from a soft-core to a hard-core pornographic ambience. *Beyond the Valley* marked the peak of his popularity. It having been demonstrated that pornography and parody could come together in feature format, the idea caught on. Such hard-core ventures as *Behind the Green Door, Deep Throat,* and *The Devil in Miss Jones* raised the pornographic ante, but this new form obviously owed a debt to Meyer.

*Ordeal* (1980), Linda Lovelace's book-length account of being forced to perform in *Deep Throat* (1972), not only exposed the unsavory and criminal atmosphere surrounding that film's production but also raised the ethical question of whether one can in good conscience see or even write about it. This question was emphatically punctuated by her testimony in hearings about the Women Against Pornography anti-pornography ordinance, where she said that to see the film is to see her being raped. Her account itself, however, is somewhat more complicated. To begin with, her white slavery was at the hands of Chuck Traynor, her husband and manager at the time. Although Lovelace recounts that the film's crew overheard a beating she got from Traynor, and one or two of them made surreptitiously futile offers of help, nowhere does she suggest that the crew knew that she was virtually a prisoner or that she was performing against her will. In fact, she specifically notes that the crew members treated her well and that she formed a humorous camaraderie with them. As for Harry Reems, the co-performer who presumably would be her principal rapist, she calls him "an ally" whose attentions she cultivated as a means of retaliation on Traynor, to the extent that she pretended to enjoy her sexual performances. She is similarly benign in her description of Gerry Damiano, the film's conceiver and director. And while she describes the film's financial backer as a sleazy Mafioso, even there she does not suggest that he knew she was performing against her will, and she in fact describes at length how opposed he was to her being hired for the role. She sums up the episode thus, "*Deep Throat* seemed just another small chapter of my life, but I hated to see it end. Maybe . . . I had to be involved sexually with an actor or two, but it was much better than it might otherwise have been. Two weeks of making a movie, even a pornographic movie, was better than two weeks of being a hooker." The issue that Lovelace raises in her book is not after all the morality or legality of the making of *Deep Throat*, but rather the white slave brutality she endured at the hands of Traynor.

While legal complexities seem to preclude Lovelace from having the film quashed, after her revelation about the circumstances of her participation in it there would seem to be an obligation not to patronize the film. But the fact is that the film was on exhibit for nearly a decade before Lovelace's revelations, so that it has a historical presence independent of its criminal framework. Not only was it perhaps the single most popular hard-core film ever made, but it was the first to go beyond the dictates of its genre by synthesizing parodic modes with pornographic conventions. Apart from the misfortunes of its star, its significance as a film is that it broke the mold of hard-core pornographic films and indicated an unsuspected artistic potential for pornographic spectacle. Thus, any serious address to the genre must take *Deep Throat* into account. The film turns on the gimmick of Linda Lovelace's impressive facility for fellatio, what she herself calls "the sword-swallowing or deep-throat trick." But that in itself would not have elevated the movie to its extraordinary success. What did that was the outrageous extravagance of its humor.

Lovelace records how production was frequently interrupted while she and Reems and the crew broke up in laughter at the absurdity of the plot and dialogue. If the pun is the lowest form of humor, it is appropriately the structural core of the movie. The first scene, after a long automobile sequence (itself a parody of movie conventions), sets the tone: Linda walks into her kitchen, where her roommate sits casually on the table smoking and chatting, as the camera gradually discovers a young man performing cunnilingus between her widespread legs; in mid-sentence she is struck with politesse—"say," she says, glancing down at her boyfriend, "do you mind if I smoke while you eat?"

For all of that, however, the movie has a plot, such as it is. Linda can't find happiness, which is to say she can't reach orgasm. So, after working her way through a veritable army of partners without success, she consults a physician, because, as she says, "There's got to be more to life than just screwing around." And besides, she wants to "really come," so that "bells ring, bombs go off, and rockets explode" ("Do you want to get off," her girl friend comments, "or destroy cities!"). The doctor, after Linda tells him that she likes it best in the mouth, discovers that her clitoris is in her throat, deep. Prognosis, he says, is good, and proceeds to administer sex therapy on the spot. And, what else, bells ring, bombs go off, and rockets explode in a montage sequence reminiscent of Bruce Conner, which is punctuated by the "1812 Overture." Thereafter, as Linda becomes a physiotherapist in pursuit of bigger and better therapeutics, we are treated regularly to the rocket's red glare. Thus Linda discovers her "mission," something more to life than just "screwing around." The plot, turning on the basic deep throat pun, builds to its final touch when Linda is made a proposal of marriage by one of her clients, a schleppy type named Wilbur. "The man I marry," Linda says gravely, looking at Wilbur's unimpressive physique, "has to have a nine-inch cock." Alas, Wilbur announces, "just four inches from happiness." What, we wonder, can poor Wilbur do? Silicone injections? A French tickler? Nope. Wilbur, poor literalist that he is, thinks he has to prune it down to size! And so Linda's deep throat finds true happiness with Wilbur's trusty thirteen-inch truncheon.

That the movie takes nearly ten minutes to set up so preposterously slight a gag suggests how much more it is committed to boffo comedy than pornography. In its use of plot as parody, *Deep Throat* follows the Russ Meyer line. But, whereas Meyer's parody projects his audience outside his films to the conventions parodied—the adventure film, for example, turned pornographic in such a way that, by being neither adventure nor pornographic, the conventions are merely rendered so silly as to amuse us in a new way—*Deep Throat* turns the audience in on the very convention it is watching and renders itself silly. It is simultaneously a smut film and a parody of such a film.

But the parody of course counterpoints the pornography. The pornographic convention is purged of its dominant effect when its eroticizing potential is compromised by laughter. In this respect, that of employing pornography and at the same time parodying it, *Deep Throat* is in the tradition of avant-garde cinema. The difference between these two uses of pornography is aesthetically profound. Meyer, with a cautious eye to the paying customers, merely alludes to hard-core pornography, that is, to explicit sexuality. His parody slides around the issue, and his audience is never threatened by the image of real sexuality on screen. His audience may or may not be erotically turned on, but in terms of sexual imagination it has hedged its bet and risked little or nothing. *Deep Throat*, on the other hand, tempts its audience by confrontation with "real" sexual energy and then purges the temptation with laughter. So pornography, being reduced to a joke, loses its lugubrious hold, the sexual imagination is freed from its oppressive association with "pornography" (i.e., Lawrence's sense of it enforcing the "dirty little secret" of sex), and the psyche gains enhanced perspective on its own sexual dynamics. The film acts, in short, as a comedy of sexual manners should act.

*Deep Throat* is a milestone. However crude, it does have an aesthetic form worth considering, and it moreover indicates an aesthetic potential for pornography until then regarded, at best, with condescension. Why, critics ask, must genitals and the paraphernalia of sex be so conspicuously flaunted? *Deep Throat* provides a uniquely cinematic answer. Visual images of genitalia in action create an erotic ambience of the sort described earlier. *Deep Throat* gives a close up view of "real" sex in action, and then manipulates the audience expectation into a more complex frame of reference. Its comedy, like Conner's, explodes the intimidation and secrecy of sexuality in laughter, thus giving us an imaginative control over our sexuality, so that it can be seen in its comic and parodic aspects rather than as the great gray Freudian Menace. When, for instance, we see Harry Reems, Linda's doctor, bent and hobbling with an elaborately bandaged penis, and he looks up with mock exasperation and exhaustion, saying "How much deep throat can a man take," our laughter is surely a liberation from the macho facade that perverts so much of our sexual imagination. And that comic catharsis requires explicit pornographic imagery to make its point. One has to see the penis deep throated into submission, with all the frame jumps, speed ups, slow downs, montage juxtapositions, and whatnot made possible by cinematic techniques, to experience that comic liberation. The medium, here, really is the message. And doesn't the macho purge require confrontation with "real" (i.e., cinematic, i.e., hyperbolic, i.e., artistic) images of the fantastic unflaggable phallus flagging?

*Deep Throat* was quickly followed by a companion feature that was unfortunately sombre and pretentious. But for its final five brilliant minutes *Devil in Miss Jones* (1973) addresses the darker flip side of the pornographic imagination, rather in the manner of Jack Smith than Bruce Conner. And here too the cinematic confrontation with actual sexuality is aesthetically imperative. This one scene is so first rate that one almost forgives the film's otherwise pretentious and tedious plot.

The plot leading up to this scene is that Miss Jones in a fit of depression commits suicide and is damned to Hell for her sin. The rub is that it is her only sin, and the gimmick is that before entering Hell she persuades the

Devil to give her a reprieve long enough to *earn* her damnation, carnally of course. But it is that final scene that retrieves the film from a merely smutty limbo. In it Miss Jones enters Hell at last. Appropriately enough, since her new damnation derives from her cultivation of sexual indulgence, she is condemned to sexual frustration. Miss Jones's Hell is a barren white-washed room without windows or exit. It is occupied by one other tenant, a man hopelessly spaced out to the point, naturally, of impotence. His only discourse is a monologue of insane precision on the procedures for watching a fly eat. All he is capable of is endless rehearsal of this monologue. Miss Jones, having sampled all the varieties of sexual experience to earn her eternity, has discovered the sexual imperative—insatiability. So, her Hell consists in eternal cohabitation with an impotent monologuist, while her own body—and soul, presumably—is in perpetual heat. Unable to distract him, she resorts to masturbation. But, by the nature of things, she is of course unable to satisfy herself. "Help me," she says, "help me. I can't get off by myself," and repeats it like a litany. The movie closes with the counterpoint of her need and his need out of phase forever. The allegory, so obvious and so true, and so sharply conceived and executed, is genuinely moving. Not so much because it echoes, as it does, so many strains of existential literature, but because it synthesizes them with an imagery unequivocally confronting a pathos inherent in the sexual imagination.

Interestingly enough both of these celebrated movies give their most concentrated imaginative energy to repudiating macho sexuality: *Deep Throat* by laughing it out of its seriousness, and *Devil in Miss Jones* by its focus on the terrible isolation and frustration so reputed a part of feminine sexuality. This motif of course contradicts the interests of traditional pornography, which exploits the myth of infinite potency and unbridled libido. This in itself, the use of pornography to deconstruct the mythologies of pornography, is an indication of the aesthetic potentials that cinematic pornography is beginning to explore. Both *Deep Throat* and *Devil in Miss Jones* indicate a very real serious pornographic form is in fact available. They are crude to be sure. But we are considering their aesthetic potential rather than their achievement. And they have suggested a complexity of interest not realized before. At their worst they are no worse, and probably better, than the miles of simple smut footage already peddled. At their best, however slight, they indicate a capacity for addressing both the comedy and pathos of the sexual imagination in a way unique to cinema.

## THE DIRTY LITTLE SECRET GOES POP

If *Last Tango in Paris* is considerably more decorous than either *Deep Throat* or *Devil in Miss Jones,* it is nonetheless far more profoundly dependent on pornographic ambience than either. When, after he and Maria Schneider have established their dingy Parisian love nest, and she asks him his name, Marlon Brando says, "In this room we don't need names. I don't want to know anything about you or your life outside. Out there doesn't matter," we are at that early moment in the film put in touch with a metaphor of classic pornographic fantasy. For, although *Last Tango* is a highly literary movie, synthesizing concerns from such works as *Story of O, Lolita,* and *No Exit,* with echoes even of Henry James, the principal allusion of its literacy is to pornographic conventions. The isolated setting, standard in pornographic fiction from *One Hundred and Twenty Days of Sodom* to *Story of O,* invokes a privately sexualized world and sets up an opposition between a fantasized pornographic ethos and the "outside." And, again characteristic of pornography, the sexual activity is to be anonymous: "In this room we don't need names." In short, the central action pivots on this construction of a purely pornographic environment. Or, more accurately, it turns on the failure of the protagonists to turn pornographic fantasy into daily reality. A predictable enough failure, but nonetheless interesting in its evolution.

The dilemma of the plot parallels the formal dilemma of the movie itself. For instance, although the movie is pornographic, it is almost ludicrously well-dressed. The first sex scene, where Brando and Schneider couple almost as soon as they meet, thus drawing on yet another pornographic convention, is an example of this. On the one hand they are swept into pornography's ubiquitous carnal vortex, but on the other they remain not only discreetly dressed but positively encumbered by a veritable jungle of topcoats, trousers, garters, and whatnot, and bang away at each other from angles impossible to execute, so encumbered, unless Brando's penis were a foot and a half long. This points up a formal problem that Bertolucci finally resolves rather neatly. The film's pornography is figural. It is, in dramatic context, convincingly pornographic, but from behind a carefully veiled imagery. In fact Bertolucci executes a fascinating reversal of normal pornographic perspective. The scene where Brando—and it is not insignificant that we see Brando himself rather more than a fictive character on the screen—has Schneider bugger him manually while he verbally indulges a crypto-sadistic fantasy is an example. We do not actually see the buggering, although we are explicitly told of it. The camera focuses on Brando's face, but the scene focuses on his urgently neurotic recitation of the fantasy, an extravagantly obnoxious one in which Brando solicits Schneider's participation in the slaughter of a pig, cutting its throat, smelling its farts, and so on. "You'll do that, won't you," Brando repeats in a heavy breathing refrain, "for me." Bertolucci has managed here to give us a persuasive pornographic drama without any of the usual pornographic spectacle. This particular scene could be as effective in a radio play as on the screen. In terms of pornographic form, it illustrates how pornographic cinema can be rescued from the domination of sexual spectacle, retain its pornographic focus, and construct a drama of the sexual imagination's dynamics of fantasy. Bertolucci has so niftily configured pornography and made it the center of his plot that he has done what no other film I know has done in so sustained a way, constructed a "tragic" cinematic pornography that shrewdly avoids the problem of sexual spectacle.

By making the sex scenes allusions to sex rather than sexual spectacle itself (a trick he may well have learned from Russ Meyer), he has effected a structural flexibility permitting him to realistically picture pornographic causality in human affairs without sexually distracting, tantalizing, or disgusting what he knows is going to be a highly distractable, tantalizable, and disgustable bourgeois audience. For the first time, hard-core pornography has been handled so as to be acceptable to popular cinema. Moreover, having had the wit to appreciate the psychic complexity and aesthetic sophistication of modern literature generally and literary pornography in particular, Bertolucci has structured his pornographic theme literarily, i.e. made it verbal, imagistic, and metaphorical. He has, in a sense, taken his audience by surprise. Without confronting a single ejaculating penis or palpitating clitoris, it has nevertheless come face to face with pornography. Working in a popular art form, which necessarily forces a contradiction between aesthetic authenticity and social acceptability, Bertolucci has found a happy resolution. And in the process he has added a dimension to the formal development of pornographic cinema.

Furthermore, his sense of spectacle has been sharply calculated. Clearly aware that his pornographic motif had a high potential for giving offense, Bertolucci's choice of Brando—a celebrity generally known for a kind of artistic integrity—was as much an aesthetic as a box-office decision. Brando as pornographic spectacle gives both artistic and moral respectability, in the popular mind, to the motif. And, whether it was Brando's or Bertolucci's doesn't matter, the decision to keep the sex visually under wraps was also aesthetically smart. Brando's performance is pornographic distillation, in effect an allusion to the illusion of real sex. And wisely so. For genitals, which are appropriate to smut films or sexual comedy, tend to be so distracting as to dissipate the pathos necessary to tragedy.

And Bertolucci is trying for pornographic tragedy, that is, a tragedy caused by the pornographic imagination projecting two people into a destructive situation they cannot control. Whether or not he achieves tragedy is not the point. What's important is that he has attempted to make tragedy turn on pornographic causality. Again, in the process he has shifted the pornographic focus from spectacle to plot, from voyeuristic sex—heretofore the pornographic staple—to a complex psychology of sex—heretofore the bane of pornography. In short, because of a very sure sense of who his actors should be and how they should appear on screen, and a sure sense of how to dramatize the illusion of pornographic spectacle, Bertolucci has found yet other means of raising pornographic action to a rhetoric for the tragic potential inherent in the pornographic imagination.

Brando's Heathcliff, to Maria Schneider's Catherine, is of course fatal; the complexities of life—love, for example—make pure romance an unworkable vision. Pornosex seems at first a possible ethos, but only until erotosex—or eros itself—comes wriggling up the caper canal. Brando's precarious ethos dominates things at first. But there is a reversal caused by the ineluctable entrance of eros, in the course of which Brando loses control and Schneider gains it. Clearly, as his bierside lamentation to his dead wife indicates, it is the loss of love which makes love's potential so threatening and confusing. It is an archetypal anxiety usually ascribed only to women. Now, neatly, the shoe is on the other foot. At the beginning Schneider wants a "normal" relationship, i.e., she wants to know who he is, his history, and the rest. But she begins to love him, even without knowing him "outside." Gradually his fantasy becomes hers. So, as long as they agree to a love moratorium, they are both "safe"; Brando is not sucked into another analogue of his destructive marriage, and Schneider's young love for her naive fiancé is not threatened. But, as Brando begins to love her, she in turn responds to the threat and, needing control, cannot let him in on her eros.

Tragic flaws having been displayed, and the reversal effected, only the tragic incident itself remains for the completion of the plot. He presses in on her, and she shoots him, an act which, despite Bertolucci's technical obeisance to Chekov's precept that a gun introduced in Act One had better go off by Act Three, is more than somewhat startling. Anyway, she chooses to live, all the healthier for the callowness of youth, in which life and love are to be enjoyed rather than misanthropically avoided as with Brando, the decadent old man of the New World. Thus, in a kind of allegory, youthful innocence (the European minx, in a slick reversal of the Jamesian motif, is all innocence) triumphs over misanthropic experience. Whereupon tragic morals fall like raindrops on Butch Cassidy's head: Pornosex is not as good as erotosex, fantasy is not reality, and tampering with this scheme is destructive all the way around.

Whatever the aesthetic achievement of *Last Tango*, it seems to have managed some remarkable things. It has brought a pornographic ambience openly into popular movies. It has made perhaps the first feature-length attempt to treat pornography in the tragic mode. It has demonstrated that cinematic pornography need not bog down in sexual spectacle. And, in that, has shown pornography to have cinematic options unrealized before.

Future development of the form will have to be in some way informed by it, and will be richer for the information.

In *Last Tango* Bertolucci's sense of the tragic is both literary and classical. He has attended to the model of the Greek tragedians; one might evoke the obscene, whether it be a matter of violence or sexuality, but to bring it on stage is to risk serious disruption of dramatic focus. Nagisa Oshima, on the other hand, has taken on the distinctly contemporary challenge of making sexual spectacle transcend itself with *In the Realm of the Senses*. Like Jack Smith, Oshima conspicuously screens genitalia with compositional meticulousness to the end of transforming sexual imagery into a larger context. But his context, like Bertolucci's, is tragic narrative. And where Smith's compositional reference point is baroque, Oshima's is classical Japanese erotic painting. In fact Oshima's tragedy is rooted in the voyeurism implicit in that tradition and in the power of sexual imagination that is implicit in voyeurism.

Oshima's story line, derived from an actual Tokyo event in 1936, translates historicity into pornographic allegory. A sometime prostitute works as a waitress and becomes the restaurant proprietor's mistress. They conduct their affair at an inn, and two-thirds of the action, mostly sexual, takes place in their room. Their sexuality becomes increasingly obsessive and turns to sado-masochistic practices that result in the strangulation death of the man (Kichizo), following which the woman (Sada) cuts off his genitals and carries them off in a trance. This final scene is of course a shocking spectacle, but so adroitly does Oshima score the cadence moving toward it that its shock value is subordinated to its punctuation of the theme of sexual possession.

The tragedy turns on two senses of possession. In one sense, Sada and Kichizo are possessed by their sexuality, and the dynamics of that possession probe an irony of sexual politics. Kichizo initiates the relationship with stereotypical male casualness, but its "pornotopian" appeal gradually takes over. The contradiction between pornotopian and ordinary life is pressed by Sada, who becomes jealous of Kichizo's relations with his wife. The wife is handsome and attentive after the Japanese fashion, but her ministrations are naturally distributed over the daily routine—household, family, and business. Sada, on the other hand, is free to focus exclusively on sexual pleasure, and she is moreover a professional at it. As she raises the ante on pleasure, so does she demand his exclusive sexuality as a *quid pro quo* for the daily life she cannot share with him. That is, she wants to transform a pornographic relationship into an erotic one, claiming his sexual fidelity as a sign that she possesses his love—in the second sense of possession.

This untenable situation would seem to have a dialectical option, in which Kichizo might synthesize normal life and sex with one woman or the other. But that would be a rational solution, and Oshima obviously sees sexual fantasy as beyond reason and in tragic conflict with the functions of ordinary life. Kichizo tries to straddle both horns of the dilemma, maintaining each liaison and thus being faithless to both. This is his tragic flaw, and Sada presages its doom when she makes him promise not to have sex with his wife on penalty of death and emasculation. Sada's tragic flaw is that she tries to subsume the whole of love into sex, the futility of which is emphasized when they personify Kichizo's penis in conversation (an allusion to *Lady Chatterley's Lover*) and is of course punctuated when she cuts it off and carries it with her after his death. While the contradiction is ultimately destructive, it is the power of sexual imagination and pleasure that possesses and lures the protagonists to their fate. If Kichizo is unable to forfeit normal life, he is even more vulnerable to Sada's sexual vortex, and in that context she becomes the dominant figure, reversing the stereotypical gender roles.

Given the dilemma, a love so single-mindedly pleasure-oriented is bound to admit pain. The pleasure/pain nexus is central to the film, in regard to both love and sex. Sada's obsessive pleasure with Kichizo's penis, for example, is concomitant with her equally obsessive pain at its absence, which generates the anguish of doubt. The theme culminates with the sado-masochism that is the plot's tragic agent. As Sada becomes increasingly possessed by the sexual imperative, she discovers that she has a taste for masochism. As they escalate their ritual to mock strangulation, Kichizo doesn't have the stomach for sadism and confesses that he cannot stand to see her suffer. She, decisively reversing their roles, promptly says then that she will be the sadist. He just as promptly complies. But mockery only whets the appetite of their ecstasy. As Sada takes Kichizo closer and closer to the point of no return, she professes her love, how happy she is, what pleasure there is in his pain. She asks if he is afraid, and he says that he is but takes pleasure in submission to it. Now in their mutual possession she truly possesses him . . . until they enact the ultimate, and she strangles him orgasmically. And the possessed are dispossessed. Her attempt to keep "him" with her by severing Kichizo's genitals is ultimately more pathetic than horrifying and informs the tragedy of possession with yet another psychic dimension. We have in an earlier chapter noted Theodore Reik's hypothesis that in coitus a woman commonly associates her lover's being with his penis and that in post-coital withdrawal she may feel an intense anxiety of loss. Oshima molds this archetypal dynamic into an allegory of erotic power and dialectical complexity.

Oshima's choreography of the spectacle of both sex and violence is carefully calculated to draw in rather than assault the viewer. The second scene subtly introduces the voyeurism motif and in the process detoxifies the obscene appearance of the penis that will become the central image and metaphor of the film. The camera discovers children gathered around a sleeping bum; they lift his ragged kimono and reveal his flaccid penis, watching intently. Their perspective becomes the viewer's perspective, and the viewer is joined with the children's curiosity, which establishes the natural and innocent source of voyeurism. As the film progresses, this pattern recycles itself in variations, for example in chambermaids spying on the protagonists at sex. Gradually the distance between seer and seen diminishes, as for example geishas at first watch and then participate in an orgy with the protagonists. By the final scenes the voyeuristic perspective has lost its innocence and shifted unequivocally to the viewer.

But Oshima distracts the viewer from being embarrassingly conscious of assuming this burden by adroit composition and allusion. The first sex scene, for example, is an allusion to classical Japanese erotic painting, where both Sada and Kichizo are dressed in flowing kimonos. This illusion is evoked throughout the film and reminds the viewer of both the aesthetic appeal of pornography and its long voyeuristic tradition. In their second sex scene Kichizo is naked while Sada is not; the scene develops deliberately, and only when the viewer has been prepared is the penis exposed and Sada fellates "him," as they refer to it. By their third sex scene both are naked but Oshima is again careful to prepare the viewer for the exposure of genitals. Thereafter, allusion to erotic painting predominates, and most of the sex is enfolded in kimonos, as Oshima shifts the focus from sexual spectacle to the sexual psyche. Thus the viewer is drawn into the sexual ambience and is retrospectively reminded of complicity via voyeurism.

Oshima is similarly astute in preparing the viewer for the violence of the final emasculation. Shots of various kinds of cutlery—straight razors, knives, shears—foreshadow the main event. Sada early has a sudden bloody fantasy of slashing Kichizo's wife's ear, which flashes on the screen so briefly as to be more a subliminal than visual impression. Kichizo cuts himself while shaving, the camera lingering briefly but distinctly on the blade and the blood. The ceremonial knife itself lies beside the lovers' bed. By the time Sada threatens at once playfully and seriously to shear "him" off if Kichizo uses his penis with his wife the viewer has been fully primed. But Oshima stretches anticipation beyond its elastic limit so that the viewer's ominous expectation has all but spent itself, and consequently the emasculation scene does not coincide with the peak of the viewer's anxiety. Thus "cooled," the viewer can apprehend the significance of the moment rather than recoil from the spectacle. In terms of obscene spectacle, then, Oshima has contrived to fascinate rather than alienate or merely titillate the viewer, rendering spectacle and theme inextricable from one another.

The viewer's voyeuristic implication is as much a part of Oshima's aesthetic purpose here as is the tragedy of sexual possession. At one level he has asserted an ontological premise: Having identified voyeurism as an extension of human curiosity, as we have noted, it follows that voyeurism is a natural aspect of human being; however, in the context of a passion, such as sexuality, it has a tragically destructive potential. While in general sexual power involves a private passion, it has its social analogies, e.g. the military. Oshima specifically, if briefly, makes this connection. His action is set in 1936, when Japanese militarism was in ascendancy and gearing up for World War II. The sex/power/military connection is made in only one scene, but it is a memorable and carefully constructed scene. Having just left his love nest, Kichizo wanders down a street where he encounters a troop of marching soldiers coming toward him. While he strolls bemusedly down one side of the street, the soldiers march with aggressive cadence down its center, and a crowd of children line the other side cheering and waving Japanese flags. Kichizo, aimlessly biding time until he can resume his passionate affair, is in counterpoint to the image of purposeful military passion, but contrast is a form of comparison and the two passions are thus associated in the scene. Its significance is compounded by what is happening in the meantime. Kichizo is wandering because Sada is off servicing a client in order to finance their pornotopian life. Her client is a schoolmaster whose principal concern is that she not be seen with him. The viewer's primary perception of him is his hypocrisy, indulging a passion that he denies so that he can be a proper example for his pupils. They meanwhile are of course indulging another passion, cheering on the military. By juxtaposing these scenes with those of the love nest at the inn, where chambermaids and the hostess, for example, both voyeuristically spy on them and chide them for their sexual extravagance, Oshima creates an associational matrix of a society fascinated by militarism and sexuality alike and at the same time denying complicity. Hypocritical refusal to acknowledge indulgence of sexual passion cultivates ignorance of the society's indulgence of militaristic passion. Similarly, while voyeurism—being at once active and passive—confirms complicity, voyeurism also permits denial, thus masking the tragic consequences. Just as voyeuristic complicity in sexual possession prevents recognition of rational alternatives, so voyeuristic complicity in militaristic possession does the same.

Given the preoccupations of not only Oshima but also Yukio Mishima, and Yoichi Takabayashi's *Irezumi*, it would seem that there is a Japanese perspective highly compatible with that European line of thought represented by Georges Bataille. Bataille sees the sexual imagination, or eroticism, as the "assenting to life up to the point of death," while death is the avenue from "discontinuous" individual being to the "continuity" of being. Just as the moment of sexual fusion is an emblem of death's fusion of separate being into continuity, there is also a strong appeal between the two. Oshima confirms this appeal for himself when he says, "Every film director has two secret cravings: first, to record on film someone actually dying; second, a man and a woman (or a man and a man or a woman and a woman or a human being and an animal) having sexual intercourse." For Bataille the appeal represents a mysterious force. *In the Realm of the Senses* is Oshima's approach to demystifying the force by exploring its function and tragic potential in both private and social life. In doing so he has demonstrated that even the most obscene of sexual spectacles can be molded to subtle and complex reflection on the continuous contradictions of human being.

But where Oshima, like Bertolucci, puts sexual dialectic in tragic perspective, Lina Wertmuller plays it as a comedy of ideas in *Swept Away*. Because her film's sexual imagery is allusive rather than genitally explicit, and focuses rather on love's ironic victimization by class consciousness, it is more properly considered erotic than pornographic. Nevertheless, her evocation of the war between the sexes makes sexuality the ultimate battleground—including, for example, depiction of the long-standing pornographic theme that women take pleasure in rape—and in that sense is pertinent to pornography. Moreover, it has been assigned notable importance in the feminist debates on pornography. In making its case for an anti-pornography ordinance, for example, Women Against Pornography suggests that this is among those pornographic films that tend to induce violence toward women, while the Feminists Against Censorship Taskforce brief opposing the ordinance characterizes its sex and power themes as "profoundly important." Similarly, feminist reviewers have described it as "sophisticated and deep, " on the one hand, and as "slick pornography," on the other. The sticking point is its integration of a complex sexual theme with class analysis.

The first half of the film establishes class conflict in the hostility between the two protagonists. Raffaella, described by a neutral party as "the worst bitch on the Mediterranean," is a rich and attractive blond from northern Italy who with her husband has chartered a yacht to entertain friends. Her antagonist, Generino, is an intensely dark, bearded worker from the south who is a deckhand and attendant on the yacht; he is also a Communist Party leader. Raffaella's rich husband is likewise a Communist, adding an irony to the Communist motif that is not fully realized until the conclusion. Meanwhile, Raffaella exhibits a relentless bitchiness, vociferously complaining about food, service, and the general situation. Most of this is directed at Generino, as Raffaella indulges her luxurious hedonism, amid which she takes particular pains to insult the competence and intelligence, if not the maternity, of Communism and Communists.

Generino mutters imprecations about capitalist caprice and decadence but is of course obliged to attempt to accommodate her whims, between each one of which she demands that he change to a fresh shirt, complaining of his body odor and calling him "a grubby southern slob." So stands the power ratio between her capital and his labor.

Both characters are meticulously stereotypical. If she manifests every predictable aspect of her arrogant class, he asserts every predictable proletarian objection to it, particularly to its unnatural acts. Generino notes with immense disgust, for instance, that its men go to bed early while its women stay up late drinking and gambling with one another. A crew mate, more tolerant of bourgeois liberalism, points out the contradiction in Generino's double standard, but his progressive politics do not extend to gender relations. Similarly, when he discovers the bourgeois indulgence of marijuana and when the ladies display their anatomies while sunbathing, Generino's cultural conservatism is prominent. These ironies hover as the plot swings toward a reversal of fortunes.

At sunset, having just awakened from the previous night's intemperances, Raffaella insists on being ferried by dinghy to a cove in the middle distance for her morning swim. Generino, mindful of the late hour and indications of uncertain weather, objects but is of course overruled. The dinghy outboard motor stalls, night falls, and the two are adrift. In the course of this misadventure Raffaella's bitchiness reaches zenith. And it is made quite clear that she is not merely arrogant but also an effete fool.

After reaching a desert isle, Generino sets about addressing the problems of survival—finding water and shelter, catching lobster, starting a fire—while Raffaella bitches and bumbles on her own, proving incompetent in the state of nature. Malappropriately, she offers him cash for his lobster, but he reminds her of the obvious—that her money is irrelevant here—and administers a lesson in labor power. She will have to work to eat. The power ratio is now completely reversed, and Wertmuller has Generino articulate this fact in the crudest possible stereotyped male terms. He not only apes her previous demands on him but asserts his total mastery, insisting that women were made to serve men and demanding that she crawl to him to kiss his fist. If there is a comedic justice in this reversal, Wertmuller is nonetheless precise in representing it as a brutish exercise of power. While the upraised fist is a sign of the proletarian revolution, the demand to kneel and kiss the fist is rather more a sign of fascism, a historical phenomenon still covertly sticking in the Italian craw. This irony of Italian Communism—that it not only numbers the idle rich among its advocates, as with Raffaella's husband, but that its vox populi resonates with the same timbre, at least in relation to women, that characterized the earlier Fascist chorale—informs Generino's subjugation of Raffaella. It is as if women play Ethiopia to Communism's Mussolini.

Still, as Wertmuller modulates the power theme from its social to its sexual basis, it appears that Generino's ironically clouded justice is nonetheless validated. Complete submission of course is signified by sexual access, made the more piquant by Raffaella's earlier contempt for his uncosmeticized body odor. For even, perhaps most especially, sex exists within the framework of class attitudes, particularly in the differentia between the civilized and the brutish. He taunts her for exhibiting her breasts on the yacht, "as if we were animals instead of men . . . but you enjoyed it, didn't you." This recognition infuriates him, and he beats her, to reduce her finally to the state of natural justice where men are men and women are women. He proclaims that she's "going to pay for everybody," and with each blow makes an indictment: *That's* for causing inflation and not paying taxes; *that's* for making hospitals too costly for the poor. . . . The social and gender conflicts merge when he threatens to rape her, determined to strip her not just of class prerogatives but of all social protection, to make her recognize that in a state of nature men are indisputably superior to women. To do that, of course, he must degrade her, purge her of the last vestige of artificial social dignity, demonstrate that she is a sexual rather than a social animal. "You're going to like it," he hisses poised above her, "You're dying with desire. . . . " But he abruptly changes tactics. "No," he says, "You will have to be a slave of love. . . . You'll have to *beg* for it," and he stalks off, saying, "You still don't understand." So, although he assaults and brutalizes her, he does not after all rape her. For that would contradict his purpose, which is her recognition of her animal being and its natural subservience. To truly know her being, she must choose it.

She thinks this over in a long pensive shot. Her recognition comes when he kills, skins, and spits a rabbit. At first she makes a sentimental protest, "You killed it. . . . " But then it comes to her . . . "It's barbarous," she says, naming the whole situation. With that she capitulates, falling at his feet, and they make love. And her submission is total. "My lord, my master," she says, "beat me, kill me, but don't stop. . . ." But her submission does not diminish his polemics. It is as if he has but scotched society, not killed it. He charges her with infidelity now, insisting that it is characteristic of the bourgeoisie. Naturally he ignores his own infidelity in assuming this bogus moral posture. And when she replies that the Communist Party has put that idea in his head, he beats her, saying that the party is "sacred" and that she's only a high-class whore. Suddenly his dialectic, which heretofore has been cogent, has become casuistic chop logic: If she does not submit, she doesn't "understand"; if she does, she's a whore. A woman, he says, is an object of pleasure . . . never did he see her so satisfied on the yacht as she is now . . . she is most beautiful when he beats her. The Communist dialectic has been reduced to simplistic male chauvinism. Nonetheless, Raffaella submits to it ecstatically. So completely has she embraced the state of nature that the more dubious his male polemic becomes the more completely she affirms it.

Wertmuller can't resist a parody of Lawrence's Lady Chatterley, and has Raffaella decorate Generino's (discreetly covered) genitals with wild flowers . The parody evokes the plot's hovering irony. Generino and Raffaella are no more able to exorcise "the world with its rotten values," as Raffaella describes it, than were Mellors and Connie Chatterley. Connie might declare that "Class is an anachronism" and hope that the rest of the world might disappear, but, as Mellors reminds her, it won't. Similarly, Wertmuller early reminds us that Generino and Raffaella are not after all in a state of nature but on a fantasy island.

That Raffaella subscribes to its romance certainly constitutes a critique of women. But the greater onus would seem to be on men. Generino's willful imposition of the power structure is not only reductive in itself, it negates the ideology to which he subscribes. Romantic idealism from a bourgeois ethos is predictable. From a Communist, however, it is the profoundest of reactionary contradictions, all the more culpable given the fascist mold into which Generino has cast it. Wertmuller emphasizes Generino's heresy in the film's conclusion. He has insisted that they be rescued as a test of their love. When he proposes that they run off together back to the island, Raffaella, en route to failing the test, says she loves him, and he pointedly replies, "Then nothing else matters." And when, as of course she does, she returns to her husband, Generino shouts after her that she's a dirty capitalist bitch and then, again pointedly, "You've left me all alone." What was earlier the "sacred" revolutionary commune has here evaporated into a romantic fog. Wertmuller has posed a dialectical situation where the power of sexuality is great, great enough to sweep the contradictions of reality into its fantastic vortex. And fantasy, in turn, will likely cultivate romantic delusions about the nature of its power. But delusion must finally succumb to reality, for it is there after all that the contradictions have to be worked out.

The last scene retrieves Generino from his fog and restores him to the proletarian fellowship. His dark, plump, quintessentially southern Italian wife is naturally furious at his panting after the rich blond bitch. She scratches and beats on him and stomps off carrying her suitcase. He chases after and wrestles the bag from her. She forges on. He tags along carrying the bag, two or three paces behind. *Swept Away*, then, is a sexual comedy that interrogates the validity of the sexual imperative even as it acknowledges its power. If the contradictions and ironies that linger in its wake are not in themselves feminist, they nevertheless probe the sexual dynamics that are central to feminism. And if its sexual spectacle is not pornographic per se, the sexual dynamics it examines are precisely the ones that have made pornography an issue in the wars between the classes and the sexes.

In terms of pornography it would not be accurate to say, after Horace, that the moving picture is like literature. The visual spectacle of sex posed an aesthetic problem to cinema that literature did not have to confront (and it would be even more complex in drama, which is perhaps why that mode has not ventured into pornography per se). While Lawrence, for instance, was presenting explicit sexual description in *Lady Chatterley's Lover*, movies were tentatively trotting a naked Hedy Lamarr through the woods in *Ecstasy*. And even several decades later—after World War II films such as *Behind the Rising Sun* had featured infanticide, rape, and general Japanese insidiousness, regarded as healthy wartime propaganda—Jane Russell's cleavage and tepid roll in the hay with Audie Murphy in *The Outlaw* were considered scandalous cinematic behavior. While movies have always been saturated with sex, it has generally been an obliquely titillating sex alluding to what could not be shown.

Avant-garde cinema has of course had a long coexistence with feature movies and had presented its own form of obscenity, as for example in *Un Chien andalou*. But it was not until the 1950s that the avant-garde film began to collectively explore the potential of erotic and pornographic imagery and make inroads on general culture. It is possible that Smith's *Flaming Creatures* effectively broke the genitalia taboo in film. In any event, the combination of Brakhage's lyricism, Smith's ornamental decadence, Conner's parody, and Noren's quotidian hedonism were certainly central in exorcising the sex taboo and suggesting aesthetic possibilities for pornographic cinema. In addition to the influence of avant-garde films, Russ Meyer's soft-core parodies pioneered the terrain of pornographic features and in the process released pornography from the simplistic hard-core closet and the protected avant-garde cloister. While hard-core features themselves have hardly achieved aesthetic distinction, the self-parody of *Deep Throat* and the concluding dilemma of *Devil in Miss Jones* showed the prospects for a more sophisticated use of hard-core contexts. Oshima's *In the Realm of the Senses*, pursuing the logic of that recognition, demonstrates that pornographic imagery is compatible with ambitious artistic enterprise. If Bertolucci's *Last Tango in Paris* adroitly maneuvers around the problem of obscene spectacle, it just as skillfully evokes pornographic ambience in its exploration of erotic tragedy. And Wertmuller's erotic comedy, *Swept Away*, although it does not employ pornographic imagery, does vividly depict sexual dominance and submissiveness in its address to the ironies of both sexual and social politics, suggesting the possibility of a pornographic cinema of ideas.

# 10

# Obscenity and the Unbearable Law of Liberalism

## BEAUTY IS TRUTH, TRUTH BEAUTY . . .

In the course of these essays I have argued that obscene poetics logically derive from the development of Western liberalism in the context of philosophical and scientific materialism. Liberalism provided the environment and materialism the methodology for challenging idealist assumptions about nature's integrally ordained symmetry and the corresponding association between aesthetics and received morality. But there has been an intriguing irony: Even as diagnostic aesthetics have pursued a materialist-oriented analysis, at least one scientific line of thought has sought to restore the univocal appeal of the idealist dispensation.

While theoretical physicists have probed and predicated asymmetry, they have at the same time uniformly invoked a faith in nature's symmetrical "beauty" as their intuitive scientific axiom. In fact the word "beauty," in the sense of symmetry, runs as a refrain through the discourse of theoretical physics and other sciences. Moreover, that vocabulary frequently has a Platonic cast. For instance, the physicist Herman Weyl noted, "My work always tried to unite the true with the beautiful; but when I had to choose one or the other, I usually chose the beautiful." This sentiment is echoed by, among others, Einstein, Bohr, and Heisenberg, and with such fervor that it has a Keatsian passion, although one might also say nostalgia. It is now a commonplace how often aesthetic intuition has led to scientific discovery. That is, science has projected a myth of nature's cohesive beauty, and it has become a self-fulfilling prophecy. This also suggests the ironic concept of a utilitarian aesthetic.

The irony is that formal theoretical aesthetics tend to consciously separate the beautiful from the useful, as George Santayana does, for example, in *The Sense of Beauty*. This is perhaps based on the Thomistic premises from which Joyce derived his aesthetic in *Portrait of the Artist as a Young Man*, where the function of beauty is to inspire contemplation rather than desire or action. Similarly, theoretical aesthetics tend to distinguish the aesthetic from the moral, the beautiful from the good. Since formal aesthetics have a rather recent history that parallels the development of materialism, it is tempting to see this distinction as a materialist differentiation reclaiming the beautiful from idealist synthesis. Be that as it may, there is a correspondence on this point between theoretical aesthetics and physics. Weyl's observation is as notable for its exclusion of the good from the Platonic trinity as for its preference for the beautiful over the true. In one sense this is predictable enough. One need only recall the belated and ineffectual efforts of atomic scientists to introduce morality into their discourse during World War II to see that morality is by and large a scientific afterthought. Then again, if one recalls Galileo or Faust one can see how morality is inconvenient for, if not incompatible with, science. The macrocosmic mission of science is to discover and explain the universe, a project in which the myth of cosmic beauty has been more usefully inspiring than the sullen freight of human morality.

In his *Scientific Autobiography* Max Planck provides a profound motive for scientific aestheticism: "It is of paramount importance that the outside world is something independent from man, something absolute, and the quest for laws which apply to this absolute appeared to me as the most sublime scientific pursuit in life." The theoretician does not merely prefer beauty to truth, its sublimity is an ontological imperative. At this level science transcends Hegelianism; it is a materialist religion positing an objective absolute independent of human perception and, of course, moral distortion. It is a paradox of modern science that its yearning for the absolute should have produced relativity and indeterminacy. Its classical predisposition is configured as well in another preoccupation, the quest for simplicity. Nobel physicist William Lipscomb describes the appeal of field theories thus, "These ideas of symmetry also introduce great simplicity where there was complexity," and goes on to say that scientists employ "the aesthetic concepts of symmetry and simplicity to great advantage because our minds work that way, and to a surprising extent so does nature." He cites Heisenberg's comment to Einstein, "If nature leads us to mathematical forms of great simplicity and beauty . . . we cannot help thinking that they are 'true.'. . . You must have felt this too: the almost frightening simplicity and wholeness of the relationships which nature suddenly spreads out before us. . . . " Theoretical physics, then, provide an objectively grand cosmic design, beautiful for its synthesis, symmetry, and simplicity, and reliable in its absoluteness. Consequently, its aesthetic utility is metaphysical. Theoretical scientists do not in fact perceive cosmic beauty, they compute it mathematically. What they perceive and so appreciate is its idea, a mythified idea altogether untouched by human doings and their problematic morality.

The situation is rather different with applied science, where ideas are unequivocally objectified and brought into the arena of human being and doing. Moreover, they are made to act on nature rather than aestheticize it. One of the early problems for resolution in the development of the atomic bomb, for instance, was whether the bomb would ignite the earth's atmosphere. Applied science, unlike theory, necessarily raises the spectre of Faust and moral consequences. In 1945, some three months after the bombings of Hiroshima and Nagasaki, Robert Oppenheimer addressed his Los Alamos colleagues about why they had produced the bomb, which had already become morally problematic:

> When you come right down to it the reason that we did this job is because it was an organic necessity. . . . If you are a scientist you believe that it is good to find out how the world works; that it is good to find out what the realities are; that it is good to turn over to mankind at large the greatest possible power to control the world and to deal with it according to its lights and values. . . .
>
> It is not possible to be a scientist unless you believe that the knowledge of the world, and the power which this gives, is a thing which is of intrinsic value to humanity, and that you are using it to help in the spread of knowledge, and are willing to take the consequences.

At the point where science intersects rather than transcends human being it restores morality to its discourse. That is, precisely where science gets morally questionable it seeks to validate itself morally. It recasts the Faustian myth; knowledge is good rather than evil. And, being mythic, that good is represented as universal and natural—knowledge has "intrinsic value." Like beauty, it becomes its own excuse for being. And its practitioners, consistently with mythic heroics, "are willing to take the consequences." Mythification is a form of aestheticizing, and in this myth science is both moralized and aestheticized.

This is where the discourses of science and post-Romantic poetics, especially obscene poetics, converge. In theoretical physics the role of the scientist is analogous to that of the high Romantic poet, a seer whose revelations are apocalyptic beyond mere morality. The role of the applied physicist is heroic enough, but the model is less vatic and more like an epistemological lab worker. Even a product so apocalyptic as the atom bomb is rationalized as just another day's work and handed rather routinely to "mankind at large." But the applied physicist is after all aware that there are consequences other than aesthetic appreciation. Similarly with post-Romantic poetics, notwithstanding Wallace Stevens' advocacy of resisting reality. Even so oracular a poet as Robert Duncan says, "I can no more 'appreciate' poetry than I can 'appreciate' the universe; I am inbound to the event." And the Surrealists, whose ambitions were aesthetic, psychic, and political apocalypse, were quite literally lab technicians in dream research. Joyce, to be sure, had his reasons for wanting to restore the tradition of holistically disinterested aesthetics. But his friend Ezra Pound had equally good, and ultimately more representative, reasons for deriving a distinctly interested aesthetic from the applied science of medicine. Where curative art addressed the situation of beauty, diagnostic art addressed the situation of ugliness. The latter had and has its own utilitarian tradition, and it essentially defines the function of obscene poetics. Like its medical model, this aesthetic line necessarily messes with the often muddling morality of human being and doing.

Obscene poetics, then, are messy in the same way that applied science is—they intrude on life. And their primarily pornographic content connects them with the sometimes scientific and sometimes aesthetic discourse of sexuality, a subject that does not permit the distancing of traditional aesthetics. The diagnostic function of obscene poetics means that their practitioners are often in the position of telling the culture that what it takes for good health is in fact the converse. Because they interrogate accepted values they are frequently taken to be immoral and anti-social. But science, too, sometimes is assigned an anti-social role.

Sex information and contraception are classic instances. In England this issue was focused around the 1877 publication by Charles Bradlaugh and Annie Besant of Charles Knowlton's *Fruits of Philosophy: An Essay on the Population Question*. Knowlton was a physician, and his pamphlet explained the physiology of sex and contraception in layman's language. Bradlaugh and Besant, both social reformers, published the pamphlet as a conscious challenge to the courts and society. Their application for the case to be tried before a higher court was reviewed by Lord Chief Justice Cockburn, whose 1867 opinion on the legal test of obscenity—"whether the tendency of the matter charged as obscenity is to deprave and corrupt those whose minds are open to such immoral influences and into whose hands a publication of this sort may fall"—specifically pertained in English and American law until the 1930s and is still an influence. In this other case he granted a jury trial, giving as his judicial opinion that Knowlton's pamphlet "really raises a fair question as to whether it is a scientific production for legitimate purposes." Bradlaugh and Besant were convicted, but the jury's verdict reflected social bemusement: "We are unanimously of opinion that the book in question is calculated to deprave public morals, but at the same time we entirely exonerate the defendants from any corrupt motive in publishing it."

Bradlaugh and Besant appealed and won, but the vindication had ironic consequences. Their appeal was that the prosecution had not specified which passages were obscene, and its success led to the requirement that prosecution in Britain and then the United States had to specify the obscene words and passages. In legal practice this came to mean that words and passages not only could but should be lifted from context. This also pertained until the 1930s but is still in fact problematic; contextualization was a central issue in the 1990 Cincinnati obscenity prosecution of an exhibit of Robert Mapplethorpe photographs.

Traditionally, the law in the West enters where scientific, intellectual, or artistic articulation is perceived to be anti-social by virtue its of moral dissent. Given liberal professions of free speech, however, this point of entry into prosecution is not called "dissent" but "obscenity." In the United States the Anthony Comstock era was a particularly virulent example of how thin the line between art, science, and obscenity can be. In 1873 Comstock successfully promoted a Congressional act, popularly called the Comstock Act, prohibiting obscene matter from the United States mail. Obscenity included contraceptive literature, and Comstock also managed to persuade the New York State Legislature to make conveying contraceptive information illegal, a prohibition that became a model for other states as well. Comstock was appointed a special agent of the Post Office for enforcing the obscenity act. He held this position until his death in 1915, and from it conducted what censorship historian Alec Craig characterizes as "a sort of reign of terror in the publishing world" for over forty years. His slogan was "Morals, not Art or Literature," although he was equally relentless in prosecuting and harassing contraceptive information. In the process, he boasted of the number of people he had driven to suicide. He himself died shortly after his successful prosecution of Margaret Sanger's husband for having given a copy of her pamphlet, *Family Limitation,* to a Post Office agent. His death marked the end of government interdiction of contraceptive literature. But the Comstock Act functioned into the 1960s and precipitated prosecutions over such literary magazines as Paul Carroll's *Big Table* and such novels as William Burroughs' *Naked Lunch,* among others in the 1950s and 1960s. For the first sixty-five years or so of this century the Post Office functioned as an extra-legal censor of literature. This was the legacy of "Comstockery," a word coined in 1905 by George Bernard Shaw.

Comstock in effect invented the modern "problem" of obscene literature. Censorship, of course, has a long history, and the concept of obscenity, although not the word, became a matter of legal record in England about 1580. "Obscenity" itself entered English law in 1728, when the court developed the charge of "obscene libel." It entered American law in 1815. But prior to Comstock there had never been so sustained a focus on obscenity as a literary and legal phenomenon. The problem was invented along the vector described by Justice Cockburn in 1867, the "tendency" of "obscene" literature to "deprave and corrupt" minds "open to such immoral influences." Until quite recently little or no research had ever been done to determine this tendency. It was assumed to be causal and therefore a social problem. The legal issue was, then, simply whether a work was in fact obscene. But since obscenity is an opinion rather than a fact, both the law and the problem had high elasticity. In Comstock's hands it was stretched to include practically anything mentioning sex.

Notwithstanding his peculiar success at criminalizing the discourse of sex, however, censorship is clearly at odds with liberal premises of a categorically free press and maximally free speech and action. Comstock had become something of a joke by the time of his death, yet not so much of a joke but that he had, as Margaret Sanger contended, "indirectly caused the death of untold thousands" and otherwise devastated the lives of "a whole generation of women." Still, as Sanger noted, he had been facilitated by the Congress and many state legislatures. Thus, Comstock reflects the complexity of the cultural situation of obscenity. On the one hand, there is the inherent contradiction of censoring the press in the face of the First Amendment. On the other there is the social dialectic between censorship advocates and civil libertarians. In this matrix the problem of obscenity defines itself according to perspective.

But, however defined, the problem of obscenity has been agonizing these United States since Comstock's time. By the late 1960s, Congress considered it "a matter of national concern" and authorized the President to appoint a commission to investigate and report on whether obscenity and pornography were socially harmful and whether "more effective methods," i.e., laws and administrative procedures, should be enacted for their control. In 1970 the commission issued its report, which proved to be somewhat ironic in terms of its mandate. It found that, while effects on minors were so far not determinable, there was little or no evidence that obscenity had harmful effects on consenting adults. It also found that obscenity was too subjective a concept to define as a workable basis for coherently enforceable laws that do not conflict with First Amendment rights, even in the context of the specifications outlined by the Supreme Court in the 1957 case of *Roth v. the United States.* Consequently prosecution of obscenity laws was unpredictable, arbitrary, ineffectual and, moreover, an unwarranted intrusion on the civil liberties of adults. The commission therefore recommended that existing obscenity laws should be repealed. The commission said, in effect, that there was no problem. The hullabaloo, both pro and con, surrounding the report, however, indicated continuing national concern. Apparently other nations were concerned also, but a British commission in 1979 and a Canadian one in 1984 reached conclusions essentially similar to those of the 1970 American report.

Nonetheless, another U.S. commission was impaneled in 1985 and reported in 1986. Its findings were rather different from those of its predecessors. While it acknowledged that evidence for a causal connection between obscenity and social harm was scarce, inconclusive, and problematic, it said it could conclude that there was an association between the two. As for a definition of obscenity that was legally workable without running afoul of the First Amendment, it did not exactly provide one but did contend that the standards established in the Roth case, as refined by two subsequent Supreme Court cases—*Miller v. California* (1973) and *Jenkins v. Georgia* (1974)—made obscenity law now coherently enforceable. The possibility of obscenity's harmful effects and the compatibility of its regulation with the First Amendment dictated a more vigorous enforcement of existing laws. While the commission did not find that new laws were needed for the prosecution of obscenity itself, it did recommend new laws and procedures for facilitating such prosecution in regard to what it regarded as ancillary aspects of obscenity—e.g., interstate commerce, organized crime, coercion and exploitation of pornography models, etc. It also proposed extra-legal citizen actions that might be taken against the distribution of obscenity. In short, where the 1970 commission found no problem and proposed a repeal of obscenity law, the 1986 commission found an urgent problem and proposed a nationwide attack on all the old fronts and several new ones.

The 1970 report had never been accepted by its conservative sponsors, which made it inevitable that another panel would be ordered to continue the project until they got it right. The wonder is that it took sixteen years. In that regard liberals possibly owe a debt to the interregnum administration of Jimmy Carter, who publicly confessed that photos of Playmates occasionally incited lust in his heart. In the march of events, however, it was the feminist assumption of the burden of pornography that was the catalyst.

The campaign for the Equal Rights Amendment had revealed a gap between feminists and conservative women, but the two groups joined in a united front on the problem of pornography. By the early 1980s

Women Against Pornography (WAP), the voice of that front, had become an influential, articulate lobby. Its most effective tactic was to raise the ante on the harmful effects of obscenity and pornography, both by emphasizing an association between pornography and violence toward women and by expanding obscenity's frame of reference to include such publications as *Playboy* and *Penthouse*, which customarily had not been included under the rubric. The 1970 commission had adopted a somewhat generic conception of harms in concluding that obscenity did not cause "social or individual harms such as crime, delinquency, sexual or nonsexual deviancy, or severe emotional disturbances." It did specifically address rape, but found no significant causal relation between it and pornography, although it allowed that the evidence was too inconclusive to close the books on the matter. WAP audited those books as they had never been audited before.

WAP introduced a whole new vocabulary of harms, itemizing such concepts as "victimization of women," "degradation of women," "subordination of women." Not only were these declared to be the basis of pornography's fraudulent currency, but pornography was held accountable for the culturally indentured situation of women in general. Andrea Dworkin and Susan Griffin had written widely acclaimed books which contended that the exploited, servile state of women was the logical conclusion of the pornographic social customs, economics, and aesthetics fashioned by the pornographic male mentality that had invented pornographic Western culture. This analysis had the advantage of a presumably immediate appeal to at least half of the population, and it became the ideological basis of WAP's attack on pornography. WAP's moral momentum surged, taking the form of an anti-pornography ordinance that was promoted across the country and provided the opportunity to broadcast WAP's case in public hearings that were natural media events. By the summer of 1984, even the American Civil Liberties Union felt obliged to give WAP's case a hearing, and on WAP's terms.

## WAP VERSUS FACT

The WAP ordinance proposed was never successfully enacted, although a Minneapolis referendum approved it, only to have it vetoed by the city's mayor as unconstitutional. The mayor's judgment was confirmed by both the U.S. District Court and the U.S. Supreme Court. Still, its spirit is alive, and its history is instructive about the legal and social dynamics of the "problem" of pornography. The principal assumption behind the ordinance is presented in Dworkin's *Pornography: Men Possessing Women*, which argues that the inexorable theme of pornography is the assertion of male power and the subordination and degradation of women. The strategy of this analysis is in its contention that the power motif of pornography has the "concrete" effect of inducing violent behavior in men toward women, ranging from psychological violence to physical beatings and rape. If accepted by the courts, this premise would, of course, disqualify pornography from First Amendment protection by virtue of being a specifically harmful action (legally analogous to falsely and maliciously yelling "Fire" in a crowded auditorium) as distinct from being a protected declaration of ideology. To give credibility to this thesis, the ordinance itself introduced sociological and laboratory studies to document a causal link between pornography and violent behavior. As for doing what Justice Brennan has said cannot adequately be done—distinguishing protected expression from that unprotected by the First Amendment, which has been the reef on which nearly all recent anti-pornography efforts have foundered—Dworkin proposed the following:

> By definition the First Amendment protects only those who can exercise the rights it protects. Pornography by definition—"the graphic depiction of whores"—is trade in a class of persons who have been systematically denied the rights protected by the First Amendment and the rest of the Bill of Rights. The question . . . is not whether the First Amendment protects pornography or should, but whether pornography keeps women from exercising the rights protected by the First Amendment. . . . Obscenity is not a synonym for pornography. Obscenity is an idea, it requires a judgment of value. Pornography is concrete, "the graphic depiction of whores."

Later Dworkin raises the ante, saying that pornography exclusively "means the graphic depiction of women as vile whores" as opposed to such "euphemisms" as "depictions of sexual acts." So Dworkin's strategy was to so describe the situation that either women or pornography, but not both, could have First Amendment rights, and to then define pornography so as to invalidate its claim.

This was the basis of the argument that Dworkin's ordinance co-sponsor, Catherine MacKinnon, presented to the American Civil Liberties Union 1984 convention. MacKinnon's debate opponent was to have been Nan Hunter, an ACLU staff member and co-author of the Feminists Against Censorship Taskforce (FACT) *amicus* brief opposing the ordinance. But, on threat of not appearing at the debate, MacKinnon had Hunter removed from the forum because she claimed that Hunter had used her ACLU position "to lever this national forum for [FACT's] position," and that Hunter's presence would increase "the exposure and legitimacy" of FACT. This suggests not only an animosity between the two feminist positions but also the power and influence of the anti-pornography movement. Still, it was clear that an ACLU audience would not likely be predisposed to concur in a logic that would appear to suppress free speech.

Perhaps that is why MacKinnon began with an analogy, placing women as victims of pornography in the company of such tortured people as South Africans, Salvadorans, blacks under slavery, and Jews at Dachau. All of the latter, she went on, are acknowledged as victims of torture and murder with rectifiable social causes, but when "these same acts" are done to women they are rationalized as sex practices. Women are being "taken and used," as are children, blacks, and Asians, used and dehumanized.

There are, she reiterated, "actual torture and murder" being perpetrated. And the reason, she said, is profit. Moreover, the profiteers claim constitutional rights. "We have been deluged with documentation," she said. "We have heard of cases of rape, we have heard of cases of battery, we have heard of cases of abuse. . . . We have come to think of these people as 'the disappeared'," she said. Given pornography's practice, she said, she and Dworkin had concluded that it should be addressed as practiced. So she would not argue the constitutionality of their ordinance under existing law but would argue why pornography should be made actionable. Pornography subordinates women, MacKinnon said, then specified four actionable harms that it constitutes: coercion, forced sex, assault, and trafficking. None of these are ideas, she said, but acts, and therefore cannot claim free speech protection. She said social and laboratory studies have documented the causal connection of pornography and these harms. Then she summed up with a peculiar analogy, given the nature of her audience. Complaining that pornographers had free speech while women did not, she said that the "First Amendment was written by those who had [free] speech. . . . They also had slaves."

Harriet Pilpel, ACLU's general counsel and MacKinnon's opponent, confronted MacKinnon's analysis of the situation of women. She said that women do in fact have free speech, and it includes the freedom to explore pain, servility, submission, and other pornographic motifs for a knowledge of femaleness that the Dworkin/MacKinnon ordinance would preclude. In fact, she argued, MacKinnon's position not only violated the First Amendment but also worked against feminist causes. For example, the past assumption that women did not have de facto free speech was behind the protective legislation that contributed to the subordination of women. She cited, among other examples, the Comstock laws that were used to prevent distribution of birth control information. Pilpel asserted that the MacKinnon/Dworkin definition was incoherently broad and idiosyncratic, and might well mean that depictions of the "missionary position" were subordinating and thus actionable, and that it also included the possibility that pictures of naked Auschwitz women would come into its purview. Moreover, she cited the dangers of prior restraint and insisted that the prospect of a pornography law so ill-defined was itself a clear and present danger.

That the debate highlighted a civil liberties schism in feminism was clear. MacKinnon had shown little or no inclination to compromise with the First Amendment. While for the most part this feminist debate merely intensified the traditional First Amendment skirmishes between its absolutist and relativist interpretations, it also added some new dimensions to the pornography issue. Whereas previous rationales for censorship relied on a relatively abstract dialectic about good, evil, and the commonweal, Dworkin and MacKinnon provided specificity: an identifiable class of "victims"—women—and a concise series of "harms"; and, since Dworkin and MacKinnon served as spokeswomen for such organizations as NOW and WAP, there was a coherent constituency focused on antipornography legislation that was not defined according to the more amorphously traditional lines of political conservatism versus liberalism. As for the feminist opposition to WAP—codified in an *amicus curiae* brief against the WAP ordinance by FACT, largely the source of Pilpel's argument—it did not merely invoke the sanctity of the First Amendment but claimed for pornography a specific epistemological potential—exploration and knowledge of female sexuality—which it linked to a specific social benefit—improvement of the situation of women. While these positions were not altogether new, the specificity of context they provide for the problem of pornography was new, and it revitalized discourse.

It was in this context that the 1986 Attorney General's Commission on Pornography (the earlier commission was presidentially appointed) received its mandate. The new commission readily adopted WAP's assumptions. Much of the testimony it heard was recycled from the WAP ordinance hearings. For the most part it followed WAP's interpretation of research data, despite caveats and even rebuttals by the researchers themselves. It used crucial terms from WAP's lexicon of harms, particularly "degrading," which permitted the commission to assign pornography a range of harms exceeded only by WAP's own ordinance brief. It apparently anticipated using the definition of pornography provided in WAP's proposed ordinance, but that ordinance was declared unconstitutional in the middle of the commission's deliberations. It was precisely for the Comstockian elasticity of definition of obscenity that a federal Appeals Court and the Supreme Court both found the ordinance in violation of the First Amendment. That modified the commission's allegiance to WAP's approach, albeit grudgingly. If the commission resorted to existing obscenity law rather than WAP's discredited one, and if its claim of obscenity's harm was less shrill and categorical than WAP's, still WAP's vocabulary and assumptions substantially informed the commission's analysis and recommendations.

Having failed to establish a new definition of obscenity, WAP found its agenda pending in the commission's report. But there was a significant difference. WAP had hoped that the urgency of harms it cited would brand nearly all forms of pornography as "a clear and present danger" that would override the definitional niceties that customarily function in First Amendment litigation. This was a severe underestimation of the authority of the First Amendment, and when WAP was whipped in court, the commission was obliged to make its case in terms consistent with the First Amendment. Obscenity had not been demonstrated to be so clear and present a danger as had been hoped, and whatever the national concern about it, that was still subordinate to even a conservative Supreme Court's concern for constitutional requirements.

Nonetheless, there is the question of whether pornography is harmful. The debate on this point is instructive as to why the 1986 commission was obliged to modify its stance and why the Supreme Court has been unable to resolve the obscenity problem. That pornography was identified by WAP as violent action rather than the image of such action made it harmful by definition. This is of course mere casuistry unless there is strong evidence causally linking pornography and violence against women. WAP cited studies which it interpreted to be such evidence. But the FACT analysis refuted each point of interpretation, asserting that in general the data were cited "in highly selective and grossly distorting ways." (It should be noted in this regard that even the 1986 commission report consistently qualifies its interpretations of essentially the same research by acknowledging that studies indicating obscenity's negative effects are scarce, problematic, and inconclusive).

To begin with, there is the contention that pornography is predominantly violent in its treatment of women. Citing content analyses of "adults only" books and magazines such as *Playboy* and *Penthouse* that show a range from 5% to 17.2% of violent depictions, FACT challenged WAP's credibility—"[WAP] asserts . . . that one study found the depictions of rape in 'adults only' paperbacks had doubled from 1968 to 1974, a statement which is simply false. The study found that the amount of explicit sexual content had doubled, but also 'that the plots, themes, and stories remained much the same. . . .'" FACT then went on to claim that, given this small volume of violence in pornography, the studies of pornographic violence are severely qualified by two aspects of their methodology. First, focusing on violence, they are skewed toward it, so they tend to measure the effects of violent imagery rather than pornographic imagery. To demonstrate, they quoted Edward Donnerstein and Daniel Linz, the authors of prominent studies cited by WAP:

> If you take out the explicit sexual content from aggressive pornographic films, leaving just the violence (which could be shown on any network tele-

> vision show), you find desensitization to violent acts in some subjects. However, if you take out the aggressive component and leave just the sexual, you do not seem to observe negative effects of desensitization to violence against women. Thus violence is at issue here. That is why restrictions or censorship solutions are problematical.

Moreover, even in the context of aggressively violent pornography, FACT concluded that "the results of the studies are not uniform," citing another prominent study "in which *no* evidence was found of changes in perceptions or attitudes following exposure to this type of pornography." There are yet other studies indicating that some kinds of "erotica" reduce aggressiveness in men.

Second, the laboratory conditions under which research on violent effects of pornography has been done have made it impossible to determine the precise cause of such violence as has been detected. As the researchers themselves note, in some cases the laboratory situation has served to condone violence, in others the design of the experiment induced irritation, and in others the phrasing of questions measuring response has made responses of marginal reliability. In general the correspondence between laboratory and real life conditions is questioned. The research, in short, is challenged as a reliable index of pornography's inducement of violence, by the researchers' own acknowledgments.

While FACT challenged WAP's interpretations and use of research data, the fact is that the researchers themselves are something of a house divided. One of the most prominent compendiums of this research (Neil M. Malamuth and Edward Donnerstein, *Pornography and Sexual Aggression*, 1984, representing some twenty-one researchers) exhibits the problem. On the one hand, they are nearly unanimous in cautioning that research on this subject is rudimentary, that its results are not uniform, that "porno-violence," as it is termed, needs to be distinguished from non-violent pornography, that the various "experiments" and studies have highly qualifying methodological shortcomings, that pornography has been inadequately separated from other possible and co-extensive social factors inducing violence, that, in short, the evidence does not warrant a causal connection between pornography and violent behavior toward women. On the other hand, the researchers are extremely anxious to validate their research in relation to its use in legal proceedings, in which context they tend to emphasize a "strong association" between pornography and violence, especially rape, while at the same time denying a causal nexus. Thus, they give contradictory signals. WAP, either willfully or wishfully, seems to have assumed that association is equivalent to cause, despite the researchers' objective disclaimers to the contrary. What the research shows at most to be problematical, WAP construed to be decisive. FACT regarded this as "distortion" of the evidence, but it has its roots in the forked tongue of the research rhetoric.

As for whether pornography is degrading and subordinating to women, FACT was similarly decisive. It argued that the key characteristics of pornography incriminated in the WAP ordinance—e.g. "subordination," "degradation," and the representing of women as "sex objects"—are too subjective for constitutional enforcement of enactments against them. For some people, any explicit sexual depictions are degrading; for others, depicting sex outside the framework of marriage and the family is degrading; for some, sexual postures other than the traditional "missionary position" are degrading; while for others that posture might well instance women's subordination; if "the absence of any indicia of personhood" is what constitutes a "sex object," which is a measure used by feminists, what objective standard distinguishes between a calendar nude and one by Edward Steichen or the depiction of a vagina by Judy Chicago? The First Amendment, FACT reminded the court, "prohibits any law regulating expression which would of necessity result in such unpredictable and arbitrary interpretations. This ordinance transgresses all three of the measures of impermissible vagueness. A person of ordinary intelligence would be at a loss to predict how any of a huge range of sexually explicit materials would be interpreted by a court."

FACT also rejected the premise that pornography causes discrimination against women. Just as it argued that violence against women is reflected and encouraged more by the general culture than by pornography, so it argued that discrimination against women has its sources in broader social structures than pornography:

> Misogynist images, both those which are sexually explicit and the far more pervasive ones which are not, reflect and may help reenforce the inferior social and economic status of women. But none of these studies and analyses identify sexually explicit material as the central factor in the oppression of women. History teaches us that the answer is not so simple. Factors far more complex than pornography produced the English common law treatment of women as chattel property and the enactment of statutes allowing a husband to rape or beat his wife with impunity. In short, the claim that "pornography is central in creating and maintaining sex as a basis of discrimination" is flatly inconsistent with the conclusions of most who have studied the question.

In short, FACT argued that the harms alleged for pornography are predicated on research that is at best inconclusive and at worst contradictory, and that WAP analysts had distorted and misconstrued research results to confirm foregone assumptions. Consequently, since pornography is not a clear cause of sexist harms, its censorship would be a gratuitous violation of constitutional rights. Moreover, FACT asserted that not only would censorship fail to diminish sexist harms but that it would reinforce sexist logic because it is itself based on sexist stereotypes—e.g., that women are in need of special protection, that women are incompetent to make contracts or independent decisions (e.g., as pornographic writers or artists or models or actresses), or that "good" women are not sexually explicit in thought, word, or deed. However, this introduces a debate on feminist strategies, which are not pertinent here.

More immediately relevant is the "chilling effect" of censorship, that to repress pornographic speech is also to repress the free exchange of ideas about it and related phenomena. WAP contended that, "The Supreme Court has determined that 'there is . . . a less vital interest in the uninhibited exhibition of material that is on the borderline between pornography and artistic expression than in the free dissemination of ideas of social and political significance.' . . . The chilling effect is simply not entitled to great weight in this context." For WAP, as we have seen, pornography by definition is a harmful act and therefore whatever "ideas of social and political significance" it may claim are not relevant. As we have seen, pornographic works by both men and women do contain ideas of social and political significance, which was precisely the point FACT made in arguing that "constitutional protection of sexually explicit speech should be enhanced, not diminished." Arguing for the obvious social value of a free exchange of ideas, FACT specified sexual speech, including pornography, as significantly political and social. FACT emphasized that it is especially important to women in exploring their social situation and personal identities, both of which are intimately connected with sexuality, as we have earlier noted in considering female pornography:

> The range of feminist imagination and expression in the realm of sexuality has barely begun to find voice. Women need the freedom and the socially recognized space to appropriate for themselves the robustness of what traditionally has been male language. Laws such as the one under challenge here could constrict that freedom. See M. K. Blakely, "Is One Woman's Sexuality Another Woman's Pornography?" Ms. Magazine 37 (April 1985). Amid fear that as more women's writing and art on sexual themes emerges which is unlady-like, unfeminine, aggressive, power-charged, pushy, vulgar, urgent, confident and intense, the traditional foes of women's attempts to step out of their "proper place" will find an effective tool of repression in the Indianapolis ordinance.

WAP's presumption that the Supreme Court was less interested in sustaining free speech than in containing pornography seems to have led it to concede that its ordinance might well have a chilling effect but that this was insignificant in comparison to the harm of pornography. But FACT seized upon this opening to promote the flip side of the harm argument. Having refuted pornography's harm to women, it now contended that suppressing pornography was not only a violation of free speech but that it would itself be a harm to women.

Moreover, even if there were convincing evidence of pornography's harm there would remain the problem of defining terms in law so that they would not impinge on legitimate free speech. This has always been the primary problem in obscenity litigation; it was so before pornography's alleged social harms were particularized, and it is so now. To take just one category of depictions WAP found censorable, it would be an instance when "women are presented in scenarios of degradation, injury, torture, shown as filthy or inferior, bleeding, bruised, or hurt in a context that makes these conditions sexual." Apart from the subjectivity of such terms as "degradation" or "inferior," all of these "scenarios" are at one point or another applicable to, for example, Alix Kates Shulman's depiction of her character Robin in her novel *On the Stroll*. In fact it is Robin's very degradation and inferiority—assuming one can have any grip at all on those terms—that Shulman is using to explore the situation of women. The ordinance specified that it shall not be a defense that there was no intention of "pornography or sex discrimination," so there is an instance where the work of a feminist author intending to explore barriers to women's liberation would be vulnerable to suppression by a feminist rationale with a different notion of how those barriers should be depicted.

Nor was the proposed ordinance at all unique in this respect. The history of modern pornography litigation is strewn with lawyers, judges, and legislators who have wasted thousands of hours attempting to plug up such definitional loopholes only to have new ones open behind them. It is true that, since the passing of William O. Douglas, no Supreme Court Justice has advocated an "absolutist" view of First Amendment rights. It is also true that the Court's 1973 decision in the landmark *Miller v. California* case confirmed the constitutional possibility of a censorship law. But in fact, as the reports from both U.S. commissions on obscenity and pornography show, and practicing lawyers and District Attorneys substantiate, there have been very few cases successfully prosecuted on that model because judges and juries alike are nearly as loathe to proscribe free speech as is the First Amendment itself. Time and again courts have been obliged to strike down censorship laws because their definitions of pornography have impinged upon the free exchange of ideas. Nor is it likely that a polemical logic will alter that record. It is, after all, a logic in contradiction with itself; to pit the rights of expression against the rights of women, for example, is to either ignore or deny that women have the right of expression. Still, there is the perception that the First Amendment is not so much the cornerstone of liberal democracy as it is an obstacle to "politically correct" social engineering.

## EXPENSE OF SPIRIT IN A WASTE OF SHAME

In the face of the proliferation of perversities cited in Chapter One, the First Amendment has been a nagging source of consternation for Americans. In January 1991, in response to public demonstrations against the Persian Gulf War, a woman wrote to a local newspaper saying that she believed in freedom of speech but nonetheless could not believe that anti-war protestors were "true Americans." In 1980, Ronald Reagan's successful presidential campaign featured the proclamation that the true Constitution excluded the Bill of Rights. In the mid-1980s, Margot St. James, a sometime prostitute and spokeswoman for the rights of prostitutes, argued that the illegality of prostitution and the legality of pornography constituted a contradiction of justice so great as to invalidate the First Amendment. If conservative feminists, patriots, presidents, and prostitutes are at odds with free speech, the foundation of democratic liberalism, can white European males be far behind?

In 1989 the University of California Press published Richard Randall's *Freedom and Taboo*, subtitled *Pornography and the Politics of a Self Divided*. The *Self* is the demos of these more or less United States, and the division is between elitist civil libertarians and the masses offended by pornography. Randall's sympathies were with what he perceived to be "the demand and felt need for control . . . , with the censorship interest, its motivation, energy, and effect, not as civic pathology but as political and social force." His argument represents an oddly conservative populism—albeit a populism that is white, European, and male—to which the free speech legacy of liberalism has finally gone too far.

His discomfort was not so much with pornography itself, which he considered natural, occasionally artistic, and psychologically informative. But, contrary to extreme liberal claims, he said, all societies have had a legitimate interest in regulating sexuality and its expression. If pornography is endemic to human nature, so does it transgress social norms, hence the divided self that generates persistent conflict. While there may be no clear objective evidence of pornography's social harm, a significant portion of society finds it offensive and disturbing. Consequently, pornography poses a challenge to liberal democracy: The felt need for control reflects a mass democratic imperative in contradiction to the prevailing free speech imperative of a social/intellectual/judicial elite.

The assumptions informing this last point are an intriguing index of the advanced state of American schizophrenia on the subject. Randall was convinced that free speech is an elitist imposition on the popular will. To demonstrate this, he subjected the Bill of Rights, particularly the First Amendment, to new historicist revisionism. "The great list of rights," he said, "was not originally intended to protect individual liberty against social control," but was rather "a concession" by a manufacturing elite seeking strong central government to other agrarian elites, who wanted it simply "to protect property and local interests." This seemed to settle the matter for him, although it in no way explained what he acknowledged to be "the uncompromising language in which they were cast." If these elites regarded "the people" as a "great beast," they nonetheless granted Grendel his voice. Nor, in light of that, would the concession seem to have alienated the Bill of Rights from what he also acknowledged, "the natural rights philosophy from which they drew much of their ideological support." Nonetheless Randall charged the Supreme Court with having arbitrarily imposed a free speech tyranny on the population over the last fifty years. This would roughly date from Justice Woolsey's *Ulysses* decision in 1933, the significance of which we shall look at shortly.

"The First Amendment itself," said Randall, "actually requires very little, because it says very little." He thought its "libertarian obscenity doctrine" was some sort of idiosyncratic invention of the Supreme Court: "Constitutional requirements are what a majority of the justices say they are, no more and no less." The First Amendment is indeed succinct; it is also categorical, that "Congress shall make no law" abridging free speech. And, given his own survey of the pertinent legal history, Randall must have been quite aware that the Supreme Court decisions themselves have twisted more than Chubby Checker in trying to evade the Amendment's simple logic. The Court has indulged its discretionary authority about as much as it can and still claim to be in touch at all with the Amendment's language.

But then it is not that Randall thought we ought to do away with the First Amendment. He probably had a pretty good idea of how that harbinger of mass oppression would go. He just thought that the Court, since its decisions are whimsical, should listen to some combination of Gallup and the *zeitgeist* and then unmake its libertarian doctrine in the same fanciful way it was made. He thought it was really a question of "management." Yes, he acknowledged, pornography was being managed, what with local laws, zoning ordinances, radio and television licensing, and even public opinion. But it wasn't being managed well. He knew this because he knew the masses found pornography "offensive" and yet it was somehow still around. Well, not all around, but the facts were less important than impressions. The masses felt it was in their faces. True, the masses were a little confused about what they thought: "Survey evidence indicates that large numbers of persons believe pornography to be harmful to individuals, but only a small fraction believe that they themselves have been harmed. The mutually contradictory nature of those two beliefs is apparent." But that is because of all that inconclusive empirical evidence, which just causes confusion. If the Court would only loosen up, management could tighten up. Since we can't seem to get the facts straight about pornography's social harm, we ought to drop that legal test and adopt one we do know about, namely offensiveness. He seriously proposed "offensiveness" as the measure of First Amendment protection. With that standard, the Court could spread the work around to local courts, whose jurors will certainly know when they have been offended.

Randall himself seemed uneasy about unleashing the offensiveness quotient of the masses. So he proposed a test: "An erotic work or expression, not otherwise obscene, may be reasonably restricted (but not altogether prohibited) . . . where it is patently offensive. . . . " If "not otherwise obscene" opened the sluice, "not altogether prohibited" closed it again, which might leave the jurors a bit puzzled about what to do that is not already being done by police and D.A. harassment, zoning regulations, and the like. He also suspected that local "triers of fact" may not have a grip on "reasonably restricted," so he defined it as "no more than necessary." That ought to clear things up. The masses may not know what's reasonable, but they'll probably know what's necessary. Given the spectre of this quagmire mucking up courts all over the country, it is small wonder Randall finally allowed as how we will probably have to keep the Supreme Court around anyway, because . . . well, you know how easily people are offended.

Randall's is a crackpot proposal only if one assumes that the principle of free speech is the cornerstone of liberal democracy. That it is is because of a history more subtle than the positivism of Randall and MacKinnon allows. Liberal democracy is inherently relativistic. The separation of powers prescribed in the Constitution is a testimonial to this imperative. But the founders were historical materialists enough to know, by example from both European and Native American history, that factions could appropriate power to neutralize or eliminate the relativity of democratic dissent. Their own dissent was symptomatic, to say nothing of their other contradictions. The Constitution, therefore, was not complete without the Bill of Rights.

Perplexity about the Bill of Rights derives from the fact that it is at once historical and ahistorical. The First Amendment is historical in its attempt to counter historically authoritarian abuses of the freedoms of religion, speech, press, assembly, and redress of grievances. It is ahistorical in that its language seeks to transcend history via the postulation of these freedoms as absolutes. Thus there is a dialectic whereby the absolute and only the absolute guarantees democratic relativism. First Amendment cynics, like Randall and MacKinnon, jump on the Amendment's historicity like a dog on a bone. But they are so polemically preoccupied with it that they ignore, or at least devalue, the holistically necessary function of its dialectic. The Supreme Court does not have this luxury. Up to 1933 it did, but that is because until that point obscenity law was defined by Justice Cockburn's 1867 British opinion cited earlier. British law has no equivalent of the First Amendment's dialectic, and Cockburn's opinion was based exclusively on the relative susceptibility of some mythically presumed mind to the presumed influence of obscenity.

By 1933 presumptions about mind and literature were somewhat different than in 1867. These presumptions informed the *Ulysses* decision, and in so doing revealed the basic contradiction of obscenity litigation in the United States. It is probably no accident that this pivotal case was decided in relation to a work of unequivocal artistic and social value. In any event, Joyce's novel obliged Judge Woolsey to articulate the law with a critical sophistication that would have been otherwise unnecessary. To address the problem, Woolsey read literary criticism pertaining to *Ulysses*, and he phrased his precedent-setting judgment according to what were in effect "new critical" standards. He determined that such a book must be read "in its entirety"—i.e., in its structural "context," as the FACT *amicus* brief more recently phrases the principle—rather than in isolated passages to determine its effect. So read, he concluded, the book was not legally obscene nor pornographic, and thus not censorable. This established the test of "redeeming" social, artistic, or scientific value, which has been the source of subsequent perturbation to the spirit of censorship. Woolsey also established another crucial principle, that obscenity should be determined, not according to the "most susceptible persons" standard inherited from British law, but according to "the Court's opinion as to its effect on a person with average sex instincts . . . who plays, in this branch of legal inquiry, the same role of hypothetical reagent as does the 'reasonable man' in the law of torts and 'the man learned in the art' on questions of invention in patent law." If Woolsey's reasoning now seems commonsensical, it had not seemed so to the Massachusetts Supreme Court just three years earlier. That court found Theodore Dreiser's *An American Tragedy* to be censorable with the following logic:

> The seller of a book which contains passages offensive to the statute has no right to assume that children to whom the book might come would not read the obscene passages, or having read them, would continue to read on until the evil effects of the obscene passages were weakened or dissipated with the tragic denouement of the tale.

Thus one can see how the critical intelligence of Woolsey's two principles has been crucial to censorship adjudication. The first has made simplistic definitions or those based on isolated passages unworkable. The second has made reason rather than morality, public sentiment, or pathology the measure of censorability.

Woolsey's decision avoided the issue of whether obscenity was entitled to First Amendment protection (clearly assuming it was not), but the Supreme Court did accept the precedent of his two key standards in the *Roth* case (1957). As Justice Brennan phrased it, the test was "whether to the average person, applying contemporary community standards, the dominant theme of the material taken as a whole appeals to prurient interest." This confirmed Woolsey's aesthetic and sociological premises in law, although they were slightly modified. But because the case involved advertising pamphlets rather than an aesthetic work, the focus was shifted to "prurient" obscenity. For the first time obscenity was declared beyond the pale of the First Amendment, and the central term in defining obscenity was "prurient." Brennan himself took up its ambiguity, but defensively: "That there may be marginal cases in which it is difficult to determine the side of the line on which a particular fact situation falls is no sufficient reason to hold the language too ambiguous to define a criminal offense." As it happened, however, the subsequent cases were not so marginal, and there were so many situations that proved intractable that the *Roth* decision was ineffective. Prosecutors found that juries and judges alike were disinclined to subordinate free speech to ambiguity. In fact, Brennan had anticipated the problem in attempting to reconcile the Court decision with the facts of life:

> However, sex and obscenity are not synonymous. Obscene material . . . [appeals] to prurient interest. The portrayal of sex, e.g., in art, literature and scientific works, is not itself sufficient reason to deny . . . freedom of speech and press. Sex, a great and mysterious motive force in human life, has indisputably been a subject of absorbing interest to mankind through the ages; it is one of the vital problems of human interest and public concern. . . . Freedom of discussion, if it would fulfill its historic function in this nation, must embrace all issues about which information is needed or appropriate to enable the members of society to cope with the exigencies of their period.

To expect ambiguity to stand up under the pressures of "a great and mysterious motive force" and "historic function" was an index of the inherent constitutional contradiction in the *Roth* decision and censorship generally.

Among the many instances where the ambiguity did not prevail were the famous cases of Lawrence's *Lady Chatterley's Lover* (1959), Miller's *Tropic of Cancer* (1962), Cleland's *Memoirs of a Woman of Pleasure* (1966) and several literary magazines. This is not to say that the ruling did not provide an umbrella for harassments and suppressions in cases that did not reach higher level courts or in some cases any courts at all, but when they did get into protracted litigation the convictions were rather more often than not overturned. But then the objective of the *Roth* decision was to validate obscenity regulation by making sure that bona fide artistic, scientific and social works, no matter how unorthodox, controversial or even hateful their ideas might be, would not be confused with obscenity. That after all was the function of the Supreme Court's confirmation of Woolsey's two principles. And to facilitate the distinction, and thus make censorship compatible with the Constitution, the Court set rigorous standards for determining obscenity. Not only was there the contextual prurience test, but material also had to be "patently offensive" to "contemporary community standards" as well as "utterly without redeeming social value." While the standards were rigorous, however, their language was somewhat too ambiguous for effective prosecution.

Moreover, in the *Stanley* case of 1969 the Court challenged, and possibly nullified, its own basic premise in the *Roth* decision, that censorship was compatible with the First Amendment. In *Stanley*, the Court determined that the private possession of obscene materials—i.e., those meeting the *Roth* standards for obscenity—was protected by the First Amendment. That is, an adult could not be legally prohibited from having obscenity in his or her possession. But did this mean only in the home, or did it include the possibility of legal obscenity in theaters or stores where admission was restricted to consenting adults? And in any case, wouldn't at least some kinds of distribution and production of obscenity be legitimized? The Court hedged its bet, saying that the government had a legitimate interest in regulating obscenity, e.g. its distribution, which might interfere with the individual's right to possess it. But, as if aware that it was speaking from both sides of its mouth, the Court emphasized that government did not have a legitimate interest in protecting an individual's mind from the effects of obscenity. And if criminal behaviors resulted—for which the Court found "little empirical basis"—the better deterrents would be education and punishment for violations of law rather than prohibition of speech and press. Thus the *Stanley* decision bemused the *Roth* decision by restoring constitutional protection to obscenity at least under some circumstances, and further muddled censorship's prospects by subordinating the legitimacy of government's concern about the harm of obscenity to its concern for maintaining First Amendment freedoms.

So in 1973 the Court girded itself for yet one more landmark decision in the *Miller* case. Justice Burger's majority opinion in *Miller* revealed his distaste for the whole subject, "The examination of contested materials 'is hardly a source of edification to members of this Court'." The Court majority hoped to dispatch not only pornography's legal claims but also the "absolutist" view of First Amendment rights held by Justice Douglas. In that regard Burger observed that, "This may not be an easy road, free from difficulty. But no amount of 'fatigue' should lead us to adopt a convenient 'institutional' rationale . . . because it will lighten our burdens." The institution to which he refers with such uneasiness is the Constitution.

The Court had been down that wearisome road several times to no avail, so it seemed somewhat wishful for Burger to suppose, as he did, that it could effectively "isolate 'hard-core' pornography from expression protected by the First Amendment," thus permitting courts to "abandon . . . casual practice." His colleague Brennan, even in voting for both the *Roth* and *Miller* decisions, had said that "no formulation . . . can adequately distinguish" protected from unprotected expression. The Court, excepting Justices Douglas and Black, ignored the irony that, forty years after Judge Woolsey's *Ulysses* decision, censorship was still in what could be described as a state of "casual practice."

Nonetheless, *Miller* reconfirms Brennan's rearticulation of Woolsey's standards about "the whole work" and the "average person's" judgment, although it relieves prosecutors from the burden of proving that obscene material is "utterly without redeeming social value" by rephrasing the clause to read that a work "taken as a whole, lacks serious literary, artistic, political, or scientific value." One notable change is in the concept of "community standard," which had been assumed to be national in *Ulysses,* been ambiguously localized in *Roth,* but is specified as "statewide" rather than "national" in *Miller.* The other notable change is, "whether the work depicts or describes, in a patently offensive way, sexual conduct *specifically defined by the applicable state law*" (italics added). These changes theoretically addressed the problem of definitional vagueness, by specifying "community" boundaries and itemizing obscene representations. However, while cognizant that specificity is the antidote to ambiguity, the Court is nonetheless unwilling to categorically enumerate impermissible sex acts—doubtless remembering that sex is "a great and mysterious motive force"—so it adds the qualification, "in a patently offensive way." But patently offensive to whom? To any given state at large? Is Cairo, Illinois, likely to have the same artistic standards or threshold of permissiveness as Chicago? And just who would the "average person" mediating the difference be? And could a Cairo distributor, let alone a New York publisher, really be held accountable for knowing the composition of that phantom average? Once again, in short, ambiguities plagued litigation, and the *Miller* guidelines proved little more useful than their predecessors.

A year later things were further complicated when the Court decided in the *Jenkins* case that a community could take "patent offense," but only sometimes. The state of Georgia, consistent with the *Miller* specification that a community standard be statewide, found that the film *Carnal Knowledge* appealed primarily to prurient interest in sex and was patently offensive to Georgians. The Court, however, decided that the Georgians' sensibility was somewhat too refined for the Constitution and in effect echoed Justice Potter Stewart's famous earlier dictum, that he may not be able to define obscenity precisely, but he knew it when he saw it . . . and this wasn't it. The Court said that Georgia was not at liberty to be patently offended by *Carnal Knowledge*.

So the situation now is that the community standard that obscenity is at risk of offending is statewide excepting when the Court prefers a national to a parochial taste. There is also the question of just what profile produces the average person in whose judgment an item is offensively obscene. Clearly the prosecutors, judges, and jurors in Georgia don't fit it. Nor, one might surmise, would those in Nevada, where prostitution is legal. Presumably the average person is drifting somewhere between Reno and Atlanta, perhaps in Lawrence, Kansas, the home of William Burroughs. And somebody will have to determine prurience, but who?

As for the last of the three *Roth* criteria, those rocks upon which obscenity law is supposed to be based, the Court's *Miller* modification has not been so helpful as it hoped. It thought that the burden of proving material to be "utterly without redeeming social value" was too great, and so demonstrating that a work, "taken as a whole, lacks serious literary, artistic, political, or scientific value," instead, would make matters easier for prosecutors. But if the Court found examining pornography to be "hardly a source of edification," is it really ready to hear mimeticists and deconstructionists square off over the artistic value of *Debbie Does Dallas*? All of these confusions and contradictions derive from rulings that assume obscenity is not protected by the First Amendment. When one factors in the *Stanley* decision, which refutes that assumption significantly, the contradiction quotient in obscenity law takes a megajump.

It is small wonder that the 1970 U.S. commission on pornography and obscenity decided to clear the legal decks. But then it assumed that pornography was not a "problem" and that, in current idiom, "If it ain't broke don't fix it." But the Court assumes that pornography is a problem and, apparently, that the First Amendment is "broke," a condition it tries to remedy with Rube Goldberg engineering. Given its assumptions and the categorical imperative of the First Amendment, the Court is in a quandary: how to evade the Constitution without violating it? The Court had hoped, with its *Miller* decision, to give coherence to obscenity law, but it is still incoherent, inconsistent, and largely ineffective. This is precisely what has so irritated Women Against Pornography, which perceives pornography to be a far more pernicious problem than even the Court does. The Court, after all, is an essentially male institution. But the obstacle is not the Court, it is the First Amendment. Even if the Court were all female, and all WAP members to boot, the quandary would be the same. The solution to the problem is either to define it out of existence, as the 1970 commission did, or repeal the First Amendment, as Margot St. James suggested. But if the fate of the Equal Rights Amendment is any index, the American electorate will be building condos on the moon long before it even considers that repeal.

The other option is to pursue the present legal muddle. For censorship advocates this has the advantage of at least permitting harassment of obscenity. If it also has the disadvantage of cultivating a cynicism about law, at any rate it does not simply cave in to the pornographers. This is essentially the posture taken by the report of the 1986 U.S. commission on pornography. Despite the commission's cheerleading for more vigorous enforcement of obscenity laws, and despite its many tactical recommendations to that end, the commission was obliged to report that pornography did not constitute a clear and present danger to society and that therefore enforcing current law, perhaps cleaned up a bit about the edges, was the best that could be done. Its confidence in current law belied its own observations about the law's ineffectiveness and the general disinclination of prosecutors, therefore, to pursue it. In any event, the commission settled for delivering a pep talk.

The commission emphasized how the *Roth*, *Miller*, and *Jenkins* cases made theoretically possible a discrimination between obscenity and protected expression, all but ignoring the theoretical counterpoint of the *Stanley* decision, not to mention the morass of confusions and contradictions that make practical application of the law a continuing snakepit for state legislators and prosecutors alike. Nonetheless, the commission conceded the authority of the First Amendment. Thus its only strategy is harassment, of pornography and possibly of the Amendment itself. This will doubtless provoke more litigation, such as that surrounding the commission's own bizarre attempt to blackmail and blacklist corporations it summarily, and lawlessly if not illegally, accused of trafficking in obscenity. Perhaps this will create more employment for lawyers, researchers, and expert witnesses. Perhaps the commission's one progressive recommendation will someday be enacted, so that performers and models in the pornography industry will be accorded the benefits and protections supposedly available to the legitimate labor force. However that may be, it is quite likely that the pornography industry will continue to be what it has become, a functional aspect of liberalism's political economy and the GNP. In that regard, perhaps harassment is as reasonable a policy as we can expect.

Still, the continuing censorship syndrome induces a wearisome cycle. At least once a decade since 1930, the higher courts have been obliged to "definitively" reconsider the viability of censoring pornography and obscenity. Each time the enterprise has proved to be an expense of spirit in a waste of shame. In the *Miller* decision, the conservative Supreme Court majority clearly ached to be able to validate censorship. But, while it curiously cited the 1970 presidential commission's minority report asserting a likely prospect of pornographic harms, and ignored the majority report denying those harms, it was not sufficiently tainted to categorically quash free speech. In attempting to accommodate First Amendment principles, which is its acknowledged responsibility, it ironically contributed to an untenable censorship legacy.

Such ironies are characteristic of censorship legislation and adjudication, and they are, however grudging and left-handed, acknowledgment of the First Amendment's absolute premise, that "Congress shall make no law . . . abridging freedom of speech, or of the press." What else is it but that, when many of the state statutes spawned by the *Miller* ruling categorically exempt the written word from obscenity prosecution? Fifty years of futile litigation should be persuasive that the inherent contradiction of censorship will not be transcended. Free speech is and is perceived to be, even by sometime censorship advocates, so vital a democratic institution that the logic of censorship cannot be sustained against it. American judicial history documents that. It also documents both major and minor abuses of free speech principles, but even these abuses have not long survived. They have perpetrated injustice, harassment, and damage, but they have not survived. Nor does censorship, by nature an abuse of free speech, solve problems. That is not its function. Its function is to negate speech. Insofar as vicious speech is a problem, its antidote is more speech. Research is speech. Art is speech. Education is speech. Censorship is not speech. It is a bad idea. My grandmother, a very strait-laced Lutheran, put it another way: "Don't cut off your nose to spite your face." She was not very enthusiastic about pornography, but she was a great believer in the Constitution.

# Bibliography

## CHAPTER 1

Apollinaire, Guillaume. *Selected Writings.* Translated by Roger Shattuck. New York: New Directions, 1971.

———. *Alcools.* Translated by William Meredith. Garden City, N.Y.: Doubleday, 1964.

———. *The Debauched Hospodar.* Paris: The Olympia Press, 1953.

Aretino, Pietro. *Dialogues.* Translated by Raymond Rosenthal. New York: Ballantine, 1973.

Barthes, Roland. *The Pleasure of the Text.* Translated by Richard Miller. New York: Hill and Wang, 1975.

Bataille, Georges. *Eroticism.* Translated by Mary Dalwood. London: John Calder, 1962.

———. *Story of the Eye.* Translated by Joachim Neugroschel. New York: Urizen, 1977.

Baudelaire, Charles. "New Notes on Edgar Allen Poe." In *Modern Continental Literary Criticism.* Edited by O. B. Hardison. New York: Appleton-Century-Crofts, 1962.

———. *Spleen and Ideal.* In *Poison and Vision.* Translated and edited by David Paul. New York: Random House, 1974.

Blake, William. *The Complete Poetry.* New York: Random House, 1941.

Breton, André. *Manifestoes of Surrealism.* Translated by Richard Seaver and Helen R. Lane. Ann Arbor: University of Michigan Press, 1972.

Burroughs, William S. *Naked Lunch.* New York: Grove Press, 1966.

Coleridge, Samuel Taylor *The Friend,* in *Complete Works.* Edited by W. G. T. Shedd. New York, 1884.

———. *Biographia Literaria.* Edited by J. Shawcross. Oxford, 1907.

De Staël, Madame. *The Influence of Literature upon Society.* Boston, 1835.

Donne, John. *The Complete Poetry and Selected Prose.* Edited by Charles M. Coffin. New York: Random House, 1952.

Ellis, Havelock. *Studies in the Psychology of Sex.* Vol. 1: *Sexual Inversion.* New York: Random House, 1936.

Foucault, Michel. *The History of Sexuality.* Translated by Robert Hurley. New York: Vintage, 1980.

Frantz, David O. *Festum Voluptatis: A Study of Renaissance Erotica.* Columbus, Ohio: Ohio State University Press, 1989.

Freud, Sigmund. *Three Essays on the Theory of Sexuality.* Translated and edited by James Strachey. New York: Basic Books, 1975.

Ginsberg, Allen. *Collected Poems: 1947-80.* New York: Harper & Row, 1984.

Giovanni, Nikki. *Black Feeling Black Talk Black Judgement.* New York: William Morrow, 1970.

Griffin, Susan. *Pornography and Silence.* New York: Harper & Row, 1981.

Havel, Vaclav. "Help the Soviet Union on Its Road to Democracy: Consciousness Precedes Being" (Speech to Joint Session of Congress), Washington, D.C., Feb. 21, 1990.

Hegel, G. W. H. *The Philosophy of History.* Translated by J. Sibree. New York: The Colonial Press, 1900.

Jarry, Alfred. *The Ubu Plays.* Translated by Cyril Connolly and Simon Watson Taylor. New York: Grove Press, 1969.

———. Selected Works. Edited by Roger Shattuck and Simon Watson Taylor. London: Methuen, and New York: Grove Press, 1965.

Jones, LeRoi (Amiri Baraka). *Dutchman and the Slave.* New York: Morrow, 1964.

———. *The Baptism and the Toilet.* New York: Grove Press, 1967.

———. *The Dead Lecturer.* New York: Grove Press, 1964.

———. *Selected Poems.* New York: William Morrow, 1979.

Joyce, James. *Portrait of the Artist as a Young Man.* New York: Viking, 1948.

———. *The Critical Writings.* Edited by Ellsworth Mason and Richard Ellmann. New York: Viking, 1966.

———. *Ulysses.* New York: Random House, 1946.

Krafft-Ebing, Richard von. *Psychopathia Sexualis.* Translation by F. J. Rebman. New York: Physicians and Surgeons Book Co., 1922.

Krich, Aron. *The Sexual Revolution.* New York: Delta, 1964.

Lawrence, D. H. *Lady Chatterley's Lover.* New York: Grove Press, 1959.

———. *Sex, Literature and Censorship.* Edited by Harry T. Moore. New York: Twayne, 1953.

Lee, Don L. *Don't Cry, Scream.* Detroit: Broadside Press, 1969.

Mallarmé, Stéphane. *Selected Prose, Poems, Essays, and Letters.* Translated by Bradford Cook. Baltimore: The Johns Hopkins Press, 1956.

Masters, William and Johnson, Virginia. *Human Sexual Response.* Boston: Little, Brown, 1966.

Raymond, Marcel. *From Baudelaire to Surrealism.* London: Methuen, 1970.

Reich, Wilhelm. *The Discovery of the Orgone.* Vol. 1: *The Function of the Orgasm.* New York: Orgone Institute Press, 1942.

Reynolds, Sir Joshua. *The Discourses.* London, New York: World's Classics Series, 1907.

Schiller, Friedrich. *Naive and Sentimental Poetry and On the Sublime.* Edited and translated by Julias A. Elias. New York: Frederick Ungar, 1966.

———. *William Tell.* Translated by Charles E. Passage. New York: Frederick Ungar, 1962.

Shulman, Alix Kates. *On the Stroll.* New York: Alfred A. Knopf, 1981.

Ullerstam, Lars. *The Erotic Minorities.* Translated by Anselm Hollo. New York: Grove Press, 1966.

Walker, Alice. *The Color Purple.* New York: Washington Square Press, 1983.

Young, Wayland. *Eros Denied.* New York: Grove Press, 1964.

## CHAPTER 2

Aristotle. *The Poetics.* Translated by Ingram Bywater. In *The Basic Works of Aristotle.* Edited by Richard McKeon. New York: Random House, 1941.

———. *Nicomachean Ethics.* Translated by W. D. Ross. *Ibid.*

Arnold, Matthew. *Essays in Criticism.* New York: Home Library, 1902.

Burroughs, William S. *Naked Lunch. Ibid.*

Cleland, John. *Memoirs of a Woman of Pleasure.* New York: G. P. Putnam's Sons, 1963.

Dryden, John. *Dramatic Essays.* London, New York: Everyman's Library, 1912.

Dworkin, Andrea. *Pornography: Men Possessing Women.* New York: Putnam, 1981.

Forster, E. M. *Aspects of the Novel.* New York: Harcourt, Brace, 1954.

Freud, Sigmund. *An Outline of Psychoanalysis.* New York: W. W. Norton, 1949.

Friday, Nancy. *My Secret Garden.* New York: Simon and Schuster, 1974.

Genet, Jean. *The Thief's Journal.* Translated by Bernard Frechtman. New York: Grove Press, 1964.

Griffin, Susan. *Pornography and Silence. Ibid.*

Harding, Esther M. *Psychic Energy.* New York and Washington, D.C.: Pantheon and Bollingen Foundation, 1963.

Hite, Shere. *The Hite Report.* New York: Dell, 1977.

Joyce, James. *Ulysses. Ibid.*

Keats, John. *Poems and Verses.* New York: Macmillan, 1949.

Kinsey, A. C., Pomeroy, W. B., and Martin, C. E. *Sexual Behavior in the Human Male.* Philadelphia and London: W. B. Saunders, 1948.

———. *Sexual Behavior in the Human Female.* Philadelphia and London: W. B. Saunders, 1953.

Kronhausen, Eberhard and Phyllis. *Pornography and the Law.* New York: Ballantine Books, 1964.

Lawrence, D. H. *Lady Chatterley's Lover. Ibid.*

———. *The Rainbow.* New York: Viking Press, 1967.

Legman, Gershon. *Love and Death.* New York: Hacker Art Books, 1963.

Marcus, Steven. *The Other Victorians.* New York: Basic Books, 1966.

Masters, William and Johnston, Virginia. *Human Sexual Response. Ibid.*

Metalious, Grace. *Peyton Place.* New York: Dell, 1957.

Nabokov, Vladimir. *Lolita.* New York: G. P. Putnam's Sons, 1958.

Newman, Frank. *Barbara.* New York: The Olympia Press, 1968.

Plato. *The Republic.* Translated by Benjamin Jewett. New York: Charles Scribner's Sons, 1956.

———. *Great Dialogues.* Translated by W. H. D. Rouse. New York: The New American Library, 1956.

Rand, Ayn. *The Romantic Manifesto.* New York: World, 1969.

Réage, Pauline. *Story of O.* Translated by Sabine d'Estrée. New York: Grove Press, 1965.

Reik, Theodore. *Of Love and Lust.* New York: Farrar, Strauss, 1949.

Robbins, Harold. *The Adventurers.* New York: Simon & Schuster, 1966.

Shelley, Percy Bysshe. *The Complete Poetical Works.* New York: Random House, n.d.

Shulman, Alix Kates. "Porn in the U.S.A.," interview. In *Rolling Stock,* No. 10, 1985.

Thomas, Donald. *A Long Time Burning.* New York: Frederick A. Praeger, 1969.

## CHAPTER 3

Barthes, Roland. *The Pleasure of the Text. Ibid.*

Bataille, Georges. *Story of the Eye. Ibid.*

Beardsley, Aubrey. *The Story of Venus and Tannhäuser.* New York and London: Award Books, Tandem Books, 1967.

———. *Collected Drawings.* New York: Crescent Books, 1967.

Breton, André. *Manifestoes of Surrealism. Ibid.*

Bryan, C. D. B. *Friendly Fire.* New York: Putnam, 1976.

Burke, Edmund. *A Philosophical Inquiry Into the Origin of Our Ideals of the Sublime and the Beautiful.* In *Works,* London, 1803.

Burroughs, William S. *Naked Lunch. Ibid.*

———. *The Soft Machine.* New York: Grove Press, 1966.

———. *Nova Express.* New York: Grove Press, 1965.

Girodias, Maurice. *The Olympia Reader.* New York: Grove Press, 1967.

Johnson, Samuel. "On the Novel," *Rambler.* In *Works,* London, 1806.

Keats, John. *Letters.* Cambridge, Mass.: Harvard, 1958.

Lautréamont, Comte de. *Les chants de Maldoror.* New York: New Directions, 1966.

Lawrence, D. H. *Lady Chatterley's Lover. Ibid.*

Mallarmé, Stéphane. *Poems.* Translated by Roger Fry. New York: New Directions, 1951.

McLuhan, Marshall and Fiore, Quentin. *The Medium Is the Massage.* New York, London, Toronto: Bantam Books, 1967.

Miller, Henry. *The Rosy Crucifixion: Sexus, Plexus, and Nexus.* New York: Grove Press, 1965.

Morris, William. *The Collected Works.* London: Longmans, 1915.

*The Pearl*, numbers 1-18. New York: Grove Press, 1968.

Pound, Ezra. *Literary Essays.* New York: New Directions, 1968.

Richardson, Samuel. *Pamela.* London and New York: J. M. Dent, E. P. Dutton, 1914.

———. *Clarissa.* London, 1848.

Sade, Marquis de. "Reflections on the Novel." In *The 120 Days of Sodom and Other Writings.* Translated by Austryn Wainhouse and Richard Seaver. New York: Grove Press, 1966.

Sterne, Laurence. *The Life and Opinions of Tristram Shandy, Gentleman.* London and Toronto, New York: J. M. Dent, E. P. Dutton, 1930.

Swinburne, Algernon Charles. *The Collected Poetical Works.* London: Heinemann, 1917.

Symons, Arthur. *The Symbolist Movement in Literature*, revised edition of 1919. New York: E. P. Dutton, 1958.

Wagner, Richard. *Tannhäuser.* London: John Calder, 1988.

Wilde, Oscar. *Essays.* London: Methuen, 1950.

Woolsey, John M. *U.S. v. One Book Entitled "Ulysses"* (1933). In Alec Craig, *Suppressed Books.* Cleveland and New York: World Publishing, 1966.

Zola, Émile. *Nana.* Translation by Lowell Bair. New York: Bantam, 1964.

## CHAPTER 4

Auerbach, Erich. *Mimesis.* Garden City, New York: Doubleday, 1957.

Beckett, Samuel. *Malone Dies.* New York: Grove Press, 1956.

Camus, Albert. *The Stranger.* Translated by Stuart Gilbert. New York: Vintage Books, 1958.

Conrad, Joseph. Preface to *The Nigger of the Narcissus.* In *Three Great Tales.* New York: Vintage Books, n.d.

Dante Alighieri. *The Divine Comedy.* Translated by Laurence Binyon. In *The Portable Dante.* New York: Viking Press, 1975.

———. *A Translation of Dante's Eleven Letters.* Translation by C. S. Latham. Boston and New York, 1891.

Faulkner, William. *Pylon.* New York: Signet, 1968.

———. *The Hamlet.* New York: Random House, 1940.

———. *Light In August.* New York: Random House, 1968.

———. "Nobel Prize Address." In *Harper's American Literature.* New York: Harper & Row, 1987.

Joyce, James. *Portrait of the Artist as a Young Man. Ibid.*

———. *The Critical Writings. Ibid.*

Lawrence, D. H. *Sex, Literature and Censorship. Ibid.*

Milton, John. *Paradise Lost. The Student's Milton, Complete Poems.* New York: F. S. Crofts, 1941.

Réage, Pauline. *Story of O. Ibid.*

Schiller, Friedrich. *Naive and Sentimental Poetry. Ibid.*

St. John of the Cross. *Complete Works.* Translation by E. Allison Peers. Westminister, MD: Newman Press, 1964.

Zola, Émile. *The Experimental Novel.* Translated by Belle Sherman. New York: Cassell, 1893.

## CHAPTER 5

Beauvoir, Simone de. "Must We Burn de Sade?" In the Marquis de Sade, *120 Days of Sodom, Ibid.*

Cocteau, Jean. *The Infernal Machine and Other Plays.* New York: New Directions, 1963.

Foucault, Michel. *The History of Sexuality. Ibid.*

Hegel, G. W. H. *The Philosophy of History. Ibid.*

———. *Philosophy of Fine Art.* Translated by F. P. B. Osmaston. London: G. Bell & Sons, 1920.

Marlowe, Christopher. *Tragical History of Dr. Faustus.* In *Elizabethan Plays.* Edited by Hazelton Spencer. Boston: D. C. Heath, 1933.

Miller, Arthur. *Death of a Salesman.* In *Collected Plays.* London: Secker and Warburg, 1967.

Nabokov, Vladimir. *Lolita. Ibid.*

Plato. *The Republic. Ibid.*

Richardson, Samuel. *Clarissa. Ibid.*

Sade, Marquis de. *120 Days of Sodom and Other Writings. Ibid.*

———. *Justine . . . and Other Writings.* Translation by Richard Seaver and Austryn Wainhouse. New York: Grove Press, 1965.

Sophocles. *Three Tragedies.* Translated by H. D. F. Kitto. London: Oxford Univ. Press, 1962.

Sterne, Laurence. *The Life and Opinions of Tristram Shandy. Ibid.*

## CHAPTER 6

Bataille, Georges. *Eroticism. Ibid.*

———. *Story of the Eye. Ibid.*

Brown, Norman O. *Love's Body.* New York: Random House, 1966.

Burke, Kenneth. *A Grammar of Motives.* Cleveland and New York: World, 1962.

Chambers, E. K. *The Medieval Stage.* Oxford: Clarendon, 1903.

Eliade, Mircea. *Patterns in Comparative Religion.* Translated by Rosemary Sheed. New York: New American Library, 1974.

Genet, Jean. *The Thief's Journal.* Translated by Bernard Frechtman. New York: Grove, 1964.

———. *Our Lady of the Flowers.* Translated by Bernard Frechtman. New York: Grove, 1963.

Lawrence, D. H. *Lady Chatterley's Lover. Ibid.*

Meyer, J. J. *Sexual Life in Ancient India.* London, 1952.

Sade, Marquis de. *Justine . . . and Other Writings. Ibid.*

## CHAPTER 7

Aristophanes. *Lysistrata.* Translated by Donald Sutherland. In *Greek Comedy.* Edited by Robert W. Corrigan. New York: Dell, 1965.

Cassanova, Jacques. *Memoirs.* Translated by Arthur Machen. New York: Dover, 1961.

Frye, Northrop. "The Argument of Comedy." In *Theories of Comedy.* Edited by Paul Lauter. Garden City, New York: Doubleday, 1964.

Joyce, James. *Ulysses. Ibid.*

———. *Portrait of the Artist as a Young Man. Ibid.*

Lawrence, D. H. *Sex, Literature and Censorship. Ibid.*

———. *Lady Chatterley's Lover. Ibid.*

———. *The Rainbow. Ibid.*

Miller, Henry. *The Rosy Crucifixion. Ibid.*

———. *The World of Sex.* New York: Grove, 1965.

———. *Tropic of Cancer.* New York: Grove, 1963.

Plautus. *Six Plays.* Translated by Lionel Casson. New York: Doubleday, 1963.

Roth, Philip. *Portnoy's Complaint.* New York: Random House, 1969.

Shakespeare, William. *The Complete Works.* Chicago and New York: Scott, Foresman, 1951.

Southern, Terry and Hoffenberg, Mason. *Candy.* New York: G. P. Putnam's Sons, 1964.

Tavel, Ronald. *Indira Ghandi's Daring Device.* New York: The Theater of the Ridiculous, 1966.

## CHAPTER 8

Barbach, Lonnie, ed. *Pleasures.* Garden City, New York: Doubleday, 1984.

Bonaparte, Marie. *Female Sexuality.* Translated by John Rodker. New York: Grove, 1965.

Di Prima, Diane. *Memoirs of a Beatnik.* New York: Olympia, 1969.

Dworkin, Andrea. *Pornography: Men Possessing Women. Ibid.*

Freud, Sigmund. *Collected Papers.* London: Hogarth Press, 1924.

Friday, Nancy. *My Secret Garden. Ibid.*

Griffin, Susan. *Pornoqraphy and Silence. Ibid.*

Hall, Radclyffe. *The Well of Loneliness.* New York: Pocket Books, 1964.

Harding, M. Esther. *Psychic Energy.* New York: Pantheon, 1963.

Hill, Eleanore. *The Family Secret.* Santa Barbara: Capra, 1985.

Hite, Shere. *Sexual Honesty by Women for Women.* New York: Warner, 1974.

———. *The Hite Report. Ibid.*

Horney, Karen. *New Ways in Psychoanalysis.* New York: W. W. Norton, 1966.

Hunter, Nan D. and Law, Sylvia A. *Brief Amici Curiae of Feminist Anti-Censorship Taskforce, et al.* U. S. Court of Appeals, Seventh Circuit, 1985.

Jelinek, Estelle, ed. *Ladies Home Erotica.* Berkeley, Ca.: Ten Speed Press, 1984.

Jong, Erica. *Fear of Flying.* New York: Holt, Rinehart and Winston, 1973.

———. *How to Save Your Own Life.* New York: Holt, Rinehart and Winston, 1977.

Jung, C. G. *The Structure and Dynamics of the Psyche.* Translated by R. F. C. Hull. New York: Pantheon, 1960.

Lamb, Charlotte. *The Sex War.* Toronto: Harlequin, 1983.

Nin, Anaïs. *Diaries.* New York: Harcourt Brace Jovanovich, 1971.

———. *Delta of Venus.* New York and London: Harcourt Brace Jovanovich, 1977.

———. *House of Incest.* Chicago: Swallow, 1958.

———. *The Novel of the Future.* New York: Macmillan, 1968.

Perkins, Michael. *The Secret Record.* New York: William Morrow, 1977.

Reik, Theodore. *Of Love and Lust. Ibid.*

Samois. *Coming to Power.* Boston: Alyson Publications, 1982.

Shulman, Alix Kates. *On the Stroll. Ibid.*

Steinem, Gloria. "Erotica and Pornography," *Ms.*, November, 1978.

Susann, Jacqueline. *Valley of the Dolls.* New York: Bantam, 1967.

Wharton, Edith. "Beatrice Palmato." In R. W. B. Lewis, *Edith Wharton, A Biography.* New York: Harper and Row, 1975.

## CHAPTER 9

Aristophanes. *Lysistrata. Ibid.*

Aristotle. *Poetics. Ibid.*

Bertolucci, Bernardo. *Last Tango in Paris.* 1973.

Brakhage, Stan. *Flesh of Morning.* 1956.

———. *Metaphors on Vision.* N.p.: Film Culture, 1976.

———. *Loving.* 1957.

———. *Wedlock House: An Intercourse.* 1958.

———. *Window Water Baby Moving*. 1959.

———. *Lovemaking*. 1968.

———. *Dog Star Man*. 1964.

Conner, Bruce. *A Movie*. 1958.

———. *Cosmic Ray*. 1961.

Damiano, Gerard. *Deep Throat*. 1972.

———. *Devil in Miss Jones*. 1972.

Lovelace, Linda. *Ordeal*. New York: Berkeley Books, 1981.

Meyer, Russ. *Fanny Hill*. 1966.

———. *Beyond the Valley of the Dolls*. 1970.

———. *Vixen*. 1968.

Mitchell, Jim and Art. *Behind the Green Door*. 1972.

Noren, Andrew. *The Adventures of the Exquisite Corpse*. 1967.

Oshima, Nagisa. *In the Realm of the Senses*. 1976.

Pound, Ezra. *Literary Essays*. *Ibid.*

Saliva Films. *The Best of the New York Erotic Film Festival*. 1972.

Smith, Jack. *Flaming Creatures*. 1963.

Spelvin, Georgina. "Speak of the Devil." *Oui*, February 1974.

Tavel, Ronald. "The Theatre of the Ridiculous." *Tri-Quarterly*, Number six. 1966.

Wertmuller, Lina. *Swept Away*. 1975.

Vatsayana. *Kama Sutra*. Translated by Sir Richard Burton and F. F. Arbuthnot. New York: G.P. Putnam's Sons, 1963.

## CHAPTER 10

American Civil Liberties Union. Biennial Conference. Boulder, Co. 1985.

*Attorney General's Commission on Pornography, Final Report*. Washington, D.C.: Department of Justice, 1986.

Cockburn, Sir Alexander. In Donald Thomas. *A Long Time Burning*. *Ibid.*

Craig, Alec. *Suppressed Books*. Cleveland and New York: World, 1966.

Donnerstein, E. and Linz, D. "Debate on Pornography." *Film Comment*, Dec. 1984.

Duncan, Robert. *The Truth and Life of Myth.* Fremont, Mich.: Sumac Press, 1968.

Dworkin, Andrea. *Pornography: Men Possessing Women. Ibid.*

Dworkin, Andrea and MacKinnon, Catherine. "Model Antipornography Law," *Ms.*, April 1985.

Friede v. Commonwealth. 271 Massachusetts 318 N.E.472 (1930).

Hunter, Nan D. and Law, Sylvia A. *Brief Amici Curiae . . . Ibid.*

Jenkins v. Georgia. 418 U.S. 153 (1974).

Knowlton, Charles. *Fruits of Philosophy.* London: 1834, 1877.

Lipscomb, W. N. "Aesthetic Aspects of Science." In Curtin, W. C., ed. *The Aesthetic Dimension of Science.* New York: Philosophical Library, 1982.

Malamuth, N. M. and Donnerstein, E., eds. *Pornography and Sexual Aggression.* New York: Academic Press, 1984.

Miller v. California. 413 U.S. 15 (1973).

Oppenheimer, Robert. In Rhodes, Richard. *The Making of the Atomic Bomb.* New York: Simon and Schuster, 1986.

Planck, Max. *Scientific Autobiography.* New York: Philosophical Library, 1949.

Pound, Ezra. *Literary Essays. Ibid.*

Randall, Richard. *Freedom and Taboo.* Berkeley: Univ. of California Press, 1989.

*The Report of the Commission on Obscenity and Pornography.* New York: Random House, 1970.

Roth v. United States 354 U.S. 476 (1957).

Sanger, Margaret. *My Fight for Birth Control.* In Craig. *Ibid.*

Santayana, George. *The Sense of Beauty.* New York: Dover, 1955.

Shulman, Alix Kates. *On the Stroll. Ibid.*

Stanley v. Georgia. 394 U.S. 557 (1969).

St. James, Margot. Speech at U.C.L.A., 1983. In *Rolling Stock*, No. 7, 1984.

Wechsler, J., ed. *On Aesthetics in Science.* Cambridge, Mass.: MIT Press, 1979.

Weyl, Hermann. In Lipscomb, W. N. *Ibid.*

Wilber, Ken, ed. *Quantum Questions, Mystical Writings of the World's Great Physicists.* Boulder and London: Shambala, 1984.

Woolsey, John M. *U.S. v. One Book Entitled Ulysses. Ibid.*